'This is far more than just another Business Economics text. Dransfield goes straight to the heart of what is important in business today. From globalization to green economics and from markets to money, the extensive range of topics and user friendly style, ensure that this text will be accessible to all students studying a business economics degree or related discipline.'

James Eden, Senior Lecturer in Economics and Finance,
Liverpool John Moores University, UK

BUSINESS ECONOMICS

The Eurozone crisis and the age of austerity, as well as challenges to the environment as a result of economic growth, have highlighted the need for a greater understanding of those facets of economics that are of most use to businesses and their decision makers.

This book introduces all of the relevant theoretical aspects of the subject and applies them to real-life examples of economics that are of particular interest to students today, including: the impact of globalization; the way in which 'green' perspectives can be built into decision making; and how the financial crisis has challenged economists, politicians and business people to rethink their existing ideas, particularly with respect to risk management. This innovative textbook features:

- A clear introduction to the features of economics and the economy that impact upon business decision making.

- Illuminating case studies that relate business examples to economic concepts.

- Summaries, activities, key terms, review questions and further reading to help reinforce your understanding.

Clear, concise and written by an expert currently lecturing in the field, *Business Economics* examines economic theory and the practical application of economics in a way that is relevant and understandable to undergraduate students studying modules in this area.

Rob Dransfield is Senior Lecturer in Economics and Strand Leader for Business Education at Nottingham Trent University, UK. He is also Tutor for the *Financial Times* Non-Executive Directors course and has written a number of introductory and international economics books – most recently, *Economics for the Caribbean School Certificate* (2011, Nelson Thornes).

360 DEGREE BUSINESS

Series Editor: Paul Smith, University of Hertfordshire, UK

The 360 Degree Series provides accessible and stimulating introductions to core business studies modules. Clear, concise and written by experts currently lecturing in the field, each title sits firmly within the business studies curriculum enabling students to meet their academic and career goals.

Published titles in this series include:

Financial Accounting
Bev Vickerstaff, Parminder Johal

Organizational Behaviour
Paul Smith, Marilyn Farmer, Wendy Yellowley

Business Economics
Rob Dransfield

360°
series

BUSINESS ECONOMICS

ROB DRANSFIELD

Routledge
Taylor & Francis Group

LONDON AND NEW YORK

First published 2014
by Routledge
2 Park Square, Milton Park, Abingdon, Oxon OX14 4RN

Simultaneously published in the USA and Canada
by Routledge
711 Third Avenue, New York, NY 10017

Routledge is an imprint of the Taylor & Francis Group, an informa business

British Library Cataloguing in Publication Data
A catalogue record for this book is available from the British Library

Library of Congress Cataloging in Publication Data
Dransfield, Robert
  Business economics/Rob Dransfield.
  pages cm. – (The 360 degree series)
  Includes bibliographical references and index. 1. Managerial economics.
  I. Title.
  HD30.22.D73 2013
  338.5 – dc23   2012048810

ISBN: 978–0–415–83765–1 (hbk)
ISBN: 978–1–4441–7045–0 (pbk)
ISBN: 978–0–203–78386–3 (ebk)

Typeset in Minion Pro and Franklin Gothic
by Florence Production Ltd, Stoodleigh, Devon, UK

Printing and binding: 1010 Printing International Ltd, China

CONTENTS

FIGURES

TABLES

SERIES PREFACE

The 360 Degree Series is an exciting new range of textbooks that provides students with a clear introduction to business and management at undergraduate level. The books are very much written with the university and college student in mind, including those who are relatively unfamiliar with this particular field of study and are seeking a clear and accessible text to help them get up to speed with the subject quickly.

The 360 Degree Series aims to inspire students' interest in the subject and to motivate them to explore further by setting out the key topics, important ideas and essential debates required for study. Relevant theories and concepts are clearly explained and applied to practice using case studies and real-life examples. Current trends are outlined and up-to-date material provided.

Within each book, chapters include an outline and objectives and are clearly structured with headings and sub-headings, so they are easy to follow and can readily be applied to lectures and seminars. Key terms are defined and case study boxes and activity questions include real-life examples that help to put learning into context. Key themes are explored, giving students a more rounded view of the subject. Students are encouraged to check their understanding at regular intervals throughout via a number of reflective questions, reinforcing the point being made and creating a solid basis for further learning. For revision, review questions and a key ideas table are included at the end of each chapter, together with recommended reading, useful websites and references to encourage further exploration of the subject.

All this combines to make titles in *The 360 Degree Series* essential companions for students studying the dynamic and exciting world of business today.

As editor of *The 360 Degree Series*, I hope the books will help to boost your understanding and enjoyment of the subject, and thus lead to success in your studies.

Paul E. Smith
University of Hertfordshire
Series Editor

PREFACE

Economics is one of the most important disciplines contributing to an understanding of the environment in which business decisions are made. News about changes in the economy features in the headlines of news reports on a day-to-day basis because economic changes have such a dramatic impact on all our lives. Headlines such as:

'Crisis in the Eurozone!'

'Rising inflation hits the value of real earnings!'

'Shock fall in economic growth!'

Studying economics will help you to develop a keener understanding of how changes in the economy arise and particularly on how they impact on business.

This book is designed to support students on a general business degree course that includes modules in Business Economics. The book is designed to focus on the essential economic information and analysis that support and illuminate business decision making. The focus in this book is on developing an understanding of economic analysis and ways of thinking that are relevant to the applied world of business decision making. An understanding of how the economy works is an essential requirement for all business students. This text is designed to provide you with an understanding of economics as it directly relates to business decision making.

The text is designed to be easy to navigate. Each chapter starts with a clear outline and objectives. This is followed by an introduction providing a narrative account of the key coverage of the chapter.

The chapters are then divided into a number of sections which link to each other. Case studies and examples are used to illustrate business examples that relate to economic concepts. Key terms are employed in each chapter to provide important definitions. Activities encourage you to read or research further. Review questions are designed to check understanding of key points covered in the chapter. The end of each chapter includes a summary of key ideas, some follow up reading, and useful websites that you can access.

This book unlocks the central concepts/knowledge and understanding of Business Economics. The writing is designed to be focused and relevant to the learning needs of business undergraduates. It covers the essential areas of economics that students following general business and management courses need to be familiar with. The emphasis is on presenting content and activities that are useful to a business and management graduate.

The text has been written with reference to:

- The QAA benchmark standards for a Bachelor's degree with honours;

- Popular courses being offered in a number of universities;

- Current core texts used to support Business Economics courses; and

- The benchmark statements, which are national guidance statements for UK Higher Education Institutions related to specific subject areas.

The benchmark statement for general business and management courses sets out that courses should provide a broad, analytical and highly integrated study of business and management, and that graduates should be able to demonstrate relevant knowledge and understanding of organizations, the external environment in which they operate and how they are managed. There is likely to be an emphasis upon understanding and responding to change and the consideration of the future of organizations and the external environment in which they operate. This external environment should be shown to encompass a wide range of factors including economic and other factors.

The emphasis in this text is therefore one of outlining the underpinning economic frameworks that influence economic decision making, and the economic factors that affect business as part of the external environment. The activities in the text are designed to encourage students to understand and outline appropriate responses to economic changes that impact upon business.

In terms of the knowledge and understanding requirements of the subject benchmark statements, particularly relevant areas for an economics for business text are:

- Markets – the development and operation of markets for resources, goods and services.

- Customers – customer expectations, service and orientation.

- Business policy and strategy – the development of appropriate policies and strategies within a changing environment to meet stakeholder interests.

- Pervasive issues – including sustainability, globalization and enterprise development.

The text consists of 17 chapters.

- **Chapter 1: Introduction to economics for business**. How economic changes impact on business. This section starts out by illustrating the impact that economic changes have upon individual businesses and the broader business community. The chapter identifies changes in the economy as presenting major risks to business. Recent events have highlighted the importance of effective risk management. The chapter shows that students need to understand economic risks and their potential impacts. On the basis of this analysis it is possible to take steps to mitigate risk in line with the risk appetite of a business. The chapter exemplifies economic risk focusing on the impact of changes in consumer incomes and spending on business, and the impact of changing interest and inflation rates. The purpose of this introduction is to immediately show the relevance of economics for business.

- **Chapter 2: Quantitative analysis for economists**. An outline of how and why economists use econometrics and visual and other ways of presenting statistical data. The chapter shows that econometrics has become an important branch of economic analysis. Econometrics is the application of statistical methods and mathematics to economic data. The chapter shows how economists can apply statistical approaches to illustrate trends. Trend data can be smoothed to take account of fluctuations such as seasonal changes. The chapter explains how and why economists use indices to measure changes in inflation and other important economic changes. The student is shown how indices are weighted to take account of the relative importance of specific classes of items represented in an index. The chapter shows that there are dangers inherent in trying to reduce everything to numbers. It shows that the emphasis in this book will be on focusing on using econometric approaches that help users of statistics to better understand economic realities. The chapter uses a number of examples using recent statistical data that are of interest to business decision makers.

- **Chapter 3: How markets work**. This chapter outlines the key aspects of the market system. The market system brings together buyers and sellers. The market establishes a market price. The chapter therefore outlines the nature of demand and supply and shows how demand and supply curves are constructed. It explains the key determinants of demand and supply and shows how demand and supply curves can alter their positions and how this impacts on price. Business managers are particularly interested in the impact of changes in price on demand, supply and revenue. An important section of this chapter therefore focuses on the concept of elasticity of demand and various ways of calculating coefficients of elasticity. The chapter then moves on to introduce different types of business units. The chapter also looks at ways in which businesses are classified according to their size.

- **Chapter 4: Costs and revenues**. This chapter introduces the student to methods of calculating the costs and revenues of a business in order to show how much profit (or loss) the business is making. It seeks to combine the analysis that is typically used in business with approaches adopted by economists. Definitions are provided of revenue and cost, and cost–volume–profit analysis before showing how break-even and profit/loss can be calculated. Simple calculations are made of contribution. The analysis then goes on to show the meaning and method of calculation of a range of important concepts and tools including average cost, average total cost and marginal cost. The text shows how different types of costs can be calculated at different levels of output and the relationship between fixed and variable costs. The student is shown how to calculate the profit maximizing point for a business based on calculating marginal cost and marginal revenue.

- **Chapter 5: Different types of market structures**. This chapter moves on to identify the different types of market structures in which businesses operate. It maps out the features of these markets in terms of numbers of competitors in the market, levels of price competition and how firms differentiate themselves from rivals. It starts out by identifying the features of 'extreme' market forms, which are referred to as perfect competition and monopoly. In perfect competition there are many rival firms producing identical products. In monopoly situations there is only one firm that dominates a marketplace. The chapter goes on to identify the point at which profits will be maximized and output determined in these markets. The chapter shows that in the real world markets are structured in different ways to the theoretical extremes. It identifies types of competition that are more representative of 'real world' reality (i.e. oligopoly and monopolistic competition). The chapter examines different models of competition in terms of how markets work, opportunities to make profits in different markets and the impact of different market forms on the efficiency of resource use in society.

- **Chapter 6: Business strategy in an economic context**. Businesses have objectives which they seek to achieve through strategies. A key objective is that of profitability, as set out in previous chapters, but in addition they may have other objectives. What a business is able to achieve is constrained by the external environment in which it operates, including the economy. This chapter therefore focuses on business strategy within the context of the external environment. Successful strategies are ones that meet a number of criteria which are explained in this chapter. These criteria include suitability, acceptability and feasibility. Business are run by directors in the interests of their stakeholders. Shareholders are important stakeholders but there are others, including consumers and suppliers. The chapter provides examples of business response to changing economic conditions. Alternative business strategies – including growth, mergers and takeovers, retrenchment and internationalization – are introduced in this chapter. The chapter focuses on the relationship between strategic decision making and consideration of economic conditions in the wider market economy.

- **Chapter 7: Government regulation and competition**. This chapter starts out by outlining important reasons why the government intervenes in the economy and in markets. It shows that in order for existing markets to become more efficient and effective the government may need to establish regulations and intervene in more direct ways (e.g. by establishing public corporations) in order to achieve a range of policy objectives. The chapter particularly focuses on government competition policy and identifies the important work carried out by the Office of Fair Trading and Competition Commission. Because the government intervenes in many ways in a modern economy it is necessary to be selective in identifying areas of government intervention. This chapter therefore illustrates government intervention in business activity by introducing sections of the Companies Act 2006 setting out the role of directors of a company.

- **Chapter 8: The wider role of government in the economy**. Whereas Chapter 7 specifically focused on government's role in markets, this chapter extends the analysis to look at a range of important roles that the government plays in the wider economy. It starts by setting out these multiple roles. The chapter then examines the government as an employer, as a stabilizer of fluctuations in the economy, its role in counteracting weaknesses in the market economy, its international role and more specific roles such as managing regional policy, debt management and dealing with inequality. The chapter also introduces the policy tools available to manage government policy, such as control of the quantity of money available in the economy and management of its own spending and taxation policies.

- **Chapter 9: Economic ideas and policy**. This chapter provides a fundamental building block in helping to develop an understanding of the contribution that economics has made to the development of ideas. It also shows that many economic ideas are contested, resulting from the differing interpretations and viewpoints held by those that seek to analyse economic interactions. In particular there are fundamental differences in viewpoints about the role of markets in the economy. Businesses play a fundamental role in the economy by producing goods and services, creating jobs and contributing to economic well-being. Businesses are continually affected by the state of the economy and the economic policy decisions that are made within it. Economic policies are significantly shaped by economic ideas. It is therefore necessary to understand how economic ideas have been shaped by key economic thinkers. The chapter starts out by outlining the development of free market economic thinking in Britain and the key contributions made by Adam Smith and later by the neoclassical economists. The chapter then shows how free market thinking was substantially challenged by Karl Marx and then reformulated by John Maynard Keynes who argued the case for state intervention in the economy. Economic policy has been a continual battlefield in recent years between those favouring Keynesian economics and those who support classical free market economics. The discussion in this chapter continues by outlining the Third Way championed by New Labour under Tony Blair and more recently the idea of Big Society championed by David Cameron's Conservatives.

- **Chapter 10: Economic indicators**. This chapter explores a range of economic indicators that a business analyst should be familiar with in order to better understand the wider economic environment within which business decisions are made. The first indicator that is studied is GDP (gross domestic product), which acts as a measure of the growth of the economy. Business activity helps GDP to grow. The opportunity for businesses to expand is also constrained and/or encouraged by the speed of growth of the economy. The chapter looks at the impact of recession on business. The chapter also looks at other ways of measuring economic well-being such as the human development index (HDI) and the happiness index. The chapter then explores the significance of employment indicators including employment, unemployment and the breakdown of employment into different sectors. Inflation is an important indicator impacting on business. You are shown how inflation is calculated and how a consumer price index is weighted. Population size and distribution also have an important impact on business and the chapter explores contemporary problems associated with an ageing population. Finally, interest rates and exchange rates are introduced because of their significance for business. These are revisited in greater detail in later chapters of this book.

- **Chapter 11: The international economy**. This chapter introduces the international business context. It starts out by showing the benefits of international trade on an international scale by outlining trade theory based on comparative advantage. It introduces ways in which businesses can enter international markets at different levels. The chapter goes on to identify the main trading partners for the UK economy and focuses on the creation of trading blocs, including the European Union (EU). The significance of exchange rates for companies that engage in international trade is outlined. Fixed and floating exchange rates are compared. The chapter outlines the process of the development of the euro and shows how the Eurozone impacts on the UK economy. The chapter concludes by examining the significance of the terms of trade.

- **Chapter 12: The economics of globalization**. This chapter shows that there are different perspectives about what is meant by 'globalization'. Globalization can be seen as having both positive and negative aspects. The chapter emphasizes the significant impact that globalization is having on businesses in the world today. The chapter then goes on to identify the key players in the globalization process, including transnational companies and governments. The chapter outlines the key international financial institutions including the World Bank and the International Monetary Fund. It shows how the growth in the influence of the World Trade Organization has led to an increasing liberalization and hence expansion of trade between countries. The chapter concludes by revisiting the theme of foreign direct investment and identifies specific markets that have proved to be particularly attractive to business in recent times. The text explores ways of entering overseas markets.

- **Chapter 13: Money, banking and finance**. This chapter starts out by describing key aspects of the recent financial crisis that have had an impact on business in the economy. It shows how stable money and banking lie at the heart of a healthy economy. Businesses flourish best when the money economy is growing in a steady and predictable way. The chapter describes the development and functions of money and how commercial banking has aided business. A description is provided of the wider monetary system including the role of the central bank. The chapter identifies issues created by an overly rapid expansion of the money supply including the impact of inflation. An analysis is provided of government measures for controlling inflation and providing a more predictable macro-environment for business.

- **Chapter 14: Government fiscal policy**. This chapter outlines ways in which the government can manipulate its own spending and the ways in which it collects revenue to 'manage' the economy. Management of the economy involves seeking to influence demand and supply at a macro-economic level. The chapter shows how the government will seek to adjust its taxation and spending policy in ways that ensure steady economic growth as well as seeking other policy objectives such as a more even distribution of income. Ways in which businesses are impacted by government fiscal policy are illustrated in the chapter.

- **Chapter 15: Green economics**. Increasingly, environmental considerations are being built into economic decision making. The concept of sustainable development involves taking into consideration a longer-term view of the use of economic resources. The chapter introduces the concept of social and environmental costs and benefits. Ways in which environmental considerations can be included in economic calculations are set out in this chapter. The chapter also outlines international collaboration on environmental initiatives. Finally, the chapter explores some sustainable business models.

- **Chapter 16: Business in the economy**. This chapter pulls together some of the threads of an earlier chapter to explore a range of ways in which the economy impacts on business decision making. It starts out by showing that the economy is one of a number of interacting environmental factors that act as constraints on business but also provide real opportunities. The chapter continues with the important theme of risk that has underpinned the book. The chapter also revisits the concept of competition between businesses and the challenge to achieve competitive advantage, as well as contrasting small and large businesses and explaining how economies of scale provide an incentive to the growth of business.

- **Chapter 17: Financial planning and investment appraisal**. This final chapter focuses on an important area of Business Economics: financial planning with particular reference to investment appraisal. The chapter shows that autonomous investment is an important economic variable. Businesses make investment decisions as a result of carrying out investment appraisal. The chapter outlines the three key methods of appraising investment: payback, discounted cash flow to calculate net present value and accounting rate of return. Another key element of financial planning is accessing appropriate sources of finance for the long-, medium- and short-term needs of a company. The chapter identifies difficulties that a business might get into resulting from fluctuations in the economic cycle in situations where the company has too high a gearing ratio.

GUIDE TO THE BOOK

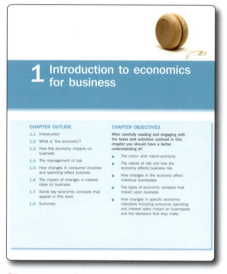

Chapter outlines and objectives
Main topics and ideas are listed clearly
at the start of each chapter to guide
you carefully through the subject

Key terms Terminology is explained as
you need it

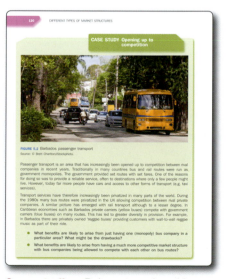

Case studies Relevant, real-world
case studies relate business examples
to economic concepts

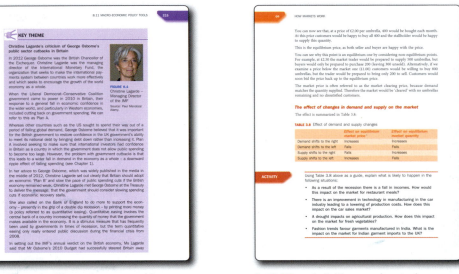

Key themes These boxes provide different perspectives and a more rounded view of particular topics

Activities Activities are located throughout each chapter to facilitate comprehension

Reflective questions Frequent and challenging questions help you apply, analyse and evaluate what you've read to reinforce your understandin

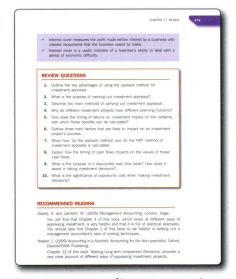

Revision support Chapter summaries, review questions, recommended reading lists and useful websites are provided to help you revise

1 Introduction to economics for business

CHAPTER OBJECTIVES

After carefully reading and engaging with the tasks and activities outlined in this chapter you should have a better understanding of:

- The micro- and macro-economy

- The nature of risk and how the economy affects business risk

- How changes in the economy affect individual businesses

- The types of economic variables that impact upon business

- How changes in specific economic indicators including consumer spending and interest rates impact on businesses and the decisions that they make

1.1 Introduction

This book has been written for business students rather than economics students. Its focus is on describing and explaining those aspects of economics and the economy that impact on business decision making. Businesses operate in a constantly changing environment. There are a number of influences operating in this environment that impact on business including political, legal, social and technological changes. Each of these is highly important. However, it is economic changes that can have the most dramatic and sustained consequences for business.

Businesses have to take risks in order to make a profit. For example, producing one type of good rather than another involves a risk. Many of the significant risks that a business takes stem from economic changes. Examples of these are illustrated at the end of this chapter. The purpose of this opening chapter is to introduce the concept of the economy. By way of illustration it sets out some examples of the ways in which changes in the economy affect business in significant ways

1.2 What is 'the economy'?

The following example illustrates the relationship between business and the economy at a local level. On 5 October 2010 the headline in the *Nottingham Evening Post* read:

> New blow to city as Boots cuts 750 jobs. Move sparks fears for the economy.

The article stated that:

> There were renewed fears for the Nottingham economy today after Boots announced 750 jobs will go at its Beeston site. About 7,500 are employed at the former head office of the health and beauty retailer. . . . Nottingham City Council deputy leader Councillor Graham Chapman feared for the impact on the local economy of the loss of 750 salaries. 'You can't reduce the spending power of 750 people out of the Greater Nottingham economy without further impact on other people's jobs', he said.

The article shows that large companies are part of the economy, and the decisions that they make affect the economy. Boots is one of the most important companies in Nottingham. The decision that it made to cut back on jobs had a knock-on effect for the wider economy of Nottingham.

CASE STUDY Alliance Boots

Jessie Boot set up his first chemist shop in Nottingham in 1877. He charged prices that were lower than rival stores and he called his shop 'The People's Store'. The formula was a success and by 1896 he had 66 stores operating in 28 different towns and cities in Britain. Today Alliance Boots is an international health and beauty business. As an international company Boots operates in highly competitive markets, and its fortunes are determined by what is happening in the economies in which it operates. Decisions made by Boots are influenced by changes in the wider world economy (including growing competition from emerging economies, and the impact of global recession).

● In what ways is Boots part of a global economic system?

● How can changes in the global economic system affect Boots?

The market – a situation (or system) through which buyers and sellers come into contact to trade goods, services, commodities or financial instruments. The market doesn't have to be a physical location. In the modern world many trades are carried out virtually through computer and telecommunications links.

KEY TERM

So what exactly is the economy? The economy is a system (or more accurately a set of interlocking systems) in which decisions are made about:

- **What goods to produce**, for example whether to use more land for agricultural production, for recreational activities, or urban development;

- **How goods and services will be produced**, for example whether to produce them manually or using modern technology systems such as factory robots;

- **Who will receive the goods and services**, for example whether they will be allocated to those with the highest incomes or whether they will be more evenly shared among the population; and

- **Who will receive the rewards for making and selling them**, for example, will the profits go to a small number of shareholders or be more evenly shared out among the community.

You can see that these are complex and potentially controversial decisions. As we shall see in later chapters, the economy plays one of the most significant roles in making these decisions, although some aspects of these decisions are additionally shaped by political, legal and social frameworks.

This economic system exists at a number of levels:

- **The local level.** Jessie Boot competing and operating in Nottingham.

- **The national level.** Boots competing and operating in 66 stores in 28 towns and cities.

- **The international level.** Alliance Boots competing and operating across the globe.

Many of the parts of the economic system are created by individuals and groups (like Boots and other companies) building relationships and making agreements with each other about trading, and prices that will be charged for trades. Other parts of the system are more centrally controlled (by governments) – for example the Bank of England produces the notes and coins that are used for cash transactions in England and Wales, and the Companies Act of 2006 is a piece of central government legislation setting out detailed rules about setting up and running companies.

Businesses are a major part of the economic system. They buy resources, transform these resources through production processes, and sell finished goods.

CASE STUDY Cargill at the heart of the international economy

Cargill is an American company that plays a significant role in the provision of food, agricultural and industrial products (as well as financial services). However, it is not a household name. The company employs over 130,000 people in 66 countries. It produces and distributes grain, oilseed, meat and poultry, as well as salt, starch, steel and many other products. Cargill therefore supplies products, that it acquires from raw material producers, to bakeries, food manufacturers, construction companies and many other businesses.

Companies like Cargill play a particularly important role today in a world of increasing shortages of raw materials. For example, in 2010 the Russian grain harvest was severely affected by soaring temperatures during the summer so that there wasn't enough grain produced in the country to meet domestic demand. The Russian government put a ban on the export of grain. The impact of this was to create a shortage of grain in many markets leading to rising grain prices. Cargill therefore had to pay higher prices to farmers to obtain grain, and then pass on these higher prices to its own customers.

- What sorts of economic decisions does Cargill make?

- Are these decisions at local, national or international level?

The Cargill example shows how a major company plays a key part in the economy, buying raw materials and foodstuffs and then supplying them to the market. It also helps to set market prices. At the same time Cargill is affected by changes in the market resulting from the actions of governments, and other buyers and sellers.

Cargill   →   supplies to the market and helps to set market prices

The market   →   influences the prices that Cargill can set

The macro- and micro-economy

The main **decision makers** in the economy are governments, suppliers and consumers. These decision makers are affected by and influence decisions at a macro and a micro level. The **macro-economy** is concerned with large changes that affect most and sometimes all of the decision makers in the economy. Examples of these changes are: the growth or slow down in economic activity in a country, and general price changes on an international scale. An example of this was the slowdown in economic activity in Britain, the United States and many other countries in 2008 and 2009. The result was falling order books for most businesses, falling profit levels, and the demise of many businesses such as Woolworths.

The **micro-economy** is concerned with small-scale economic decision making, such as the pricing of individual products such as shoes, chocolate bars or computers. The study of micro-economic decision making is useful in that it not only helps to understand influences that affect individual business units but it also helps to develop more general theories that can then be developed to create a better understanding of many types of economic situation.

KEY TERMS

Micro-economics is concerned with analysing the behaviour of individual consumers and producers and how households and firms make decisions. An important part of this analysis is concerned with how prices are set, and alter over time.

Macro-economics is concerned with the workings of the whole economy. It therefore involves taking a bigger picture than micro-economics. It examines changes in the national and international economy, analysing patterns and trends and seeking explanations and theories for macro-economic problems such as unemployment and inflation.

1.3 How the economy impacts on business

The business environment consists of a range of major influences that are outside a business. These include political, social and legal changes that affect business. However, most business people will tell you that it is changes in economic factors that they fear most because they can have such a dramatic effect, as witnessed by the global economic crisis of 2008–2009. The years 2008–2009 saw one of the biggest recessions in the UK in recent years.

Recession – when for at least two consecutive three-month periods (quarters), the value of all the goods produced and sold in the economy falls.

A recession in the economy tends to have ripple effects that spread out in increasing waves to affect more and more businesses.

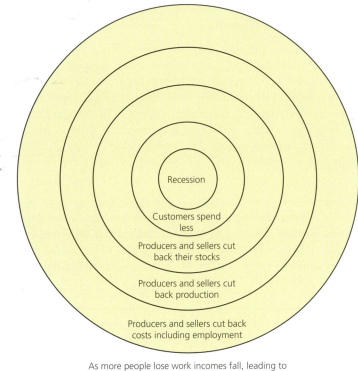

Recession

Customers spend less

Producers and sellers cut back their stocks

Producers and sellers cut back production

Producers and sellers cut back costs including employment

As more people lose work incomes fall, leading to further cutbacks in customer spending

FIGURE 1.1 A ripple effect resulting from initial changes in economic activity

In the second half of this book a range of economic factors that affect business is explored, including the rate of growth of the economy, inflation rates, changing foreign exchange levels and other factors.

1.4 The management of risk

Businesses are decision-making units that need to manage risk if they are to survive and prosper. The 2008–2009 recession highlighted issues associated with poor risk management, particularly in the financial sector of the economy. In response to the crisis, and what was seen as a systemic failure in banking and financial institutions, the government set up the Walker Review (2009) to come up with recommendations about improving the effectiveness of this sector, including better controls on risk management. The resulting Walker Report recommended that in banks and other financial intermediaries (BOFIs) there should be a separate 'risk committee' made up of independent directors responsible for monitoring and reviewing risk. The Report also recommended that there should be an officer specifically responsible for risk management and control in BOFIs.

> **Risk** – the chance of damage or loss resulting from an event or activity. Risks are taken in order to secure benefits (such as shareholder returns or profits).

KEY TERM

The two key variables determining the magnitude of risk are the likelihood of the risk and the impact that results.

Different organizations will have different risk appetites – in other words, they will be prepared to take on larger or smaller risks. Some industries are characterized by a higher risk appetite (e.g. speculative finance), while others have low risk appetites (e.g. insurance). Business by its very nature involves risk – there is a chance that a business may make a profit but there is also a chance that a business may make a loss. The owners of the business (entrepreneurs) must decide on how much risk they are prepared to take. As stated above, the insurance industry is typically conservative in the amount of risk that shareholders in insurance companies expect to take. Detailed calculations are made over time to ascertain the likely risk of particular accidents occurring. Premiums charged to those taking out insurance can then be set to make sure that the insurance company makes a healthy profit. In contrast, there are industries where far more speculation takes place. For example, in the search for precious minerals and oil and gas reserves entrepreneurs may take more of a gamble on profits materializing. Should abundant deposits of precious resources be found then the entrepreneur may make a substantial gain. People who seek higher returns from riskier ventures are said to have a strong risk appetite – more cautious investors are described as being 'risk averse'.

It should be clear from the above that organizations cannot eliminate business risks. However, they can choose from a number of alternatives:

- To **minimize risk**. To only choose the options with the lowest risk.

- To **maximize returns**. To choose risky options that yield the highest returns.

- To operate in a **prudent** way. To err on the side of caution – limiting the risks to what is regarded to be safe.

- To **balance risk and return**. To choose a combination of risk and return based on the risk appetite of the organization.

- To use some other formula for balancing risk and return.

Many of the risks that businesses face stem from the economic environment. Examples of the major risks are highlighted in Sections 1.5 and 1.6.

UK Company Law requires companies to produce a Business Review as part of the Directors' Report to shareholders. This process is still in development, but good practice typically involves three steps:

1. The identification and description of key risks.

2. Outlining the potential impact of these risks.

3. Detailing the steps that an organization has taken to mitigate these risks.

For example, a food company might list some of its principal risks as including:

• Increasing competition, product innovation, technical advances and changes in the market.

• Global economic downturn.

• Volatile global market trends.

• Change in the cost of supplies.

• Foreign currency and interest rate exposure.

Each of the uncertainties listed above is an economic risk. Business graduates and business managers need to understand the causes and effects of these economic risks because they can have such a dramatic effect on business performance.

A business needs to be able to respond to these risks in an appropriate way, as illustrated by Figure 1.2 (based on just one of the risks identified above).

FIGURE 1.2 Illustrating how a business can mitigate a specific risk

It is important therefore to develop a clear understanding of economic factors that constitute business risk. Knowing the potential impact of a risk enables a business to identify the seriousness of the consequences. For example, it is possible to argue that failures to fully identify economic risk factors have led to serious problems for many economies such as Greece, Ireland and Portugal in the wake of the 2008–2009 crisis.

Today these governments and many others are taking action to mitigate future risks – for example, by demanding that banks hold more liquid assets (cash and near cash equivalents), and that they ring-fence the impact of speculative bank activity so that it does not impact so severely on other banking operations. Requiring banks to hold more liquid assets means that should depositors withdraw deposits from the banks then the banks will have more reserves to meet customers' demands for liquidity.

Identify what you consider to be some of the principal risks facing a business of your choice that you would consider to be economic risks.

● **What are the potential impacts of these risks on the chosen business?**

● **What courses of action can the business take to mitigate these risks?**

Risk mitigation – involves controlling risk to a level that is compatible with the risk appetite of the company. Measures should be taken to limit risk.

Liquid assets – the financial reserves that a bank (or other business) holds in a form that can quickly be converted to cash.

In this introductory chapter it is helpful to provide some clear examples of ways in which changes in the economy have a direct impact on business. The next two sections therefore focus on the effects of some of the principal risks and uncertainties that are likely to face a business:

• Changes in incomes and spending; and

• Changing interest rates.

1.5 How changes in consumer incomes and spending affect business

One of the most direct ways in which economic changes affect business is the impact of changing incomes on expenditure. Most people's incomes consist in the main of the wage or salary they receive in return for their work. When wages fall or employees lose their jobs this leads to a fall in income. Common sense tells us that the knock-on effect will be a reduction in consumer spending (although initially people will try to maintain their existing standard of living and hence their spending levels).

In the UK in 2008–2009 **consumer spending** fell substantially as a result of falling incomes and rising unemployment. This fall in spending impacted directly on the sales of High Street retailers such as Next.

Consumer spending – consumers are people who spend money on consumer goods and services such as visits to clubs and the cinema (service expenditure) and on food, clothing and household goods (expenditure on physical goods).

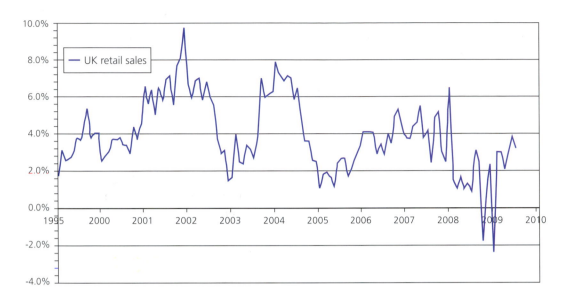

FIGURE 1.3 Changes in UK retail sales

Source: © Marketoracle.co.uk 2009. Data source ONS.

Figure 1.3 shows the impact of falling consumer spending at a macro (in this case UK-wide) level. Look carefully at the diagram and you will see that retail sales in 2009 were lower than they had been in the same period one year earlier. Shops were able to sell less because consumers weren't spending as much.

The chart shows that there was a pronounced fall in sales in 2009, in stark contrast to the period 2002–2004 when the economy was booming (with higher growth, low unemployment and low, stable inflation),

CASE STUDY Falling sales at Next

In August 2010, the fashion retailer Next announced that like-for-like sales could be down by between 1.5 per cent and 4.5 per cent in the second half of the year. The company also forecasted that their prices would rise by between 5 and 8 per cent because of rising costs – including higher cotton prices, the increase in Value Added Tax to a rate of 20 per cent in January, and changes in the exchange rate between the pound and other currencies.

Next stated that its research and sales figures indicated a falling level of consumer demand in the economy. Partly as a result of these predictions share prices for Next fell by 8 per cent.

- What has been happening to the sales of Next and other UK retailers in recent times?
- What does this tell you about the state of the economy?

The Next case highlights the way in which a specific high-street business was suffering from changes in the macro-economy. The money going into its tills was falling as consumers cut back ('a falling level of consumer demand in the economy').

A number of other macro factors were also affecting Next's costs. These included:

- Higher cotton prices;

- An increase in VAT; and

- Changes in the exchange rate.

Each of these factors helps to push up Next's costs. These factors would have contributed to Next's decision to raise prices. Business decisions that companies like Next make are therefore affected in a major way by changes in the macro-economy.

Reflective questions

1 Why do you think that share prices in Next are likely to have fallen as a result of the changes outlined above?

2 In what ways do you think that changes taking place in the economic environment that affected Next would also affect other firms in the economy? Would there also be further effects for households?

1.6 The impact of changes in interest rates on business

Another economic variable that has a major impact on business is the interest rate. Interest is the cost of borrowing money. It is typically expressed as a percentage. Later on in the book (see Section 10.7) we look in detail at how interest rates are set.

There are many different rates of interest in an economy. The interest charged depends on how big a risk the lender is taking, the length of the loan and other factors. However, interest rates will follow a pattern which is strongly influenced by the monetary authorities in a country which may be the government's bank, or a committee of experts brought together to set the interest rate that the government will lend at. In recent years the interest rate set by the Bank of England's Monetary Policy Committee has become more important than ever before in determining other interest rates. This is because many large banks and other financial institutions have had to borrow from the government during the 'financial crisis'. Other institutions therefore set their own interest rates at a little above the rate that they are charged when they borrow from the government's bank. As such, the monetary authorities have a strong influence on national interest rates. When they raise the central bank's interest rate all other interest rates will tend to rise shortly afterwards. When they lower the interest rates all other interest rates are likely to fall.

KEY TERMS

Monetary authorities – groups and institutions with responsibility for overseeing the supply of money to, and financial arrangements within, an economy. They include the central bank of a country, and committees specially set up to set the government's official interest rate and to licence and regulate banks.

Financial crisis – a period of uncertainty in the banking and financial sectors of the economy in 2008 and 2009. During this period a number of banks found that they did not have enough ready funds to meet potential withdrawals. The UK government response was to provide new funding to the financial sector provided that certain criteria were met, including cutting back on risky lending activities. The government also partially nationalized a number of banks, including Lloyds and HBOS.

Businesses favour low interest rates, for two obvious reasons:

- They can borrow more cheaply.

- Their customers can borrow more cheaply and are therefore likely to spend more.

During the recent recession, the Monetary Policy Committee in the UK continually lowered interest rates until they reached 0.5 per cent, as illustrated by Figure 1.4.

This cheap money policy was designed to encourage greater spending during the recession. Figure 1.4 shows how interest rates had fallen to 0.5 per cent from the first quarter of 2009, and were retained at this level in 2010 and 2011.

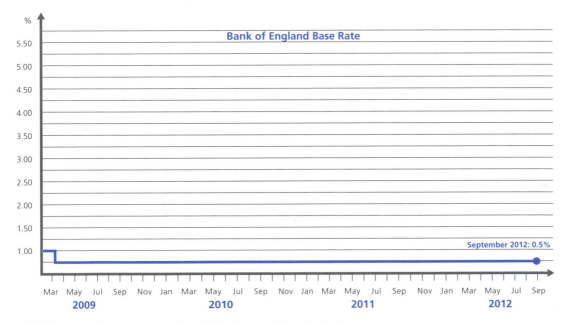

FIGURE 1.4 UK base interest rates established by the monetary authorities

Source: Bank of England.

CASE STUDY Keeping interest rates down

In September 2010 Charlie Bean, the Deputy Governor of the Bank of England, said that interest rates were being kept low in order to encourage consumers to spend more. In an interview he stated that low interest rates would act as an incentive for people to spend rather than to save.

In the period from April to June 2010, households were only saving a very low 3.2 per cent of their income. This figure masks substantial differences between poor households who might have to spend all of their income (and then borrow some), and higher-income households who would have been able to save.

Lowering interest rates would have the impact of encouraging higher-income households to spend more and save less at a time of falling demand in the economy.

- **What has been happening recently to interest rates in the UK?**
- **What is the likely impact on saving?**

While businesses generally welcomed the cheap cost of borrowing money, it did not mean that they were easily able to access funds. In fact, during 2010 businesses found it increasingly difficult to borrow from many parts of the financial sector. Banks were reluctant to lend in a period in which demand in the economy was sluggish. They feared that the loans they made might not be repaid despite the best intentions of the business community.

The examples outlined above make it very clear that business is affected in a substantial way by changes in the wider economic environment. Business people need to constantly monitor economic conditions, forecasts and changes in economic indicators. Understanding of how the economy operates is therefore essential to all business students.

1.7 Some key economic concepts that appear in this book

Economists use a range of concepts that have been developed over time and which are helpful in informing business decision making. A brief introduction to four of these is outlined below.

The opportunity cost of making a choice

When we use resources to produce an item, we are taking these **resources** away from the production of something else.

Decision making over the use of resources involves:

- Making a **choice** (we can do one thing or the other).

- Making a **sacrifice** (if we choose to do this with a resource, we cannot also do the other).

Daily life for individuals and businesses involves solving many economic problems where choices have to be made. For example, as a student you have to decide whether to buy this book or borrow it from a library. If you buy the book, you 'sacrifice' the opportunity to buy something else with the money you would have saved by borrowing it.

Opportunity cost refers to the next best alternative that we give up when we make a particular choice. For example, when a farmer decides to sell his produce to Tesco rather than to a local fruit and vegetable wholesaler, then the opportunity cost principally consists of the return that he could have made from supplying the local wholesaler.

Many first-time business owners fail to appreciate the opportunity cost of decisions they make. For example, when they start to work for themselves the opportunity cost includes the income or wage that they had previously been earning.

The concept of opportunity cost needs to be considered in any business decision that involves weighing up alternatives. Another example is in investment appraisal. There is always a cost to investing money in a business project because that sum of money could have been used in an alternative way. The returns from the next best alternative project foregone should be seen as the opportunity cost of an investment.

The importance of incentives in decision making

An **incentive** is a reward that encourages an individual, business or other economic unit to take a particular course of action. Incentives help to motivate many different types of economic behaviour. For example, profit acts as an incentive to supply more of a product. Bonuses act as an incentive for city bankers to work harder or to achieve better results. If incentives can be employed to encourage certain types of activity then penalties (negative incentives) can be used to discourage other activities. A tax on pollution might discourage businesses from emitting harmful waste into water or into the air.

The importance of the market

One of the ongoing themes in economics has been the analysis of how the **market** works and how the workings of the market can be improved. Adam Smith is generally regarded to be the founding father of economics as we know it. In his book *An Inquiry into the Nature and Causes of the Wealth of Nations*, written in 1776, he identified the market as a situation in which buyers and sellers come together to trade. In his view buyers and sellers pursue their own personal selfish interests, but this typically leads to an efficient use of resources in society. Millions of decision makers signal their preferences through the market and this determines how resources will be used.

Economic efficiency

Economists are also concerned with how resources can be used in an efficient way. **Efficiency** refers to getting maximum results from the inputs that go into any activity. Some economists believe that allowing free competition is the best way to achieve economic efficiency. Businesses seek to compete with each other by lowering costs and prices, or by somehow differentiating their products from those of other firms. However, other economists believe that efficiency is best achieved by producing on a large scale, enabling 'economies of scale' in production.

1.8 Summary

There is a two-way relationship between business and the economy. The economy provides a constantly changing environment in which business decisions need to be made. The decisions that businesses make then impact on the economy. Business decisions have a direct impact on the local economy (e.g. the decisions that the Boots company makes in Nottingham). The decisions that a number of businesses make have a wider macro-economic effect. Business students need to understand a range of micro-economic and macro-economic concepts, and how economic changes impact on business decision making. Economic changes comprise some of the principal risks and uncertainties facing business decision makers. By understanding economic influences on risk it is possible to mitigate these risks by taking appropriate actions.

KEY THEME

Businesses are independent units that set out to meet the objectives of their owners. Each business paves its own path to success. Some do well while others struggle. Many of their experiences are particular to the business itself – for example, does it have the right products for the market it is selling in? Is it more efficient than competitors? Is it in the right location? And so on.

However, there are experiences that are common to a broad range of businesses, resulting from the state of the economy and changes taking place in the wider economy. For example, Lloyds Bank produces a monthly 'barometer' of business confidence based on a survey of UK businesses. The barometer involves surveying businesses to find out if business people feel more or less confident about business prospects. In March 2012, Lloyds reported that 51 per cent of businesses were more optimistic whereas only 20 per cent were more pessimistic than they had been in the previous month. This backed up Lloyds Bank's view that the economy would pick up in the second half of 2012. This came on the back of falling concerns by economists about the Eurozone crisis (i.e. worries that countries such as Greece and Portugal, with high debts, would either need to be bailed out by other Eurozone countries, or might default on some of their debts).

However, it is interesting to note that more recently the concerns of economists have again risen about uncertainties in the Eurozone, and whether the structural problems faced by economies such as Greece, Spain, Ireland and Portugal will go away. A key theme from this chapter is that businesses do not operate in isolation from changes around them. The different parts of the economy are interlinked and businesses are impacted on in a major way by changes in the wider economy.

● **What major changes in the wider economy have been taking place recently that impact on businesses in your locality?**

KEY IDEAS

Some of the main points covered in this chapter are listed below. If you feel unsure about any of them, then revisit the appropriate section. If you would like some additional reading on the topic, try the books listed below in recommended reading.

What is the economy?

- The economy is a system that exists to resolve key economic problems such as what to produce, how to produce, and how goods and services will be distributed between members of society.

Risks and uncertainties

- A basic fact of business life is risk.
- Many of the principal risks and uncertainties facing businesses stem from the economic environment, including market conditions and changes in variables such as the exchange and interest rate.
- Business managers need to take appropriate steps to mitigate risk through a process of risk management.

How the economy impacts on business

- Changes in the economy are major concerns for all businesses. Some of these changes, such as the onset of a recession, can have a dramatic ripple effect that affects businesses and households across the economy.

How changes in consumer incomes and spending affect business

- The major determinant of how much revenue a company receives is the expenditure pattern of consumers.
- If consumer incomes fall they will have less to spend.
- This may lead to a downturn in demand for goods and services for many firms.

The impact of changing interest rates on business
- The interest rate is the cost of borrowing money.
- Businesses like to be able to borrow at low interest rates.
- However, when interest rates are low it is not always easy to borrow.

Some key economic concepts
- There are some central economic concepts that appear many times when exploring how the economy works.
- These concepts include opportunity cost and economic efficiency.

REVIEW QUESTIONS

1. What is an economy? What are the main decisions made in the economy?

2. What is the difference between the macro- and the micro-economy?

3. What is risk and how can risks be mitigated? Provide an example.

4. What is the relationship between consumer income and spending?

5. Who are the monetary authorities and how do they control interest rates?

6. What is opportunity cost? Give an example of how opportunity cost impacts on business decision making?

7. What is the role of incentives in the economy?

8. What is the market? Who are the participants in the market?

9. What is economic efficiency?

10. Who makes economic decisions?

RECOMMENDED READING

Harford, T. (2006) *The Undercover Economist*, Oxford, Oxford University Press.

> This book provides a very interesting and easy to understand introduction to economics, and the theories and concepts that economists use in their day-to-day work.

Levitt, S.D. and Dubner, S.J. (2005) *Freakonomics*, London, Penguin Books.

> Chapter 1 explores the nature of incentives in economics.

REFERENCES

Smith, A. (1776) *An Inquiry into the Nature and Causes of the Wealth of Nations*, republished (1976), edited by R.H. Campbell and A.S. Skinner, Oxford, Clarendon Press.

USEFUL WEBSITES

www.guardian.co.uk/business/interest-rates – latest news, and comments, on UK interest rates from *The Guardian* newspaper.

www.ons.gov.uk – The Office for National Statistics site provides a range of useful data relating to macro-economic indicators.

www.timharford.com – provides a range of interesting articles about economics that Tim Harford has written for the *Financial Times*.

2 Quantitative analysis for economists

CHAPTER OBJECTIVES

After carefully reading and engaging with the tasks and activities outlined in this chapter you should have a better understanding of:

- The meaning of the term econometrics and situations when an econometric approach can be applied

- Situations in which economists use diagrams to illustrate simple statistical relationships

- The nature and uses of predictions

- How a relationship can be illustrated between two variables

- How to construct index numbers and the uses of index numbers

- How to calculate a share price index

2.1 Introduction

Economists frequently use quantitative techniques to identify trends and patterns. Statistical techniques help economists to demonstrate relationships between variables – for example, between the growth of the economy and the level of employment. Quantitative techniques have been helpful in enabling economists to develop theories. However, in some instances they have also proved a hindrance in overcomplicating explanations and sometimes in oversimplifying reality.

Some readers may want to read all of this chapter during their first reading of this text. Alternatively, you may want to quickly review some of the content and then re-read various sections of the chapter in greater detail when you come across the various quantitative approaches later in the book. The chapter outlines some of the major quantitative approaches that economists employ. Because economics leans heavily on them it is important to be familiar with key quantitative techniques. Some of these techniques have been simplified in order to make economics more accessible to the reader.

One of the most widely respected books on economics, *Principles of Economics,* was written by Alfred Marshall and first printed in 1890. Marshall came into economics having trained as a mathematician. His book used very clear explanations with only a limited use of mathematical treatment. Marshall argued that economists should only use mathematics as shorthand language when developing theories and ideas. He argued that they should always write their explanations in clear English and illustrate points by examples rather than by mathematical theories. The examples used should be relevant to real life.

In a letter of 27 February 1906 Marshall gave some very useful advice (Pigou, 1925: 427–8):

> a good mathematical theorem dealing with economic hypotheses was very unlikely to be good economics; and I went more and more on the rules –
>
> 1. Use mathematics as a shorthand language, rather than as an engine of inquiry.
> 2. Keep them till you have done.
> 3. Translate into English.
> 4. Then illustrate by examples that are important in real life.
> 5. Burn the mathematics.
> 6. If you can't succeed in 4 burn 3.

Marshall's emphasis is therefore on making economics useful, and this is the approach that the author has sought to take in writing this book. Marshall (1920: 1.IV.1) stated that 'Economic science is but the working of common sense aided by appliances of organized analysis and general reasoning, which facilitate the task of collecting, arranging and drawing evidence from particular facts.' You can learn a lot from Marshall – in other words, apply common sense reasoning to facts that emerge from your reading and study.

Unfortunately some of the economists who followed after Marshall tended to overuse mathematical treatment so that some aspects of the subject became impenetrable. Fortunately some of the leading economists in recent times have reversed this trend and have gone back to writing in a way that everyone with an interest in the economy should be able to understand.

2.2 An econometric approach

KEY TERM

Econometrics – the application of statistical methods and mathematics to economic data.

Many important developments in economics have traditionally relied heavily on mathematical treatments of topics. In this chapter we will identify some of the reasons why this has been the case, as well as some of the problems of over-reliance on mathematical formulations. The chapter then goes on to look at how economists use diagrams and models to help them to understand and explain economic relationships and how the economy works.

The earliest economic works, such as Adam Smith's *An Inquiry into the Nature and Cause of the Wealth of Nations* (1776), provided typically descriptive accounts of how the economy worked. For example, Smith described how economies developed from simple subsistence models to more advanced industrial ones, and how specialization of tasks leads to increases in production. However, it was not long before mathematical formulations were introduced – for example, Thomas Malthus' (1798) essay on population, which provided the base for the assumption that population increases at a geometric rate (e.g. 2, 4, 8, 16, 32, 64, etc.) while food production increases at an arithmetic rate (e.g. 2, 4, 6, 8, 10, 12, etc.). Using a mathematical approach Malthus was able to show how the rapid acceleration of population would lead to crises in the form of famines and other problems.

In 1817 David Ricardo's work, *The Principles of Political Economy and Taxation,* set out trade theory, showing how countries benefit from specialization using a mathematical treatment to show the advantages of this arrangement. He was able to show that when countries specialized it was possible for the combined output from economies to be greater than without specialization.

By the twentieth century econometrics had become a major branch of economics. Econometrics is concerned with economic measurement, and has been defined by Samuelson *et al.* (1954) as 'the quantitative analysis of actual economic phenomena based on the concurrent development of theory and observation, related by appropriate methods of inference'.

KEY TERMS

Statistical inference – refers to the way in which we learn or 'infer' something about the real world as a result of the analysis of a sample of data.

Monetarism – a branch of economic theory which relates rises in prices (inflation) to changes in the quantity of money in circulation. In simple terms, as the quantity of money circulating in the economy increases this is likely to be followed by an increase in prices (after a time lag). A reduction in the quantity of money might lead to a fall in prices (deflation) after a time lag. The relationship between the quantity of money and the average level of prices can be recorded by measurement (quantitative analysis).

CASE STUDY Applying economics to monetary policy

An excellent example of how econometrics has been applied with some success in the real world is in charting the relationship between the quantity of money in circulation and prices. One of the best explanations of monetary inflation was provided by the American economist Milton Friedman in the book he wrote with Anna Schwartz, *A Monetary History of the United States, 1867–1960*, published in 1963.

Friedman and Schwartz argued, on the basis of the econometric data that they had collected, that price levels are linked to the quantity of money available. In other words, 'inflation is always and everywhere a monetary phenomenon'. This work became a model of good practice in using detailed statistical analysis over a long period to make the link between prices and the quantity of money.

Gujarati (1988) states that economic analysis typically proceeds in the following way:

1. Statement of theory or hypothesis.
2. Specification of the econometric model to test the theory.
3. Estimation of the parameters of the chosen model.
4. Verification or statistical inference.
5. Forecasting or prediction.
6. Use of the model for control or policy purposes.

FIGURE 2.1
Milton Friedman – an economist whose work on monetary policy in the United States was based on a detailed econometric approach

Source: Milton Friedman, 1971 © CSU Archives, courtesy Everett Collection/Alamy.

Friedman's thinking and previous work (as well as his understanding of previous economic theory) postulated the hypothesis that there was a link between money supply and changes in price. This was then tested by detailed analysis of US figures over a period of time. From this it was possible to compare money supply figures with prices and price changes. On the basis of the findings from the research it is now possible to make forecasts and predictions. Friedman's model today predicts that an increase in money supply will lead to an increase in prices after a time lag.

This gave rise to a growing emphasis in the West, particularly in the 1980s and 1990s, on monetarism. During this period many governments paid particular attention to the supply of money. For example, in Britain and elsewhere we have money supply targets in order to control monetary inflation. The example shows how painstaking research using econometrics provides the basis for economic policy-making.

Reflective questions

1   Why do you think that relating the quantity of money to prices lends itself to an econometric approach?

2   Can you think of three other situations in which an econometric approach might be helpful in studying economic relationships?

Benefits of applying econometrics

Using econometrics is potentially very helpful:

- Econometrics helps us to test out important economic hypotheses – for example, that the level of education in a country impacts on the rate of growth of the economy.

- Econometrics helps us to estimate the relationship between economic variables using econometric methods such as being able to calculate the impact of a change in the price of a good on the change in the quantity purchased and the change in revenues and profits.

- Econometrics also helps us to predict economic outcomes – for example, what the impact of the government raising the level of income tax will be on tax revenues and consumer spending.

Criticisms of over use of econometrics

Most economic journals that can be accessed in libraries and through electronic searches contain many articles that are based on econometric research. For many economic researchers it has become standard practice to test out a problem or question by constructing an econometric model based on testing out theories related to the question or problem being investigated. Predictions are made and tests are carried out to identify the relationship between economic variables.

Once the relationship between variables has been analysed using statistical techniques, then statistical inferences can be drawn out. Sometimes this is set out in a descriptive way – for example, the relationship between changes in the quantity of money and prices is x. At other times economists may go further and set out the policy implications of their findings – for example, the government can control price inflation by limiting the increase in the supply of money in a particular period to y per cent.

However, there have been criticisms from some quarters about the over-reliance and overemphasis on statistical modelling. While it may be possible to outline the relationship between money supply and prices in some situations, there may be other situations in which mathematical modelling is less valid. This is particularly so when there is a stronger human dimension to behaviours associated with economic activity. Humans make economic decisions in human ways – and these cannot always be subjected to mathematical modelling. In 2008 an economics journal called the *Post-Autistic Economic Review* was launched. The title was intended to be critical of rigid econometric modelling and an over-focus in economics on abstract theory. More recently the journal has changed its name to the *Real World Economic Review*, partly in recognition that the original title was not sympathetic to the condition of being autistic.

Reflective question

3   What do you see as being the benefits and the drawbacks of relying heavily on econometrics in economic and business analysis?

The interpretation of economic data

Economists use economic data to indicate what is happening in the economy and to identify relationships between economic variables.

However, the data that economists present may be used by different people in different ways. For example, statisticians may gather data showing changes in the level of employment. By analysing this data, economists may be able to show that unemployment rises during a period of economic recession when the economy slows down. The data supplied by the statistician and the economist may then be used by a politician to make a political point. For example, an opposition politician may use the rising unemployment figures to suggest that the existing government has engaged in poor economic management. It is very important therefore to understand that the analysis carried out by economists may be distorted by others for their own purposes.

There are two broad approaches that an economist can use which enable us to identify two main branches of economics:

- **Positive economics** is concerned with studying and making statements about what is demonstrable. For example, the GDP of the UK in February 2012 was £x as measured by the Office for National Statistics.

- **Normative economics** is based on value judgements. Whereas positive economics focuses on what 'is', normative economics is concerned with what 'ought to be'. For example, normative economics might make the case that raising the minimum wage is a good thing because it will reduce poverty.

There has been considerable debate over the years as to whether economists should operate from a positivist or from a normative stance. Some economists believe that the approach of an economist should be to find out the 'facts' whereas others believe that 'facts' rarely exist so it is better for an economist to state their beliefs and to identify a coherent case explaining why particular actions and policies are likely to lead to 'better' and 'different' ends.

2.3 Using diagrams and simple statistical relationships

In this book we use diagrams to model the inter-relationships between economic variables. We have also employed some basic statistical techniques that can be used to help provide an understanding of the relationship between key economic variables.

Statistics begins with the collection of raw data. This is obtained by collecting observations or measurements. The type of data that economists are principally interested in is made up of numerical quantities such as changes in unemployment levels, or consumer spending figures.

All data must be stored in a databank or catalogued as a list. An inventory is a document setting out a basic set of data from which different types of inferences can be made. In most situations the first step of analysis is to determine the frequency distribution of the collected data. This can refer to either:

- The frequency of occurrence of each listed value or quality; or

- The frequency of occurrence of values or numbers which fall within a certain range – for example, households with an income between £10,000 and £19,999.

Once data has been collected, there are three important steps in making sense of statistical information. These are:

- Interpreting: establishing what the information means.

- Presenting: choosing the best way of showing the information.

- Organizing: assembling the information in a structured way.

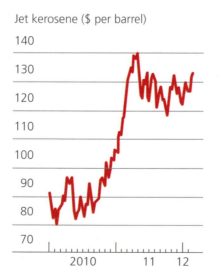

FIGURE 2.2 Fuel price of jet kerosene

For example, data may be collected about aircraft fuel prices. It makes sense to examine this data over a period of time (e.g. 2010–2012). This can then be presented in the form of a time-series chart (see Figure 2.2). The chart and the information that it presents can then be organized into a review of airline costs and the implications for the airline industry.

CASE STUDY Business application – regression analysis

Regression analysis is a major approach used by economists to study business and economic data. Regression analysis is helpful in identifying patterns and trends and is useful for predicting future business and economic conditions.

Regression analysis uses statistical equations (known as models) to predict the values of a dependent variable based on the values of one or more independent variables. The value of the independent variable is used as a predictor of the value of the dependent variable. Univariate regression analysis estimates the value of a single dependent variable based on the value of an independent variable. So for example we could use regression analysis to predict the consumption of cigarettes based on the price of cigarettes. Here the consumption of cigarettes is the dependent variable and the price of cigarettes is the independent variable.

Multivariate regression analysis predicts the impact on a dependent variable of changes in a number of variables. For example, the consumption of cigarettes may be affected not only by the price of cigarettes, but by changes in consumer income and government initiatives to deter smoking. Multivariate regression analysis therefore examines the change in a dependent variable resulting from a change in a dependent variable while holding other variables that might impact on the dependent variable constant.

- What is the main difference between univariate and multivariate regression analysis?
- What would you expect to be the relationship between the price of a good and the quantity demanded of that good, where the price is the dependent variable and the quantity demanded is the independent variable?
- Why might it be helpful to use multivariate analysis to investigate the demand for a good or service?

Values that change over time

Line graphs are particularly useful in showing how values or quantities rise and fall over a period of time. Graphs showing changes in the value of variables over time are also called time series charts. Time series charts can be used for showing a wide range of economic variables such as:

- Interest rates.
- Unemployment rates.

- Inflation rates.

- Exchange rates.

- The rate of growth of the economy.

- Changes in population.

- Fluctuations in share prices.

Time series line charts are a particularly effective way of making comparisons between two economic variables – for example, comparing the rate of inflation with the unemployment level.

The illustration here (Figures 2.3a, 2.3b and 2.3c) shows a general fall in inflation rates at a time of rising unemployment (as a result of recession) in the period September 2011–January 2012.

Reflective questions

4 Studying the diagram for inflation and unemployment does there appear to be a relationship between the level of unemployment and the rate of inflation?

5 If so why do you think that there might be a relationship between these two variables over time?

Illustrating trends

Economists seek to identify trends as well as to predict future trends. What is happening to exchange rates, economic growth rates, etc. – is it possible to make predictions about the future based on trends?

Trend – a general direction or tendency whereby a variable appears to rise, fall or fluctuate over a period of time.

KEY TERM

Business and economic data is affected by:

1. Seasonal movements – for example, the highest proportion of retail sales take place in the Christmas period.

2. Cyclical movements – business and economic activity is strongly influenced by movements in the trade cycle. As we shall see later in the book, economies experience an economic cycle of booms and recessions in economic activity.

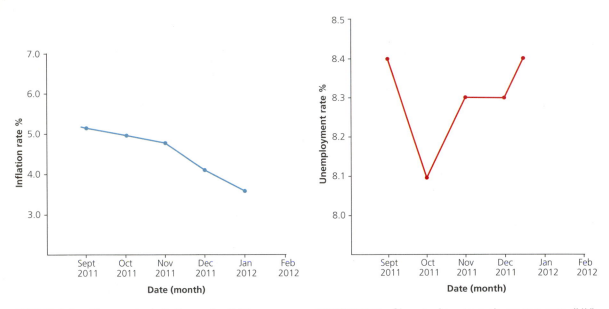

FIGURE 2.3a Change in inflation rate (UK)
Source: ONS.

FIGURE 2.3b Change in unemployment rate (UK)
Source: ONS.

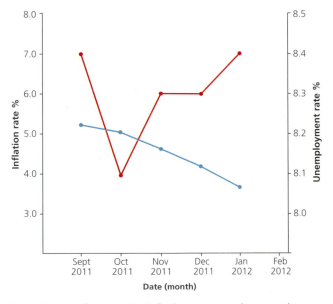

FIGURE 2.3c Change in inflation rate and unemployment rate (UK)
Source: ONS.

CASE STUDY Seasonal variation

In Figure 2.4 you can see two elements causing fluctuations in sales figures. One is an underlying trend towards increasing sales as the company in question steadily raises its public profile and market share. This underlying trend is represented by the rising dotted line.

In addition, you can see a seasonal trend for increased sales in December (pre-Christmas) and January (due to January sales).

On the graph, Point X is higher than Point Y for two reasons:

*   Because of the upward trend over time.
*   Because X is December while Y is in the summer period.

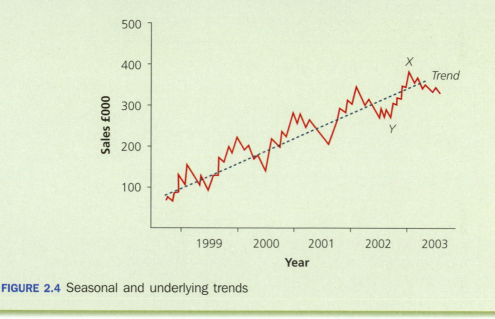

FIGURE 2.4 Seasonal and underlying trends

Moving averages

A good way to calculate a trend is by using a moving average. To create the moving average you need to think carefully about the basis on which the average is calculated. For example, in calculating unemployment figures it makes sense to take account of seasonal changes.

Using the four seasons of the year may be appropriate when there are clear quarterly patterns. However, other patterns may need to be considered in other situations. For example, in calculating supermarket sales it is important to consider distinct daily sales patterns. Averages would need to be worked out over a seven-day period to allow for the effect of higher sales on Fridays and at weekends.

CASE STUDY Supplying oil for central heating

A firm supplying oil for central heating faces high demand in autumn and winter and lower demand in spring and summer.

In order to find out the long-term trend in demand for its product, the business needs to eliminate the seasonal variation from its demand picture. It does this by creating a moving average which smooths out demand for the four seasons of the year.

The first step is to calculate the average for the first group of four seasons. Then an average is taken for a second group of four seasons, starting with spring, and so on.

The demand patterns and resulting moving averages are shown in Figure 2.5.

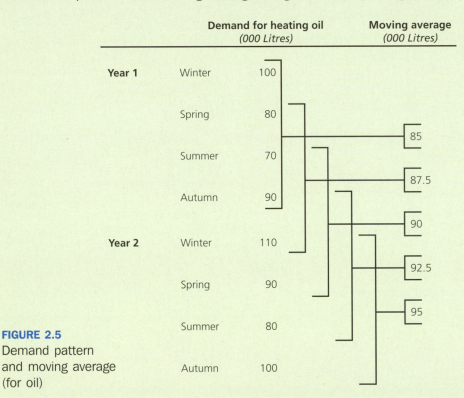

		Demand for heating oil (000 Litres)	Moving average (000 Litres)
Year 1	Winter	100	
	Spring	80	
			85
	Summer	70	
			87.5
	Autumn	90	
			90
Year 2	Winter	110	
			92.5
	Spring	90	
			95
	Summer	80	
	Autumn	100	

FIGURE 2.5
Demand pattern and moving average (for oil)

You can see from the illustration that in each of the seasons in Year 2, values have risen by ten from the previous year. Having removed the seasonal variation, it is therefore possible to identify a steady upward movement.

Plotting a trend simply involves finding moving averages which are relevant to the sequence of quantities that we are studying.

If we are studying figures where there are four seasons, then we take moving averages covering every four sets of figures.

> **Moving average** – an average of a data set calculated over a period of time. For example, it is often used to measure the average price of securities over 20, 30, 50, 100 or 200 days. Each day the data for the new day is entered into the series and the oldest data (i.e. data that is no longer included in the time period) is removed from the series.

Seasonally adjusted figures

To identify underlying trends it is important to account for seasonal variations. For example, the unemployment figures for the summer of 2012 may look particularly bad until we notice, for example, that they are lower than at the same time in a previous year. It is quite usual for unemployment to rise when school leavers and university students swell the numbers of those looking for work.

Statisticians need to be aware of – and adjust for – these seasonal patterns.

'Smoothed data'

Most economic data – and a lot of business data, such as sales and employment figures – is produced monthly and quarterly. This data is often obscured by regular seasonal events such as changes in the weather, opening and closing of schools or major holidays.

Because of the British climate, for example, employment in the building industry typically slows down in winter and picks up again in spring. Given that this increase is seasonal, how do we know if an increase in building employment is higher or lower than normal?

Removing or neutralizing regularly occurring increases or decreases during a given month results in 'smoothed' data that give us a better perspective from which to see the true size of the over-the-month change.

Eliminating random fluctuations

In addition to seasonal fluctuations, there can be a number of random fluctuations, which affect data. To identify a trend we need to remove both the seasonal and these random influences.

We can therefore say:

Trend = Data – Seasonal Effect – Random Error

2.4 Making predictions

Predictions are statements which are probable or credible (using reasoning and common sense) in that they attempt to take the 'don't know' out of economic and business decision making and replacing it with 'I predict'. However, in the economic world, predictions and forecasts have to take into account many different variables and uncertainties – so a

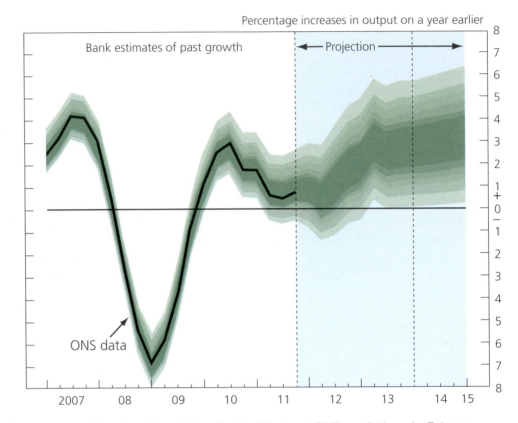

Percentage increases in output on a year earlier

FIGURE 2.6 Fan chart illustrating Bank of England GDP predictions in February 2012

wide range of alternative predictions are often made. For example, the fan chart shown in Figure 2.6 indicates the wide range of alternative GDP predictions made by the Bank of England in February 2012.

In business and economic forecasting, it is possible to establish expected values based on careful analysis of trends and other fluctuations.

One formula for forecasting data such as unemployment levels, sales revenues and profit is:

Forecasted Figures = T + S + R

Where T is the expected trend, S is the expected seasonal variation and R is a random variation.

Establishing the trend

In establishing a trend we need to examine the most recent patterns and any causal explanations that may underlie them.

The process of extending a trend outside the time range of the original data is called extrapolation.

Estimates of future figures can be based on extending the trend and seasonal variations from previous periods.

Establishing the seasonal variation

In establishing the seasonal variation, we need to examine the most recent seasonal variations and examine whether these are likely to change over time.

Estimating the random variation

The random variation is the most difficult to estimate. One method is to calculate random changes on the basis of how significant random factors have been in the past. Sometimes it makes sense to ignore random factors or discount negative random factors altogether. If we are feeling pessimistic or cautious, however, we may want to make a generous allowance for negative random factors.

2.5 Relating two variables

A statistical investigation often involves the observation of two variables that are related in some way. For example, the amount spent on consumables by families is often related to their disposable income.

In order to explore the relationship between two variables, the first step is to collect data and to set them out in a table. For example, Table 2.1 shows data for family income and the amount of consumer spending by each family over a year.

Once the information has been collected it can be set out in what is known as a scatter graph. On Figure 2.7 one variable is measured from the horizontal axis and the other from the vertical axis. Each intersection of the two measurements represents an observation, and each observation shows the relationship between the two variables.

TABLE 2.1 Income and consumption expenditure by families

Income (£000s)	Consumption (£000s)
5	8
40	32
15	20
30	25
50	40
10	12
6	10
60	45
20	20
25	24

'Line of best fit'

Where the relation between two variables is a simple or direct one, the result can often be represented by a straight line sloping down from left to right or vice versa.

The easiest way to carry out this work is to use a computer package such as Microsoft Excel – it is easy to set up a scatter graph and then simply to ask the programme to draw the line of best fit for you.

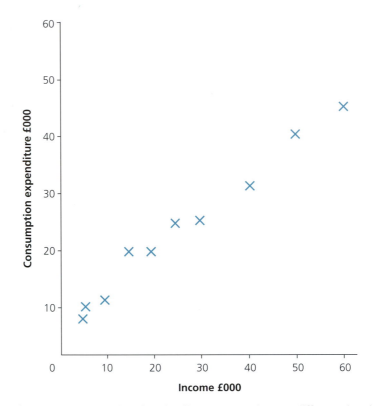

FIGURE 2.7 Scatter diagram showing family consumption at different levels of income

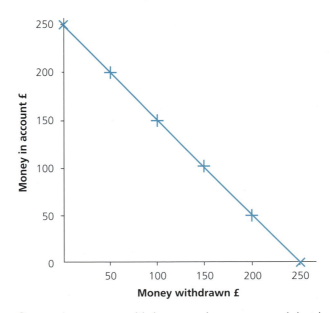

FIGURE 2.8 Comparing money withdrawn and money remaining in account

For example, a graph showing sums withdrawn from a bank account on one axis and the resulting bank balance on the other axis would look like Figure 2.8.

However, in the real world relationships are rarely as exact as this. In plotting points on a graph, we often find that they are scattered on either side of a straight line drawn to show the typical relationship between two variables.

The straight line that can be drawn through the dots to show the 'typical' relationship between the two variables is called 'the line of best fit'. This is a measure of the central tendency, which seeks to iron out the variations between the scattered points.

In Figure 2.9, the line of best fit shows the central tendency in relating family income to family expenditure. It shows the straight line from which the scattered points deviate.

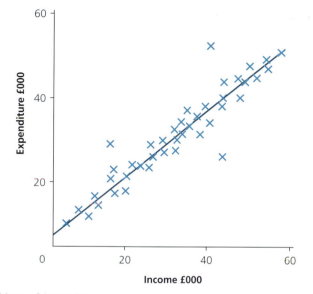

FIGURE 2.9 Line of best fit

Correlation – describes the relationship between two variables. Correlation refers to situations where there is an association between the behaviour of two variables.

KEY TERM

Reflective questions

6   Why do you think that correlation is likely to be an approach that is relevant to economics?

7   Can you think of situations where correlation will occur between economic variables?

- When both variables are moving consistently in the same direction (e.g. when consumption increases as incomes increase) we say there is a positive correlation.

- When one variable moves consistently in the opposite direction to the other variable (e.g. when one falls while the other rises), we say there is a negative correlation (e.g. as my withdrawals increase, the amount of money in my bank falls).

- When there is no pattern to the relationship between two variables we say there is no correlation.

Correlation coefficient

The correlation coefficient is a numerical measure of the strength of a correlation. It is represented by the letter r. It measures the closeness to which a sample of paired values fit a straight line.

The most common form of correlation coefficient is the Pearson correlation coefficient, which measures the extent to which each value differs from the mean of its own distribution, the standard deviation of the two distributions, and the number of pairs of values. Most computers and calculators include a function for calculating Pearson's coefficient.

Using the Pearson correlation the value of r varies from +1 for perfect positive correlation to −1 for perfect negative correlation. In both cases of perfect correlation, all the points would lie on an imaginary straight line. A zero value of r indicates that X and Y are independent of each other.

Figure 2.10, which is widely used in statistics, provides a good way of visualizing different strengths of correlation.

A rough guide to the strength of correlation (both positive and negative) is sometimes given as:

0.0–0.2	=	very weak
0.2–0.4	=	weak
0.4–0.7	=	moderate
0.7–0.9	=	strong
0.9–0.10	=	very strong

The purpose of correlation analysis is to show the association between data – for example, to show the association between an increase in sales of two separate products.

Very often, decision makers need to identify the causal relationship between one variable and another – for example, the relationship between interest rates and consumer spending, income and consumption, or between advertising expenditure and sales of a product.

Where the magnitude of one variable depends on the other, we say that:

- The variable that causes the change in the other is the independent variable.

- The variable that responds to the change in the other is the dependent variable.

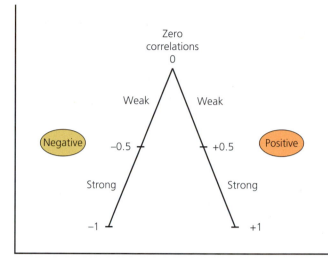

FIGURE 2.10 Different strengths of correlation

For example, the Chancellor of the Exchequer may want to analyse the relationship between an increase in taxes on spending (independent variable) and consumer spending patterns (dependent variable).

However, we need to be careful in interpreting the relationship between variables. It may be the case that the 'independent' variable is also dependent on the other variables. In some cases there may be a third variable that affects the other two.

Leading and lagging indicators

In studying economic data there are many situations where movements in economic variables are closely followed by changes in other variables. For example, a rise in disposable income is typically followed, after a period of time, by a rise in the demand for consumer goods. Business managers are therefore particularly interested in leading indicators because this enables them to forecast future changes in demand.

So for example, if you are a business manager in a company selling a brand of perfume where you know that the sales are affected by consumer income – then you will carefully follow changes in consumer incomes in order to forecast changes in demand.

Leading indicators in the UK which are good indicators of changes in the economy are:

- New house building.
- New orders for producer (capital) goods.
- Changes in manufacturing stocks.
- Changes in consumer credit.
- Stock exchange prices.

Leading indicator – a variable that goes up before the trade cycle has bottomed out and falls before the peak of the trade cycle.

Lagging indicator – a variable that goes down after the peak of the trade cycle and rises before the trade cycle bottoms out.

Economic models

Economic modelling has been a key aspect of the development of economics over time. For example, we have models which seek to illustrate how prices are determined in markets, and models which show the impact of government spending on the economy.

Economic model – a theoretical construction set out to show economic processes involving sets of variables and (logical or quantitative) relationships between them (e.g. if demand rises what is the impact on price?).

Models help us to simplify the complex real world to identify key relationships between important variables. Reasoned choices need to be made about which variables and relationships to focus on in our models. Economists first construct models and then they check these models for accuracy. Models are only useful to the extent to which they reflect the relationships they claim to be identifying.

In recent years a number of economic models have been criticized for oversimplifying reality to such an extent that the models lack value. In this context the models can be problematic. For example, following the recent global financial crisis a group of economists presented the following conclusion as a result of discussions that took place over a week-long workshop:

> The economics profession appears to have been unaware of the long build up to the current worldwide financial crisis and to have significantly underestimated its dimensions once it started to unfold. In our view, this lack of understanding is due to a misallocation of research efforts in economics. We trace the deeper roots of this failure to the profession's focus on models that, by design, disregard key elements driving outcomes in real-world markets. (Colander *et al.*, 2010: 2)

2.6 Index numbers

Index numbers are used widely in economics – for example, indices of industrial production, indices of consumer prices, indices of the terms of trade, etc. They are a convenient way to make comparisons of changes in quantities over time.

Instead of measuring changes in a variable in terms of units such as £s of sales or tonnes of output, values are expressed in abstract numbers, rather like percentages.

Index numbers can also be set out in a time series to illustrate how prices, production levels, etc. have changed over time. This conveys an overall picture much more clearly and directly than a chart or table based on the original units of measurement.

To calculate an index value, we first need to establish a base position, or benchmark from which changes can be measured. This is given an index number of 100. The index values are calculated by dividing the new value by the base value, multiplying by 100/1 and adding 100.

If the base position is set at 50, then an actual value of 60 is therefore given an index number of 120.

CASE STUDY Constructing a simple index

In constructing an index, we need to start with a base value of 100 against which comparisons can be made.

For example, to monitor sales figures we might establish a starting point at the year 2010, when sales were £50 million. Using the method outlined (above), sales figures for the following years could then be given index values as shown in Table 2.2.

TABLE 2.2 Sales figures with their index values

Year	Actual sales (£m)	Index number
2010	50	100
2011	60	120
2012	70	140
2013	100	200

One of the main advantages of setting out figures in this way is that it helps us to make comparisons between the relative rate of change of different variables.

For example, even though the exports and imports of a country such as the UK are vastly different (exports include whisky and exams, while imports range from wine to televisions) we can still make comparisons of changes in export prices compared with import prices.

Using index numbers, it is possible to measure the terms of trade – the relationship between export prices and import prices – as follows:

$$\text{The terms of trade} = \frac{\text{Index of export prices}}{\text{Index of import prices}} \times \frac{100}{1}$$

- How can the use of index numbers help economists and business people to make comparisons?

- Why do these comparisons need to be made with base year figures?

Reflective question

8 In choosing a base year why do you think it would be important to choose a year that is not abnormal in terms of the figures for that year (e.g. exceptionally high or low figures)?

Calculating percentage changes

Once an index number has been assigned to a set of variables, it is possible to calculate the percentage change from one index number to another.

This is done using the formula:

$$\% \text{ Change} = \frac{\text{New Index} - \text{Old Index}}{\text{Old Index}} \times 100$$

Example – a simple price index

Suppose that we want to compare changes in the price of three items that feature heavily in a typical family budget: a standard loaf of bread, six eggs and half a litre of milk. Table 2.3 shows the actual price of these items in pence over a three-year period:

TABLE 2.3 Price of items over a three-year period

	Price (pence)		
	2010	**2011**	**2012**
Bread	30	40	60
Eggs	50	60	80
Milk	100	110	120

To create a simple price index we need to calculate the ratio of the new prices to the base year for each item. The ratio of the new price to the original (base year) price is known as the price relative.

A formula for a simple price index is:

$$\text{Index} = \frac{Pn}{Po} \times 100$$

Where Pn represents the price in a particular year (Year n) and Po represents the base year price (Year 0).

We can set this out in the new table (Table 2.4). You can see that during the period covered in the table, bread has gone up in price by 100 per cent (i.e. from 30 to 60), eggs by 60 per cent and milk by 20 per cent.

TABLE 2.4 Measuring price changes over time using index numbers

Year	Bread			Eggs			Milk		
	Price	Pn/Po	Simple price index	Price	Pn/Po	Simple price index	Price	Pn/Po	Simple price index
2011	30	1.00	100	50	1.00	100	100	1.00	100
2012	40	1.50	150	60	1.20	120	110	1.10	110
2013	60	2.00	200	80	1.60	160	120	1.20	120

In the example above, we looked at the increase in price of three separate items. But it is also possible to work out a simple price index for the three items combined. This is known as a simple aggregate price index.

The sum of the three prices is represented by the symbol Σ. The simple aggregate price index is therefore:

$$\frac{\Sigma Pn}{\Sigma Po} \times 100$$

The new calculations are set out in Table 2.5.

TABLE 2.5 Simple aggregate price index

Price in given year (pence)	Bread	Eggs	Milk	$\Sigma Pn/\Sigma Po$	Simple aggregate price index
P(2011)	30	50	100	180/180 = 1.0	100
P(2012)	40	60	110	210/180 = 1.16	116
P(2013)	60	80	120	260/180 = 1.44	144

The problem with this approach is that it ignores that fact that the typical family will spend more in their weekly shopping on some of these items than others – for example, more on bread than eggs.

As a result, changes in the price of eggs are being given more significance than they warrant, while changes in the price of bread are being given less significance than they warrant.

To avoid this distortion, it is necessary to introduce a form of weighting that takes into account the relative importance of different items in the aggregate index.

Weighting an index

In order to reflect the relative importance of different items in an aggregate or composite index, it is necessary to include an element of weighting.

CASE STUDY Weighting business expenditures

A company manufacturing chairs has two basic inputs: materials and labour.

In Table 2.6 you can see that between 2012 and 2013 the amount spent by the firm on materials and labour has increased.

TABLE 2.6 Consumer spending on materials and labour

	2012 (1)	2013 (2)	Index number 2/1 × 100	Expenditure weight (£s)
Labour (unit costs)	50	55	110	150
Materials (unit cost	200	250	125	200

However, what the table does not show is the relative magnitude of the increases – which of the price increases has affected the firm most significantly. Labour unit costs have gone up from 50 to 55 and material unit costs from 200 to 250, but what impact has this had on the firm?

In order to answer this, we need to calculate what is known as the price relative of both labour and materials.

The unit cost of labour has risen from 50 to 55. Taking 2012 as the base year, we can calculate the price relative of labour from 2012 to 2013 by expressing it in terms of an index of unit labour costs:

$$\frac{55}{50} \times 100 = 110$$

We can do the same for materials, giving us a price relative index of 125. Immediately you can see from the index that materials have risen 2.5 times as much as labour.

We can also find the combined effect of the rise in price of labour and materials. This can be done using a simple averaging technique:

$$\frac{110 + 125}{2} = 117.5$$

However, this would only be a useful figure if the amount spent by the company on materials were the same as the amount spent on labour – which is not the case. From the table (by reading the expenditure weight) you can see that the firm buys 3 units of labour for £150 and 1 unit of materials for £200. The simple averaging technique used above has therefore underestimated the importance of materials.

More weight needs to be given to materials because materials make up a bigger proportion of total costs than wages.

The true percentage increase in total cost is obtained from the weighted average of the individual indices, as follows:

$$\frac{(£110 \times 150) + (£125 \times 200)}{(150 + 200)} = 118.5$$

This shows that the total cost increased by 118.5 rather than 116.5.

This can be confirmed as follows. If 3 units of labour and 1 unit of materials are required to produce a chair, then in 2012 the total cost of producing a chair was:

$$50 \times 3 + 200 \times 1 = £350$$

In 2013 the total cost was:

$$55 \times 3 + 250 \times 1 = £415$$

So the total cost in 2013 as a percentage of 2012 is:

$$\frac{415}{350} \times 100 = 118.5$$

Reflective questions

9 Why is it important to weight items when constructing a complex index?

10 Table 2.7 below shows prices and quantities for a basket of consumer goods over a two-year period. Calculate a price index for this basket using the year 2010 as your base year.

TABLE 2.7 Prices and quantities of consumer goods over two years

Goods	2010 (pence)		2012 (pence)	
	P1	Q1	P1	Q1
Beans	30	200	45	200
Milk	50	500	60	500
Eggs	20	300	30	300

In Chapter 10 we show how the government calculates price inflation in Britain using a weighted index to measure average changes of prices.

Between 2010 and 2014 the prices of five items bought by a typical household changed in the way illustrated by Table 2.8.

TABLE 2.8 Changes in prices of typical items bought

Item	Price (pence)				
	2010	2011	2012	2013	2014
Bread	80	85	90	95	100
Cheese	100	120	130	140	160
Eggs (6)	90	95	100	110	120
Wine	400	410	420	430	440
Cigarettes	700	710	740	750	800

1. Set out indices to show how the prices of these goods changed in the period shown.

2. Set out a composite index to show average price changes of the five items in each of the years, using the year 2010 as your base year.

2.7 Share price indices

Share price indices are widely quoted in the business and financial press. Some of the most important are as follows:

- The FTSE ('Footsie') 100 Index gives hourly market movements for the most significant 100 companies listed on the London Stock Exchange. It is used as an indicator of the health of the economy. This index started with a base of 1,000.

- The FTSE 250 Index is made up of the next range of companies, just below the size that would qualify them for the FTSE 100. The FTSE 350 combines the 100 and 250 indices. There are separate indices for smaller companies.

- The FTSE TechMark Index tracks the progress of technology-related shares.

- The FTSE All Share Index covers all listed companies.

- Within the European Union, the most important index is the Euro Top 200, which covers top European companies.

- The Dow Jones Industrial Average covers the New York Stock Exchange, while the Nikkei 225 covers the Tokyo market.

Movements in a share price index are usually measured in points. For example, if the FTSE 100 drops from 5,000 to 4,900, it is said to have fallen 100 points.

Share price indices tend to fluctuate with business confidence.

2.8 Summary

In the wrong hands the use of econometrics can be confusing, and can also oversimplify relationships in the real world. However, econometrics can be useful both as a descriptive and as an analytical tool.

The use of econometrics picks up important trends (e.g. changes in GDP over time) and relationships (e.g. the relationship between the supply of money and prices). Techniques such as correlation enable economists to analyse the relationships between variables. The use of index numbers enables economists to translate lots of separate patterns (e.g. individual price changes) into general price changes (e.g. rises in general consumer prices). Econometrics not only enables economists to describe economic changes more clearly but also to analyse and understand those changes in greater depth.

KEY THEME

Lies, damn lies and economic statistics

The following post recently appeared on the Internet (Mike Ivey, *The Capital Times*, March 2012).

> I enjoy reading the economic tea leaves as much as the next guy, although I'll admit to skipping the Philadelphia Federal Reserve Bank monthly forecasts.

But the reports – written by economist for economists – have turned into ammunition in the ongoing debate over whether Republicans have Winsconsin heading in the right direction.

The latest exchange came this week when Governor Scott Walker's office sent out a press release touting the Philly Fed's latest economic growth forecast.

The report forecasts Wisconsin's economy to grow at a 1.9 per cent annualised rate over the next six months. That's the best forecast for the state since 2003. 'Strong signals suggest we are turning things around for Wisconsin's economy, and the Federal Reserve Bank of Philadelphia' news report of state leading economic indexes provides yet one more indicator that our pro-jobs policies are moving us in the right direction', said Walker in a statement.

And almost within the hour Republican Brett Hulsey was out with his own press release touting a different Philadelphia Fed Report.

'We have the second worst economic performance in the nation in the last three months', said Hulsey.

Hulsey is referring to the 'coincident index' where the Fed uses four variables – non-farm payroll, average hours worked in manufacturing, unemployment rate and inflation-adjusted wages – to track actual economic performance.

Walker is referring to the Fed's 'leading indicators', which combine the four variables above with four others – housing starts, new unemployment claims, manufacturing delivery times and interest rates – to predict economic growth going forward.

- **Why do you think that the Democratic Governor Walker and the Republican representative Hulsey are using different sets of figures?**

- **What does this tell us about the interpretation of economic data?**

- **What do you think an economist's approach would be to setting out the data outlined above?**

KEY IDEAS

Economists frequently use econometrics to analyse economic data. In most of the chapters of this book there is some emphasis on econometric approaches. However, econometrics should not obscure or oversimplify important economic relationships.

Diagrams and charts are a good way of illustrating economic data. Time series data can be used to demonstrate trends and patterns that are taking place over time.

Correlation is a very helpful technique to show the relationship between variables. Positive correlation shows that two variables are moving in the same direction over time. Negative correlation shows that as one variable rises over time the other falls. However, we need to be careful in applying correlation because this can sometimes confuse the relationship between the dependent and the independent variable. Also it is important to recognize that changes in economic data often arise from the impact of a variety of often inter-related factors.

Index numbers are a convenient way to compare changes in quantities over time. Values are expressed in terms of an index number. Index values can be compared with a base value. It is important to choose a base date which is a representative rather than an unusual figure.

In order to reflect the relative importance of items that are used in an index it is important to weight them according to their relative importance in the index.

Index numbers are used by economists for a variety of purposes, including a consumer price index, a terms of trade index and share price indices.

REVIEW QUESTIONS

1. What are econometrics and how do economists use them?

2. What is the difference between positive and normative economics – give two examples to illustrate the difference.

3. What criticisms can be levelled at the use of econometrics?

4. What is a trend and how can it be calculated by use of a moving average?

5. What are 'smoothed' data?

6. What is a forecast? What factors militate against making accurate forecasts?

7. What is a consumer price index? How would you construct such an index?

8. Why is it important to weight an index?

9. How could an index be used to measure changes in the terms of trade?

10. What is a share price index? How could this be calculated?

RECOMMENDED READING

Caplin, A. and Schotte, A. (eds) (2008) *The Foundations of Positive and Normative Economics, A Handbook*, Oxford, Oxford University Press.

Colander, D., Follmer, H., Haas, A., Goldberg, M., Juselius, K., Kirman, A., Lux, T. and Sloth, B. (2010) *The Financial Crisis and the Systemic Failure of Academic Economics*, 9 March 2009, University of Copenhagen Department of Economics, Discussion Paper No. 09–03.

Putman, H. and Walsh, V. (eds) (2012) *The End of Value Free Economics*, Abingdon, Routledge.

REFERENCES

Friedman, M. and Schwartz, A.J. (1963) *Monetary History of the United States 1867–1960*, Princeton, Princeton University Press.

Gujarati, D.N. (1988) *Basic Econometrics*, 2nd edition, New York, McGraw-Hill.

Malthus, T.R. (1798) *An Essay on the Principles of Population*, London, J. Johnson.

Marshall, A. (1890 [1920]) *Principles of Economics, An Introductory Volume*, 8th edition, reprinted 1961, London, Macmillan and Co. Ltd.

Pigou, A.C. (ed.) (1925) *Memorials of Alfred Marshall*, London, Macmillan and Co. Ltd.

Ricardo, D. (1817) *On the Principles of Political Economy*, London, John Murray.

Samuelson, P.A. (1954) *Economics*, New York, McGraw-Hill.

Smith, A. (1776) *An Inquiry into the Nature and Causes of the Wealth of Nations*, republished (1976), edited by R.H. Campbell and A.S. Skinner, Oxford, Clarendon Press.

USEFUL WEBSITES

http://economics.about.com/cs/studentresources/f/econometrics.htm – a useful site providing links to useful materials about econometrics.

3 How markets work

CHAPTER OBJECTIVES

By the end of this chapter you will understand:

- The role of the market in the economy

- The four laws of supply and demand

- Reasons why demand and supply change and the impact on market equilibrium

- How to measure elasticity of demand and supply

- The relationship between price elasticity and revenue

- The part that private business organizations play in the market

3.1 Introduction

This chapter shows how prices are determined as a result of the decisions of consumers and producers of goods. Prices act as signals indicating to producers what goods they can make at a profit. Relative prices also signal to consumers which goods they should purchase in order to get value for money.

Today, economies in most parts of the world are structured around market systems. The market relates to any situation in which buyers and sellers are in contact with each other for the purpose of making transactions. Consumers express their willingness and ability to purchase goods in the form of demand. Producers express their willingness to make goods available in the form of supply.

3.2 The nature of the market economy

The economy as a system

The economy is a system that creates wealth for citizens. There are three main sectors in the economy:

- Firms
- Households
- Government

An economic system:

- Organizes resources for the production of goods and services; and
- Satisfies the wants and needs of people who are part of that system.

In all modern economies the government plays an important role in making economic decisions through government spending, and through government production (i.e. through government-owned and -funded industries). However, in this chapter we will be focusing on the operation of the market primarily by considering the non-government sector of the economy (the private sector). We will be looking at how the market works by examining the interactions between firms and households.

The market

The market brings together buyers and sellers. This might be in a traditional market, where buyers and sellers come together to trade for vegetables, sweets, crockery, clothing and other items. The term 'market' also describes any other situation where buyers and sellers contact each other. They might do this over the telephone or on the Internet.

The alternative to the market is to have a central planning authority such as a government department decide what goods will be produced, what prices will be charged for them and who will receive these goods. During the twentieth century a number of countries experimented with this approach – for example, the Soviet Union, China, Cuba and a number of other states. In many instances this led to a range of problems associated with the inefficient manufacture and distribution of goods. The key problem of central planning was that it required the planning authorities to second-guess the choices of consumers. Frequently they got this wrong so that in some instances the wrong goods arrived, in the wrong places, at the wrong times – and quality was often poor.

 KEY THEME

Inefficiency of alternative to the market – Golub

Slavenka Draculic, the Croatian writer, tells how she finally realized that there was no future for communism in her book *Forward to the Past* (1992). She argues that communism foundered in a soggy mire of scratchy brown lavatory paper. She describes the coarse, dark sheets of 'Golub' she used in her childhood, then the soft, pink rolls eventually achieved by 'socialism with a human face' of the 1970s, then the day, in 1985, when she stood with her 17-year-old daughter in a chemist's shop, arguing bitterly because the recent price rises meant that they had to go back to Golub. Her daughter refused point blank to adopt this symbol of poverty and Draculic knew then that it was all over: 'This was how the communists lost; when the first free elections came in May 1990, the entire younger generation voted against Golub, against shortages, deprivation, double standards and false promises.'

A particular strength of the market is that it is self-regulating. Millions of individual consumers are able to make choices every day about purchasing decisions. Some of these decisions are spontaneous (you see a good and buy it) whereas others are carefully budgeted for and planned. The information about what consumers purchase is fed through the cash registers and stock control systems of suppliers. Suppliers are thus provided with a wealth of data about consumer preferences. Armed with this data, suppliers are able to make intelligent decisions about what to produce and supply to the market. The beauty of this system is the speed with which decisions are communicated and responded to. Adam Smith (see article at the end of this chapter) likened the market to an 'invisible hand' guiding economic decision making.

The market brings together two sets of people: those who are willing and able to buy products (demanders), and those who are willing and able to supply products (suppliers).

- **Draculic's daughter was brought up in a centrally planned economy. What weaknesses does the case study indicate exist in such an economic system?**

- **Do you think that the market might provide better solutions? Why?**

Demand and supply

Economists use **demand** to mean the quantity of a good or service that consumers will be prepared to buy at a particular price. For example, at a price of 20 pence per apple, demanders at a fruit market in Sheffield are willing and able to buy 1,200 apples on the 15 July 2012.

Supply – the quantity of a good or service that suppliers will be prepared to supply at a particular price. For example, at a price of 20 pence per apple, suppliers at the fruit market in Sheffield are willing and able to supply 1,200 apples on the 15 July 2012.

Benefits of the market

The principal benefits of the market are as follows:

- It brings together buyers and sellers.
- It helps to allocate resources to goods that are in demand. For example, if a firm supplying yoghurt to supermarkets knows (on the basis of information supplied by the supermarket buyers) that a particular flavour (e.g. raspberry) is popular, then they will allocate more resources to the production of raspberry yoghurt.
- It coordinates decision making. The market system coordinates billions of decisions. Across the world, every second, billions of consumers are making purchasing decisions. They make their decisions known through the purchases that they make. Sellers also make their own decisions about what to produce and sell.
- It provides plenty of choice. In a market that is working well, customers have choices – there will be plenty of competing rivals providing goods.
- Competition in the market helps to keep prices down. Rival businesses will seek to beat the competition by providing lower prices than those offered by rivals.

Reflective question

1   What do you see as being the main role/s of the government in a market economy?

3.3 The relationship between price, demand and supply

Price, demand and supply

There are four basic laws that you should learn about the relationship between supply, demand and the market price. The market price is the price at which goods and services are exchanged as a result of the interaction of market forces.

The four laws are:

1. If demand increases and supply remains constant, then market price will increase and suppliers will be encouraged to increase the quantity supplied.

2. If demand decreases and supply remains constant, then market price will fall and suppliers will be likely to reduce the quantity supplied.

3. If supply increases and demand remains constant, then market price will fall.

4. If supply decreases and demand remains constant, then market price will rise.

CASE STUDY The supply and demand for dry coconut

Table 3.1 illustrates the demand and supply of dry coconut. It shows the quantity that suppliers are willing to supply to the market and the quantity that demanders (companies purchasing dry coconut) are willing and able to buy at different prices.

TABLE 3.1 Initial demand and supply for dried coconut

Price per tonne (£)	Demand for coconut (tonnes)	Supply of coconut (tonnes)
500	900	300
750	800	400
1000	700	500
1250	600	600
1500	500	700
1750	400	800
2000	300	900

- Describe the relationship between the price of dry coconut and the demand.

- Describe the relationship between the price of dry coconut and the supply.

- What is likely to be the market price of coconut, and why?

In the case study the equilibrium market price is $1,250 per tonne of dry coconut. This is the price determined by market forces. Demanders are willing to buy 600 tonnes of coconut and suppliers are willing to supply this quantity.

The two laws of demand

What would happen if the demand for dry coconut increased or decreased while the supply remained constant? These situations are illustrated in Table 3.2. You can see that at each price 200 more tonnes are demanded when demand rises, and 200 fewer tonnes are demanded when demand falls.

TABLE 3.2 Supply and demand of dried coconut

Price per tonne (£)	Original demand (tonnes)	Supply (tonnes)	Demand rises (tonnes)	Demand falls (tonnes)
500	900	300	1,100	700
750	800	400	1,000	600
1,000	700	500	900	500
1,250	600	600	800	400
1,500	500	700	700	300
1,750	400	800	600	200
2,000	300	900	500	100

The table illustrates the two laws of demand. You should be able to see that when demand rises (the fourth column), demand and supply will now match at a price of £1,500 per tonne – suppliers are willing to supply 700 tonnes and demanders are willing to buy 700 tonnes.

In contrast, when demand falls (the fifth column), demand and supply will now match at £1,000 per tonne – suppliers are willing to supply 500 tonnes and demanders are willing to buy 500 tonnes.

The two laws of supply

What will happen if the supply of dried coconut increases or decreases while the demand remains constant? These situations are illustrated in Table 3.3:

TABLE 3.3 The two laws of supply

Price per tonne (£)	Demand (tonnes)	Original supply (tonnes)	Supply rises (tonnes)	Supply falls (tonnes)
500	900	300	500	100
750	800	400	600	200
1,000	700	500	700	300
1,250	600	600	800	400
1,500	500	700	900	500
1,750	400	800	1,000	600
2,000	300	900	1,100	700

Demand is initially equal to supply at a market price of £1,250 per tonne, that is where demand is 600 tonnes and supply is 600 tonnes. Columns 4 and 5 of the table illustrate a rise in supply (column 4) and a fall in supply (column 5).

When supply rises by 200 units at each price (column 4), demand and supply will be in equilibrium (equal to each other) at a price of £1,000. At £1,000, demand will be 700 tonnes and supply will be 700 tonnes.

In contrast, when supply falls at each price by 200 units (column 5), demand and supply will be in equilibrium at a price of £1,500. At £1,500, demand will be 500 tonnes and supply will be 500 tonnes. The new price is higher than the original price.

Demand and supply for most products change frequently.

Market forces – changes in demand and supply. The relative strength of demand and supply determines the market prices of goods.

KEY TERM

Market prices act as signals to producers about the strength of demand for the products they supply. Rising prices act as an incentive for producers to produce more of certain types of goods. In contrast, falling prices will encourage consumers to buy more goods as they become relatively cheaper. Gaining a clear understanding of the four laws of demand and supply will enable you to have a good grasp of how the market works.

Changes in demand and shifts in demand – economists distinguish between a 'change' in 'demand' (where the whole demand curve changes its position, e.g. as a result of a change in tastes or incomes), and 'changes' in 'quantity demanded' (i.e. movements along a given demand curve). Changes in quantity demanded result from a change in the price of the good whose demand is being examined.

KEY TERM

3.4 The construction of demand and supply curves

Demand and supply curves

A demand curve is used by economists to illustrate the relationship between price and quantity demanded. It shows demand and changes in quantity demanded. It is useful for business organizations trying to predict the effect of different prices on demand for their products. It helps them to decide how much of a good to make in order to meet quantity demanded.

Common sense and personal experience explain the shape of the demand curve. The curve slopes down from left to right because more people can afford to buy goods at lower rather than at higher prices. Existing purchasers of a good will be tempted to buy more of a good at a lower price because they have to give up less of their income to make the purchase. Table 3.4 and Figure 3.1 show the quantity demand for dried coconut at different prices per tonne.

TABLE 3.4 Demand for dried coconut at different prices

Price per tonne (£)	Quantity demanded (tonnes)
500	900
750	800
1,000	700
1,250	600
1,500	500
1,750	400
2,000	300

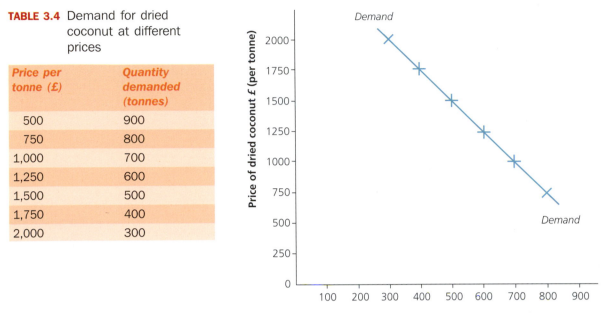

FIGURE 3.1 The demand curve for dried coconut

The demand curve is constructed by showing prices on the vertical axis and quantities demanded along the horizontal axis. You can see that:

- Higher prices lead to lower quantities being bought.

- Lower prices lead to higher quantities being bought.

Supply curves

The supply of a product is the quantity that a supplier is willing to provide at different prices. Typically, suppliers will supply more at higher prices than at lower prices. Higher prices enable producers to cover costs and increase their profits.

Table 3.5 and Figure 3.2 show the supply curve for dried coconut at different prices. The supply curve is constructed by showing quantity supplied along the horizontal axis and price along the vertical axis. You can see that:

- Higher prices lead to greater quantities being supplied.

- Lower prices lead to smaller quantities being supplied.

TABLE 3.5 Supply of dried coconut at different prices

Price per tonne (£)	Quantity supplied (tonnes)
500	300
750	400
1,000	500
1,250	600
1,500	700
1,750	800
2,000	900

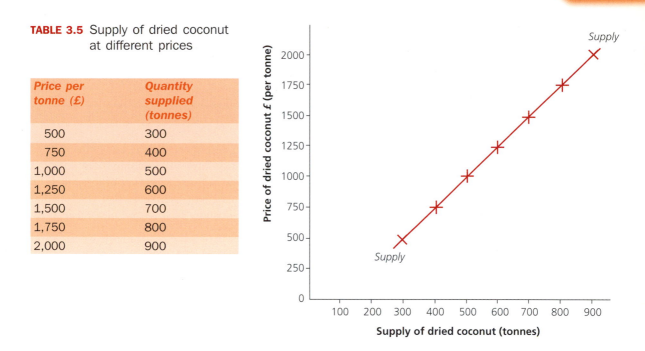

FIGURE 3.2 The supply curve for dried coconut

Combining the demand and supply curves

Demand and supply curves for a product can be plotted onto a single diagram. Where the demand and supply curves intersect is the equilibrium price. Figure 3.3 shows the demand and supply curves for dried coconut – the economist's way of representing the market for this product. Note that the equilibrium price is at £1,250.

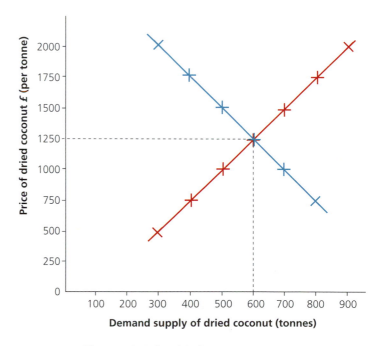

FIGURE 3.3 The market for dried coconut

Ceteris paribus

Ceteris paribus – economists use a Latin term *ceteris paribus*, which means literally 'with the rest being the same' or, more freely, 'assuming everything else remains the same'.

The nature of the modern world is that many things do not remain the same: they change regularly. This makes it difficult to identify direct relationships. For example, many scientists think that global temperature is rising because of the increased burning of fossil fuels by humans. However, it is difficult to prove this because there are many other changes that affect climate – volcanic eruptions for example, or changes in the orbit of the Earth.

When economists want to examine the relationship between one economic variable and another they make the *ceteris paribus* assumption, that all other factors remain the same. In our climate example, this is the equivalent of studying the relationship between human activity and climate change while holding factors such as volcanic activity constant.

For example, economists look at the relationship between:

• The demand for a product and its price *ceteris paribus*.

• The supply of a product and its price *ceteris paribus*.

This enables us to draw a demand curve showing the relationship between price and quantity demand *ceteris paribus*. We can also draw a supply curve showing the relationship between price and quantity supplied *ceteris paribus*.

When we assume *ceteris paribus*, the only factor affecting the quantity demanded or supplied of a product is its price.

The determinants of demand and supply

The demand and supply of a product in the real world are affected not only by its price but by other factors in the economic environment. To take account of these other environmental factors we need to remove the assumption of *ceteris paribus*.

When one or more of these environmental factors changes the demand and/or supply curve will shift in position. For the purpose of our analysis we will look at situations where the demand curve shifts to the left or right, and situations where the supply curve shifts to the left or right.

The environmental determinants of demand therefore include all the other factors that influence demand (not including the price of the product itself). The environmental determinants of supply include all the other factors that influence supply (not including the price of the product itself).

Movements along a curve

It is important to distinguish between movements along a demand curve (and a supply curve) and shifts in the position of the curve. Movements along curves result from changes in price of the good whose demand or supply is being plotted. Economists use the terms contraction (reduction) or expansion (increase) to describe changes in demand (or supply) (see Table 3.6).

Movements up or down a curve – when the only factor influencing demand or supply is the price of the product itself, this will lead to a movement up or down the demand or supply curve.

Shifts in a curve – when factors other than the price of the product change, this is likely to lead to a shift in the demand or supply curve.

Figure 3.4 shows a movement down a demand curve resulting from the fall in price of a product.

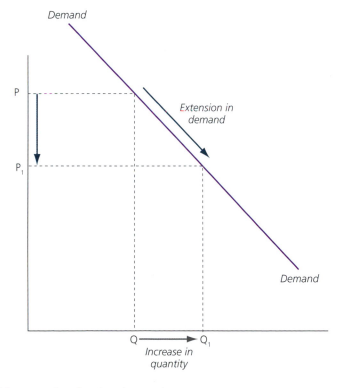

FIGURE 3.4 Movements along a demand curve

TABLE 3.6 Economists' uses of the terms extension and contraction

What happens	Term used
Demand increases as a result of a fall in price (ceteris paribus)	Extension in demand
Demand falls as a result of a fall in price (ceteris paribus)	Contraction in demand
Supply increases as a result of a rise in price (ceteris paribus)	Extension in supply
Supply falls as a result of a fall in price (ceteris paribus)	Contraction in supply

3.5 Changes in the conditions of demand and supply

Changes in the conditions of demand

In addition to price there are a number of factors that influence the demand for a product. If one of these factors alters, the conditions of demand are said to have changed. These factors include:

- Tastes or fashion
- Income
- Number of buyers/population
- Price of other products
- Expectation of price changes

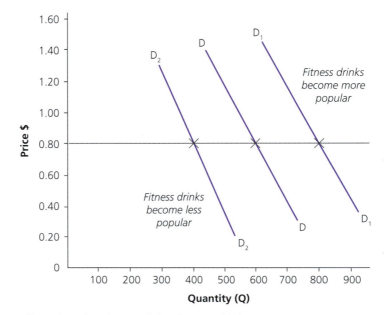

FIGURE 3.5 Changing the demand for fitness drinks

Changes in one (or a combination) of these factors will cause a shift in the demand curve. The demand curve will shift to the left if smaller quantities are wanted than before at given prices. A shift to the right indicates that larger quantities are wanted than before at given prices.

Tastes and fashion

Figure 3.5 shows that originally a quantity of 600 fitness drinks would be bought per month at 80 cents. However, if the drinks become more popular with consumers, more will be demanded at all prices so that, for example, at 80 cents perhaps 800 will be bought.

Alternatively, if the drinks become less popular fewer will be bought at all prices so that at 80 cents 400 drinks will now be demanded.

Income

It is obviously easier to buy goods if you have the money to spend. The amount of income people have to spend on goods – that is, after deductions for taxes – is known as their disposable income. Average incomes tend to rise over time, which leads to a general increase in demand for most goods, noticeably expensive branded goods. An increase in incomes leads to a shift to the right in the demand curve.

However, some products may become less popular as income rises: as spending power increases they may be regarded as inferior. An example is a bicycle being replaced by a motor scooter or car. In the case of inferior goods, when incomes rise demand shifts to the left.

Note that the term 'inferior' in economics is not a pejorative term and does not indicate substandard or shoddy goods. Also, what is inferior in one nation or for one income group may not be so in another country or income group. At very low incomes people may not even be able to afford public transport, yet once income rises they can do so. For these people public transport is a normal good.

Number of buyers and population

The size of the population can affect demand. For example, in the holiday season thousands of tourists visit seaside tourist resorts, increasing the demand for food, accommodation and many other items, thus pushing up prices.

Price of other products

The demand for products that have close substitutes will often be strongly influenced by the price of the substitutes. This would be the case, for example, with different brands of tinned fruit or different brands of petrol – there are many similar brand names from which consumers can chose.

The demand curve for a product is likely to shift to the right if a substitute product rises in price. The demand curve for a product is likely to shift to the left if a substitute product falls in price.

Some products are used together (complementary products), and the demand for one is linked to the price of another. An example might be cars and petrol – if the price of cars falls this is likely to lead to an increase in demand for petrol.

Expectation of price changes

The expectation that prices will change in the future will also affect the demand for a product. For example, if people think that prices are due to rise shortly they will want to hoard goods to protect themselves against the rise. For example, in years when winter weather is particularly bad householders may stock up with food supplies in anticipation of heavy snow.

Changes in the conditions of supply

The cost of producing an item is determined by the price of the various inputs, including the raw materials and machinery used to make it. Rises in the prices of some resource inputs will increase production costs, which in turn will result in a reduction in supply at each prise rise (see Figure 3.6). The supply curve will shift to the left when, at any given price, fewer items are produced and offered for sale.

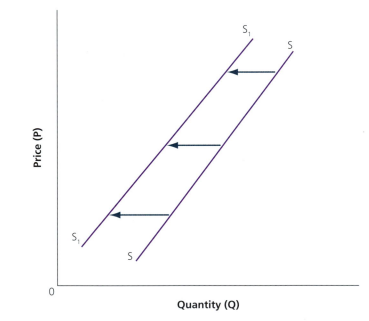

FIGURE 3.6 The effect of a shift in the supply curve to the left

Causes of changes in supply conditions

There are several factors that can cause changes in supply:

- Rising or falling production costs
- Changes in technology
- Changes in physical conditions
- Changes in taxation and subsidies
- Changes in joint supply conditions
- Changes in the number of producers

Rising or falling production costs

A rise in production costs pushes the supply curve to the left (it will cost more to produce each level of output), and a fall in production costs pushes the supply curve to the right.

This can be explained by an appeal to common sense – following a rise in production costs firms will produce less at the same selling price in order to preserve revenues; similarly, at lower production costs firms are able to produce more at the same selling price.

Rising resource prices lead to rising production costs. War and conflict can restrict the supply of important resources such as oil and can lead to rapid increases in product costs. Production costs fall when the price of resources falls. So when the price of oil falls, energy costs for all industries are reduced.

Changes in technology

The development of new technology in the form of computer-based processing systems and computer-controlled machinery has reduced production costs in many industries, pushing the supply curve to the right.

Physical conditions

Changes in the weather, the quality of soil and natural disasters such as drought or wind damage can have a dramatic impact on production capacity. For example, in countries and areas in the hurricane belt the sudden impact of bad weather can dramatically impact on the production capacity of the countries affected.

Taxation and subsidies

Rises in taxation and subsidies pull in opposite directions on the supply curve. A production tax of 10 pence per unit on a good would increase the cost of its production by 10 pence per unit. In contrast, a subsidy would reduce the costs of production. Supply therefore shifts to the left as a result of rising taxes on a product, and to the right as a result of a subsidy (see Figure 3.7).

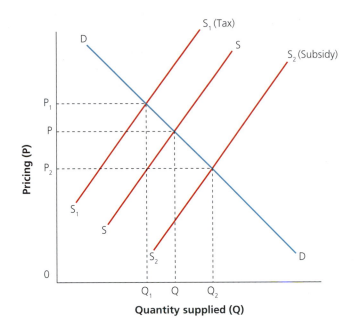

FIGURE 3.7 The impact of taxes and subsidies on the supply of a product

Joint supply

Some production processes create more than one product (joint supply). For example, oil and natural gas are frequently produced as part of the same process. Increases in oil supply therefore drive down the prices of these by-products as more of them are supplied to the market.

Number of producers

An increase in the number of producers will usually increase the supply of a product. Where suppliers leave the market this can reduce the supply. In recent years we have seen a rapid increase in the number of Internet-based suppliers of many goods and services.

Effects of changes in supply on the market

An increase in supply results in a fall in the price of a product. This leads to a movement along the demand curve (more is bought in response to the lower price).

A decrease in supply results in a rise in the price of a product. This leads to a movement along the demand curve (less is bought in response to the higher price).

Equilibrium price

As an example of how an equilibrium price is reached, a market stall holder at Cambridge market provides bargain umbrellas which he sells to customers – particularly in wet weather.

KEY TERM

Equilibrium – a state of balance. An equilibrium price occurs when there is a balance between demand and supply: the quantity demanded by consumers is equal to the amount that suppliers are willing to provide.

Competition is fairly intense for other suppliers such as TK Maxx and local garages. The higher the price the market trader can get the more inclined he is to supply more. The lower the price that the stallholder charges, the more customers will buy from him.

These demand and supply curves can be illustrated on a single drawing (see Figure 3.8).

TABLE 3.7 The demand and supply schedules for umbrellas from the stallholder

Price of umbrellas (£)	Stallholder's supply per month	Demand per month
2.50	500	200
2.00	400	400
1.50	300	600
1.00	200	800

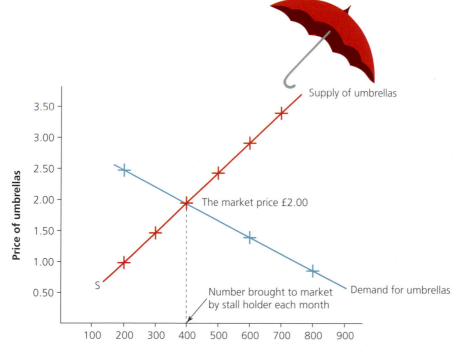

FIGURE 3.8 How the price of umbrellas is determined

You can now see that, at a price of £2.00 per umbrella, 400 would be bought each month. At this price customers would be happy to buy all 400 and the stallholder would be happy to supply this quantity.

This is the equilibrium price, as both seller and buyer are happy with the price.

You can see why this point is an equilibrium one by considering non-equilibrium points. For example, at £2.50 the market trader would be prepared to supply 500 umbrellas, but buyers would only be prepared to purchase 200 (leaving 300 unsold). Alternatively, if we examine a price below the market one (£1.00) customers would be willing to buy 800 umbrellas, but the trader would be prepared to bring only 200 to sell. Customers would soon bid the price back up to the equilibrium price.

The market price is often referred to as the market clearing price, because demand matches the quantity supplied. Therefore the market would be 'cleared' with no umbrellas remaining and no dissatisfied customers.

The effect of changes in demand and supply on the market

The effect is summarized in Table 3.8:

TABLE 3.8 Effect of demand and supply changes

	Effect on equilibrium market price	Effect on equilibrium market quantity
Demand shifts to the right	Increases	Increases
Demand shifts to the left	Falls	Falls
Supply shifts to the right	Falls	Increases
Supply shifts to the left	Increases	Falls

ACTIVITY

Using Table 3.8 above as a guide, explain what is likely to happen in the following situations:

- As a result of the recession there is a fall in incomes. How would this impact on the market for restaurant meals?

- There is an improvement in technology in manufacturing in the car industry leading to a lowering of production costs. How does this impact on the car sales market?

- A drought impacts on agricultural production. How does this impact on the market for fresh vegetables?

- Fashion trends favour garments manufactured in India. What is the impact on the market for Indian garment imports to the UK?

Changes in the market equilibrium

Changes in market equilibrium result from changes in the market environment – that is, shifts in the demand and supply curves.

Figure 3.9 shows the effect of an increase in demand for an expensive brand of trainers. This might be triggered by the rising popularity of the brand, an increase in consumer incomes and an increase in the population of consumers (mainly young people), or a fall in the price of a good that complements the trainers – for example, designer clothes or tracksuits. The diagram illustrates the impact of the change. Demand shifts from DD to $D_1 D_1$, leading to an increase in price from P to P_1 and an increase in the quantity traded on the market from Q to Q_1.

Figure 3.10 shows the effect of a fall in demand for tourist holidays to a popular destination. This might be the result of adverse weather conditions in the region, political unrest or steep price rises in the visitors' home markets. You can see that the market price charged by tour operators would fall from P to P_1, and the quantity of holidays traded in the market would fall from Q to Q_1.

Figure 3.11 shows the impact of an increase in the supply of fish to a city centre fish market. There are a number of reasons why the supply might increase, including an increase in the number of wholesalers supplying that market, an increase in fish stocks in the sea, the use of better techniques to catch the fish (including better equipment), a fall in fishing costs (for example cheaper fuel) or a subsidy paid by the government to encourage fishing.

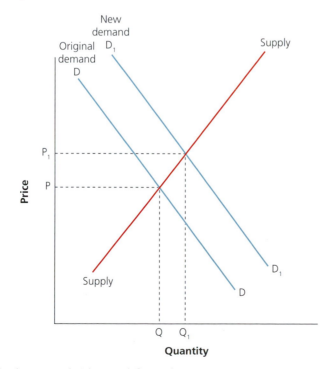

FIGURE 3.9 An increase in demand for trainers

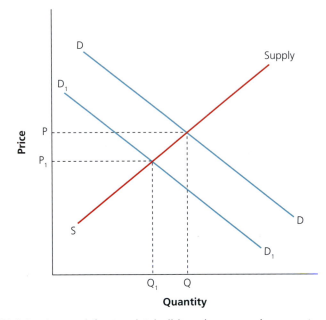

FIGURE 3.10 Fall in demand for tourist holidays in a popular resort

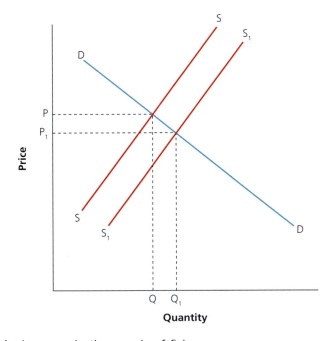

FIGURE 3.11 An increase in the supply of fish

FIGURE 3.12 Reduction in the number of bars and cafés

You can see that the impact of the shift in the supply to the right is to increase the supply to the market and to lower the market price.

The final illustration in this sequence (Figure 3.12) shows the impact of a reduction of bars and cafés in a student city. What factors can you think of that would cause the supply curve to shift to the left?

3.6 How to measure elasticity of demand

It is important to understand the key economic concept of elasticity. Elasticity is a measure of how demand or supply responds to a change in another variable. In the previous section you will have read that there are many variables that can impact on the demand or supply of a good.

KEY TERMS

Elasticity – the measurement of how changing one economic variable affects others.

Price elasticity of demand – measures the percentage change in quantity demanded caused by a percentage change in price. As such, it measures the extent of movement along the demand curve.

Price elasticity of supply – measures how the amount of a good firms wish to supply changes in response to a change in price. Price elasticity of supply captures the extent of movement along the supply curve.

In the analysis that follows we will first review elasticity of demand before going on to examine elasticity of supply.

Business managers are particularly interested in the extent to which demand is likely to respond to a price change. Measuring the response is referred to as the measurement of price elasticity.

In addition, it is helpful to measure the responsiveness of demand to variables other than price – for example:

- The responsiveness of demand for a good to changes in the prices of other goods – referred to by economists as cross-price elasticity.

- The responsiveness of demand for a good to changes in income – referred to by economists as income elasticity.

The econometric technique that economists use to measure elasticity is referred to as the coefficient of elasticity:

$$\textbf{The coefficient of elasticity} = \frac{\text{Percentage change in quantity demanded}}{\text{Percentage change in a relevant variable}}$$

So, for price elasticity of demand:

$$\textbf{Coefficient of price elasticity} = \frac{\text{Percentage change in quantity demanded of good A}}{\text{Percentage change in price of good A}}$$

For cross-price elasticity of demand:

$$\textbf{Coefficient of cross elasticity} = \frac{\text{Percentage change in quantity demanded of good A}}{\text{Percentage change in price of another good}}$$

For income elasticity of demand:

$$\textbf{Coefficient of income elasticity} = \frac{\text{Percentage change in quantity demanded of good A}}{\text{Percentage change in income}}$$

Price elasticity of demand

A restaurant owner who is considering increasing prices will first want to know what teffect this will have on the customers. Will there be no effect, a small fall in customers, or a large fall? If the number of customers remains the same or falls by a smaller percentage than the price change, the business will make more revenue. The calculation used to estimate this effect is price elasticity of demand, which measures how quantity demanded for a product responds to a change in its price. Anyone wishing to raise or lower prices should first estimate the price elasticity.

Measuring price elasticity

> **Price elasticity** – where falls in price have a more than proportional effect on quantity demanded, quantity demanded is said to be elastic. If instead quantity demanded changes by a smaller proportion than the change in price, it is said to be inelastic.

Price elasticity of demand is calculated as follows:

$$\text{Price elasticity of demand} = \frac{\%\ \text{change in quantity demanded}}{\%\ \text{change in price}}$$

Table 3.9 illustrates different price elasticities. Price elasticity of demand is always a minus figure. This is because an increase in price (+) leads to a fall in quantity demanded (–). A fall in price (–) leads to a rise in quantity demanded (+). Another way of putting this is that there is an inverse relationship between price and quantity demanded.

If the demand for a good is inelastic, an increase in its price will lead to an increase in revenue to the seller. In contrast, where demand is elastic, an increase in a good's price will lead to a fall in revenue to the seller. This is why producers of price inelastic goods do not engage in heavy discounting or get involved in price wars.

TABLE 3.9 Relative elasticities

Relative elasticity	Description	Example
Elastic demand	Quantity demanded changes by a larger proportion than the change in price	Price of a good rises by 5% while quantity demanded falls by 10% Elasticity = –2
Inelastic demand	Quantity demanded changes by a smaller proportion than the change in price	Price of a good rises by 5% while quantity demanded falls by 2.5% Elasticity = –1/2
Unitary elasticity of demand	Quantity demanded changes by the same proportion as the change in price	Price of a good rises by 5% while quantity demanded falls by 5% Elasticity = –1

How to make simple calculations

1. Calculate the percentage change in quantity demanded. This is the change in quantity demanded as a percentage of the quantity originally demanded (before the price change).

2. Calculate the percentage change in price. This is the change in price as a percentage of the original price (before the price change).

3. Divide the percentage change in quantity demanded by the percentage change in price. Remember to include the minus sign.

4.　If the figure is greater than –1, demand is relatively elastic. If it is less than –1, demand is relatively inelastic. (Please note that care needs to be taken here. It is important to stress that we are talking in absolute terms. –0.5 is greater than –1 if we are talking in the normal sense and a figure of –0.5 is relatively **inelastic**. A useful way to decide if a good is price elastic or inelastic, or to compare two elasticity results, is to ignore the negative sign when making your comparison.)

Example 1: A railway company reduces rail fares from £10.00 to £9.00. Daily demand for tickets rises from 100,000 to 120,000.

Price elasticity is therefore –2 (elastic demand):

$$\frac{20\ \%}{-10\ \%}\ =\ -2$$

Example 2: A bus company reduces bus fares from £1.00 to 90 pence. Daily demand for tickets rises from 10,000 to 10,500.

Price elasticity is therefore –0.5 (inelastic demand):

$$\frac{5\ \%}{-10\ \%}\ =\ -0.5$$

CASE STUDY Indian Railways lowers price

Railways in India are government-owned. Indian Railways is India's largest employer.

In July 2001 an expert declared that India's railway network was on the edge of bankruptcy. The cost of running the railway was 107 per cent of revenue, a loss-making position. By 2005 costs have been cut to 84 per cent of revenue, a surplus position, and in 2009 costs were 78 per cent of revenues. By 2009 the railways had become the second largest cash generator in India's public sector.

Instead of raising fares, the Railway Board cut them. This led to much higher passenger numbers. At the same time the trains were lengthened. Because each train pulls more carriages the cost per passenger has fallen.

●　What was the prime economic case for cutting rail fares?

●　What would have been the effect on revenues and profit of cutting rail fares?

The impact of altering price on sales revenue

It is important for business firms to calculate the impact of raising or lowering prices on sales revenues. The elasticity of demand varies from one product to another. Demand for a product may be more elastic at high prices than at low prices.

It is important to understand that the elasticity of demand depends on the price range in question for a price rise or price reduction. A supplier needs to consider: 'What will be the impact of changing my original price to a new price.' When the supplier raises price and demand is inelastic this will lead to a rise in revenue. When the supplier lowers price and demand is elastic this will lead to a rise in revenue.

Impact of raising price from current price: An increase in price causes a reduction in the quantity demanded, but total revenue increases (where demand is price inelastic). An increase in price causes such a large fall in quantity demanded that total revenue falls (where demand is price elastic).

Impact of lowering price from current price: A reduction in price causes an increase in quantity demanded, but total revenue earned declines (where demand is price inelastic). A reduction in price causes such a large increase in the quantity demanded that the total revenue rises (where demand is price elastic).

The time period in question also affects elasticity. In the short period elasticity of demand may be more inelastic than in the longer period. For example, if petrol prices increase consumers may continue to buy almost as much as before – however, in the longer term they may economize as the impact of the rise in prices on their income becomes more obvious.

Another factor that should be considered is the 'width' of the definition of a product. For example, if we consider simply 'bread', it is price inelastic in demand as there are very few substitutes. On the other hand Hovis bread is price elastic as there are other substitute brands such as Allinsons, Sunblest, etc. The same is true of jeans and many other products where a variety of 'brands' is available.

Reflective question

1   Why might a producer or seller want to know what the price elasticity of their good or service is, should they choose to change their price from the existing price they are charging?

Income elasticity of demand

In most countries average incomes increase over time. As this happens, people alter their consumption patterns – for example, they are likely to purchase more luxury goods. It is useful therefore for sellers to know how the demand for the goods they are selling is likely to alter as incomes rise. Income elasticity of demand is measured in the following way:

$$\text{Income elasticity of demand} = \frac{\text{Percentage change in demand}}{\text{Percentage change in income}}$$

For normal goods – that is, goods that people are more likely to buy when their incomes rise – income elasticity will be above zero.

Some goods have an income elasticity greater than 1, showing that the percentage change in demand is greater than the percentage change in income.

This situation is described as income elastic.

Normal goods – these are goods that experience rising quantities demanded when incomes rise. They include necessities which tend to have an income elasticity of less than 1, and include basic food stuffs and day-to-day essential clothing items. Luxuries are ones which can be afforded once a consumer exceeds a minimum income level – income elasticity therefore tends to be greater than 1.

Other goods may have an income elasticity of less than 1, showing that the percentage change in demand is less than the percentage change in income. This situation is described as income inelastic. Inferior goods are goods which consumers buy less of when their incomes rise. The value of income elasticity is therefore negative for these goods. Examples might include some varieties of low-quality potatoes, and cheap package holidays.

Table 3.10 shows examples of the effects of some different income elasticities.

TABLE 3.10 Different income elasticity

Relative elasticity	Description	Example
Income elastic	Demand increases by a greater proportion than the change in income	Income increases by 5%; demand for good increases by 10% Income elasticity = 2 (10/5)
Income inelastic	Demand increases by a smaller proportion than the change in income	Income increases by 10%; demand for good increases by 5% Income elasticity = 0.5 (5/10)
Inferior good	People buy fewer of them as incomes rise	Elasticity less than zero

Identify three goods in each of the following categories:

- Those which are income elastic;
- Those which are income inelastic; and
- Inferior goods.

● **In each case explain why you have put it in the category that you have selected.**

Cross-price elasticity of demand

Cross-price elasticity – a measure of the extent to which a change in the price of one good affects the demand for another good, whether it is a substitute good or a complementary good. Consider the rival demand for different types of fish – for example, cod and plaice. An increase in the price of cod is likely to lead to a rise in demand for plaice, which are now cheaper by comparison.

Cross-price elasticity of demand is measured in the following way:

$$\text{Cross-price elasticity of demand} = \frac{\text{Percentage change in demand for good x}}{\text{Percentage change in price of product y}}$$

If the cod (product x) and plaice (product y) are rivals, then as the price of plaice rises, the demand for cod will also rise.

The cross elasticity of demand between cod and plaice will lie somewhere between zero and plus infinity. The cross elasticity of demand between cod and a complementary good (e.g. tomato sauce) will lie somewhere between zero and minus infinity. This is because there is an inverse relationship between demand and price for complementary goods.

CASE STUDY Making price decisions

A household decorating store is seeking to make pricing decisions for products that it has in stock based on calculations to hand about the coefficient of elasticity for various products that it stocks. The store is in competition with rival sellers that are very close to its premises. The business is concerned to make sure that it doesn't end up with too much unsold stock. Using your understanding of the concepts of elasticity, what advice would you give about pricing decisions for the following products?

1. The store stocks standard white emulsion paint which is a top-selling line. Recently it has experienced a 20 per cent fall in quantities sold of the paint as a result of a 10 per cent fall in the price of similar paint in rival stores.

2. The store stocks an exclusive range of gloss paint that has recently proved to be very popular with better-off home owners and professional decorators. It has priced these paints at a competitive pricing point in order to win market share.

3. As a result of recession in the economy the store has suffered from a decline in sales of a range of highly profitable painting-related items such as brushes and rollers. This has been further impacted upon by aggressive discounting in rival stores.

● **In each of the above situations how might the store use a knowledge of elasticity to adjust its pricing strategies?**

Price elasticity of supply

When the price of a good rises or falls this leads to an extension in supply – that is, a movement up or down the supply curve. The extent to which quantity supplied responds to a change in price is determined by how elastic supply is.

Price elasticity of supply – the extent to which quantity supplied alters in response to a change in price. It is measured by the formula:

$$\text{Price elasticity of supply} = \frac{\%\ \text{change in quantity supplied}}{\%\ \text{change in price}}$$

In the case of supply there is a positive relationship between the two variables. As a result price elasticity of supply will typically be represented by a + sign.

Elasticity of supply occurs when the percentage change in quantity supplied is greater than the percentage change in price – for example, if supply increased by 10 per cent as a result of a 5 per cent increase in price.

Factors influencing price elasticity of supply

The main factor influencing price elasticity of supply is time. At a particular moment in time it may be impossible to increase supply, for example reprinting a popular book, however much price increases. Supply in this instance is perfectly inelastic. In the short term it may be possible to increase supply using existing equipment and machinery. In the longer term it may be possible to increase supply further by acquiring more machinery and equipment. The longer the period of time, the more elastic supply is in response to a price change (see Figure 3.13).

In Figure 3.13, S_1 shows perfectly inelastic supply at a moment in time, S_2 relatively inelastic supply in the short period, and S_3 represents relatively elastic supply in the longer period.

Other factors affecting the price elasticity of supply are:

*   The ease with which a product can be stored. If stores of a product can be kept easily, supply will be more elastic. Coffee can be stored in jars (making supply elastic), but fresh strawberries go off very quickly (making supply more inelastic).

*   The cost of increasing supply. The less costly it is to increase supply, the more elastic supply will be.

Making simple calculations

Example 1: A rise in the price of rice in a country from $1.00 per bag to $1.20 per bag leads to an increase in quantity supplied by farmers from 1,000 bags per month to 1,300 bags per month.

$$\text{Price elasticity of supply} \quad = \quad \frac{30\%}{20\%} \quad = \quad 1.5 \text{ (relatively elastic supply)}$$

Example 2: There is a shortage of flour in a country. A rise in the price of bread from 50 cents to 60 cents a loaf leads to an increase in quantity supplied by bakers from 1,000 loaves per month to 1,100 loaves per month.

$$\text{Price elasticity of supply} \quad = \quad \frac{10\%}{20\%} \quad = \quad 0.5 \text{ (relatively inelastic supply)}$$

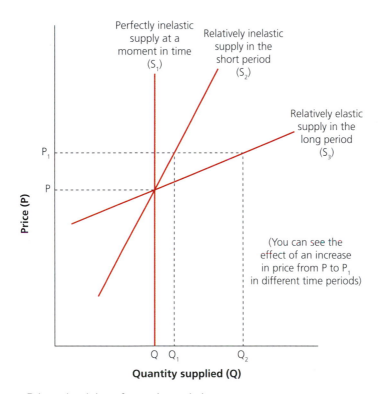

FIGURE 3.13 Price elasticity of supply and time

3.7 The role of firms in the market

Business firms provide the enterprise that enables a market economy to supply the right goods. Entrepreneurs are people that are willing to take a risk when they provide goods and services that they hope will be in demand. However, it is not just a matter of having a good idea and hoping – in addition, successful entrepreneurs must know the market sectors in which they operate (marketing). Successful modern enterprise is well illustrated by the founders of Google.

Larry Page and Sergey Brin arrived relatively late in the Internet search-engine market behind front-runners such as Yahoo, Altavista and Ask Jeeves. However, they were convinced that they had stumbled on a 'big idea'. Today Google is the major Internet search engine. In 2004 the company went public to raise more capital (see below).

Brin and Page set up Google in 1998 in a Silicon Valley garage. Initially family and friends funded the pair. Google (the name derives from Googol, the term for a number starting with 1 followed by 100 zeros) is the major search engine dealing with hundreds of millions of search requests every day. Google's major innovation was in searching out web pages according to their popularity and inter-relationship, not just according to key words. The results are therefore more likely to be what the customer needs (effective marketing).

Reflective question

2   How can Google be seen as a market-focused company?

Size of UK companies

The Office for National Statistics (formerly the CSO) classifies companies in the UK according to whether they are small, medium or large companies:

* A small company employs up to 50 employees;

* A medium-sized company employs up to 250 employees; and

* A large company employs over 250 employees.

Small and medium-sized businesses are often grouped together as SMEs – small and medium-sized enterprises.

There are approximately 1.2 million SMEs and there are approximately 7,000 large companies in the UK.

Like Google, most companies start out on a small basis. If they can attract a sufficient number of customers and share of the market they can grow and prosper.

Types of enterprise

Sole trader is the most common form of business ownership and the easiest to set up. A sole trader is a business owned by one person – although it may employ a large number of people.

To start up as a sole trader all you need to do is inform the tax authorities and open your door. There is no complex paperwork to be filled in beforehand. In addition, you can keep the affairs of your business private, because you are not required to publish reports – simply to fill in your tax return for the HM Revenue and Customs each year.

Is there a demand for our product?

Innocent Smoothies is a good example of a company that identified a demand for its product through common-sense marketing techniques. The company was set up by three friends who had recently graduated from university. They came up with the idea of producing a fruit drink made from 100 per cent natural ingredients.

In order to assess whether there was a demand for it they developed a simple marketing technique. They visited a local fête with supplies of their product and paper cups. They then used two containers to dispose of the finished drinks cups. They asked consumers to dispose of their cups either in a container labelled that the consumer had enjoyed the drink, or another container showing that they had not enjoyed the drink. By the end of the day the first container was full and they knew that they had a winning idea.

● **Can you identify a novel idea for a good or service that would be relatively easy to produce and sell?**

● **How would you go about finding out if there was a demand for your product?**

Typical examples of sole traders are plumbers and small building firms, graphic designers, providers of personal services such as mobile hairdressers, small shops and a number of information technology services such as web design.

Partnerships are business associations between two or more owners of an enterprise. Partnerships usually have between two and 20 members, although there are some that have more. Partnerships are found in many different areas of business where more capital, skill or expertise is required than can be provided by a single owner.

Companies are groups of people who share responsibility for a business venture. The owners (shareholders) jointly put a stock of capital (money) into the business. They are then entitled to a share of the profits in the form of a dividend. Private (limited) companies issue shares which can be bought and sold only with the permission of the board of directors, who are appointed to represent shareholders. In contrast, a public company (PLC) has shares that are traded on the stock exchange, and can be bought and sold freely.

Franchises are a 'business marriage' between an existing proven business (the franchisor) and a newcomer. The newcomer (known as the franchisee) buys permission to copy the business idea and use the name of the established company in a certain location. The franchisee commits his or her capital and effort. The franchisor commits the trading name and management experience, and often supplies material and equipment.

The types of enterprise outlined above are the sources of supply to the market. Through market research they will identify the demand for the products they want to supply. They will make careful calculations of potential costs and revenues in order to make a decision as to whether to supply particular markets, the quantities that they will be prepared to supply and the prices they will charge.

3.8 Summary

This chapter has introduced the way in which the market works. It has shown how the market coordinates decisions made by consumers and producers through the forces of supply and demand. It has demonstrated how demand and supply for particular products can be illustrated on demand and supply curves. It then went on to explain how the interaction of demand and supply creates a market price.

The market is continually changing as a result of changes in the factors that influence the position of the demand and supply curves. Business people are interested in the elasticity of demand for the goods and services that they provide. In particular, they are interested in the impact of changing prices on the revenues earned from their products. The market is a particularly efficient way of coordinating the use of resources because it is self-regulating rather than having to be managed by the state.

KEY THEME

Capitalism and the growth of the market

Adam Smith's book *The Wealth of Nations*, published in 1776, is seen as providing one of the first coherently argued justifications for the market. Smith was centrally concerned with the analysis of economic advancement. Smith showed how business and individual enterprise could contribute to the well-being of economic society.

Smith identified a propulsive force that would put society on an upward growth path and a self-correcting mechanism that would keep it there. The propulsive force was the 'desire for betterment' – or the profit motive. In Smith's words 'it impels every manufacturer to expand his business in order to increase his profits'.

The main road to profit consists in equipping working people with machinery that will increase productivity. Thus the path to growth lies in what Smith called accumulation or, in modern terms, the process of capital investment.

The rising demand for working people pushes up wages. As people become better off they become healthier and mortality rates fall. More people would become available to swell the working population. As a result the demand for products would increase and the rising working population would prevent wages from rising and eating into profits. Because profits are sustained we have a self-correcting mechanism that enables growth to be maintained.

We can illustrate market-led growth in Figure 3.14 as an engine providing a propulsive force and a set of tracks that serve as a self-correcting mechanism enabling growth to take place.

At the same time competition between producers in the marketplace keeps prices down and ensures that goods are produced in line with consumer requirements. If a baker tried to charge more than competitors trade would disappear, or if employees asked for more than the going wage they would not be able to find work.

FIGURE 3.14 Illustrating growth

 ## KEY IDEAS

The market
- The market is any situation where buyers and sellers are involved in making an exchange.
- The market is an efficient way of coordinating the decisions of demanders and suppliers.

Demand and supply
- Demand is the quantity of a product that consumers are willing and able to buy at a given price.
- Supply is the quantity of a product that suppliers are willing to supply to the market at a given price.
- *Ceteris paribus* changes in demand are dependent on changes in price.

Changing conditions of demand and supply
- The market price is determined by the forces of supply and demand.
- There are a number of factors that lead to changes in the condition of demand and supply.

- A demand curve can shift position as a result of a change in income, tastes, the price of substitutes or complements, and the number of buyers.
- A supply curve can shift position as a result of changes in technology, the weather and the costs of production.

Elasticity

- Elasticity is a measure of the extent to which demand or supply alters as a result of a change in price, income or the price of other goods.
- Price elasticity of demand shows the percentage change in quantity demanded resulting from a (percentage) change in price.
- The elasticity of supply is primarily affected by the time period in which supply can be altered.

Firms and the market

- The market is supplied by small and medium-sized enterprises as well as large companies.
- Profit provides a propulsive force which stimulates enterprise.

REVIEW QUESTIONS

1. What is a market and who are the key decision makers in markets?

2. Draw a diagram to show how the market price is determined by the interaction of demand and supply.

3. Illustrate what happens to the market price as a result of: a rise in income; a fall in the popularity of a product; an improvement in the technologies involved in producing the product; and a rise in the costs of manufacturing the product. In each case start from the market price and show whether the demand or supply curve changes position, and what the impact on market price is.

4. Define the following: price elasticity of demand; income elasticity of demand; and cross elasticity of demand. Explain each of these in relation to the demand for trainers.

5. Draw a diagram to illustrate the relationship between price elasticity of supply and the time period in question.

6. Explain why price elasticity is typically a negative number while income elasticity is typically a positive number.

7. What is the relationship between enterprise and supply?

8. How does the market operate as a means of meeting the wishes of consumers?

RECOMMENDED READING

Friedman, M. and Friedman, R. (1980) *The Power of the Market*, San Diego, Harcourt.

Chapter 1 of this book is entitled 'The Power of the Market'. This sets out the case for the power of free markets. It is accompanied by free Google-accessed content – based on the ten-chapter television series that Friedman established.

Harford, T. (2006) *The Undercover Economist*, London, Abacus.

In Chapter 2 of this book Harford sets out a fascinating discussion of how prices are determined in the marketplace, including an interesting discussion of how much you pay for a drink in different types of coffee shop.

REFERENCES

Draculic, S. (1992) *Forward to the Past: How We Survived Communism and Even Laughed*, London, Hutchinson.

Smith, A. (1776) *An Inquiry into the Nature and Causes of the Wealth of Nations*, republished (1976), edited by R.H. Campbell and A.S. Skinner, Oxford, Clarendon Press.

USEFUL WEBSITES

www.timharford.com – provides some interesting and useful economic insights into the way the market operates in a series of popular economics articles by the author Tim Harford.

4 Costs and revenues

CHAPTER OBJECTIVES

By the end of this chapter you will understand:

- How to analyse the cost–volume–profit relationship

- The relationship between average, total and marginal cost

- The importance of increasing and diminishing returns

- How to illustrate costs and revenues

- How to combine cost and revenue to illustrate profitability

- Marginal analysis as a means of identifying the profit maximizing point

4.1 Introduction

Having outlined in Chapter 3 how the market works we now need to focus on how businesses operate in the market, particularly in relation to studying how costs and revenues vary with the quantity of goods produced.

All organizations are concerned about the relationship between the costs of running the organization and the revenues and other income received by it. Costs need to be managed and controlled. Generating revenue helps the organization to carry out its essential activities.

This chapter introduces you to some simple techniques for analysing the costs and revenues of a business. The approaches employed are based on a combination of approaches used in business and economic analysis with a focus on relevance to real world business decision making. The chapter shows you how to calculate and record different types of costs and revenues incurred and received by businesses. You are shown how to measure and illustrate different types of costs and revenues and methods that can be used to identify break-even, loss making and profit making positions for a business.

4.2 The nature of cost–volume–profit analysis

A business model

All businesses will receive revenues from selling products. They will incur costs in making and providing these products. The relationship between costs and revenues can be illustrated by taking the example of the giant multinational company BIC. BIC is a company that is able to benefit from what economists refer to as economies of scale. Economies of scale are the cost savings per unit of production that a large firm is able to achieve from producing on a very large scale. For example, BIC is able to spread its marketing costs across billions of units of product that are sold across the globe.

KEY TERM

Business model – a description of the operations of a business, including its plans to increase revenues and control costs.

For example, BIC is an international business that focuses on producing biros, razors and cigarette lighters among other products. Its core lines are functional in meeting customer needs for standard useful items at value for money prices. BIC's business model includes maximizing **revenues** by providing useful goods at attractive prices, and in controlling its **costs** through efficient operations including exploitation of economies of scale. These economies of scale include mass production and distribution.

The relationship between revenues and costs determines the profit that a business makes.

KEY TERM

Revenue – the receipt from selling a good or service.

There are a number of different ways of measuring revenue which are explored later in this chapter. In the context of this chapter cost will be defined as the money outlay to produce, and/or sell a good. The relationship between costs and revenues can be introduced by the application of cost–volume–profit analysis.

Cost–volume–profit analysis

Cost–volume–profit analysis is used to examine the relationship between:

- The volume – quantity produced or sold.
- The cost of producing or selling that quantity.
- The profit from producing or selling.

Businesses will make a profit when they can exceed the 'break-even' point.

Break-even point – the point at which sales levels are high enough not make a loss, but not high enough to make a profit. At the break-even point the total cost of producing a given volume of goods would be equal to the total revenue.

Break-even analysis – shows how a business will cover costs or make a profit/loss at different levels of operation.

Let's look at this by examining how a fictional business – Donna's Kebabs – can break even.

Donna's Kebabs sells one main type of kebab, which costs £2 to produce. The costs that go directly into making each kebab include:

- Raw materials – pitta bread, meat and salad; and
- Staff wages – which are based on how many kebabs each employee sells.

The kebabs are sold for £3 each. On the face of it, it seems that the business is making a profit of £1 on each kebab sold (£3 – £2).

However, we haven't accounted for all the costs yet. So far we have only accounted for what we call variable costs – how much it costs directly to produce each kebab. They are called variable costs because they vary directly with the numbers of items produced or sold:

The variable cost of 1 kebab = £2

The variable cost of 2 kebabs = £4

The variable cost of 3 kebabs = £6

However, we haven't included the overhead or fixed costs which are the costs of running the business, regardless of how many kebabs we produce. These overheads include the rent on the shop, local business taxes, fuel bills, insurance, the manager's salary and so on. Let's say these overheads or fixed costs add up to exactly £20,000 per year. The business has to sell enough kebabs to cover these fixed costs too, or it will make a loss.

As we saw above, every kebab sold brings in (or contributes) £1 towards covering the overheads. This £1 contribution comes from the sale price of £3 minus the variable cost per kebab of £2.

Calculating contribution:

> Sale price per kebab = £3
>
> Variable cost per kebab = £2
>
> Contribution per kebab = £1

Contribution – the sum that a particular unit of sales contributes to paying off the fixed costs of a business. It is calculated by deducting the variable cost of producing that item from the sales revenue from selling that item.

The business therefore has to sell 20,000 kebabs per year to cover all of its fixed costs (£20,000/£1 = 20,000 kebabs).

If the business is open for 50 weeks in the year (being closed for two weeks' holiday) this means that 400 kebabs will need to be sold each week (20,000/50 weeks). As long as Donna's Kebabs sells 400 kebabs on average each week it will be safe!

Break-even analysis can be converted into a formula or rule that goes like this:

$$\text{Break-even sales} = \frac{\text{Fixed costs}}{\text{Contribution}}$$

Another way of expressing this is:

$$\text{Break-even sales} = \frac{\text{Overheads}}{\text{Contribution}}$$

In this case:.

$$\text{Break-even sales} = \frac{£20,000}{(£3 - £2 = £1)} = 20,000 \text{ kebabs}$$

Let's try these calculations again with a different business example. Imagine you run a hairdressing salon and charge £15 on average to each customer. If the cost per customer in terms of staff wages and materials is £5 and annual overheads are £50,000 how many customers do you need to serve each year in order to cover your total costs and break even?

Answer:

$$\frac{\text{Overheads}}{\text{Contribution}} = \frac{£50,000}{£10} = 5,000 \text{ per year}$$

If we assume again that your business operates for 50 weeks a year, then you need to serve 5000/50 = 100 customers each week (on average) to break even.

ACTIVITY

Use this formula to work out the weekly break-even sales level for the following three examples, assuming each business operates for 50 weeks per year. You will need to use a calculator. There are three key pieces of information we will be using: fixed costs, variable costs per unit and sale price per unit.

● A taxi driver charges an average of £10 per customer for a cost per trip of £5 and has fixed costs of £25,000 per year.

● A beauty salon charges an average of £12.50 per customer for a cost per visit of £5 and has fixed costs of £100,000 per year.

● A recording studio charges £25 per customer per hour, with a variable cost of £7.50 per hour and annual fixed costs of £50,000.

CASE STUDY Illustrating break-even

Break-even analysis can also be shown on a chart produced either manually or on a computer using a program like Microsoft Excel. We can do it manually by using a sheet of graph paper and plotting sales on the horizontal axis, and costs and revenues on the vertical axis. The numbers to plot can be illustrated by Table 4.1 for the kebab shop example used earlier.

We need to plot sales per week up to 800 on the horizontal axis and cost/revenue figures up to £120,000 per year on the vertical axis. This will allow us to draw the following line graphs against weekly sales of 100–800 kebabs:

   D: Annual fixed cost
   E: Annual total cost   = C + D
   G: Annual total revenue   = A × 3 × 50

You can draw all these lines by mapping the figures in each column against the right sales level.

Let's start with annual fixed costs (line D). We know that these are £20,000, however many kebabs are made and sold. We can therefore plot these as a straight line at £20,000.

Now we can plot annual total cost (line E). Total cost is made up of two parts, total fixed costs (which we have already drawn), and total variable cost. The variable cost is £2 per kebab. We can therefore plot the total cost as a diagonal line starting at £20,000 and rising at £10,000 for every 100 kebabs sold each week. For 1,000 kebabs, total cost = £20,000 of fixed costs + £10,000 of variable costs (100 kebabs × £2 × 50 weeks).

Now let's take line G (sales revenue). Where sales = 100, plot revenue of £15,000 and mark a small x on the graph paper. Where sales = 200, plot revenue of £30,000. Keep going for the rest of the revenue figures compared to sales and then join all the points up to create a line graph.

We can now illustrate profit or loss at any level of sales. This is simply G (total sale revenue) minus E (total costs) at any level of sales.

Once you have drawn all the lines you will be able to see:

1. That the most profitable volume of sales is 800 per week.
2. That the break-even volume (which must be met to avoid making a loss) is 400 per week.
3. The way in which total revenue and total cost alter with volume sold.
4. The profit making zone where the total revenue line is higher than the total costs line (this is where sales volume is higher than 400 per week).
5. The loss making zone, where the total revenue line is below the total cost line (this is where sales are lower than 400 per week).

TABLE 4.1 Break-even and profit

A Sales output (kebabs/ week)	B Variable cost/ week £2/kebab (£)	C Annual total variable cost (£)	D Annual fixed costs at £20,000 (£)	E Annual total costs (C + D) (£)	F Sales revenue/ week £3/kebab (£)	G Annual total revenue (£)	H Annual profit/ loss (£)
100	200	10,000	20,000	30,000	300	15,000	−15,000
200	400	20,000	20,000	40,000	600	30,000	−10,000
300	600	30,000	20,000	50,000	900	45,000	−5,000
400	800	40,000	20,000	60,000	1,200	60,000	0
500	1,000	50,000	20,000	70,000	1,500	75,000	5,000
600	1,200	60,000	20,000	80,000	1,800	90,000	10,000
700	1,400	70,000	20,000	90,000	2,100	105,000	15,000
800	1,600	80,000	20,000	100,000	2,400	120,000	20,000

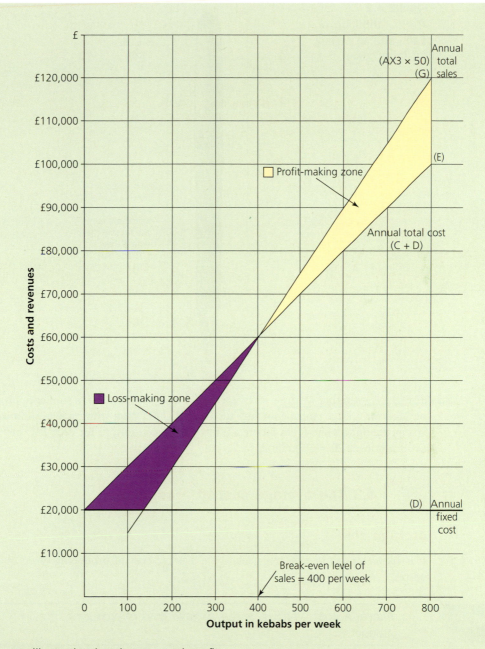

FIGURE 4.1 Illustrating break-even and profit

- Set out a table for one of the other examples given in the text.

- Now try drawing these figures as a chart using a software program such as Microsoft Excel.

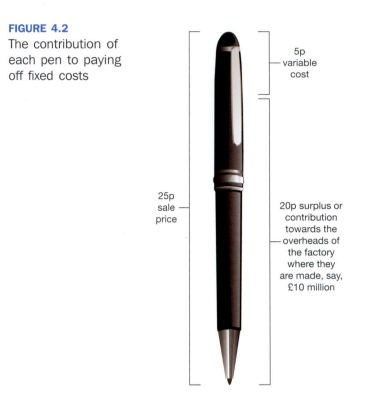

FIGURE 4.2
The contribution of
each pen to paying
off fixed costs

5p
variable
cost

25p
sale
price

20p surplus or
contribution
towards the
overheads of
the factory
where they
are made, say,
£10 million

The illustration that we drew was for a small business. However, a similar approach could be used for a large global company such as BIC operating with huge economies of scale. Using the figures shown in Figure 4.2 the break-even output for each BIC pen would be £10 million/£0.20 = 50 million.

4.3 The average cost of production

Average cost

It is important to be able to calculate the average cost of producing given quantities of output.

Average cost – shows us the average cost of producing or selling units of a product.

Average cost is normally illustrated by a U-shaped curve. This shows that the average cost of producing a small number of units is high. The average cost will then fall as output increases. Common sense provides an explanation for this. Production involves combining factors of production. When only a small quantity of factors of production are combined they are not combined together very effectively. For example, a large factory machine may

TABLE 4.2 Output per head per hour with different numbers of operatives

Number of operatives	Output per head per hour
1	20
2	22
3	25
4	30
5	35
6	30
7	27

work most efficiently with five or six operatives. With fewer operatives it would be run less efficiently. Output per head from operating the machine might therefore change in the way illustrated in Table 4.2.

You can see from Table 4.2 that productive efficiency increases up to the point at which five employees are working with the machine and then it starts to fall.

This point can also be illustrated with reference to another economic concept –marginal output. In economics the marginal unit is the extra unit of something that you want to measure. In this case we can measure marginal output per head per hour. The first worker was able to produce 20 units per hour. An additional (marginal) worker was able to increase the output to 22 units per head per hour – a marginal increase of 2 units per head. You should be able to see that marginal output per head per hour increases up to the point at which five workers are employed. Beyond this point marginal output per head starts to fall (see Figure 4.3a). Logically therefore (assuming each operative receives the same wage) average labour costs (variable costs) per unit of production will decrease up to a point at which five operatives are employed and will then start to rise (see Figure 4.3b).

The law of increasing and diminishing returns to a factor of production

Economists use the laws of increasing and diminishing returns to describe what we have just explained.

Increasing returns – as increasing quantities of a variable factor of production (in this case labour) are combined with a fixed quantity of another factor (in this case machinery) initially there will be increasing returns to the variable factor.

Decreasing returns – at a certain point decreasing returns set in. Beyond the most efficient point of production adding increasing quantities of the variable factor will lead to falling efficiency and rising cost per unit.

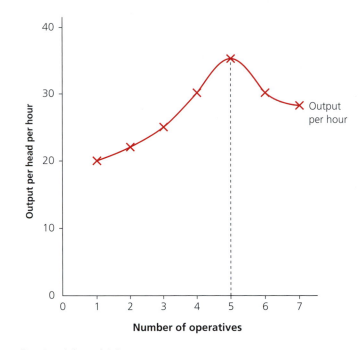

FIGURE 4.3a Productivity of labour

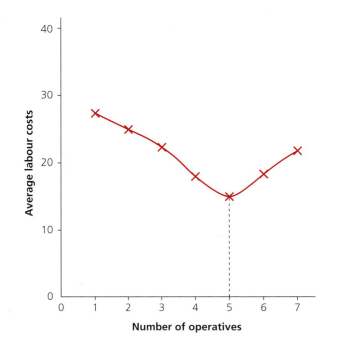

FIGURE 4.3b Average labour costs

CASE STUDY Returns to a small company

Office Services is a company with five computers. With no staff the capital lies idle and is therefore inefficient. With one member of staff only four computers remain idle and output and efficiency start to increase. With a second member of staff the process continues (with increasing efficiency). Once five members of staff are employed efficiency is maximized, but if we keep adding staff then they start to argue over computer usage and have to wait to use computers so efficiency starts to decline.

- Over what range of output does the firm benefit from increasing returns in terms of computer usage?
- What problems set in once the firm expands its staff beyond the most efficient point?
- How might the firm seek to resolve this inefficiency (i.e. beyond the most efficient point)?

Average variable cost

Variable costs of production usually include the raw materials. Variable costs increase as more labour is added to produce more goods, and average variable costs (AVCs) alter as output increases.

CASE STUDY Costs at different levels of output

A business has variable costs, as illustrated by Table 4.3.

- Illustrate the average variable cost curve on a graph.
- Explain why it has the shape that it does.

TABLE 4.3 Average variable cost at different levels of output

Output	Average variable cost per unit (pence)
100	10
200	8
300	6
400	8
500	10

Average fixed cost

In working out the cost of producing individual units we also need to account for fixed costs.

The fixed costs per unit of producing a small output will be relatively large. This fixed cost per unit will then fall progressively as output is increased. The more units a business produces the lower will be its unit costs. This is illustrated in Figure 4.4 showing average fixed cost.

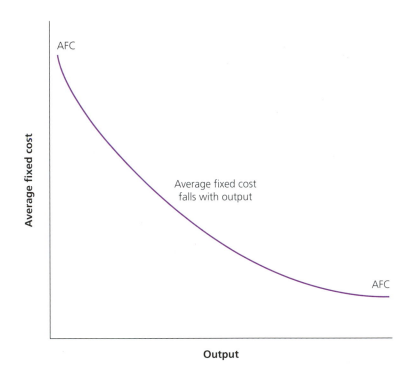

FIGURE 4.4 Average fixed costs

Total and average costs

Total costs can be calculated by adding the fixed and variable costs at different levels of output. Figure 4.5 shows in graph form the total, fixed and variable costs given in Table 4.4.

The fixed costs are £200 whatever the level of output. Variable costs start from zero – in other words, there are no variable costs if nothing is produced. Variable costs then increase, as more variable factors are required to produce increasing quantities of output.

On the graph the total cost at any level of output is the fixed cost (200) + the variable cost (e.g. £50 to produce 15 units of output). The total cost of producing 15 units of output is thus £250.

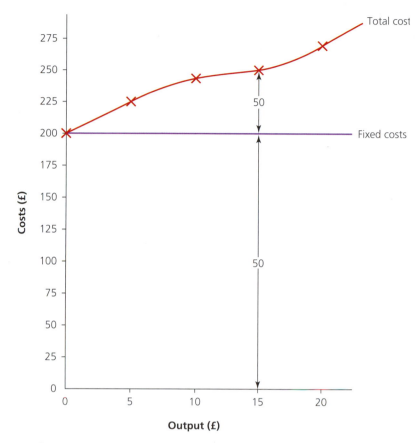

FIGURE 4.5 Total cost = fixed cost and variable cost

TABLE 4.4 Costs at different levels of output

Output per week	Fixed costs (£)	Variable costs (£)	Total cost (£)
0	200	0	200
5	200	25	225
10	200	40	240
15	200	50	250
20	200	70	270

Average cost

KEY TERM

Average cost – the cost of producing a unit of product at a particular output.

To calculate average cost, use the following formula:

$$\text{Average cost} = \frac{\text{Total cost}}{\text{Output}}$$

For example, in the table above the average cost of producing 10 products would be £24 (240/10). The average cost of producing 20 products would be £13.50 (270/20).

The shape of the average cost curve

It is important to know and understand the shape of a typical average cost curve. Figure 4.6 shows its characteristic U-shape.

It has this shape because:

1. Average fixed cost is falling as output levels increase. This effect pulls the curve down at a slower and slower rate. So if total fixed costs are £1,000, producing two units rather than one will lower the fixed cost from £1,000 to produce 1 unit to £500 to produce 2 units. However, at much higher levels of output – for example, producing 1,000 units rather than 999 – you will only be reducing the average fixed cost from £1.11 to £1.00 – that is, by just a few pence.

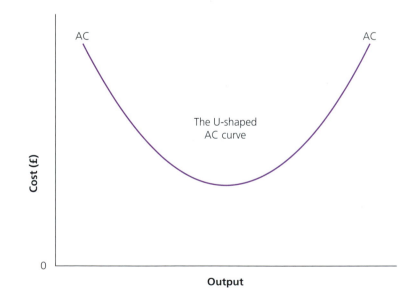

FIGURE 4.6 U-shaped average cost curve

2. Average variable cost falls initially as the firm is able to combine its factors of production more efficiently. However, there comes a point at which inefficiencies creep into the production plant.

The lowest point on the average cost curve shows the point at which the business is combining its resources most efficiently. We call this lowest point the optimum output level or minimum efficient scale.

4.4 Costs at different levels of output

Costs and output

We are now in a position to examine the relationship between the various types of costs and output levels.

Total and average cost

CASE STUDY Manufacturing paint

A paint manufacturer has calculated that fixed costs for the business are £1,000 per week. These are made up of the costs of advertising, transporting paint to the store, lighting and heating, as well as the rent and rates of running the business. The variable costs of manufacturing the paint consist of the materials that go into the paint and the labour required to manufacture it – the more that is produced, the greater the number of people employed (so their wages vary with the quantity produced).

The fixed and variable costs are set out in Table 4.5.

TABLE 4.5 Costs at different levels of output (2)

Number of tins produced	Total fixed cost (£)	Total variable cost (£)	Total cost (£)	Average cost (£)
0	1,000	0		
100	1,000	1,000		
200	1,000	1,800		
300	1,000	2,300		
400	1,000	3,200		

- Copy the table and complete the columns for total cost and average cost.
- What is the optimum output? How did you work this out?
- Explain the changes in the average cost curve as output increases.

Fixed variable and total cost

Table 4.6 summarizes some key terms and their meanings.

TABLE 4.6 Definitions of different types of costs

Total fixed cost	The sum of all of the different types of fixed costs at different outputs
Total variable cost	The sum of all of the variable costs at different outputs
Total cost	The sum of total fixed cost and total variable cost at different outputs
Average fixed cost	The total fixed cost divided by the level of output
Average variable cost	The total variable cost divided by the level of output
Average total cost	The total cost divided by the level of output

CASE STUDY Canning tomatoes

The total costs for a canning plant that specializes in canning tomatoes are:

- The fixed costs – interest paid on a loan, rent and rates, and the cost of energy to run the plant.
- The variable costs – the tomatoes, the cans and the labels.

TABLE 4.7 Costs at different levels of output (3)

Output (units)	Total fixed costs (£)	Total variable costs (£)	Total cost (£)
0			
100		1,200	
200			3,800
300		2,400	
400	2,000		4,700
500			5,400

- Some of the figures are missing from Table 4.7. Copy the table and fill in the missing numbers.
- Now calculate the average fixed cost, the average variable costs and the average total cost at each of the levels of output shown in the table.

4.5 Illustrating revenues

Revenue – the sum of money that a business receives from making sales. Obviously sales revenue increases with the quantity of goods sold.

Total revenue

To calculate total revenue (in order to calculate the value of sales made by business) multiply the quantity of goods sold by the price they are sold for:

Total revenue = quantity of goods sold × price; or

$$TR = Q \times P$$

Average revenue

Average revenue – the price received for selling a given quantity of goods.

This can be illustrated in the following way:

$$AR = TR/Q;$$

and as $TR = P \times Q;$

then $AR = (P \times Q)/Q = P$

It is helpful for a business to know its average revenue because this can be compared with the average cost of making and/or selling that item.

The best way of illustrating this is to show the market price – that is where demand and supply meet. Take the example of footballs produced by a major sports goods producer. The market price (where demand cuts supply) is £10. At this price the business is prepared to supply 1,000 footballs a week to sports shops. Sports shops are happy to buy 1,000 footballs a week.

So what is the total revenue?

$$1,000\,(Q) \times £10\,(P) = £10,000$$

In Figure 4.7 this is illustrated by the shaded area OPAQ.

So what is the average revenue?

The average revenue is simply the price: £10. This is because every ball will be sold to shops for £10.

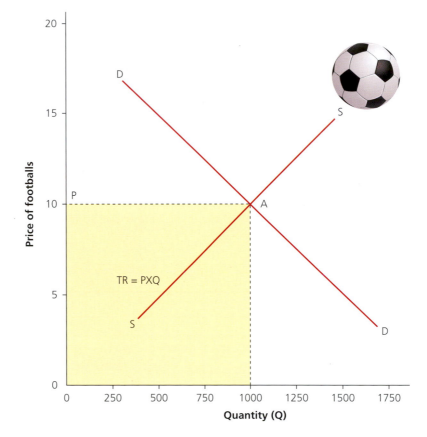

FIGURE 4.7 The market price and total revenue

TABLE 4.8 Revenues at different levels of sales

Sales	Average revenue (price) (£)	Total revenue (total value of all sales) (£)
100	10	1,000
200	10	2,000
300	10	3,000
400	10	4,000
500	10	5,000
600	10	6,000
700	10	7,000
800	10	8,000
900	10	9,000

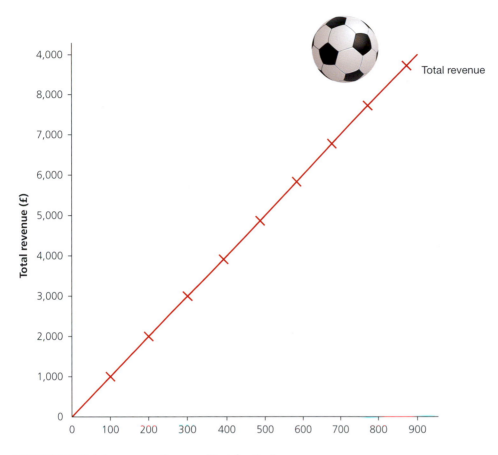

FIGURE 4.8 Total revenue from selling footballs

Total and average revenue

The total revenue is the sum of all of the revenues received by a supplier. Table 4.8 shows the weekly average and total revenue of a company that supplies footballs to shops in a particular country for a price of £10 each.

Figure 4.8 shows this data in graph form. Notice the straight line starting at zero and then rising by £10 for each sale made.

4.6 Combining cost and revenue to illustrate profit

Making a profit

The main aim of a business is to make a profit. There may be wider goals, such as building a reputation for quality or helping to build a stronger community, but most businesses will place an emphasis on profit.

One group that is very interested in the profits is the shareholders. The shareholders are the owners of a company. A portion of company profit will be distributed to shareholders. These are called 'dividends'. Shareholders will receive a dividend for each share owned. They will want to see their business making healthy profits over time. They will be interested in figures illustrating:

- Operating profit margins – the amount of profit made compared with sales figures. This is often expressed as a percentage – for example, a profit margin of 6 per cent. A 6 per cent margin shows that the business is making 6 pence of profit for every £1 of sales revenue.

- Earnings per share – the amount of profit a company makes for each share in the business. This is calculated by dividing the profit by the number of shares in the company.

- Return on capital employed – the profit made by the business as a proportion of the capital employed by the business, including both the shareholders' capital and borrowed capital.

Maximizing

To maximize is to make something as large as possible, and many businesses seek to maximize profits in the long period. Analysis of costs and revenues helps us to find out

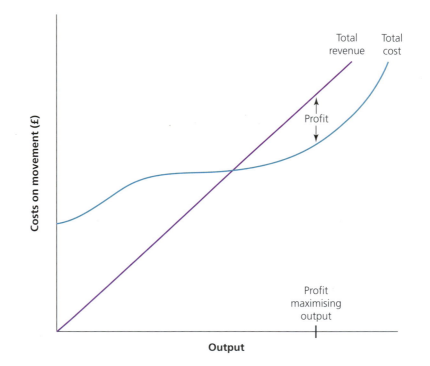

FIGURE 4.9 The profit maximising output

how much businesses should produce, and what prices they should charge, in order to maximize their profits. The profit maximizing point of a business is the point at which there is the greatest difference between total revenues (TR) and total costs (TC). Figure 4.9 shows this.

Please note that total revenue is represented by a straight line assuming that the business charges a standard price as it increases output. Total cost increases more than proportionally to the increase in output at first (because of diminishing returns). Total cost then rises less than proportionally to the increase in output because of increasing returns. Beyond the most efficient point total cost will again start to rise more than proportionately to output because of diminishing returns.

The profit maximizing output is the point at which there is the greatest vertical difference between cost and revenue.

Reflective question

1   Will producers always want to maximize profit? If the answer is no, what are the alternatives and why might they choose one of these alternatives?

Marginal cost and marginal revenue

Economists use marginal cost and marginal revenue analysis as a tool to identify the profit maximizing point of a firm.

The logic behind this is simple. The margin is the extra unit of something – for example, the additional cost or the additional revenue from producing one more unit.

When the marginal cost of producing an extra good is less than the marginal revenue of the good, the producer or seller will make additional revenue from selling that unit.

For example, a producer knows that the 1,000th unit of production will cost 50 pence to produce but will yield 60 pence worth of revenue. So it makes sense to make that unit.

The producer knows that the 1,100th unit will cost 59 pence to produce but will yield 60 pence worth of revenue. So it makes sense to make that unit.

However, the 1,101st unit will cost 60 pence to produce and will yield 60 pence worth of revenue. So that is the last unit that will be produced. You can see why.

The 1,102nd unit may cost 61 pence to produce – so the producer would be making a loss of 1 penny from producing that unit.

4.7 A marginal approach to profit maximizing

At the start of this chapter we showed how a business can carry out cost–volume–profit analysis to identify how much profit can be made at different levels of output.

What we want to show you now is an approach used by economists to identify the profit maximizing point for a firm. The approach is based on marginal analysis. This analysis involves:

1. Explaining how marginal revenue can be derived from a demand curve.

2. Explaining the relationship between marginal costs and average costs.

3. Illustrating how the point at which marginal cost equals marginal revenue is the profit maximizing point.

Deriving average revenue from the demand curve

In Chapter 3 we saw that a typical demand curve is downward sloping. To sell more goods we have to lower prices.

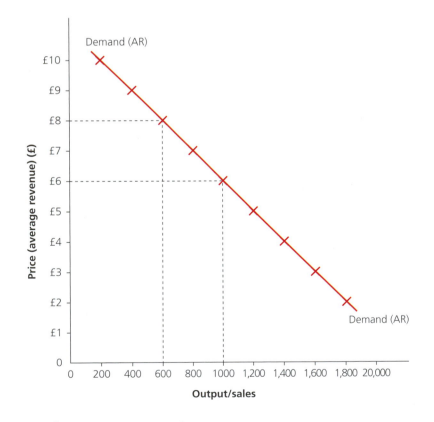

FIGURE 4.10 Average revenue = price

Another way of thinking about the demand curve is that it illustrates 'average revenue'. For example, in Figure 4.10 when the business charges a price of £8 the demand for its product is 600 units. The average revenue for each of these units is therefore £8.

If the business charges a price of £6 the demand for its product is 1,000. The demand curve and average revenue are thus the same.

Deriving marginal revenue from the demand curve

In order to increase sales a business needs to lower the price of the units that it sells. As a result the marginal revenue generated will always be less than the price the firm is able to charge for the unit sold (because the firm has had to lower the price of all of the units that it sells in order to make additional sales).

Marginal revenue thus always lies below average revenue (see Figure 4.11 illustrating this).

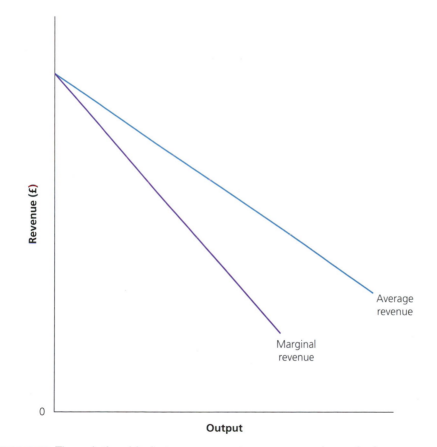

FIGURE 4.11 The relationship between average revenue and marginal revenue

Average cost and marginal cost

The average cost is the total cost of producing a given output divided by the quantity produced.

The marginal cost is the cost of producing an additional unit of output.

When a business produces a relatively small output marginal costs will be lower than average costs. This is because of increasing returns. As the firm increases output it becomes more efficient at using its resources.

However, beyond a certain level of output, inefficiencies (diminishing returns) will step in. The initial impact of diminishing returns is that marginal costs will start to rise. Average costs will however continue to fall (as long as the marginal cost of production is lower than the average cost).

However, once marginal costs become greater than the average cost of producing a given quantity of output then average cost will also start to rise. This sounds complicated, but actually it can be deduced using common sense. Follow through the logic in Figure 4.12 showing marginal cost and average cost.

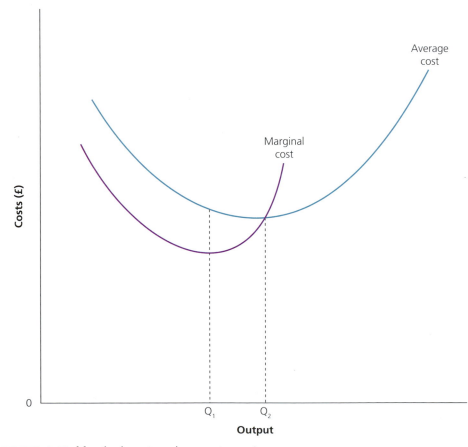

FIGURE 4.12 Marginal cost and average cost

At levels of output up to Q_1 both the marginal cost and average cost of production are falling. Because each additional unit of output can be produced more cheaply (because of increasing returns) average cost will fall.

Beyond Q_1 and up to Q_2 marginal cost is starting to rise. However, because the cost of producing additional units is less than the average cost, average cost will continue to fall (just in the same way as your grade average falls if additional grades are lower than your average grade).

However, beyond Q_2 both marginal cost and average cost will rise. This is because the marginal costs are now greater than the average costs – pulling the average up.

Optimum point – the point at which marginal cost cuts average cost (and average cost starts to rise). The optimum output is the output that can be produced at the lowest unit cost.

Combining cost and revenue curves

We are now in a position to combine costs and revenues into a single diagram to identify the profit maximizing point. To do this we need to set out a diagram showing average revenue and marginal revenue, and average cost and marginal cost.

Before we do this let us return to our marginal analysis. We showed earlier that the profit maximizing point for a business is the point at which marginal revenue equals marginal cost. We can illustrate this in a diagram that just includes marginal revenue (MR) and marginal cost (MC).

We have seen that marginal revenue falls as output increases. In contrast, after initially falling marginal cost will rise. Figure 4.13 therefore shows the profit maximizing point using marginal analysis.

Now we are in a position to set out a diagram showing the profit maximization point of a firm using four curves.

Figure 4.14 illustrates this situation. The firm will produce at the point at which MR = MC. At this level of output we are able to calculate total cost and total revenue in order to calculate profit.

- Total revenue is simply average revenue multiplied by output (at the profit maximizing point).
- Total cost is simply average cost multiplied by output (at the profit maximizing point).
- OQ_1 will be the quantity produced. At an output of Q_1 profit is maximized (i.e. MC = MR).
- Total revenue at OQ_1 is represented by the area on the diagram OQ_1CB.
- Total cost at OQ_1 is represented by the area OQ_1DA.
- Total profit is represented by the rectangular area ABCD. ABCD is total revenue minus total cost.

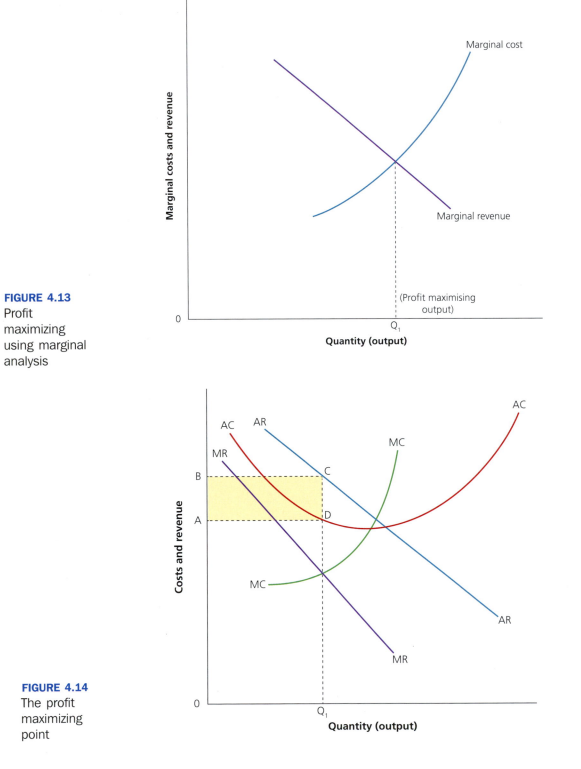

FIGURE 4.13
Profit
maximizing
using marginal
analysis

FIGURE 4.14
The profit
maximizing
point

Reflective questions

2 Why would a producer lose out by producing less than the profit maximizing point?

3 Why would a producer lose out by producing more than the profit maximizing output (relate your answer to Figure 4.14)?

When is marginal costing used in business?

Marginal costing tends to be used on an ad hoc basis as a management technique to aid decision making. Marginal costing is appropriate for short-term decision making where the knowledge of cost behaviour can maximize the contribution to paying off overheads and to generating profit.

The change in the contribution of producing an additional unit of product is the marginal revenue minus the marginal cost:

> Change in contribution = Marginal revenue – Marginal cost

For example, if a business can sell 10 units for £100 or sell 11 units at £95, then the marginal revenue for the eleventh unit is just £45 (11 × £95) – (10 × £100).

In this case, if the marginal cost is less than £45 selling the 11th unit will add to profits (or reduce losses).

Marginal costing is often used in the following situations:

- Make or buy? For example, when a business needs to decide whether to manufacture a product in-house or subcontract to a supplier.

- Terminate a business activity? Part of a business or a particular product line may be reporting losses using other types of costing systems. The business needs to find out how closure or termination will affect total business profits. What costs will be saved and what revenues lost?

- Setting the selling price. A business needs to know where to pitch the selling price of its products.

Raising profit levels

At the start of the chapter we showed that a business model helps a business to be successful. An existing business model can often be improved by raising sales levels or by lowering costs.

How can we raise sales?

For a firm like BIC, making millions of biros can increase its sales revenue by:

- Improving the quality of its product – for example, by making a more colourful and appealing pen.

- Successful promotion and advertising.

- Entering new markets, such as new countries.

Each of these strategies could increase the demand for BIC pens and help to raise the revenue line, so that a profit is made at a lower level of output than previously.

This is illustrated in Figure 4.15a below where total revenues increase at a faster rate – so that the profit zone is reached at a lower output or level of sales than previously.

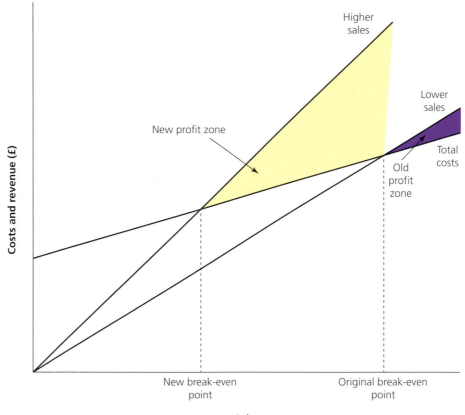

FIGURE 4.15a Raising sales to increase the size of the profit zone

Alternatively, a firm can increase its profits by lowering it costs. A firm like BIC can lower its costs per unit sold by:

•   Buying materials from cheaper sources.

•   Paying less for resources such as staff or materials.

•   Producing more efficiently, for example by generating less waste.

In Figure 4.15b you can see that a firm can break even more quickly and increase the size of its profits by lowering its costs.

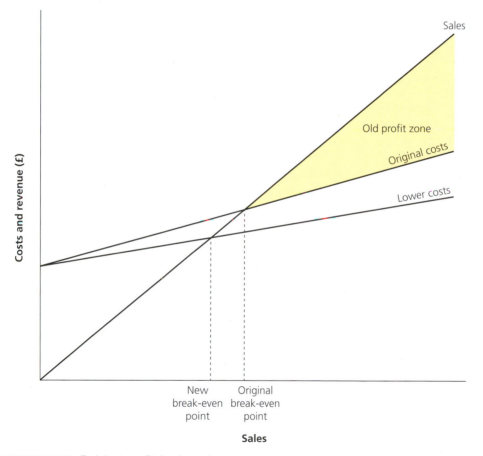

FIGURE 4.15b Raising profit by lowering costs

4.8 Summary

This chapter has examined ways in which businesses can calculate costs and revenues of production. An important aspect of business decision making is that of identifying the costs and revenues of producing alternative volumes of output in order to calculate profits. Businesses need to be aware of total, average and marginal costs and revenues of production. Armed with this information they are able to make decisions about how much

CASE STUDY Making a profit – costs and revenues for Sainsbury's in 2011

Table 4.9 shows highlights from J Sainsbury plc annual group income statement for the 52 weeks to 19 March 2011.

This statement shows that J Sainsbury plc sold roughly £21 billion worth of goods (total revenue). Its cost of sales consisted principally of buying in goods to resell through its stores. Its profit from trading activities was therefore £1,160 million. From this it was able to take away costs of running the business such as head office costs (administrative costs).

From carrying out the day-to-day operations of the business an operating profit was generated of £851

TABLE 4.9 J Sainsbury plc annual group income statement

	£m
Revenue	21,102
Cost of sales	(19,942)
Gross profit	1,160
Administrative expenses	(417)
Other income	108
Operating profit	851
Earnings per share	34.4

million. After making further deductions from this total, including the income tax expense, J Sainsbury plc were able to make a profit for the financial year of £640 million.

Earnings per share is calculated by dividing the profit by the number of shares in the company. You can see from the above that J Sainsbury plc would thus be very interested in the relationship between costs and revenues.

Decisions would have to be made about which products to stock and which suppliers to work with. The company seeks to secure maximum returns per square foot of store space. Regular analysis would be carried out to find out how particular product lines are generating profits in order to justify stocking them in the supermarket. This would involve comparing the revenue per square foot for a particular product line with the cost per square foot of stocking that item in a particular period of time. Items which fail to generate sufficient profit margins would be cut out to be replaced by more profitable lines.

- How does the profit maximizing process outlined for Sainsbury's above fit in with: (1) the concept of cost–volume–profit analysis; and (2) maximizing at the margin?

to produce. An understanding of costs and revenues helps us to understand the business models that businesses employ. Marginal analysis enables us to identify the profit maximizing point of a business.

KEY IDEAS

Cost–volume–profit analysis
- Cost–volume–profit analysis enables the analysis of costs and profits at different levels of output.
- The break-even point is the point at which costs are exactly matched by revenues and can be calculated by overheads/contribution.

Average costs of production
- The average cost of any level of output can be calculated by dividing the total cost by the number of units sold or produced.
- The average cost curve has a U-shape.

Examining costs at different levels of output
- Total cost rises with the level of production.
- Average costs will initially fall but will rise beyond an optimum point – largely because of diminishing returns.

Revenues
- Total revenue is calculated by multiplying sales by the price charged.
- Average revenue is the same as the price charged for uniformly priced goods.

Combining costs and revenues
- Comparing costs and revenues makes it possible to assess the profit that a business makes. The difference between the total revenue and the total cost of producing a given level of output is the profit.

A marginal approach to profit maximization
- Marginal costing looks at how additional output contributes to fixed costs and profits.

Review questions

1. Define the terms fixed cost, variable cost, contribution and break-even.

2. How can break-even be calculated from contribution?

3. Explain why the average cost curve has its characteristic U-shape.

4. When and why do diminishing returns set in when more of a variable factor is added to a fixed factor?

5. What happens to the following costs as output increases: (a) total cost; (b) average cost; and (c) marginal cost?

6. What is the relationship between average and marginal revenue? Show how average and marginal revenue can be illustrated on the same graph.

7. What is the relationship between marginal revenue and marginal cost? How can the profit maximizing point be identified by comparing marginal cost with marginal revenue?

8. Draw a diagram to illustrate the profit maximizing point – by combining average cost, average revenue, marginal cost and marginal revenue on the same illustration.

9. What business decisions can be informed by a process of marginal costing?

10. How can a firm increase its profit from producing a given level of output?

RECOMMENDED READING

Dransfield, R. (2004) *Accounts Made Easy*, Chapter 5, Cheltenham, Nelson Thornes.

USEFUL WEBSITES

http://www.globusz.com/ebooks/costing/00000012.htm – an e-book publication identifying useful aspects of absorption and marginal costing that might be helpful for your wider reading on costing.

5 Different types of market structures

CHAPTER OBJECTIVES

By the end of the chapter you will understand:

- How to identify different types of market structures

- The features and benefits of a perfectly competitive market

- The features and benefits of a monopoly market

- The features and benefits of oligopoly markets

- The features and benefits of monopolistic markets

- Pricing strategies in the real world

5.1 Introduction

One of the most important topics that economists have analysed is the market for goods and services. They are particularly interested in how competition between firms in the market affects market outcomes such as prices, output levels and differentiation between products. Economists are particularly interested in the extent to which competition in the market leads to an efficient use of resources.

At the start of this book we saw that the fundamental economic problem is of scarcity and choice. If resources and goods are scarce they need to be used efficiently. A key question therefore is to what extent does a particular market lead to efficient use of resources? One of the main arguments presented to support competition and competitive markets is that this leads to a highly efficient use of resources. Many economists believe that where there is less competition this can lead to waste and less efficient use of resources. In Chapter 2 we saw that economists use models to simplify the relationship between economic variables to aid understanding. In this chapter we present some models of different market structures.

5.2 What is market structure?

Market structure means the characteristics under which a market operates. An understanding of market structure is very important in business because it helps to identify the nature of competition in the market. Knowledge of market structure helps entrepreneurs to consider the nature and scale of competition. The more competitive the market the greater the influence of rivals/competitors on pricing and other competitive decisions that a business makes.

Market structure consists of four main elements:

- How easy is it for new firms to enter the market or for existing firms to leave?
- The number of buyers and sellers.
- The types of goods and services sold in the market.
- How price is determined in the market.

Extreme market structures

It is possible to identify two extreme market structures. At one extreme is a situation where the market is controlled by one supplier. This is referred to as a monopoly. For example, pharmaceutical companies such as GlaxoSmithKline can apply for a patent to produce a newly researched medicine or drug for a given period of time during which they would be the sole supplier.

At the other extreme there are competitive markets in which many sellers provide almost identical products, for example farmers producing sugar beet. However, even with agricultural products there is some differentiation in quality. For example, hens' eggs come

COMPETITIVE MARKETS   **MONOPOLY MARKETS**

Sugar beet,
eggs

Patented
pharmaceuticals

FIGURE 5.1 The range of market structures

in different sizes and colours, and some are produced by intensive farming whereas others are free range (see Figure 5.1).

 5.3 Types of market structure

Economists have identified four main types of market structure, shown in Table 5.1.

The purpose of identifying market structures is to be able to identify the different characteristics of such structures and the implications for effective use of resources in the economy. For example, if monopolists restrict price or output what will be the likely impact on consumer choice – will some or all consumers lose out? If monopoly is harmful does the government need to step in to limit monopoly powers?

TABLE 5.1 Types of market structure

Market structure	Number of buyers and sellers	Types of goods	Freedom of entry	Price controls
Perfect competition	Many buyers and sellers	Goods all the same	Perfectly free entry	Firms are price takers
Monopolistic competition	Large numbers of buyers and several sellers	Goods are similar but differentiated	Free entry or easy access	Firms are price setters
Oligopoly	Large numbers of buyers, only a few sellers	Goods can be differentiated or homogeneous	Restrictions to entry	Firms are price setters
Monopoly	Many buyers, one seller	Only one producer	Very difficult for new firms to enter	Firms are price setters

CASE STUDY Opening up to competition

FIGURE 5.2 Barbados passenger transport

Source: © Brett Charlton/iStockphoto.

Passenger transport is an area that has increasingly been opened up to competition between rival companies in recent years. Traditionally in many countries bus and rail routes were run as government monopolies. The government provided set routes with set fares. One of the reasons for doing so was to provide a reliable service, often to destinations where only a few people might live. However, today far more people have cars and access to other forms of transport (e.g. taxi services).

Transport services have therefore increasingly been privatized in many parts of the world. During the 1980s many bus routes were privatized in the UK allowing competition between rival private companies. A similar picture has emerged with rail transport although to a lesser degree. In Caribbean economies such as Barbados private carriers (yellow buses) compete with government carriers (blue buses) on many routes. This has led to greater diversity in provision. For example, in Barbados there are privately owned 'reggae buses' providing customers with wall-to-wall reggae music as part of their ride.

- What benefits are likely to arise from just having one (monopoly) bus company in a particular area? What might be the drawbacks?

- What benefits are likely to arise from having a much more competitive market structure with bus companies being allowed to compete with each other on bus routes?

Features of market structures

The number of buyers and sellers

Most consumer markets have many buyers. In some markets for producer goods – for example, machinery – there may be a smaller number of buyers. The number of sellers varies from just one in a pure monopoly situation to an infinite number in a perfectly competitive market.

Consumer market – one in which consumer goods are sold. These goods are those that will be used by the end consumer (e.g. food, clothing, entertainment).

Producer market – one in which producer goods are sold. These goods are those that will be used by producers of goods (e.g. the market for industrial machinery and equipment).

Types of goods

Some goods are identical (or almost identical) in nature – for example, bags of white sugar. Other goods are highly differentiated – for example, works of art painted by skilled and celebrated artists. The more sellers there are, the higher the level of competition.

Freedom of entry and exit

Some markets are difficult to enter. For example, many professions, such as medicine, involve high skill levels so there are relatively few practitioners. Other markets are easy to enter – for example, setting up a small grocery store. The greater the ease of entry the more intense the competition.

Controls on price

In most markets firms compete with each other through the prices they charge. However, in monopoly markets the monopolist is able to set prices. In some instances the government also sets price controls in the form of maximum prices that sellers can charge.

5.4 Perfect competition

As a way of analysing how businesses compete with each other, economists have developed a theory of perfect competition. Perfect competition does not exist in pure form in the real world because there are always differences between sellers. For example, one street vendor of plain colour t-shirts might be more friendly than another vendor of identical items.

The idea of perfect competition that economists have modelled is based on the following assumptions:

- There would be lots of firms competing with each other;
- Each firm would produce an identical product;

- Each producer would know exactly what the others were producing and the prices they were charging;

- There would be no barriers to new firms entering the market and no barriers to exit, so firms enter or leave the market easily;

- Each firm would produce only a small percentage of the overall production in the market; and

- There would be lots of buyers, each of whom would know the prices charged by all the sellers.

Given these conditions, economists believe that:

- Businesses would all charge the same price;

- This price would be the minimum that a business could charge without going out of business;

- The price would just enable each business to cover its costs and to make the minimum (normal) profit required to keep operating in the market; and

- No firm would risk charging more than the market price, because they would make no sales if they did so.

Normal profit – the profit that a business needs to make to stay in a market. The normal profit that an entrepreneur will need to make is equivalent to what they could make from using their capital and their talent in its next best use – that is, the opportunity cost of remaining in an industry.

Abnormal profit – any profit made in excess of normal profit. The normal profit is included by an economist in the costs of producing goods.

Price takers

Firms operating under perfect competition would charge the market price. They are thus price takers rather than price makers.

We can illustrate this situation in the following way. Figure 5.3 shows:

1. The U-shaped average cost curve that was described in Chapter 4.

2. The marginal cost curve illustrating the marginal cost of producing additional units of output. The marginal cost curve cuts the average cost curve at the lowest point on the average cost curve.

3. Average revenue – the price which the perfectly competitive firm 'takes' from the market. The firm can only sell units at the market price so average revenue is a horizontal line.

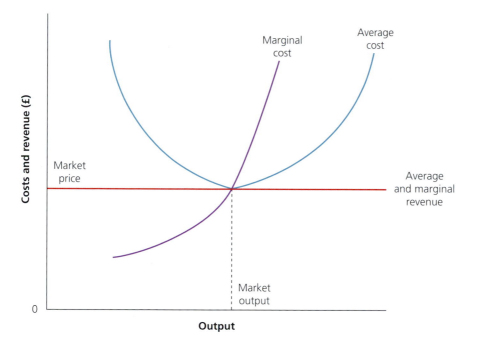

FIGURE 5.3 Output and price under perfect competition

4. Marginal revenue – the revenue that the firm will receive from selling additional units of the product. Because the firm can only sell at the market price then marginal revenue is also a horizontal line.

5. The business will produce additional units of output if the marginal revenue from producing the extra unit is greater than the marginal cost. The firm will therefore produce at the point where marginal revenue is equal to marginal cost.

6. The point where marginal revenue equals marginal cost will be at the lowest point on the average cost curve.

7. The average revenue line (sometimes referred to as curve) also cuts the average cost curve at its lowest (optimum) point.

> **Financial returns** – these are financial performance indicators. Examples are operating profit margin (i.e. the profit a company makes on its everyday operating activities such as retailing goods in a supermarket) or return on capital employed, which measures the profit a company makes as a percentage of the capital invested in the business.

KEY TERM

We can also illustrate the total cost and total revenue under perfect competition (Figure 5.4). The total cost is the average cost (AC) multiplied by the number of units produced = 0ABC. The total revenue is the average revenue (price) (AR) multiplied by the number of units produced = 0ABC.

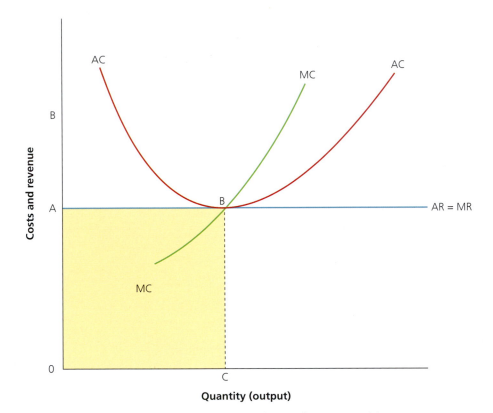

FIGURE 5.4 Total cost and total revenue under perfect competition

The firm in a perfectly competitive market would therefore only be able to make normal profit (remember that normal profit is included in the cost of production).

You may wonder why economists are so interested in 'perfect competition' if it doesn't exist in the real world. The reason is because it points out the benefit of competition. It shows that the competitive firm is not raising prices to exploit consumers. The perfectly competitive firm is also forced to use resources efficiently in order to survive.

Many economists are advocates of competition and they constantly seek to identify ways of enabling greater competition in order to achieve competitive efficiency.

5.5 Monopoly

A monopoly is the opposite of perfect competition. In a pure monopoly there is only one firm in an industry, so there is no competition. There are very few pure monopolies in the real world, but there are local examples. For example, there may only be a single shop in a remote area, or there may only be one ferry company operating a service between islands. There are also businesses that are so large that they can benefit from the same advantages as monopolies, for example Microsoft which provides the operating system for most computers. Microsoft is able to use its virtual monopoly position to create exclusive deals with computer manufacturers.

In some countries government-owned corporations have monopoly powers. For example, state-owned oil companies sometimes manage all of the oil resources in that country.

Price makers

One of the main features of a monopoly is that it acts as a price maker. A price maker chooses what price to charge rather than having to charge a price that is identical or very similar to the prices charged by rivals. Microsoft is (within limits) able to choose the price it charges to computer manufacturers, although of course it would not want to make this price unaffordable for the manufacturers.

The demand curve for a monopolist

Monopolists are faced with a highly inelastic demand curve. As a result, when monopolists raise prices they tend to lose a relatively small number of sales (see Figure 5.5).

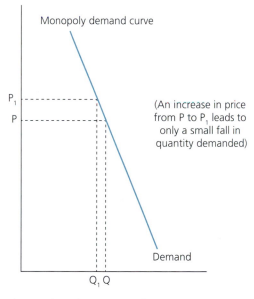

FIGURE 5.5 Inelastic demand under monopoly

The features of a monopoly

A monopoly has the following market characteristics:

* There is only one firm and it controls the market.

* It is almost impossible for new firms to enter the market.

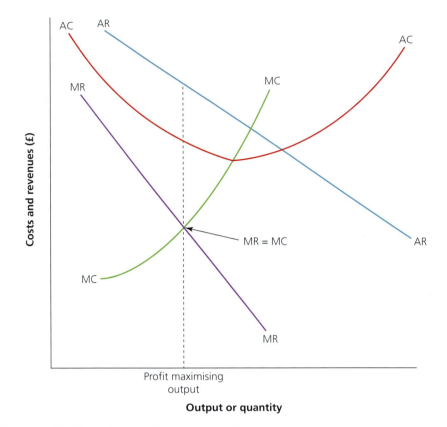

FIGURE 5.6 Profit maximizing for a monopoly

- The monopolist is a price-maker, setting the market price.

- Monopolists make abnormal levels of profit.

- Because monopolists control the market, they can restrict the quantity of goods they supply in order to raise prices and make abnormal profit.

Figure 5.6 shows the profit maximizing output under monopoly.

Please note that:

- The average revenue (AR) and marginal revenue (MR) curves slope down from left to right. This is because the monopolist will only be able to sell more output by reducing price.

- The profit maximizing point will be where marginal cost (MC) cuts marginal revenue (MR). If the monopolist produced less output their profit would be lower. If they produced more output their profit would be lower.

We can also illustrate the amount of profit made by the monopolist (see Figure 5.7).

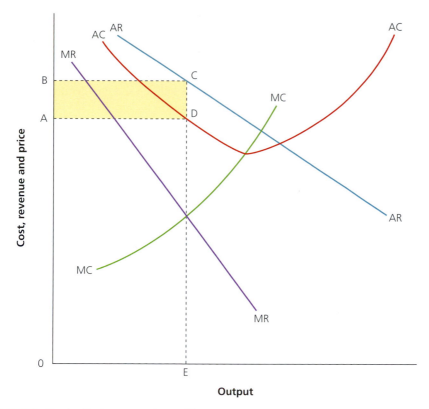

FIGURE 5.7 Illustrating monopoly profit

Monopoly profit is the amount of abnormal profit made at the profit maximizing output. We have already seen that the profit maximizing point is where MR = MC. To find out the level of abnormal profit at this output we need to find out total cost and total revenue. Looking at Figure 5.7:

- Total revenue is represented by the area OBCE. It is the average revenue (price) multiplied by the quantity produced (E).

- Total cost is represented by the area OADE. It is the average cost multiplied by the quantity produced (E).

We are now in a position to illustrate abnormal profit (i.e. the shaded rectangle ABCD).

You should immediately be able to see some of the main criticisms levelled at monopoly represented in the illustration:

- In contrast to perfect competition the monopolist is not producing at the optimum cost. Output is less than the point of lowest average cost.

- In contrast to perfect competition the monopolist is charging a price OB which is higher than the cost of producing that output. The price is OB whereas the average cost is only OA.

It is possible to argue that the monopolist is thus using society's resources in an inefficient way in order to make abnormal profit for itself (usually its shareholders).

Sources of monopoly power

A business gains a monopoly when it is the exclusive producer of a particular product. For example, a large part of the world's supply of 'rare earths' used in the production of magnetic motors for electric cars and windmills come from China. This gives China a monopoly in the sale of these products enabling them to raise prices. So one of the main sources of monopoly power is having a 'natural' (nature provided) monopoly. Interestingly, in the case of rare earths customer countries such as Japan, with its developing electric car industry, have re-engineered their cars so that they are no longer dependent on these rare earths – effectively destroying some of China's monopoly powers.

Another source of monopoly is a government monopoly. In some countries the oil industry is totally dominated by a government-run company giving it the effective monopoly.

There are other sources of monopoly power stemming from 'intellectual property'. In the UK the government's Intellectual Property Office manages intellectual property in relation to patents, trademarks, copyrights and designs:

- A patent grants exclusive rights to production, sale, use and even importation. A patent can last for up to 20 years. A company that develops a new product, technique or process can seek exclusive rights known as a patent. For example, pharmaceutical companies spend billions of pounds on research. They want to have protected payback on that research for a period of time.

- A trademark is something that distinguishes one companies product from those of competitors. The symbol ® shows that a company has a registered trademark. This trademark will typically appear next to a company's logo. Trademarks are very important to distinguish the brand of one business from another – enhancing monopoly power.

- A copyright is protection provided for music, lyrics, books, plays, photographs and other types of work. For example, there is a copyright associated with this book. The symbol for copyright is ©. For example, for a book it will last for the author's life and for 70 years afterwards.

- A design right protects a design from copying. The design relates to a three-dimensional product's visual appearance. This covers aspects of appearance such as shape, contours and texture – for example, the design of a garment, or the shape and structure of a bicycle. The design right can last for up to 25 years.

5.6 Market structures in the real world

Perfect competition only exists as a model created by economists to identify the characteristics of intense competition. Monopolies do exist in the real world, for example when the government is responsible for water supply and electricity, or one private firm has cornered the market. However, most markets have the combined features of monopoly market structures and competitive market structures. Economists have therefore analysed two other forms of market structure that are closely representative of how businesses compete with each other in the real world: oligopoly and monopolistic competition.

Oligopoly

Oligopoly means 'competition between a few producers'. Many markets on a global, regional, national and local scale are dominated by a few suppliers. For example, many airline routes to the Caribbean are dominated by just a small number of airlines. If you wanted to travel between London and Bridgetown (Barbados) you would have to choose between Air Canada, Caribbean Airlines, Virgin Atlantic, British Airways or American Airlines. Although there are only a few suppliers, the competition between these airlines can be intense. They will compete with each other in a number of ways – for example, on price, service, reliability or the days on which they operate.

The market structure of oligopoly markets consists of the following features:

* There are only a few firms in the market.

* Barriers to entry and exit are high, often because of economies of scale. The few firms that dominate the industry may employ expensive technologies.

* Products offered may be very similar or they may be differentiated.

* Firms tend to be price setters rather than price takers. However, there may be a market leader whose prices other firms tend to copy.

The key features of oligopoly are that there are only a few firms. The reason for there only being a small number of firms is typically barriers to entry. The most common barrier to entry is the cost of setting up. Large firms are able to benefit from economies of scale (economic advantages of being large). To become a large firm takes time and investment in resources.

Many industries in the UK are characterized by scale economies leading to domination by oligopolists. Examples include:

* Detergents and household cleaning fluids. There are three main companies that dominate this market in the UK – Unilever, Procter and Gamble and Reckitt Benckiser. These companies produce a high volume of output using large manufacturing units and extensive advertising. The high cost of setting up and operating acts as a barrier to entry.

* Other examples are fast food (McDonalds, KFC, Burger King), mobile phone operating companies, national newspapers, breweries, confectionery and sugar processing.

Concentration ratios

A good indicator of the extent of oligopoly is a concentration ratio. A concentration ratio is a measure of the percentage of market share held by the largest firms in an industry. Concentration ratios vary, as illustrated in Figure 5.8.

← Monopoly – Oligopoly – Monopolistic competition – Perfect competition →

FIGURE 5.8 The range of different competitive situations (and concentrations) – Monopoly = 100 per cent

The oligopoly range starts from about 50 per cent upwards. In the UK, for example, sugar production is dominated by two firms (Tate & Lyle and Silverspoon) and weapons and armaments manufacture is dominated by a small number of firms, the largest of which is BAE.

Two common concentration ratios are the four-firm concentration ratio (measuring the total market share of the four largest firms in an industry) and the eight-firm concentration ratio (measuring the share of the eight largest firms).

CASE STUDY Market share for smart phones (US, April 2011)

A Nielsen market research survey revealed the following market shares in the US market for smartphones in April, 2011:

Microsoft Windows Mobile	10%
Apple iOS	27%
RIM Blackberry OS	22%
Android OS	37%
Symbian OS	2%
Palm/WebOS	3%

- Calculate the four-firm concentration ratio at the time.

- To what extent does this appear to constitute an oligopoly market?

- What would you expect to be the main forms of competition between rivals in this market?

- How might competition have changed in this market since the time that these figures were published?

An approach to analysing competition in oligopoly markets

One way of analysing oligopoly markets is through formulating a 'kinked' demand curve. This is based on the idea that in oligopoly markets there is intense competition at the prevailing market price. We often see intense price wars in markets dominated by oligopoly structures – for example, in price cutting at the petrol pumps, or price wars between tabloid newspapers.

Between periods of price wars there can be periods of relative calm and stability during which there is a more stable market price. The reason for this is that oligopolists keep a very close eye on the actions taken by their rivals.

Should an oligopolist raise their price this is likely to lead to a greater than proportional decline in sales (elastic demand) as consumers switch to buy from rivals. However, if the oligopolist chooses to lower prices they are unlikely to increase sales by much because rivals will follow suit and lower their own prices. When the oligopolist lowers price they are therefore faced by an inelastic demand curve.

Therefore the price can become stuck at a prevailing market price (P), followed by periodic price wars as oligopolists jostle for increased market share.

Note that the MR curve splits in two at the output (Y) where the AR (demand curve) kinks. This is because to sell an additional unit beyond the current market output would

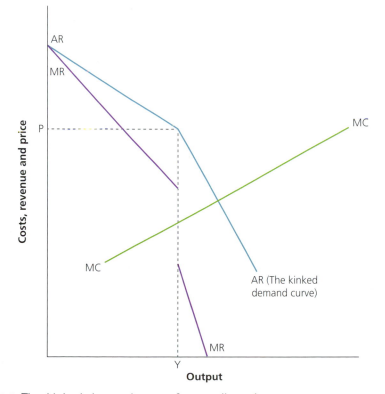

FIGURE 5.9 The kinked demand curve for an oligopoly

involve reducing prices at a faster rate than on higher ranges of the AR curve. The profit maximizing output occurs where MR cuts MC which occurs at the break in the MR curve.

The key implication that you should understand from the above analysis is that the actions of oligopolists are strongly influenced by those of rivals. This is particularly true in relation to pricing decisions but is also relevant to other aspects of competition.

Game theory

Game theory is today a significant branch of economics. Game theory can be applied to oligopoly (and to other situations where competition exists, e.g. in international trade). A game occurs where there are two or more interacting decision takers (players) and each decision or combination of decisions involves a particular outcome (pay-off). The fate (or pay-off) of a player in a game depends not only on the strategies employed by the player but also on the strategy of other players.

Much of the analysis that has been carried out by economists focuses on the benefits/drawbacks of the players collaborating or competing with each other. Important ground-breaking work in game theory was carried out by the US economist John Nash. Nash developed the concept of the Nash equilibrium – a situation in which each of the players in the game arrives at an optimal solution given the potential response of a rival player.

CASE STUDY A competitive duopoly

Let us consider an example of pure conflict in an oligopoly market by looking at a situation of a duopoly (i.e. a market containing two firms). We can call these two firms Shell and BP. Each firm controls half of the market. The illustration below shows that both firms have a wide range of possible strategies that they can employ to try to increase their market share. Each firm will hope that its strategy will increase consumer preference for its particular brand.

As with a game of chess, the moves of each player will affect the other's situation. Between them they satisfy the total market for petrol. Any increase in the market share of one will result in a reduction of the market share of the other. The total market is a constant sum. The game the two firms play is thus called a constant sum game.

Let us now assume that Shell and BP have narrowed down the effective strategies that they can employ to increase market share. Shell is considering four possible strategies to gain the largest possible market share. It is, however, aware that it is impossible to disguise its strategy from BP.

The four possible strategies are:

1. To offer free gifts with petrol
2. To spend more on advertising
3. To cut petrol prices
4. To open new petrol stations.

TABLE 5.2 Percentage market share for Shell as a result of applying different strategies

Shell strategies	BP strategies			
	Free gifts	More advertising	Price cuts	New petrol stations
Free gifts	60	50	45	60
More advertising	70	60	50	55
Price cuts	75	60	51	65
New petrol stations	60	40	45	50

Table 5.2 shows the percentage of the market that Shell would expect to control after the implementation of each strategy. A further dimension is added to the table because BP can respond to Shell's chosen decision in four different ways. For example, if Shell cuts petrol prices, BP could respond by a reactive strategy – for example, by opening new petrol stations. For each of Shell's potential strategies there will be four possible outcomes. (It is important to remember that this model is only a simplification of the real world in which there is a range of possible strategies, and degrees to which they can be applied.)

If, for example, Shell offers free gifts and BP responds by opening new outlets then Shell's market share will reach 60 per cent. If BP had responded instead by cutting prices then Shell's share would have fallen to 45 per cent.

It is likely that Shell will expect BP to respond in those ways that will minimize the effectiveness of Shell's own initiative (which are sometimes referred to as damage limitation policies). For example, if Shell offers free gifts it would expect the response – price cuts. The response to opening new petrol stations would be increased advertising. Because Shell expects BP to respond to each of its strategies in the way that will have the worst effects for Shell, then Shell will concentrate its attention on those figures underlined in the table. The effects for these worst responses (for Shell) are called row minima.

If Shell wants to make the most of situations in which it can predict BP's reactions to its own policies it will carry out policies which produce maximum gains from dynamic situations. These 'best possible' policies are referred to as the maximin. The maximin will be the highest figure from the row minima. Shell will therefore resort to the strategy of price cutting which will give it 51 per cent of the market. This is because by price cutting in this situation it will gain whatever BP does. Of course, the table only applies to a given moment in time. Changing circumstances will lead to changing figures – for example, if Shell improves its advertising performance then this will give it an increased advantage in the advertising column.

- **To what extent does the above theory give an insight into the strategies employed by oligopolists?**

- **What competitive strategies do oligopolists employ to outsmart their competitors? Relate your answers to specific industries that you are familiar with.**

In making a decision each player (e.g. an oligopolist) must first consider the options available to, and likely actions of, its rivals. Before Shell decides to reduce the price of its petrol it must first consider what BP is likely to do and what the potential impact will be.

Monopolistic competition

> **Monopolistic competition** – exists where many competing producers are selling products that are differentiated from each other.

Products are substitutes for each other but they have differences of brand and different features. In the short run a firm can make abnormal profits because of this differentiation. However, in the longer term new firms can enter the industry attracted by these profits, so abnormal profits will be competed away.

The market structure under monopolistic competition has the following features:

- There are many producers and consumers and no individual firm can control the market price.
- Consumers believe that there are differences between the products being offered by the firms competing in the market.
- There are few barriers to entry and exit from the market.
- Producers have some control over the prices they charge in the short period.

Producers often gain more market control, and so more monopolistic power, by applying for patents or trademarks. A patent is a grant provided by the official patent office giving the creator of an invention the sole right to apply it. A trademark is the exclusive right of one party, such as a business, to apply a word, phrase, symbol or design that is protected in law.

Profits made in different market structures

- Monopolists can make abnormal profits in the short and long periods.
- Oligopolists can make abnormal profits in the short and long periods.
- Monopolistic competitors can make abnormal profits in the short period but not in the long period.
- Perfect competitors can make abnormal profits in the short period but only normal profits in the long period.

Porter's analysis of competitive forces

Michael Porter (a Harvard academic) made an important contribution to competition theory. He has argued that the 'key aspect of [an organization's] environment is the industry or industries in which it competes'. He refers to five basic forces which he calls 'the structural determinants of the intensity of competition' (1979: 2). These, he feels, determine the profit potential of the industry. The five forces are:

- Rivalry among existing competitors (competition);
- The bargaining power of buyers;
- The bargaining power of suppliers;
- The threat of new competitors entering the industry; and
- The threat of substitute products.

Porter argued that the strength of these five forces will determine not only the sort of competition a business has to face but also the profitability of the whole industry. Existing competition between competitors can be shown to be influenced by the other four factors (see Figure 5.10).

Three of Porter's five forces focus on some aspect of competition from rivals:

1. Existing competition with firms already in the market;

2. The competitive threat from new entrants; and

3. The threat of substitute products.

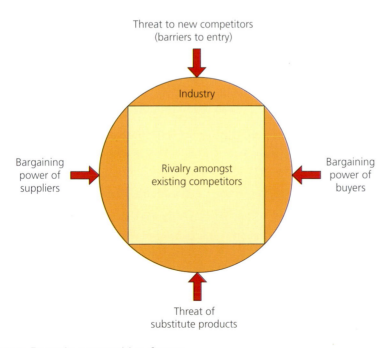

FIGURE 5.10 Porter's competitive forces

The other two forces relate to what Porter refers to as the micro-environment: relationships over which the business has some control (e.g. through the relationships it builds with suppliers and customers).

Porter's model may be used to improve an organization's analysis of the nature of competition by weighing up the relative strengths of the other four forces (i.e. forces other than direct competition between firms in the industry). We shall briefly explain each of these four forces:

The threat of new competitors

A new entrant to an industry poses a threat which influences the market share and profitability of others already in the marketplace. In some industries businesses may constantly enter or leave the marketplace – examples would include restaurants and clothes retailing. In other markets it may be difficult for newcomers to enter the market because of barriers to entry. Porter lists seven main barriers to entry:

- Economies of scale. Large-scale producers are typically able to cut their average costs through economies of scale. For example, they may be better placed to use advanced technology, or to spread costs through using machinery and equipment that process goods in bulk. New entrants to some industries may be put off by the scale of investment required.

- Product differentiation. Existing companies may develop a brand heritage and customer loyalty. Product differentiation may have taken years to build. In contrast newcomers have to invest to establish their brand identity.

- Capital requirements. Start-up costs and investment in research may be high. For example, the high costs of research in pharmaceutical and agrochemicals deter new entrants.

- Switching costs. These are the costs of switching from existing products and production technologies to new ones. Switching costs may deter firms from moving from one industry to another (e.g. the need to retool production lines and to retrain staff).

- Access to distribution channels. Existing firms establish efficient distribution channels enabling them to lower costs. New entrants have to build up these channels, which is likely to be costly.

- Other cost disadvantages. New firms are faced with other cost disadvantages such as the need to relocate.

- Government policy. Government regulations may deter new entrants to an industry by restricting the number of firms or creating rules that are expensive to comply with (e.g. regulations about the nature of products).

The bargaining power of buyers

Buyers will try to obtain the best possible deal for themselves. They will want better quality products at value-for-money prices. The more power that buyers have the bigger the share of profits they will be able to take for themselves.

CASE STUDY Service stations and levels of competition

Lighter hoses?

Cheaper petrol?

Lead free?

Better logo?

Attendant service?   Free car wash?   Better locations?

More grades of petrol?   Easier forecourt entry?

What else?

FIGURE 5.11 Competition faced by service stations

In any town you will find a number of service stations (selling petrol, newspapers, confectionery, soft drinks, fresh milk and a range of household goods). These service stations are in close competition with large supermarkets (although the service stations are usually open for longer hours).

Service stations need to be highly competitive, particularly in relation to price, because by law prices have to be advertised on hoardings outside the service area. Passing motorists can quickly compare prices. Service stations are typically located on the major roads leading into a town in order to pick up the most passing trade.

In contrast, motorway service stations have much less competition because they may be many miles from the nearest competitor. Typically therefore the price of buying petrol and other goods will be much higher at a motorway service station than within a town. The service station is able to exert monopoly powers while the town service station operates in a strongly competitive market.

However, the costs of operating a motorway service station may be higher than a town service station because the owners of the motorway sites on which the service stations are based are able to charge higher rents because of the superior location.

- **What other markets can you think of where parts of the market are highly competitive, while other parts of the market are dominated by monopoly producers?**

- **Why is it that motorway service stations tend to be dominated by the large petrol retailers, whereas smaller firms are able to operate in town areas?**

The bargaining power of suppliers

Suppliers are providers of raw materials, components and manufactured goods to a firm. The greater the market power that suppliers have the bigger the impact that they can have on firms in an industry. For example, if there are just a few suppliers they will be in a stronger position to dictate prices and terms to the firms that they supply (and hence will be able to capture a greater share of the profits in the industry). In contrast, where a company can select from many different suppliers they will be in a better position to dictate the terms on which they conduct business. Companies like Tesco have much more power when dealing with lots of small producers (e.g. suppliers of eggs) than they do when dealing with giant consumer goods companies such as Cadburys and Unilever.

The threat of substitute products

Suppliers not only compete with producers of the same product, they also compete with suppliers of similar products that are competing for the same share of the consumer's purse. For example, while at one level Coca-Cola and Pepsi are competing with each other to sell Cola products, at another level they are competing with suppliers of other forms of refreshment (e.g. tea, coffee, water). The closer the substitutes are the greater the intensity of the competition (which helps to explain why increasingly Coca-Cola and Pepsi have differentiated their offering by branching out into producing bottled water, coffee and tea.

5.7 Price setting in the real world

One way of assessing the competitiveness of a market is to identify the frequency of price changes. If competition exists you would expect to see prices changing at regular intervals.

KEY TERM

Price stickiness – the extent to which prices tend to stick at the same level over a period of time.

One way of investigating price stickiness is to identify the frequency with which prices change in a given year or the average time that elapses between one price change and the next.

Research into UK consumer prices shows that about 19 per cent of prices change each month. This compares with comparable figures in the United States of 26 per cent. A survey carried out by Greenslade and Parker, reported in 2012, asked firms: 'At what intervals do you change the UK price of your main product or activity?' One-fifth of companies reported that they changed prices at least monthly, and a third of firms annually.

Studies carried out in the United States show that price changes are more frequent for goods (about 30 per cent) compared with services (21 per cent) (Bils and Klenow, 2004). Transportation prices (such as new cars and airfares) are most flexible with over 40 per cent of these changing monthly. In contrast, prices for medical care and entertainment are much less flexible with only about 10 per cent changing on a monthly basis. For producer prices in the Eurozone energy prices are the most flexible whereas capital goods (e.g. machinery and equipment) are much stickier.

Some interesting additional data found by Greenslade and Parker (2012) is that larger firms are more likely to set prices at high frequencies, with a quarter of large firms resetting prices at least monthly but only 15 per cent of small firms doing so. Firms with a higher market share sometimes changed their prices less frequently than those that had a lower market share. Companies with a lower market share may have had a stronger incentive to check that their price was not out of line with a competitor's price.

The research also showed that in reviewing prices (which firms do more frequently than they change prices) they are particularly aware of current and future market conditions, indicating that the competitive environment is important in establishing prices. Table 5.3 illustrates this information.

TABLE 5.3 Relationship between the frequency of price change and information used when reviewing prices (share of response, %)

	Rule of thumb	Primarily past conditions	Primarily current conditions	Primarily future conditions	Total of each frequency
Daily	11	9	63	17	100
Weekly	5	10	48	38	100
Monthly	5	2	55	38	100
Quarterly	12	3	55	30	100
Half-yearly	11	12	41	36	100
Annually	17	9	38	36	100
Irregularly	12	10	48	30	100
Other	5	5	47	43	100
Total of each information type	12	8	45	35	100

Source: Based on research by Greenslade and Parker (2012).

A recent survey carried out by the same authors asked: 'How are UK prices for your main product or activity primarily determined?' The answer that was most commonly given a ranking of 'important' or 'very important' was that prices are primarily determined by competitors' prices (68 per cent). The next most common answer was mark-up over costs.

These findings about price setting in the real world therefore back up important aspects of theory, showing that:

- Prices charged by large firms are either adjusted frequently (e.g. in competitive oligopoly situations) or less frequently (e.g. in non-competitive oligopoly situations).

- Competition is a key factor leading to more frequent price changes in the market.

- The degree of stickiness or flexibility of market prices is influenced by the level of competition.

Identify goods and services that you buy on a regular basis. Identify sets of products whose prices change regularly (e.g. every month) and those that change less frequently.

- **In which of these product markets are there the greatest levels of competition?**

- **How do firms in these markets compete with each other apart from price competition?**

Pricing strategies

There are a number of pricing strategies that a company can employ:

Competitive pricing

Competitive pricing simply involves establishing a price which is competitive compared with that of rivals. In a market where goods are highly similar then a competitive price will be one which is the same or lower than that of rivals.

In contrast, in a market where goods are differentiated then a competitive price is one which, coupled with differentiating factors such as the quality and branding of the product, leads the consumer to believe that they are getting better value for money than that offered by rivals.

The important point to understand with competitive pricing is that this does not necessarily mean charging a lower price than that of rival producers.

Cost plus pricing

Cost plus pricing involves identifying the cost of producing a desired level of output or sales and then adding a margin for profit. This margin is referred to as a mark-up. For example this might be 20 per cent on top of the cost price. The more control that the business has over sales (i.e. monopoly powers) the more opportunity that it has for cost plus pricing.

Penetration pricing

A penetration price is an appropriate strategy for entering an existing market with a new product. There are likely to be high fixed costs involved with entering that market so it is important to cover those fixed costs as quickly as possible through large sales/volume selling.

A typical example might be a new breakfast cereal. By charging a relatively low price in the first instance it will be possible to win market share. The price can be raised once the market is effectively penetrated.

Expansion pricing

Similarly, expansion pricing can be used to expand existing market share by lowering prices and then benefitting from economies of scale in manufacture and sales. Today we can often see this policy applied to the sale of existing motorcars – where discounting can be used to drive up sales.

Destruction pricing

This is a practice that can be applied where a company has an existing monopoly position. A policy of destruction pricing can be used to undermine the sales of rivals or to warn potential new rivals not to enter a particular market. Destruction pricing involves reducing the price of an existing product or selling a new product at an artificially low price in order to destroy customer sales. For example, when a new discount supermarket sets up in an area existing supermarkets may slash their prices to try and force the new rival into a loss-making position.

Customer pricing

Another approach to pricing is to identify the price that customers are willing to pay for a good through a process of market research. This enables producers to identify what consumers consider to be an appropriate price. However, research by Greenslade and Parker (2012) suggests that firms are less likely to use this approach than they are to use competitor pricing and cost plus pricing strategies.

FIGURE 5.12
The destroyer pricing range

5.8 Price setting in different market settings

In this chapter we have explored different market models. So how are prices set in these different situations?

- In perfectly competitive markets all good are identical. Managers would only be able to set a price at the market price. Consumers would be perfectly aware of all prices. The price would thus be the market price (i.e. where marginal cost = marginal revenue, and where average revenue = average cost).

- In monopoly markets firms will be price markers. Because the firm is not faced by competition it will have discretion in setting prices at levels that maximize its profits. Demand for the goods provided is more price inelastic. The price that the firm decides to charge depends on its objectives – for example, to maximize profits, to maximize sales, etc. If the firm seeks to maximize profits it would produce at the point where marginal cost is equal to marginal revenue. Alternatively, if it wants to control market share then it will produce at a point that maximizes total revenue (i.e. average revenue multiplied by output).

- In monopolistic markets firms are faced with many competitors producing similar but different products. It will set a price that enables it to make a profit. They will therefore need to consider their revenues and costs at different levels of output to identify an appropriate price to charge.

- In oligopoly markets the price charged will depend on the level of competition. We have seen that some oligopoly markets are highly competitive whereas in others there is considerable scope for profit making. Prices can be relatively sticky in some oligopoly markets. Oligopolists need to be aware of how rivals will react to the prices they charge. Competitive pricing is likely to be a key feature of oligopoly price setting.

KEY THEME

The Rule of Three

In 2002 Jagdish Sheth and Rajendra Sisodia developed what they referred to in a business context as 'the rule of three'. In a nutshell their argument was that originally competitive markets start out in an unorganized way with only small firms servicing the market. However, in the course of time these markets consolidate.

The market then evolves to a situation where there are 'full-line generalists' in the market providing a range of relevant goods and services, and then a number of 'market specialists' and 'product specialists'. The full-line generalists provide a range of different products (e.g. like in a department store) whereas your 'product specialists' focus on a specific type of product (e.g. trainers), whereas your market specialists focus on a particular group of customers (e.g. affluent consumers).

Sheth and Sisodia investigated 200 industries. They argued that there is an uncanny tendency for just three 'full-line generalists' to emerge whose market

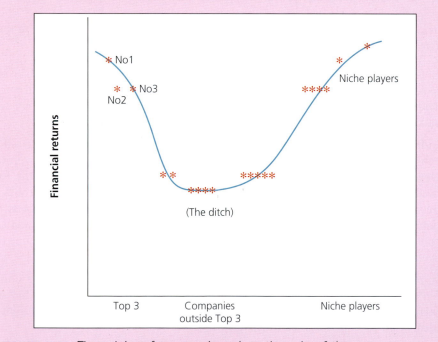

FIGURE 5.13 Financial performance based on the rule of three

Note: For example in retailing the top 3 would be Tesco, Morrisons and Sainsbury's. Niche players would include Waitrose (upmarket), and Aldi and Lidl (downmarket). The implication is that if you are one of the top 3 or a niche provider your returns are relatively secure. Out of the top 3 and you are in the ditch.

share is generally about 70 per cent (between 70 per cent and 90 per cent) of the market (broken down into proportions of 40, 20 and 10). This breakdown relates to the ongoing development of the market through various stages – local, regional, national and global.

In the overall market therefore you have your generalists and your product and market specialists. Where the product and market specialists concentrate on retaining a relatively small market share they will prosper. However, if they expand their offering to become more generalist their profits will fall. Sheth and Sisodia therefore set out the diagram illustrated in Figure 5.13 to compare financial performance with market share.

It shows that where product or market specialists increase their market share to beyond 5 per cent by becoming more generalist their profits will dip. As generalists increase their market share from 10 per cent up to 40 per cent their financial performance will improve.

They therefore coined the term 'the ditch' to describe a position where market or product specialists lose financial performance from becoming too large and where generalists lose out from being too small. The implication is that it is more beneficial to be either a relatively small niche player or a generalist benefitting from economies of scale.

- **Where a firm is a product specialist or a market specialist, how is this likely to give the firm more monopoly powers? What would be the implication in terms of the pricing policy of the company and the ability to make abnormal profit?**

- **Where a firm is a large full-line generalist, what type of market structure is it most likely to be operating in? What would be the implication in terms of the pricing policy of the company and the ability to make abnormal profit?**

Reflective question

1 Some economists suggest that perfect competition in markets leads to an effective use of resources. Is it possible to argue that some elements of large-scale monopoly may also lead to an efficient use of resources?

5.9 Allocative efficiency

It is important to have key criteria for assessing whether a market structure is 'better' under perfect competition or where some element of monopoly power exists. A key criterion is to examine what type of situation supports allocative efficiency.

Allocative efficiency – occurs when the value that consumers place on a good or service (reflected in the price they are prepared to pay) equals the cost of resources used up in production.

The economists would identify this condition as being met if the price of a good is equal to the marginal cost of producing that good. When this condition is met this will lead to the greatest economic welfare – because society is using resources well.

Our previous analysis shows that the perfectly competitive firm produces at a point where marginal cost = marginal revenue = average revenue (price). In contrast, a monopoly business will produce at a point where marginal cost is equal to marginal revenue, but where marginal cost is less than average revenue. The price of goods is thus higher than the marginal cost of producing them, enabling a monopoly business to take abnormal profits for themselves. Monopolists gain at the expense of consumers.

The Italian economist Vilfredo Pareto defined allocative efficiency as a situation in which no-one could be made better off without making someone else worse off to at least the same degree. Using Pareto's definition monopoly pricing does not lead to allocative efficiency.

However, there are some counter arguments that can be put forward in support of monopoly powers, including:

- Monopoly and oligopoly businesses may operate on a large scale. They are thus able to benefit from economies of scale and pass some of the advantages of lower cost on to consumers.

- Monopoly powers (e.g. in the form of patents/copyrights and other restrictions) may be necessary for research and development. For example, in the pharmaceutical industry protected businesses are able to engage in expensive research knowing that they will be able to recoup the costs of this research through future monopoly profits. Without the opportunity to make monopoly profits they would probably not take the risk of investing in this research.

KEY THEME

Differentiating in a competitive market

New markets continually emerge and firms entering these markets will seek to differentiate their products in order to win competitive advantage. Through differentiation a firm is better placed to raise prices relative to those charged for competing products. Calculations of price elasticity of demand and cross elasticity of demand (see Chapter 3) are particularly important in estimating the impact of pricing decisions.

A market that has grown quickly in recent years is that of breakfast biscuits in the UK. By late 2012 this market was estimated to be worth between £33 million and £40 million. In September 2012 Premier Foods launched a range of breakfast biscuits under its well-known Hovis brand umbrella. At the time the market was dominated by other key food companies that focus on the breakfast market (i.e. Kellogg's and Kraft Foods).

The dominant player in the breakfast biscuit market in late 2012 was Kraft Foods' BelVita brand, which positions itself as a healthy breakfast option. In order to win market share therefore the new Hovis breakfast biscuits have to compete with BelVita and other leading brands such as Kellogg's Nutri-Grain and Special K brands. The new Hovis biscuits are targeted at women in the 25 to 45 age category. The Hovis brand is instantly recognizable and in advertising the new biscuits Hovis have focused on healthy aspects coupled with innovative stand-out packaging. Hovis is placing its biscuits in the biscuit aisles of supermarkets so that they sit side-by-side with rival products.

- **What challenges do you see that Hovis breakfast biscuits will face in this competitive market?**

- **How will differentiation enable Hovis to be successful?**

- **How might competitors respond to the arrival of Hovis in the market?**

- **What advantages do existing firms have in the market that give them a competitive advantage?**

- **What will be the impact for: (1) retailers such as supermarkets; and (2) consumers of Hovis entering the breakfast biscuit market?**

5.10 Summary

Different markets are structured in different ways depending on the number of firms in the market and the intensity of the competition between them in terms of similarity of the good and or service offered and the level of price competition. The two extreme situations are perfect competition (intensely competitive) and monopoly (one producer/seller) situations. The real world reality is that most firms lie somewhere between these extremes.

Most firms enjoy some level of differentiation from rivals and this enables them to manipulate price to a certain extent. The number of firms in a market is by no means a measure of the intensity of competition in the industry. Some industries with relatively small numbers of competitors can be intensely competitive, whereas in contrast some may be less competitive.

In the real world the models that best explain how firms compete are imperfect (monopolistic) competition and oligopoly structures. In these situations firms have some ability to alter their prices but they need to be keenly aware of the pricing and differentiation strategies employed by rivals. Economists are particularly interested in how efficient different market structures are in allocating scarce resources. Competitive markets encourage businesses to charge prices that reflect the cost of producing goods. However, there are benefits of scale associated with monopoly/oligopoly markets that may outweigh some of the disadvantages resulting from firms charging prices higher than the marginal cost of production.

KEY IDEAS

Some of the main points covered in this chapter are listed below. If you feel unsure about any of them then revisit the appropriate section. If you would like some additional reading on the topic try the books listed below in recommended reading.

What is market structure?

Market structure is the characteristics under which a market operates. It consists of four main elements: (1) ease of entry for new firms; (2) numbers of buyers and sellers; (3) types of goods and services sold; and (4) how price is determined.

Types of market structure

The four main types of market structure are: perfect competition, monopolistic competition, oligopoly and monopoly. Perfect competition and monopoly are seen as extreme forms that don't fully match up with real world reality. Monopolistic competition and oligopoly fit more closely to real world reality.

Perfect competition

Perfect competition is a theoretical state whereby lots of small firms produce identical products and only normal profit is made. Normal profit is the minimum profit required for a firm to remain in an industry. Perfectly competitive firms are price takers.

Monopoly

In a pure monopoly there is only one firm in an industry. The monopolist is a price maker and is faced by a downward sloping demand curve. Sources of monopoly power include patents, being a 'natural monopoly', economies of large-scale production and government bestowing monopoly powers on a specific business (e.g. a state-run corporation).

Market structures in the real world

In the real world markets are more closely represented by oligopoly and monopolistic market structures. In these structures firms produce differentiated products and are able to manipulate prices to a certain extent. A concentration ratio shows the extent to which a market is dominated by the largest firms in the market.

Price setting in the real world

Price stickiness can be investigated by analysing the frequency of price changes over a specific period of time. Research into price stickiness shows that prices change more frequently in some markets than in others.

Pricing in different market settings

In perfectly competitive markets firms are price takers. In monopoly markets firms are price setters. In monopolistic markets firms have some leeway in setting prices. In oligopoly markets pricing depends on the level of competition.

Allocative efficiency

The concept of allocative efficiency (i.e. the extent to which the value that consumers place on a good or service equals the cost of resources used up in production) is important in making comparisons between the efficiency of markets. It is also helpful in making decisions about whether a market can be made to operate in a more efficient way. There is a strong case that perfect competition leads to an efficient use of scarce resources. However, perfect competition assumes that there are lots of small firms, which limits the opportunity to produce using economies of scale.

REVIEW QUESTIONS

1. What are the key characteristics of market structures?

2. Compare monopoly and perfect competition in terms of: (a) the number of buyers; (b) the number of sellers; (c) market price; (d) how output is determined; (e) the homogeneity of the product or service; and (f) type of profit made.

3. How many firms will there be in an oligopoly structure? How do oligopolists compete with each other?

4. What are the main points of difference between a monopoly market and a monopolistic market?

5. Explain the main point of difference between 'price taking' and 'price making'. What types of firms will be price makers and what firms will be price takers?

6. What is allocative efficiency? Discuss whether allocative efficiency is likely to occur in an oligopoly market situation.

7. What does a concentration ratio measure? Identify three industries with high concentration ratios and three with low concentration ratios.

8. What is the rule of three as applied to business? Can you identify industries where the rule of three applies?

RECOMMENDED READING

Greenslade, J. and Parker, M. (2012) 'New Insights into Price Setting Behaviour in the UK: Introduction and Survey Pages', *The Economic Journal* 122 (558): 1–15.

This journal article provides a useful outline of some of the key considerations involved in shaping pricing strategy as well as examining the frequency with which UK firms alter prices.

Nellis, J. and Parker, D. (1997) 'Unit 6, Understanding Pricing Strategies', in *The Essence of Business Economics*, London, Prentice Hall.

Although this text is a little dated it provides a useful outline of pricing strategies employed by firms operating in different market structures.

Porter, M.E. (2008) 'The Five Competitive Forces that Shape Strategy', *Harvard Business Review*, January: 78–93.

Michael Porter developed his concept of the competitive forces in the late 1970s. This article revisits some of these important ideas.

Sheth, J.N. and Sisodia, R.S. (2002) *The Rule of Three: Surviving and Thriving in Competitive Markets*, New York, Free Press.

REFERENCES

Bils, M. and Klenow, P.J. (2004) 'Some Evidence on the Importance of Sticky Prices', *Journal of Political Economy*, 112 (5): 947–85.

Greenslade, J. and Parker, M. (2010) 'New Insights into Price-setting Behaviour in the United Kingdom', *Bank of England*, Working Paper No. 395.

Porter, M.E. (1979) 'How Competitive Forces Shape Strategy', *Harvard Business Review*, March/April: 2–10.

USEFUL WEBSITES

www.ccp.uea.ac.uk

The Centre for Competition Policy is based at the University of East Anglia and undertakes interdisciplinary research into competition policy that has 'real-world policy relevance without compromising academic rigour'.

It takes an interdisciplinary approach, with members drawn from a range of disciplines, including economics, law, business and political science. They produce a working paper series, run weekly seminars, hold a number of events throughout the year (including an annual conference), and publish a regular newsletter and e-bulletin. The Centre maintains links with practitioners, both policy-makers and those in the private sector.

The main themes of research include: consumers, institutions, market power/regulation, mergers, agreements/collusion, regime dynamics, enforcement and remedies, developing principles and methodology. The website has information on research projects, events, job opportunities, resources and published papers.

6 Business strategy in an economic context

CHAPTER OBJECTIVES

By the end of this chapter you will understand:

- Why businesses need to have an effective strategy

- The components that need to be in place to create a business strategy

- How to judge a strategy in terms of suitability, acceptability and feasibility

- How to create a PEST analysis

- Why it is important to evaluate the economic environment and its impact on business strategy

6.1 Introduction

Businesses need to have a sense of the direction in which they want to move. Once they are clear about this they can formulate their plans – strategies to achieve their desired goals. However, the process is not as simple as it sounds. Businesses operate in uncertain environments. They need therefore to be continually prepared to adjust their strategies to accommodate for environmental change.

Perhaps the biggest uncertainty in the business environment is economic change. This is one of the reasons why an understanding of economics is so important to business students. You need to be able to understand the impact of major macro-economic changes such as changes in the gross domestic product (GDP) of a country, and the relative growth of different economies. This chapter therefore explores corporate strategy in the context of an uncertain economic environment. It illustrates the sorts of strategies that businesses have employed to survive and prosper against a background of economic uncertainty.

6.2 What business strategy involves

KEY TERM

Strategies – the means through which a company achieves its desired ends.

A company will set out the ends it wants to achieve in the form of aims and objectives – for example, to become the market leader, to increase sales every year and so on. The strategy is then the means through which it achieves these objectives, through carrying out careful market research to identify new areas of customer demand, developing new products and markets and so on.

FIGURE 6.1 The relationship between aims, objectives and strategy

The board of directors of a company plays a key part in formulating the strategy. The board of directors is made up of two groups:

1. Senior executive directors. These are directors that are employed by the company to oversee the major day-to-day running of the business. Their job is to execute (i.e. carry out) the major strategies formulated by the board. The executive directors consist of the chief executive officer (CEO), the finance director, and other key executives (e.g. the chief operating officer (COO)) responsible for the operational decisions and activities of the company.

2.   Non-executive directors. These are independent directors who advise the board and help to formulate and to question strategy. They do not work directly for the company – rather, they have service contracts to provide advice and other services to the company. They are chosen because of their wealth of experience of business, enabling them to contribute independent insight to strategic decision making. Non-executive directors include the chair of the company. The chair runs the board meetings and encourages constructive interaction within the board. There is also a senior independent director (SID) in most large companies who acts as an intermediary between the chair and the CEO. Independent directors play key roles in staffing board committees – for example, to decide on directors' remuneration and to nominate new directors.

The Companies Act 2006 set out the role of directors. The role consists of a number of elements including serving to promote the interests of the company and to act in an independent way as well as to help formulate strategy. Directors are expected to take into consideration the requirements of all of the various stakeholder groups in making decisions, although clearly they will listen very closely to the interests of the major stakeholder group – the shareholders.

The board of directors will help to shape the objectives of a business organization. Traditionally management texts focused on a single business objective: profit maximization. This is based on a view that shareholders (the owners of a business) are primarily interested in making a profit.

Although profits are still seen as important to business it is recognized by economists and business analysts that other objectives are also important, particularly in the short and medium term. This is particularly the case in companies with a range of powerful stakeholder interest groups – for example, environmental pressure groups, consumer lobby groups, community groups, trade unions, etc.

The board of directors and executive managers have to balance a range of stakeholder interests in decision making. So it is possible to recognize a range of different business objectives including:

- Providing shareholder value. This includes enhancing the returns which shareholders value (e.g. earnings per share, dividends, increase in share price, reputation of a company).

- Maximizing sales revenue over time – particularly at the expense of rival companies.

- Meeting company growth targets – the scale of output, scope of operations (e.g. in terms of products and markets), growth of physical capacity of the company, etc.

- Objectives that meet personal goals of managers (e.g. pay and bonuses, status, power and personal security).

- Maximizing value for other stakeholders – for example, winning government support through paying taxes and contributing to public projects, winning loyalty of customers through high-quality service, building an environmental reputation etc.

6.3 The ingredients of strategy

Strategy involves:

- Long-term planning (often 3–5 years and longer);

- Major resource decisions (e.g. to build a new plant);

- Deciding on the scope of an organization (i.e. the range of products and services it produces and in which markets);

- Planning that needs to be overseen by senior executives in the company; and

- Flexible planning – strategies should be subject to review and alteration where appropriate.

6.4 The criteria for an effective strategy

Suitability – appropriate to the external environment.

Acceptability – accepted as appropriate by stakeholders, particularly shareholders. It is important to make a distinction between shareholders and stakeholders. A shareholder is a part owner of a company. They are entitled to a share in the profit. Stakeholders consist of any individuals or groups who have an interest in a business. Stakeholders include shareholders but in addition include many other groups such as employees, customers, suppliers and the local community that interacts with the business.

Feasibility – able to be achieved with the existing resources of an organization.

Strategies need to meet three criteria. Firstly they need to be suitable to the environment in which the organization is operating.

Suitability

To check that a strategy is suitable an organization needs to scan the external environment – particularly checking on economic factors. A useful starting point is to carry out a PEST analysis. A PEST analysis is an analysis of the wider environment in which a business operates. It is an analysis of political, economic, social and technological factors that are likely to impact on business decision making. The political, economic, social and technological environment acts as a constraint on choices that a business might want to take, but also presents opportunities – for example, the development of new technologies, new social changes (perhaps ones that make specific goods more popular), etc.

CASE STUDY PEST analysis Tesco in China

Tesco is a British company, but in recent years it has expanded into international markets including Thailand and China. China is demographically the largest economy in the world with over 1.3 billion people.

Before moving into China Tesco scanned the environment to identify whether China would be suitable as a potential market. It considered the following factors:

- Political factors. In doing business in China it is important to gain approval from national and local government. The government in China looks favourably on companies that work with local partners. There are a lot of regulations that need to be complied with in doing business in China. Tesco therefore created a partnership with a large Chinese distributor and retailer. In addition most of Tesco's employees are local people.

- Economic factors. The Chinese economy has been growing rapidly for the last ten years – outperforming nearly all of the world's economies by a substantial margin with growth rates in some years of almost 10 per cent. China has a large urban population made up of industrial employees and tertiary sector employees whose incomes have been steadily increasing. The economy in China is well run with careful government management of the economic system – employment is high, inflation and interest rates are relatively low.

- Social factors. Households in China are relatively affluent because of a one-child policy. Increasingly urban shoppers in China buy a substantial proportion of their weekly shop in large shopping malls. Supermarket shopping is an established way of buying goods in China's cities.

- Technological factors. Technological fit is important in developing international links. Tesco gains a competitive advantage through the quality of its electronic marketing carried out at point of sale. The growing use of credit and debit cards in China enables Tesco to develop much greater customer insights by finding out what individual customers are purchasing at point of sale. Technological factors that are relevant in the supermarket industry also relate to supply-chain links and distribution factors such as availability of refrigerated transport vehicles.

Tesco has invested heavily in China with its distinctive Tesco Legou brand. Legou in the Chinese language Mandarin means 'happy shopper'. Tesco have invested in large shopping malls, with the ground floor being dedicated to the Tesco supermarket and other floors being rented out to other retailers.

Tesco's strategy for China is **suitable** because it:

- Meets political and legal requirements – through a partnering arrangement and by employing local managers and staff.
- Is based on a sound economic model – a rapidly growing, stable and large economy.
- Is well matched to social patterns of consumption and shopping in China.
- Fits with new technologies – related to distribution, purchasing and marketing in China.

Tesco's strategy for China is **acceptable** because it promises shareholders the potential for growing dividends at a time when Tesco's earnings from some of its international ventures are relatively less successful (e.g. poor results/losses in the United States).

Tesco's strategy is **feasible** because Tesco has a sufficient basket of spare resources (e.g. finance) to invest in China coupled with appropriate resources in the form of technological and marketing expertise to penetrate new markets.

● Why is it important for new (and existing) strategies to be suitable for the environment in which an organization operates?

● Can you identify another organization whose current strategy appears to be successful because it is suitable to the environment in which it is operating?

● Can you identify an alternative organization whose strategy you believe is unsuitable to the current economic environment?

KEY TERM

The economic environment – the external economic factors that impact on an organization and the decisions it makes, including whether the economy is growing and whether interest rates, inflation rates, savings rates, exchange rates and other economic indicators are changing in ways that impact the business.

The economic environment is particularly relevant to the criteria of suitability:

- When the economy is growing is often a good time for a strategy of expansion.
- Conversely, in a recession it may be an appropriate time for a company to make cutbacks or to put expansion plans on hold. Of course there are exceptions. For example a recession is often a good time for a company selling lower-priced items to expand. For example during the recession in the period 2008–2009 in the UK there was an expansion in the number of cut-price stores such as Poundland.

Acceptability

The criteria of acceptability relates to whether a strategy is acceptable to the stakeholders in a business. In public and private companies strategy should enhance shareholder returns. Shareholders will seek measurable returns that they consider to be acceptable. For example, a strategy designed to gain an increase in market share (say from 15 to 20 per cent) will need to be linked (for instance) to a minimum profit margin that is acceptable to the shareholders.

Feasibility

Then of course the strategy selected needs to be feasible. A key consideration here will be the resource base of the organization. A strategy can only be delivered when an organization has enough of the right sorts of resources to deliver that strategy. A company like Tesco is able to expand internationally because it has a sufficient capital base and the management experience and expertise to move into new markets. However, it can only move into so many new international markets at a particular moment in time. Even Tesco's resources are finite (the basic economic problem of limited resources).

CASE STUDY A new strategy for Facebook

In April 2012 Facebook announced that it was taking over Instagram – what was then a profitless, two-year-old photosharing application – for $1 billion.

At the time of purchase Instagram had been loaded by 30 million people. The app allows people to share photos taken with their mobiles with friends on its own site and on Facebook, Twitter or via text. Having taken photographs on their own phones it enables photographers to alter the look of their pictures, giving their images a vintage, old-world feel. Users can then share high-quality and interesting photographs.

The owner of Facebook, Mark Zuckerberg (2012) announced the news in the following way:

This is an important milestone for Facebook because it is the first time we've ever acquired a product and company with so many users.

He went on to state that:

> providing the best photo sharing experience is one reason why so many people love Facebook and we knew it would be worth bringing these two companies together.

- Analyse the acquisition in terms of suitability, acceptability and feasibility.

- What do you think would be the key driver behind the strategy of acquiring Instagram for $1 billion.

6.5 How an environmental analysis helps to determine the suitability of a strategy

An environmental analysis is a study of the external environment (i.e. everything influential outside the business). The process of carrying out an environmental analysis is usually described as scanning the environment.

The process is described in textbooks in various ways:

- A PEST analysis – a study of the political, economic, social and technological environment.

- A SLEPT analysis – a study of the social, legal, economic, political and technological environment.

- A PESTLE analysis – a study of the political, economic, social, technological, legal and natural environmental environments.

In scanning the environment it is important to identify the key factors that will affect the business and to prioritize them rather than just providing an extensive list.

Typically there will be a relatively small number of factors which have a significant impact, and then a list of other factors that are also important. It is important to identify the principal risks and uncertainties and to prioritize these, as well as to put in place appropriate control mechanisms to make risks manageable.

The nature of economic change is that it has such an impact on businesses that economic factors will typically be significant features in the principal risks and uncertainties.

Quantifying risk

Business involves risk. However, it is important to make sure that the risks taken by a company are in line with its risk appetite. It is helpful to use analytical techniques to assess risk to make sure that any risks that are taken are acceptable to the company and its stakeholders. Many individuals are risk averse so it is important that risks are aligned with the willingness of stakeholders to take risks.

There are a number of techniques for assessing risk. For example, risk can be assessed on the likelihood of an event occurring and the consequence of that event occurring. This can be illustrated in a matrix showing levels of risk (see Figure 6.2).

Consequences	Insignificant	Minor	Moderate	Major	Severe
Likelihood					
Almost certain	Medium risk	High risk	High risk	Critical risk	Critical risk
Likely	Medium risk	Medium risk	High risk	High risk	Critical risk
Possible	Low risk	Medium risk	Medium risk	High risk	Critical risk
Unlikely	Low risk	Medium risk	Medium risk	Medium risk	High risk
Rare	Low risk	Low risk	Medium risk	Medium risk	High risk

FIGURE 6.2 A risk assessment matrix

Where risks are likely to materialize and the consequences are severe, the impact is classified as critical. For example, the island of Madagascar faces regular cyclones and the impact of these is, in many cases, severe. Cyclones therefore present a critical risk to Madagascar. In parts of Japan earthquakes happen on a regular basis – often with severe impacts – thereby presenting the country with a serious risk. Japanese architects and planners have therefore had to identify suitable building materials and structures to limit the impact of earthquake damage. In a similar way businesses are faced with economic risks such as the impact of a recession that can rapidly destroy the value of the business.

In business, rivals will from time to time develop new products or services that can transform their share of the market, or new legislation may be passed by governments that require new production techniques or that will affect the costs of production in different ways. It is important to identify the emergence of these risks and to consider the likely impact on a business.

Assigning a value to the risk involves calculating the probability of the occurrence of an event and then multiplying this by the predicted cost of the impact. In choosing between different alternatives, an organization may weigh up the predicted costs of various strategies in the light of the risk appetite of the organization.

In terms of choosing strategies it is important to calculate risk and then to choose strategies that fit the risk appetite of the business.

6.6 The nature of strategic vision, objectives, focus and architecture

Vision and objectives

Before a company develops a strategy, it needs to have a clear picture of the direction in which it is heading. The term for this is strategic direction.

The board, with the chairman playing a prominent role, needs to articulate the vision for the company. A vision statement provides a clear description of a desired outcome to inspire and energize people directly involved with the organization. It should comprise between two and four sentences.

For example, Amazon's vision statement is: 'Our vision is to be the earth's most customer centric company; to build a place where people can come and find and discover anything they may want to buy online.'

The vision of an organization needs to be backed up by a more specific set of strategic objectives. The strategic objectives should be SMART:

- Specific
- Measurable
- Agreed
- Realistic
- Time related

Often SMART strategic objectives will be set out in quantitative terms:

- To increase market share **over the next three years**.

- To increase turnover **by 10 per cent per annum**.

- To reduce emissions into the air and water **by 20 per cent by 2020**.

ACTIVITY

Identify the key objectives of a well-known organization as published in their company report or website. Analyse these objectives in terms of whether they are SMART.

Strategic focus

Some theorists believe that in selecting a strategy it is appropriate to focus on the following three aspects (although other writers argue that two or three aspects can be combined):

1. Achieving a competitive position in the industry or market.

2. Resources, capabilities and core competences of a business.

3. Integration of dispersed operations.

For example, Tesco focuses primarily on the first two of the above. In the UK it has the largest share of the market enabling it to benefit from economies of scale – for example, buying in bigger bulk than rivals which helps to drive down costs. Additionally, it is able to do some things better than its rivals by concentrating on the things it does really well – described as core competences. A core competence for Tesco is high-quality database marketing.

Some car manufacturers, such as the Japanese company Toyota and the German manufacturer Volkswagen, are particularly effective at creating globally integrated manufacturing systems that bring together components that are produced at large manufacturing hubs in different parts of the world.

Measuring the effectiveness of strategy

In developing business strategies, it is also important to be able to evaluate them. Performance measures are therefore required. Business relies heavily on key performance indicators (KPIs) to measure business performance and the effectiveness of strategies over time.

Traditionally, businesses have used KPIs related to the financial and economic performance of a business. Typical KPIs have included:

- Turnover; and

- Operating margins (i.e. total revenue less costs, before deductions).

TABLE 6.1 Examples of Triple Bottom Line KPIs

Economic KPIs	Social KPIs	Environmental KPIs
Earnings per share	% of profit donated to charity	Volume of waste emissions
Operating profit	Number of days of volunteering: – to community projects – by company employees	% of products recycled

In the modern business world, in which businesses are accountable to a range of stakeholders, there has been an increasing emphasis on Triple Bottom Line indicators (see Table 6.1).

The board of directors needs to decide which indicators to measure and report on.

Strategic architecture

The term strategic architecture refers to the building of interlinking competences to enable organizations to develop competitive advantage.

Core competences – the things that a business does particularly well. It is important to focus on and build these core competences because they provide a competitive advantage over rivals.

Competitive advantage – being able to or being perceived to be able to do something better than rivals. Competitive advantage may relate to being able to provide a product or service at a lower cost, or it may relate to differentiation – being able to offer a superior product or service.

Organizations need to identify the main sources of competitive advantage in the sector or market segment that they are operating in – for example, having the fastest and most reliable distribution links, the most rapid response to consumer requirements or the most reliable components. They then need to design and build the core competences – the strategic architecture that enables them to gain and maintain this competitive advantage.

For example, the strategic architecture for a low-cost airline may include:

- Developing links and contacts with aircraft suppliers and developing preferential links with airports.

- Building a reputation for reliability, safety and customer care.

- Developing skilled pilots and airline crews who provide a quality service.

- Making sure that all of the processes involved in running the airline fit in with the concept of value for money at low cost.

The strategic architecture is therefore concerned with enabling the organization to combine processes, resources and competences to put the strategy into effect. Specific actions and tasks are then implemented in order to put the strategy into effect.

Reflective question

1   Strategic architecture is fundamental to giving an organization competitive advantage and strength. Identify what you consider to be the main elements of the strategic architecture of an organization that you are familiar with.

TABLE 6.2 External economic pressures and their impact on business strategy

Economic pressure	Impact on business strategy
Rate of economic growth in a country	The rate of growth of GDP in an economy has profound implications for business. When the economy is growing consumers have more disposable income to spend on business products. In a period of growth the strategy may be one of growth and investment. In contrast, in a period of recession businesses will seek to make cutbacks.
Rate of economic growth in other countries	Most large businesses engage in international business strategy. The relative rate of growth of different economies, and the level of consumer spending power, will determine strategic decisions about the selection of markets.
The rate of inflation (inflation is the general increase in the price level)	Inflation is a disrupting force for business strategies. Inflation creates uncertainty about whether the money received when businesses get paid (for goods supplied on credit) will be as great as that originally anticipated. When developing strategies it is important to calculate likely future rates of inflation in order not to be caught out.
Changes in the rate of interest	Interest rates are the costs of borrowing money. When interest rates are raised they impact on the return on business investment by raising business costs. High interest rates will discourage business growth strategies.
Changes in the exchange rate	The exchange rate is the rate at which one currency (e.g. the pound) exchanges for another (e.g. the dollar). Changes in relative exchange rates will determine which overseas markets become more attractive in terms of international expansion strategies.
Changes in wage levels	Wages are an important business cost. In deciding on strategies businesses need to examine the relative wage costs of operating in different markets. Similar logic can be applied to other production costs – such as the costs of raw materials.
Changes in tax rates	Business taxes also have an impact on business strategy. The lower business taxes are the more likely a business is going to be able to expand.

Strategic control

Strategic control is concerned with monitoring the performance of strategy and then taking appropriate actions to make sure that the strategy is effective. Control is concerned with identifying what is going well and what is going badly and then taking appropriate actions to remedy problems.

6.7 Business strategy in an economic context

The economic environment is external to the organization. However, it constitutes a number of real pressure points that impact on business strategy. Table 6.2 illustrates some of these external economic pressures, showing how they impact on business.

There are a number of generic business strategies that a business can engage in and these are clearly impacted on by the economic environment:

- A growth strategy. Businesses are most likely to expand when the national and international economies are expanding – such as when interest rates are low, inflation rates are relatively low and taxes are low.

- A retrenchment strategy. Retrenchment is when businesses cut back to focus on key activities. Retrenchment is most likely to occur when there are gloomy economic prospects (e.g. during a recession).

- An internationalization strategy. Businesses are most likely to explore an international strategy when there are clear opportunities available in other countries and when the costs of internationalization are not too high – for example, lower taxes and wage costs in other countries, or a ready and growing market in other countries.

CASE STUDY Retrenchment at Sony

In April 2010 Sony announced 10,000 job cuts as a process of retrenchment. At the time Sony had been making losses for four years and the retrenchment strategy was seen as a means to bring the company back into profit. Sony was not the only Japanese company that was downsizing – others included mobile phone maker NED and electronics firm Panasonic.

A major problem for Japanese companies was an ongoing recession coupled with the high value of the yen when compared with other international currencies. A major problem for Sony was a reliance on selling TVs – a product where sales typically fall during a recession. Part of Sony's restructuring involved selling off non-core parts of the business such as a chemical products division. The company also asked a number of executives to return their bonuses because of the poor results of the company.

- What is the strategy that Sony was adopting and why? Relate your answer to the economic environment.

- Consider the strategy in terms of suitability, acceptability and feasibility.

KEY THEMES

What is strategy?

In his article 'What is Strategy?' Porter has the following to say:

> What is strategy? Strategy is the creation of a unique and valuable position, involving a different set of activities. If there were only one ideal position, there would be no need for strategy. Companies would face a simple imperative – win the race to discover and pre-empt it. The essence of strategic positioning is to choose activities that are different from rivals. (1996: 61)

If the same set of activities were best for producing all varieties, meeting all needs and accessing all customers, companies could easily shift among them and operational effectiveness would determine performance.

- **What is Porter telling us about why companies need to develop strategies?**

- **Why do these strategies need to change over time? What part does the economic environment play in requiring these changes?**

6.8 Summary

The selection and development of strategy is the most important long-term activity of the board of a company. Strategy involves complex high-level decision making and has major resource implications for a business.

The strategy that a board selects needs to meet the criteria of suitability, acceptability and feasibility. The strategy is the means to achieve ends that are set out in the vision and objectives of the organization.

In preparing, monitoring and evaluating strategies it is essential to continually scan the external business environment. The economic environment is perhaps the single most important external factor impacting on business decision making. The economic environment comprises changes in GDP and consumer spending, as well as a range of other important changes such as interest rates, exchange rates and wage rates. Changes in the economic environment present a key risk and uncertainty facing businesses.

KEY IDEAS

Some of the main points covered in this chapter are listed below. If you are unsure about any of them then revisit the appropriate section. If you would like some additional reading on the topic try the books listed below in recommended reading.

What are business strategies?

- Businesses strategies are the means through which organizations achieve their objectives.
- Strategies involve long-term decisions that have major resource implications for an organization.
- The board of a company plays a key part in helping to formulate, question and monitor the effectiveness of strategy.
- Typically strategies relate to the longer period, although strategies should be flexible so that they can be adjusted in the light of changing circumstances facing an organization.

Criteria for effective strategies

- Strategies should meet three main criteria: (1) they should be acceptable to stakeholders including shareholders; (2) they should be suitable to the environment in which a business is operating (e.g. a growth strategy might be suitable when the economy is growing, but not necessarily in a period of contraction); and (3) they should be feasible given the resources and capability of an organization at a particular time.

PEST analysis

- A PEST analysis is a useful tool for scanning the environment facing an organization.
- This involves carefully analysing and reviewing the political, economic, social and technological changes that are taking place in the business environment.
- Carrying out a PEST analysis enables an organization to develop strategies that adjust to changing environmental factors.

Quantifying risk

- Businesses live in a risk environment and need to be prepared to take risks.
- However, different companies will have different risk appetites.
- The risk appetite of a company should be aligned with the willingness to take risks by stakeholders.

- Calculating risk can be achieved by calculating the probability of the occurrence of an event and then multiplying this by the predicted cost of the impact.
- By quantifying risk an organization can select strategies that match its risk appetite.

Vision, objectives, focus and architecture

- The vision of an organization is a clear description of what the company is seeking to achieve outlined in a desired outcome.
- The vision can be backed up by SMART objectives, which are more specific ends to be achieved.
- It is helpful if measurement is attached to the objectives and that they are agreed by the members of the organization.
- The objectives should be realistic and a time should be established for when the objectives should be attained.
- Strategic focus sets out what the central direction of strategic planning will be – for example, to achieve a competitive position (e.g. to be the market leader), to focus on building resources and capabilities, or sometimes to be good at integrating dispersed operations.
- The strategic architecture of an organization refers to the interlinking of those things that a company does particularly well (i.e. its core competences).

Measuring the effectiveness of strategy

- Senior managers and the board of a company will agree on Key Performance Indicators (KPIs) to measure the effectiveness of its strategies.
- The KPIs focus on measuring those aspects of strategy that are particularly important (e.g. making a profit or cutting out waste).

Competitive advantage

- Competitive advantages are what gives a company a distinctive edge over rivals.
- Organizations need to identify those factors that give them a competitive edge in a particular industry or group of industries and then focus on building these advantages.

Types of business strategy

- There are a number of strategies that a business can pursue.
- The main ones are growth of products and markets, retrenchment (i.e. cutting back to focus on core activities) and internationalization (i.e. building up a presence in international markets).

REVIEW QUESTIONS

1. What is corporate strategy and why is it important for organizations to formulate a clear strategy?

2. What are the main characteristics of an effective strategy?

3. Why is it so important to scan the economic environment in formulating a strategy?

4. What are the key changes that can take place in the economic environment that will impact on corporate strategy?

5. How can securing competitive advantage enable an organization to develop a successful corporate strategy?

6. What do you see as being: (a) the controllable elements of strategy formulation; and (b) the uncontrollable?

7. Who in the organization should be responsible for formulating corporate strategy? Why is it important for those that shape strategy to have a good understanding of the economic environment?

8. Explain how each of the following economic factors are likely to impact on strategy formulation: (a) changes in interest rates; (b) recession; (c) economic growth; and (d) changes in wage rates in different countries.

RECOMMENDED READING

Johnson, G., Scholes, K. and Whittington, R. (2008) *Exploring Corporate Strategy: Text and Cases*, 8th edition, Harlow, Financial Times/Prentice Hall.

This is one of the best texts on corporate strategy.

You will also benefit from looking at the classic works about corporate strategy written by Michael Porter:

Porter, M.E. (1987) 'From Competitive Advantage to Corporate Strategy', *Harvard Business Review*, May/June: 43–59.

Porter, M.E. (1996) 'What is Strategy?', *Harvard Business Review*, November: 61–78.

REFERENCES

Zuckerberg, M. (2012) Facebook Just Bought Instagram. Available at: https://www.facebook.com/zuck/posts/10100318398827991 (accessed January 2013).

USEFUL WEBSITES

A useful Internet search is to use the key phrase 'videos of Michael Porter on strategy' which will provide you with some interesting materials. For example:

www.youtube.com/watch?v=ibrxIP0H84M

You can also access Porter's important article from Harvard Business Review 'What is Strategy' directly online:

http://www.thefreelibrary.com/Michael+Porter+%3a+What+is+Strategy %3f-a085608624

7 Government regulation and competition

CHAPTER OBJECTIVES

After carefully reading and engaging with the tasks and activities outlined in this chapter you should have a better understanding of:

- Why the government intervenes in the economy

- Why the government intervenes in markets

- Why the government creates rules about fair competition

- The key strands of UK competition law

- How to identify other forms of government regulation including regulations covering directors' duties

7.1 Introduction

If all markets were characterized by competitive businesses and this led to the allocation of resources in an efficient and equitable (fair) way then there might be a strong case for arguing that government intervention would not be required in business activity. However, as we saw in the previous chapter the concept of perfect competition is only a theoretical ideal and there may be economic disadvantages from having too many small suppliers.

Market models illustrate different levels of competition ranging from perfect competition to monopoly. The nature of uncompetitive markets is that there is asymmetry of power in those markets. This suggests that there may be a role for the regulation of markets in order to address imbalances of power.

This chapter introduces the role of the government in the market economy. It shows that there is considerable difference of opinion about the appropriate role of government interference in the marketplace. Some economists believe that the best role for government is a minimal role. In contrast, other economists believe that there is an important role for government in making markets more efficient and for protecting the interests of consumers. This chapter focuses on how markets can be made to work more efficiently and effectively.

KEY TERMS

Efficiency – involves making best use of existing resources – for example, by producing more with the same quantity of resources. Efficiency involves getting the most out of present resources and production capacity. It is sometimes referred to as 'doing things right'.

Effectiveness – involves focusing on how things can be done better in the long-term (i.e. it focuses on ends, as opposed to efficiency which focuses on the means to achieve particular end purposes). Effectiveness is sometimes referred to as 'doing the right things' – for example, by being entrepreneurial and innovative to come up with better solutions.

Government plays a key role in enabling markets to work by facilitating the creation of effective markets. In particular the government can help to make sure that businesses can compete freely with each other without restraints resulting from the activities of businesses that seek to distort the market. The government also plays a role in providing protection for consumers. The government needs to strike a fine balance between enabling markets to work well and creating rules and regulations governing market relations that may limit competition or which create so many rules and regulations that compliance with these rules adds to business costs to the extent of blunting the entrepreneurial impact of business innovation. In the UK the main public bodies that support the government in creating competitive markets are the Office of Fair Trading and the Competition Commission.

7.2 Government intervention

Governments intervene on a regular basis in many areas of life, ranging from imposing a tax on a litre of petrol, to determining the appropriate sentence for mugging an old-age pensioner.

In the period from the Second World War until 1979 governments tended to become more involved in economic decision making (than had previously been the case). For example, immediately after the Second World War a number of major industries were nationalized and operated as public corporations where the government owned the industry and appointed its own managers in a range of enterprises including railways, water and gas supply, iron and steel, coal and telecommunications. At the same time the government and agencies that it set up became increasingly involved in setting the rules related to how firms would be allowed to compete with each other – for example, by establishing a Monopolies Commission and a range of laws designed to protect consumers against unfair dealings and price fixing by suppliers.

From 1979 this emphasis was to change with the election of Margaret Thatcher's Conservative government. Between 1979 and 1997 the Conservatives went about privatizing state industries and reducing the role of the government in the economy. This move to reduce the role of government was partly based on ideological beliefs that individuals should be free to make their own decisions rather than having decisions dictated to them by government. It also stemmed from the economic beliefs of its supporters (neoliberal economists) who believe that the market is the best system for allocating scarce resources. The government of the time also set about deregulating business by seeking to remove restrictions and paperwork that complicated the business process.

Businesses in the economy operate in two main sectors:

1. The public sector – businesses (and other organizations) owned and run by the government and its appointed managers.

2. The private sector – businesses (and other organizations) owned by private individuals including shareholders of companies.

Figure 7.1 shows how industries can be privatized or nationalized.

KEY TERMS

Privatization – the transfer of public corporations and other government enterprises to the private sector.

Nationalization – involves the takeover of private companies by the government so that they become part of the public sector.

Typically, Conservative governments are ideologically inclined to reduce the influence of the government in the economy whereas Labour governments have a tendency to increase the role of the state in the economy.

FIGURE 7.1 Privatization and nationalization

During the most recent period of Labour government, from 1997 to 2010, there was an emphasis on seeking what was referred to as a 'third way' – seeking to develop a partnership arrangement between the private sector and government in the economy. For example, in some cases enterprises took the form of public/private partnerships (e.g. the construction of the Docklands Light Railway system in London).

The most recent period of Liberal Democrat–Conservative Coalition government, led by David Cameron, has seen a sharp move to reduce the role of the public sector in the economy. Moves towards more or less government controls over economies tend to ebb and flow over time depending on political preferences as well as on perceptions of how the state or the private sector is performing in a particular country at the time. The last decades of the twentieth century were very much an era of global liberalization and the spread of the private sector, but the financial crisis at the end of the first decade of the twenty-first century has raised questions about this approach. There are still many countries in which the government plays a key part in the economy (e.g. Venezuela in South America, North Korea in Asia and Zimbabwe in Africa). The following case study illustrates that in some countries there has been some movement towards greater state influence in recent times (bucking the trend to reducing the role of the state).

CASE STUDY Nationalization in Argentina

Argentina has a socialist government led in 2012 by an economist called Cristina Fernandez. Increasingly the country has moved in the direction of nationalization – for example, nationalization of the pensions industry in 2008, nationalization of Aerolíneas Argentinas (the main airline) in 2008, and most recently the renationalization of the largest oil company YPF which was formerly Spanish-owned.

The trend to nationalization of the oil industry in Argentina was a move in the opposite direction to that of many other resource-rich countries that increasingly welcome foreign investment.

Many countries have sought partnerships with overseas private oil companies as they look to exploit some of their more technically challenging resources – such as shale oil and gas – that their national oil companies lack the expertise to develop. For example, in the first few years of the twenty-first century the government increasingly took oil companies away from private ownership. However, by 2012 this policy had changed, as exemplified when Rosneft (the Russian state oil company) formed a partnership with ExxonMobil (a US oil company) to access some of the largest untapped hydrocarbon resources – the Arctic fields of Russia's Kara Sea. Similarly in Colombia and Ecuador national oil companies have been encouraged to join together with foreign private oil companies leading to a boom in oil production.

- Why might the government of Argentina have decided to nationalize industries such as the oil industry?

- In contrast, why might other countries such as Colombia, Ecuador and Russia have moved towards public/private partnerships with foreign oil companies?

- Can you identify other economies where: (1) there has been a move to increasing state interference in recent years; and (2) there has been a reduction in state interference in recent years?

There are a number of reasons why the government intervenes in the economy, including:

- To deliver goods and services that the private sector is not able to provide – because the state has access to more resources.

- To deliver goods and services that are most appropriately provided by the state – because the state may have different criteria for the production and distribution of goods (e.g. using criteria such as fairness and social inclusion).

- To counteract some of the failings of the market economy. The market economy has a number of failings referred to as 'market failures', such as the failure to provide goods that are beneficial to society as a whole (e.g. the universal inoculation of children against smallpox).

- To make markets more competitive. This point is developed in Sections 7.3, 7.4 and 7.5.

Note that support for the above motives for government intervention may be based on economic arguments or political beliefs (or a combination of the two).

Economists who favour free markets argue that when the government increases its influence in the market it 'crowds out' private sector spending and investment. For example, if the government raises taxes for its own spending then this money is not available to private businesses to expand and grow. They are 'crowded out'.

However, economists who favour more government influence in the market present a different version of 'crowding out'. They argue that when the government reduces taxes and its own spending then important government welfare spending (e.g. on health and education) is 'crowded out' by spending on other items (by the non-government sector of the economy) – for example, more money is spent on consumer goods such as visits to the cinema, petrol consumption, visits to the hairdresser, etc.

KEY TERM

Crowding out – where one sector of the economy (private or public) acquires resources at the expense of the other sector.

Reflective questions

1   What is your view of 'crowding out'?

2   What type of expenditure do you think should be 'crowded out' more – private spending or government spending? Justify your answer with appropriate examples.

7.3 The government and the market

In previous chapters we have examined ways in which the market operates. Figure 7.2 illustrates three alternative market models.

KEY TERMS

A **free market** is one in which there is no government involvement at all. All decisions about what to produce, how to produce goods and who will receive goods are determined by the interaction of consumers and producers (i.e. through the forces of supply and demand).

Planned economy – in contrast to the free market, at the other end of the spectrum we have a situation in which all decisions are made by the state.

Mixed economy – between these two extremes we have a mixed economy in which there is a combination of private decisions made by consumers and producers and by the government.

FIGURE 7.2 Three alternative market models

When we look at government's role in the economy we should look much further than direct government ownership and employment. The influence of government is also felt through the many ways in which it creates structures, rules and frameworks which impact on businesses and households. In Section 7.4 we examine a range of ways in which the government influences the working of markets.

One of the central debates in economics relates to the best way of organizing economic society. Some economists believe that the market will best serve the needs of citizens if government is not allowed to meddle. The belief here is that 'least government is best government'.

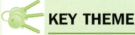 **KEY THEME**

The ideology behind the free market

In his book *The State to Come* (1997) Will Hutton identified the ideology of the free market in the following way:

> The vocabulary of western liberalism – of freedom, choice, independence and even morality – has been captured and recast into thought categories consistent only with competitive economic individualism. Freedom is defined as the freedom to buy and sell; choice as the right to exercise choice in markets; independence is independence from the state; moral conduct is the exercise of individual choice.

With the words programmed to have these meanings, any questions that use them have their answers prefigured. Thus enlarging freedom means enlarging economic freedom; maximising choice means maximising the operation of markets. No public institution can be independent because, of necessity, it is government-owned and financed and the state is collectivist; to be independent therefore implies that an institution be private. An independent university, for example, in this vocabulary is impossible, unless it is a private university.

This language is but the first step in the construction of a sealed thought process impregnable to criticism or evidence from the real world. The great achievement of classical economics has been to demonstrate that, under highly artificial assumptions, the act of freely buying and selling in markets in response to price signals produces a perfect economic outcome.

- What is an ideology (look this up if you are not sure)?
- What is the ideology of the free market?
- What is the role of the government in the free market?

An important area of disagreement between economists is whether the economy works better in situations where the government intervenes more or in situations where the government intervenes less. Those who are opposed to government interference argue that governments can only 'second guess' the wishes of consumers leading to poor decision making. For example, if I spend my own money on healthcare will I use that money more wisely than when the government taxes me and then spends on healthcare on my behalf? The problem with this type of discussion is that it is not one that can be resolved by 'positive economics'. It involves 'normative judgements'. Some economists are ideologically disposed to support private healthcare, whereas others favour state provision of healthcare.

KEY TERMS

Positive economics – economic analysis based on a study of factual information, on evidence and on the reporting of this evidence (e.g. analysis of how much is spent by the government on healthcare in 2013).

Normative economics – economic analysis based on ideas of what ought to be (based on value judgements) – for example, the government should carry out a policy that gives everyone more access to scarce resources because this is fairer.

Why does government intervene in markets?

Free markets in the modern world need help to exist and flourish. Perhaps ironically they need the help of government to make sure that free market conditions are in place. The government then uses a range of agencies to provide the enabling structures to secure free and competitive markets. These agencies include the law courts and specific bodies with a remit to enable competition, such as the Competition Commission and the Office of Fair Trading (see below).

Government intervention in markets sets out to achieve two main purposes:

1. To make markets work more effectively. This will involve making sure that there is an appropriate framework in the market. In simple terms the market will need to be free and open so that competition can take place. This will involve establishing the fundamental 'rule of law' in which contracts are upheld, and property rights recognized. This will be backed up by competition and consumer protection law. Businesses will need to be free to compete with each other without impediment and consumers should be able to exercise their free choice without being coerced or defrauded by unscrupulous suppliers.

2. To influence market outcomes. This will include minimizing the external impacts of markets (e.g. pollution and waste). The government will also use markets to deliver public services such as state education and refuse collection.

Direct or indirect participation

The government can intervene in markets through direct or indirect participation (see Table 7.1).

TABLE 7.1 Government intervention in markets through direct or indirect participation

Direct participation	Indirect participation
• As a supplier (e.g. by maintaining the railway network in the UK) • By providing state education, etc. • As a buyer of goods (e.g. purchasing medical supplies through the NHS, by commissioning and purchasing ready-made films, documentaries, etc. through the BBC)	• Through regulation of industries (e.g. regulation of public utilities) and by establishing the rules through which firms can compete with each other (as well as consumer protection) • Through taxation and subsidies

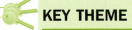 **KEY THEME**

When to intervene in the market

In 2009 the Office of Fair Trading produced a guidance document for policy-makers – *Government in Markets*. The executive summary set out the following key points for policy-makers:

> At a minimum, the aim for policy makers should be to minimise the distortions to markets, subject to achieving the desired policy objective. That is, where Government has a reason for intervening in markets, it should try to do so in a way that avoids unintended consequences as far as possible.

In assessing the effectiveness of existing or proposed Government interventions in a market, policy makers should consider the associated costs and benefits, including the impact on competition within a market.

Some interventions are more likely to distort or restrict competitive markets, either intentionally or inadvertently. To identify these, policy makers should consider the following questions:

- Does the policy affect the possibility of entry and exit in a market – for example by granting exclusive right to supply, limiting the number of suppliers, or significantly raising the cost to new firms of entering the market?

- Does it affect the nature of competition between firms in a market, either through direct restrictions (such as price or product regulation) or by reducing the incentive for firms to compete strongly?

- Does it affect the ability of consumers to shop around between firms and exercise choice – for example, does it raise costs of switching?

When a proposed intervention is likely to adversely affect competitive markets, policy makers should consider possible alternatives which might be less restrictive of competition. Government can often play a beneficial role in stimulating competition in markets, either through setting up market mechanisms, or, for example, through its wider role in procurement.

- **How useful do you find the advice outlined above as general guidance for government policy-makers in relation to taking actions that will have an impact on markets?**

- **Identify one or more situations where the government has recently taken action which will have an impact on a specific market – for example, as a result of the government awarding a contract to a specific supplier, or the government taking an action that will benefit particular suppliers. How could the points outlined above enable the government to achieve its policy objectives while minimizing distortions in the market?**

The case study that follows should be read in conjunction with the key theme set out above.

Types of government intervention in the market

The Office of Fair Trading (2009) has identified the following six forms of government intervention in the market:

1. Regulation
2. Subsidies and taxation

CASE STUDY Energy market shakeup raises fears of higher bills

At the end of May 2012 the government set out its plans for the most significant reforms to the UK energy sector since the privatization of this sector 20 years earlier. This generated an immediate negative response from consumer groups and green campaigners concerned that this would raise energy bills and penalize renewable energy while boosting nuclear power.

The changes outlined in the draft bill provide the government with much greater powers to intervene in the energy market. Key changes recommended were that low-carbon generators (including nuclear companies) will receive a fixed price for their energy that is likely to be higher than they would be able to sell it for on the open market. In addition the bill recommended that a 'capacity market' should be created to ensure a reliable supply of power and prevent blackouts.

Another change that is designed to benefit the environment is that a minimum price will be established for carbon dioxide emissions, and an emissions performance standard will be set with the practical impact of stopping any new coal-fired power stations being built without technology to capture carbon.

The reforms will mean major changes to the way the market is regulated and the way utilities and their smaller rivals operate.

A key benefit that the Conservative government expects to see arising from the reforms is that this will encourage substantial private sector investment in new low-carbon energy capture. Provisional estimates suggest that this may create up to a quarter of a million jobs.

This radical restructuring makes sense at a time when Britain's energy production sector includes a number of ageing power stations based on old-fashioned energy-inefficient technology. Failure to invest in new technologies and new capacity could potentially lead to soaring energy bills for consumers in Britain coupled with the reliance of the economy on imported energy – making Britain vulnerable to political instability in countries that supply gas and other fuels and hikes in imported energy prices.

However, there are those that believe that the government's energy policies do not face up to the real changes required to deal with climate change, while at the same time they risk exacerbating 'fuel poverty'. Fuel poverty results when the poorest and most vulnerable members of the community have to spend a disproportionate percentage of their income on energy.

Green groups and some renewable energy companies also attacked the draft bill. They accused ministers of breaking promises not to subsidize nuclear power, because the 'contracts for difference' by which low-carbon power generators will be guaranteed a price for their electricity will favour the nuclear industry.

By giving generators a fixed price guarantee in advance for their power, the 'contracts for difference' system should offset the risks taken by renewable and nuclear developers, which have to shoulder high upfront costs before they can start reaping the returns from their investment. This is seen to favour established nuclear energy providers who already benefit from economies of scale and are further down the road in developing energy technologies than new and emerging forms of energy.

- How are the government energy proposals outlined here likely to distort the market?

- Who is likely to benefit and who to lose out from the new market arrangements?

- Which of the questions outlined in the previous key theme should policy-makers have taken into account and why?

3. Government as influencer

4. Government as market maker

5. Public procurement

6. Government as supplier

Regulation

KEY TERM

Regulations – sets of rules administered by the government (in the context of business economics) to influence the behaviour of businesses.

Regulations range from rules setting market frameworks (e.g. relating to how firms can and cannot compete in the water industry) to detailed regulations (e.g. relating to the control of emissions from power stations and other energy suppliers in the energy industry). Examples of regulations include permits, quotas, quality standards and price controls. A key aspect of government regulation of business behaviour in markets is to ensure that consumers are not harmed by firms abusing their size in the market.

From a competition perspective regulations should be framed in such a way as to minimize regulation while maximizing the benefits of competition.

Regulations on price, quantity and who can enter a market will have a direct impact on competition. For example, imposing a minimum price restricts price competition between suppliers.

A key issue relating to regulation is that of 'regulatory capture'. This is where regulations have the outcome of benefitting firms in the industry being regulated rather than the wider public. Regulators need to be aware of this issue and seek to take mitigating actions to prevent this from occurring.

Subsidies and taxation

The government subsidizes some business and activities and taxes others. Subsidies and taxes distort costs. Subsidies reduce costs to a supplier and taxes raise costs. Examples of subsidies are tax exemptions for business, soft loans (at low rates of interest) and direct grants. Subsidies can distort markets in a number of ways – for example, by enabling inefficient firms to continue in the market, by enabling some firms to gain a dispropor-tionate (monopoly) share of a market, and by creating other inefficiencies and market restrictions. A key issue of using taxes to raise competition is that many taxes are general so that all firms have to pay them so that taxation cannot be used as a means of targeting businesses that are seeking to restrict competition.

Subsidies can be used in a beneficial way to increase competition in markets by subsidizing new and dynamic businesses that will in the future help markets to become more competitive.

Government as influencer

Government can seek to influence businesses and consumers by seeking to encourage greater levels of competition in markets. Influencing can be carried out through information campaigns, and discussion forums led by government as well as by government policy statements. These actions encourage change rather than directly imposing change. For example, the government can carry out advertising campaigns highlighting the negative impacts (on individuals and society) of excessive alcohol consumption to encourage moderation in drinking. Similarly governments can encourage industries to be self-regulating to create better market outcomes (e.g. the self-regulation of advertising through the Advertising Standards Authority). Where this is effective it removes the need for an additional cost of government regulation.

Government as market maker

The basic principle of the government acting as a 'market maker' is to enable competitive market structures to develop. As a market maker the government helps to design the market, as well as supervising and enforcing the effective operation of the market. There are three main ways in which the government can intervene as a 'market maker'.

1. Competitive tendering – principally in relation to delivering public services. Making sure that the process of tendering for contracts is open, fair and transparent (e.g. in public service provision of education, health and defence).

2. User choice – again principally in relation to the delivery of public services. Allowing the users of services to choose a provider. For example, if children/parents are provided with 'educational vouchers' to spend on an education of their choice, or allowing GPs to choose which medicines from an appropriate list to prescribe to patients.

3. Tradable permits – principally a means of dealing with negative externalities such as pollution. The government grants businesses permits to create a certain level of waste or pollution. Efficient firms will cut back pollution and exceed targets. They can then be allowed to trade their permit to create pollution by selling it to another firm that is less effective. This acts as an encouragement to be efficient in dealing with negative externalities.

Public procurement

Government can use its own buying as a means to make markets more competitive in a number of ways:

- Instead of the public sector providing a good or service the government can buy in from firms in the private sector. This helps to increase the level of competition especially if it buys from two or more firms.

- Using government buying power to encourage competition (e.g. by buying from new and emerging businesses). Government buying can also encourage the development of new technologies and products.

- Purchasing departments in the public sector should therefore consider ways in which they can use their buying to encourage greater competition in markets.

Government as supplier

Sometimes the government will provide goods and services directly –for example, the Met Office providing weather reports and the Office for National Statistics providing official statistics. The government may be able to provide these essential goods and services more efficiently than private providers. However, government suppliers should be aware of the dangers of crowding out the private sector, and ensure that competition is fair where it exists with private providers. The emphasis here is that where the government supplies directly to the market it should do so in ways that enhance competition in the market rather than employing monopoly powers or restrictive practices.

KEY TERM

Restrictive practice – any form of action by a firm or agreement between firms that restricts competition in a market. Examples of restrictive practices include only dealing with certain suppliers and customers, price fixing and collusion with others to prevent free competition.

7.4 Creating a competitive environment

All societies create rules that enable better interaction between members of that society. For example, imagine that two cars are heading for each other on a collision course. Each driver can veer either to the left or the right. If both veer to the right or both veer to the left, a collision is avoided. There must be some form of coordination of the decisions if disaster is to be avoided.

One way to ensure cooperation is to establish conventions or ground rules – in this case, rules about driving on the left- or right-hand side of the road. These rules of the road are formalized in the UK Highway Code.

If people simply pursue their own interests, this may be harmful to society as a whole. 'What is best for me alone' may not be best for the rest of the community. It is necessary in some instances to have a referee or umpire who makes sure that all parties in society keep to rules that are of benefit to the community as a whole.

Part of this rule-making needs to relate to the regulation of competition. For example, there need to be rules which prevent 'gangs' of producers fixing prices so that consumers are faced by high prices because of lack of competition. There need to be rules about single monopoly producers restricting their output in order to charge exorbitant prices. There needs to be some oversight of the joining together of firms through takeovers and mergers so that they do not gain a dominant position in a market to the detriment of consumers.

7.5 UK competition law

UK competition law is based on both UK law (the Competition Act, 1998, and the Enterprise Act, 2002) and European Union law where an aspect of competition involves a European-wide dimension. The Competition Act was introduced to ensure that businesses compete on a level footing.

Competition law is focused on three main activities:

1. Prohibiting agreements and practices that limit free trading and competition between businesses.

2. Banning abusive behaviour that results where a firm dominates a market, or where groups of firms engage in practices that lead to a dominant position.

3. Supervising merger and acquisition activity by large companies.

The two main bodies responsible for supervising competition law are the Office of Fair Trading (OFT) and the Competition Commission. The OFT's slogan is that it 'makes markets work well for consumers'. It believes that this will happen when companies are in open, fair and vigorous competition with each other. In addition there are a number of 'watchdog' agencies responsible for monitoring competition in markets that have been privatized – for example, Ofcom in the telecommunications industry and Ofwat in the water industry.

The OFT is a government department. It is responsible for supervising consumer protection and competition law. Its purpose is to secure vigorous competition between rival firms and fair dealing to benefit consumers.

KEY TERMS

The Office of Fair Trading (OFT) – a not-for-profit and non-ministerial government department that was originally set up by the Fair Trading Act in 1973. It is the UK's economic regulator and enforces competition law and consumer protection. As a result of the Enterprise Act (2002) the role of the OFT was extended to include the exploration of how market sectors operate, in order to help markets work well.

The Competition Commission – a public body responsible for investigating mergers, markets and other enquiries related to regulated industries under competition law in the United Kingdom. The Enterprise Act (2002) gave the Competition Commission the power to make decisions on enquiries which it conducts.

The OFT analyses markets, enforces consumer and competition law, and seeks to control mergers and to educate consumers about their rights. It also provides consumer advice.

A major part of the work of the OFT is to investigate markets to see whether they are working in the interests of consumers and customers. When it believes that it is appropriate it will refer a market to the Competition Commission for investigation. The OFT can make recommendations to the government – for example, that a market is insufficiently competitive and that action needs to be taken.

The Competition Commission is an independent public body that carries out in-depth inquiries into mergers, markets and the regulation of major regulated industries.

For the Competition Commission to carry out an investigation this has to be referred to it by the OFT or another authority. Under the Enterprise Act (2002) the OFT has a function to obtain and review information relating to all anticipated and completed merger situations, and a duty to refer to the Competition Commission for further investigation any relevant merger situation where it believes that it is or may be the case that the merger has resulted or may be expected to result in a substantial lessening of competition in a UK market.

It may be asked to investigate a particular market (e.g. the supermarket industry). In its investigation it will then have to decide whether any feature of the market or combination of features prevents, restricts or distorts competition. If this is so it will recommend remedies.

The Competition Commission can also review mergers (under the Enterprise Act, 2002). In considering the merger the Commission will want to make a judgement about whether the merger will lead to a substantial lessening of competition (SLC).

In order to qualify for investigation by the OFT the merger must meet all three of the following criteria:

1. Two or more enterprises must cease to be distinct.

2. The merger must not have already taken place, or must have taken place not more than four months ago.

3. One of the following must be true:

    (a) the business being taken over has a turnover in the UK of at least £70 million; or

    (b) the combined business supplies (or acquires) at least 25 per cent of a particular product or service in the UK (or in a substantial part of the UK) and the merger results in an increase in the share of supply or consumption.

The Competition Commission can prevent a merger from going ahead. It can also require a company to sell off parts of its business.

The OFT and consumer law

The OFT is also responsible for consumer protection law. Consumer protection law is designed to ensure that consumers are not disadvantaged by businesses that are not meeting legal requirements. Key aspects of consumer protection law include:

- Unfair Terms in Consumer Contracts Regulations, 1999. This protects consumers against unfair terms that are set out in contracts made with traders. The OFT (and some other bodies) can take legal action against the use of such terms. Unfair terms are not binding on consumers. In legal language a term in a contract is deemed to

CASE STUDY Creating more competition in Britain's Airport Authority

The control of Britain's major airports (e.g. the provision of airport infrastructure) was, until 1986, in government hands and the responsibility of the British Airports Authority (BAA). However, in 1986 BAA was privatized. In 2006 the company was taken over by a Spanish consortium.

With the expansion of BAA many airlines complained about the growing concentration of market share in the hands of a single provider. Britain's airports market was then referred to the Competition Commission which has since decided to require BAA to sell off Gatwick, Stansted and Edinburgh airports to reduce its monopoly powers.

Among its many recommendations the Competition Commission proposed to introduce measures to ensure that investment and levels of service at Heathrow, Gatwick and Stansted more effectively meet the needs of airlines, passengers and other airport users.

In making their report the Competition Commission announced that 'having provisionally identified competition problems at each of BAA's seven airports, we are proposing remedies which address them directly and comprehensively through a combination of divestment and other measures to improve investment and levels of service'. The Competition Commission went on in its announcement to state that: 'the most effective way to introduce competition in the South-East and in lowland Scotland is to require the three London airports and the two principal Scottish airports to be separately owned'. The Competition Commission recommended the sale of Gatwick, Stansted and Edinburgh to new independent owners with the operating capabilities and financial resources to develop each of them as effective competitors. Previously under the common ownership of BAA there was no competition.

- **How will the break up of BAA's control of airports in parts of the UK be likely to lead to better provision of services for customers?**

- **Do you think that it is important for the government to create more effective market structures in this example?**

- **Can you think of parallel examples where the break-up of monopoly control by a single firm can lead to better market outcomes for customers?**

be unfair 'if contrary to the requirement of good faith, it causes a significant imbalance in the parties' rights and obligations arising under the contract, to the detriment of the consumer' (Office of Fair Trading 2008).

- Consumer Credit Act, 1994. This sets out that only licenced traders can provide credit. They can only do so using acceptable credit and hire agreements (as defined by the Act). The OFT is responsible for administering the licencing arrangements.

- Consumer Protection from Unfair Trading Regulations, 2008. Traders have a general duty not to trade unfairly. They should be honest and fair in dealings with customers.

CASE STUDY Reference to the Competition Commission

A recent example helps to illustrate the process through which cases are referred to the Competition Commission for investigation. In 2012 the private healthcare industry was worth about £5 billion a year and was a rapidly growing market as a result of government health reforms which encourage private providers of health care to tender for extra National Health Service contracts.

The original complaint to the OFT was made by a new private health care provider, the Circle Partnership (the complaint being made in September 2010). The Circle Partnership alleged that anti-competitive agreements were being made between some existing national private health care providers and private medical insurance providers. In the industry these agreements are known as 'network agreements' and they act as a barrier to new firms entering the industry. Consumers therefore lose out because their choice is limited.

The OFT then held a public consultation to find out if there was a case to be answered. In January 2012 it published preliminary findings from that consultation stating that there was a case to answer – they believed that there was sufficient evidence that competition was being restricted. In addition the OFT was concerned that there was only a limited number of health care providers and insurers, which restricted the availability of private health care facilities to consumers. The OFT reported that there appeared to be significant barriers to new competitors. Removing these barriers would create greater choice. The OFT felt that some of the larger existing providers were raising their prices above what should be the case in a more competitive market.

Some examples of the way in which the market was being distorted included:

* Private clinics and hospitals offering incentives to consultants to treat a higher number of patients at their facilities.
* Private clinics and hospitals offering incentives to GPs to encourage them to refer patients to their facilities.

As a result of the initial investigation the private healthcare industry was referred by the OFT to the Competition Commission.

● What was the role of the OFT in this case example?

● What evidence was provided of restrictive practices?

● Why has the case been referred to the Competition Commission?

● How does this case illustrate the way in which the government can play a part in helping markets to work more effectively?

The list below sets out the general rules relating to bans and prohibitions on unfair trading:

- A general ban on unfair commercial practices.

- A prohibition on misleading practices – for example, false or deceptive advertising, or leaving out important information.

- A prohibition on aggressive practices that use harassment, coercion or undue influence.

- 31 specific practices that are banned in all circumstances.

Consumer law along with competition law is therefore designed to make sure that markets work better. Consumers and sellers should be able to interact in fair, open and transparent markets. The role of government is to facilitate the creation of these markets and to oversee the working of markets. Government, through its agencies (e.g. the OFT and Competition Commission), has an enabling role. In enabling markets to work well government policy-makers should be continually alert to the dangers of 'enabling' actions becoming 'distorting' ones. There is a fine line to be drawn between enabling markets to be more effective and heavy-handed distorting interference in those markets.

7.6 Other forms of government regulation

A former Conservative government minister, Michael Heseltine, stated that in reality 'the government [Conservatives 1979–1997] like all its predecessors for at least the last fifty years, is up to its neck in the business life of this country, stimulating one enterprise here, stifling another there and interfering everywhere'. Most (if not all) aspects of business life are regulated in one form or another. Obvious areas are health and safety, employee law, environmental protection, and many other areas of corporate life.

From the point of view of making markets work better the government needs to establish a balance between regulation and enabling the free flow of market forces. Too much regulation, and economic decision making becomes bogged down under a mountain of regulations, rules and form filling that acts as a brake to enterprise and economic efficiency. Too little regulation brings with it the danger of market abuse by unscrupulous individuals.

Regulations governing business activity stem from national government, from local government and perhaps most significantly from European Union regulations and directives. It would not be possible to review all of the rules governing business simply because they are so extensive in nature. This section therefore exemplifies one aspect of regulation by examining part of the Companies Act 2006.

The revised Companies Act was the longest legal document produced in British history. The Act covers many aspects of business law including how companies are set up and formed, as well as their legal responsibilities. An important aspect of the Act was the duties that it set out for directors of companies. These duties are particularly pertinent in the way that they shape the board decision-making process in relation to creating strategy and steering the board against a background of an uncertain economic environment.

The Act sets out seven general duties for directors. The overarching principle underpinning the general duties is that a director must act in the interests of the company and not in the interest of a group or groups within the company, such as shareholders. The company comes first. The company should be seen as an organization with a variety of stakeholders – including suppliers, employees, shareholders and local communities – each with an interest in the company.

The duties are:

1. Duty to act with the company's powers.

    The powers of a director are typically set out in the company's constitution (i.e. in the articles of association of the company). Directors are expected to follow the rules as set out in the constitution.

2. Duty to promote the success of a company.

    Directors have a duty to act in a way that they consider in good faith to be most likely to promote the success of the company. Directors need to consider a number of different factors:

    - The long term consequences of decisions;
    - The interests of the employees;
    - Relationships with suppliers and customers; and
    - The impact of decisions on the community and environment.

    They also need to consider:

    - The desirability of maintaining the reputation of the company; and
    - The need to act fairly when considering the interests of the various members of the company.

    You can see from this list that it may be perceived that there are some conflicting requirements in securing 'success'. For example, it could be argued that shareholder interests might conflict with environmental impacts. The introduction of new technologies may be better for the environment but may also create job losses.

3. Duty to exercise independent judgement.

    Directors are required to form judgements for themselves. They may have a personal interest in a particular issue but they are expected to listen to the views of others. However, the important point is that they need to arrive at a point of view based on their own independent judgement and not one shaped or influenced by others' views.

4. Duty to exercise reasonable care, skill and dilgence.

    Directors are usually appointed because they possess specialist skills that are going to be valuable in giving a company direction. These skills need to be employed for the benefit of the company and its stakeholders.

5. Duty to avoid conflicts of interest.

   Directors are required to avoid situations where they have a direct or indirect interest that conflicts with the interests of the company. This duty particularly applies to situations where directors have multiple directorships.

6. Duty not to accept benefits from third parties.

   The requirements of this duty is that a director does not benefit from a third party as a result of:

   - Being a director; or
   - Doing or not doing something as a director.

The requirement covers both monetary and non-monetary benefits.

7. Duty to declare any interest of the director in a proposed transaction or arrangement.

   Before a company engages in any transaction, directors must disclose the nature and extent of their interest, if any. This also includes disclosing the interests of persons connected to the director.

The duties of directors as set out by the Act are particularly pertinent to the steering role that directors provide for companies in an uncertain economic environment. Directors should contribute to better board decision making – for example, in helping a board to steer its way through a recession by taking a long-term view of strategic decision making.

One of the problems of many large British companies in recent years has been an emphasis on short-term results rather than long-term performance. The Companies Act requires that boards place more of an emphasis on the long term and see the company as an organization with responsibility to a wide range of stakeholder groups. For example, the interests of employees should be taken into account in making hard decisions about cutbacks and in merger and takeover situations. In relation to making markets work better directors also have a fundamental responsibility to consider the company's relationship with customers and suppliers. In all strategic decision making the board needs to demonstrate (particularly through minutes of meetings) that it has taken these considerations into account.

A key aspect of corporate governance and regulation in the UK is that we have a relatively flexible, less regulated market than many of our competitors (for example, in the wake of the financial crisis the United States established a much more regulated corporate governance environment). If this framework is to be successful it requires that the players in the market – government, businesses and consumers – take part in a responsible manner. If markets are to work then we can't just rely on the OFT and the Competition Commission to make the market work – business must also act responsibly. Businesses can only fully benefit from operating in a market environment if they abide by the rules of fair competition. It is when unscrupulous businessmen and women start to break and bend the rules of fair competition that the system becomes less efficient and critics start (with some justification) to demand more regulation.

KEY TERM

Competition and Markets Authority (CMA) – the current government's (2012) Department for Innovation and Skills has announced reforms that are likely to see the development of the CMA which is likely to combine many of the roles of the OFT and Competition Commission.

7.7 Summary

This chapter has reviewed the role that the government plays in a market economy. There will always be debate about the appropriate role for government – should there be more or less government interference in the economy? The government can intervene directly in the economy (e.g. by running public corporations in key industrial sectors), or indirectly through disseminating information that encourages the formation of effective markets, or targeting its purchasing in such a way as to encourage the development and growth of competition. It is very difficult to get the balance right between helping markets to be more effective and taking actions that distort a market or limit competition. Government agencies such as the OFT and the Competition Commission play a major role in identifying anti-competitive practices and then seeking to eliminate such activity. The case studies in this chapter help to exemplify what are regarded as anti-competitive situations in this country and the work being carried out by government agencies to make markets work better.

KEY IDEAS

Government intervention

- There is a fundamental distinction in economies between the public (government owned) and private sectors (owned by private individuals).
- The relative balance between the size of these two sectors in economies has ebbed and flowed, particularly during the twentieth century, but generally in recent years there has been a movement towards the expansion of the private sector.
- Government intervention doesn't just take the form of direct control of industries or government departments but also involves a range of regulation and other interventions in the market economy.

Government and the market

- Economies range from ones in which there is substantial state control to free markets. Typically the mixed economy is the dominant model.
- Government intervenes in markets to make markets work better and to influence market outcomes.

Creating a competitive environment

- The government in the UK seeks to make the market work more effectively.
- Making the market work more effectively not only involves creating an environment in which private industries can compete effectively. It also involves making sure that government policy and action operate in such a way as to enhance the market.

UK competition law

- The main government agencies for ensuring and enhancing competition are the Office of Fair Trading (OFT) and the Competition Commission.
- The OFT makes an initial investigation into situations where it is suspected that competition is being limited, and where there appears to be evidence that this is the case it asks the Competition Commission to carry out an investigation.
- Competition law also provides protection for consumers against unfair commercial practices.

Other forms of government regulation

- Government regulation covers most, if not all, areas of business activity.
- A particularly extensive piece of legislation is the Companies Act (2006) which provides rules governing many aspects of company formation and the running of companies.
- In the UK the emphasis is on enabling businesses to be more effective in the markets in which they operate rather than tying them down in a welter of rules and regulations.
- If a market economy is to work efficiently then this requires responsibility on the part of business, the government and consumers. There is no room for unscrupulous business people in a smoothly running market economy.

REVIEW QUESTIONS

1. What are some of the key reasons why the government becomes involved in economic decision making in a market economy?

2. What are the main benefits of a market economy when compared with a planned economy?

3. Why might the government choose to nationalize an industry?

4. Why might the government choose to privatize an industry?

5. What is the significance of 'crowding out' in economics?

6. What sort of ideology underpins support for the free market model?

7. What are some of the main actions that a government can take to make markets work better?

8. What sorts of considerations should a government take into account so as to ensure that its interventions in markets do not distort them in such a way as to limit competition or to hurt consumers?

9. What are the three main types of activity that competition law is based on?

10. What is the relationship between the Competition Commission and the Office of Fair Trading?

RECOMMENDED READING

Hutton, W. (1997) *The State to Come*, London, Vintage Original/Random House.

This book examines the vital choices that need to be made in society. Drawing on the concept of a stakeholder society the author shows how a future government could create both a stronger economy and a fairer society.

Office of Fair Trading (2009) *Government in Markets, Why Competition Matters: A Guide for Policy Makers*, London, Office of Fair Trading.

An excellent guide provided by the OFT setting out why competition matters for policy-makers and the thinking that should underpin decision making in relation to ensuring that markets are competitive.

REFERENCES

Office of Fair Trading (2008) Unfair contract terms guidance: Guidance for the Unfair Terms in Consumer Contracts Regulations 1999. Available at: http://www.oft.gov.uk/about-the-oft/legal-powers/legal/unfair-terms/guidance#named1 (accessed January 2013).

USEFUL WEBSITES

www.competition-commission.org.uk – the site of the Competition Commission outlining the nature of its work in creating more effective markets and providing examples of its investigatory work and recommendations.

8 The wider role of government in the economy

CHAPTER OBJECTIVES

After carefully reading this chapter you should be able to:

- Identify the key roles that the government plays in the economy

- Explain how the government produces goods and provides employment

- Analyse approaches to stabilizing the economy

- Explain government measures to increase competition

- Identify government solutions to market failure

- Analyse ways of managing the national debt

- Evaluate approaches to redistributing income

- Identify and explain industrial and regional policies

- Outline key macro-economic tools

8.1 Introduction

This chapter examines the very important roles that the government plays in managing the economy. Although the UK is predominantly a market economy the shape and integrity of our markets are dependent on effective government management of the economy. Government plays multiple roles in the economy all of which impact on business in one way or another.

Although there is considerable disagreement in the economics profession about the appropriate role of government there is also considerable agreement about the fundamental role that the government can play in providing the environment in which business can flourish.

This chapter reviews a range of roles including the government's international and national economic roles. It also focuses on specific roles such as seeking to create a fairer society through its policies to combat inequality and to ensure development of an effective industrial and regional structure. The chapter concludes by examining a range of macro-economic policy tools as an introduction to later chapters in the book.

8.2 Government's multiple roles and policies

Governments have a fundamental responsibility to try and make sure that the economy runs smoothly. In a smoothly running economy there should be a steady yearly growth in the production of useful goods and services. The economy then generates high levels of employment and rising wage levels. At the same time it is essential that the government ensures that general prices of goods and services only rise slowly and that there is not too much inequality of incomes. A growing economy is good for business confidence and business investment. With economic stability businesses can make sound investment decisions based on well-thought-out expectations of likely future returns.

Governments play a direct role in economies as producers of goods and employers of labour, particularly in the provision of public goods. Governments play an important stabilizing role in the macro-economy seeking to ensure that the level of aggregate (total) demand in the economy is appropriate to aggregate supply.

Governments also have an important international role in terms of participating in negotiations about trading agreements with other countries, as well as cooperating with other governments and international financial institutions to create international liquidity and payments arrangements to ensure the stability of currencies and to facilitate international payments.

The government is responsible for the national debt which needs to be kept in manageable proportions. The government also plays a key role in managing 'fairness' within the economy, particularly in relation to tackling inequality. Additionally, the government has an important role in creating and administering industrial and regional policies.

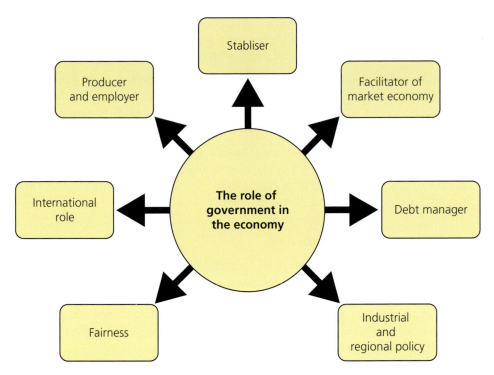

FIGURE 8.1 The role of government in the economy

8.3 The government as producer and employer

In some countries – Cuba and North Korea, for example – the government plays a major part in owning and running many large industries or important businesses in an industry. In some other countries, such as Singapore, the government owns major holdings of shares in large businesses considered to be of national importance. In other countries the government owns some of the key industries which are of national strategic importance – for example ARAMCO, the state-owned oil company in Saudi Arabia.

In the UK the main period of state ownership was between 1946 and 1997. For 50 years the government owned many key industries and public utilities in the form of public corporations including coal and steel, electricity, water, gas, telecommunications, the railways, the post office and many more. However, from 1997 these industries were privatized (i.e. transferred from public ownership to private ownership). Since this time the public sector has been substantially cut back.

Governments typically take responsibility for production for the following reasons:

- **To produce essential goods and services**. Some products are regarded as essential – for example, health and education. In Sweden employees pay about 50 per cent of their income in tax to pay for education, health care, care of the elderly and other social service industries provided by local and national government.

- **To supply merit goods**. Merit goods are produced on the basis of individual or societal needs rather than ability to pay. Again these would include health and education services to which everyone is entitled. Some governments provide these for all citizens.

- **To supply public goods**. These are goods that the private sector would be reluctant to provide because it is difficult, and often impossible, to get people to pay for them. Examples are road repairs and traffic lights – goods from which everyone benefits but which not everyone would be prepared to pay for.

- **To control natural monopolies**. Some industries are natural monopolies, such as the supply of water and electricity coming from a huge dam. If this were owned by a private company it might charge high prices. Government ownership of natural resources can make sure that everyone gets them at a fair price.

The government as an employer

The government is a major employer in all countries. Some people work directly for the government as civil servants (e.g. as tax collectors, accountants and immigration officers), or carry out office work on behalf of the government (e.g. producing reports that evaluate recent research). Another group of government employees includes workers in public services such as education and health care. A third group works for state-controlled businesses – the BBC or the Meteorological Office, for example.

Some people think that employees in the public sector may have more secure employment because the government can raise the funds through taxes to pay them. However, the financial crisis from 2007 onwards and the return of a Conservative government (as part of the Liberal Democrat–Conservative Coalition) in the UK has challenged these assumptions, with public sector employment being scaled back.

8.4 The government as a stabilizer of the economy

In Chapter 9 you will see that there has been considerable debate for many years about the role that the government should play in managing the macro-economy.

The nature of the wider economy is that it doesn't grow evenly over time. There are periods of increasing economic activity, followed by periods of recession. This is referred to as the trade cycle.

Trade cycle – a cycle of booms and recessions in economic activity. A boom is characterized by rising output, employment and income whereas recession is a decline in real GDP that lasts for at least two consecutive yearly quarters.

The trade cycle is a wasteful process involving fits and starts in economic activity. In a recession resources are wasted and the uncertainty in the economy makes it difficult to make rational business decisions.

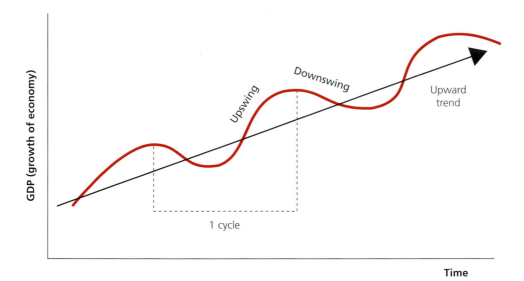

FIGURE 8.2 The trade cycle

The work of the economist John Maynard Keynes provided a basis for government to stabilize issues associated with the trade cycle. His ideas were widely adopted by governments in the post-Second World War world.

Prior to the development of Keynes' ideas economists had assumed that unemployment on a substantial scale could not exist in a market economy. They believed that any fall in employment (occurring in a recession) would be counteracted by a fall in wages which would encourage employers to recruit more labour. Similarly in a recession other prices would fall – for example, the interest rate (the price of money) – and cheaper interest rates would encourage businesses to invest more.

If these economists were right then there would be no need for the government to intervene in the economy to stabilize it because the market would do that automatically.

However, Keynes detected what he considered to be a flaw in this thinking and set this out in his book *The General Theory of Employment, Interest and Money* in 1936. Keynes' work showed that in a market economy workers could be involuntarily unemployed if they would like to work during a recession but are not able to do so because of general demand deficiency.

Keynes showed that the level of output and employment of resources depend on the following:

- Total demand for goods and services in the economy (aggregate demand); and

- Total supply of goods and services in the economy (aggregate supply).

Keynesian economists have illustrated this relationship by means of aggregate demand and supply curves.

Aggregate demand curve – an illustration (curve) showing the total demand for goods and services from all sources.

Aggregate supply curve – an illustration (curve) showing the total supply of goods and services by all producers in an economy.

As with micro-economic supply curves, the aggregate supply curve will slope upwards from the bottom left as the economy increases its output, towards higher prices, but there will always be a limit to supply at the point where factors of production are fully employed. At this point the supply curve will be vertical (given the current state of technical progress). The aggregate demand curve will slope downwards from the top left because, as prices fall, total demand for goods and services will tend to increase.

The actual level of national income (OQ) is where the aggregate supply and aggregate demand curves intersect. The difference between the equilibrium national income and the full employment point shows the extent to which it is possible to expand national income to minimize the employment of resources. This difference between national income and the full employment position is known as the deflationary gap (QR).

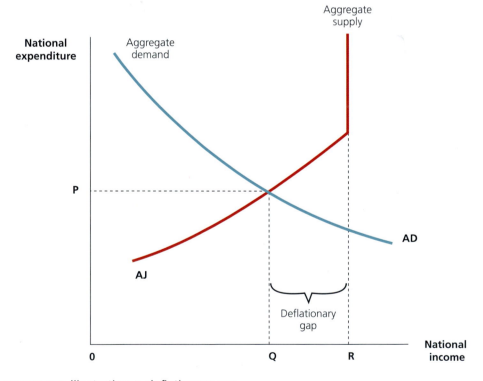

FIGURE 8.3 Illustrating a deflationary gap

Stabilizing demand

Keynes believed that aggregate demand might need to be manipulated in order to create desired levels of employment in the economy. To do this it would be necessary to adjust one or more of the components of aggregate demand. The components of aggregate demand are:

1. **Consumption** itself. Keynes showed that consumption is largely a function of income.

2. **Investment** in capital equipment. Private investment largely depends on the level of business confidence. When the economy is doing well business people are likely to invest. During a downturn, business people lose confidence in the economy and cut back on investment expenditures.

3. **Net exports**. The relationship between exports and imports depends on the competitiveness of a country's foreign trade sector.

4. **Net government spending**. The government's budget position depends on whether it spends more money than it takes in revenue (from taxes) or not. Prior to Keynes economists had believed that the government should seek to balance its budget (i.e. match expenditure with taxes).

Having examined the components of aggregate demand Keynes believed that investment was the most volatile of these aggregates. He argued that during a downturn in the economy business people would become reluctant to invest. As a result savings would not be initially channelled into investment. This would lead to demand deficiency in the economy, causing supply to be reduced, and an ongoing downturn in economic activity until savings were once again in balance with investment at a lower level of national income.

Keynes' solution to the deflationary gap was therefore the deficit budget.

KEY TERMS

Deflationary gap – situation when there is not enough demand in the economy to ensure aggregate supply at the full employment level.

Deficit budget – where, in any given time period, the government spends more than it raises in revenue.

Government intervention in the economy for stabilization purposes would involve:

1. Increased government spending to stimulate demand; and

2. Reductions in taxes to encourage consumers to spend more.

Keynes' solution to the deflationary gaps was therefore the deficit budget. In Keynesian analysis the cause of recession is demand deficiency.

Reflecting on the era in which Keynes was writing (the Great Depression of the 1930s) the American economist J.K. Galbraith commented:

> There remained one – just one – course. That was government intervention to raise the level of investment spending – government borrowing and spending for public purposes. A deliberate deficit. This alone would break the underemployment equilibrium by, in effect, spending – wilfully spending – the unspent savings of the private sector. It was a powerful affirmation of the wisdom of what was already being done under the force of circumstance. (1987: 68)

When the credit crisis hit hard in 2007–2008 it is interesting to note what the policy of the UK government and the US government was when faced with a sudden downturn in demand and spending as a result of the banking crisis. The immediate reaction was to increase government spending. The term 'quantitative easing' was used to describe a situation in which the UK government, through the Bank of England, pumped money into the economy to prevent a crash similar to that which occurred in the 1920s and 1930s.

In effect the government resorted to deficit spending in order to try and counteract the recession.

KEY TERM

Quantitative easing – this refers to increasing the available quantity of money in the economy. When a government wants to raise the amount of lending and economic activity in the economy one way of doing this is to directly pump money into the economy. This is done by the central bank (e.g. the Bank of England in the UK) buying financial assets such as government and company bonds using money it has created. It will buy these assets from commercial banks and other financial institutions so that they now have more money to lend to customers.

However, within a short space of time Gordon Brown had lost the general election and a new Coalition government had been elected with a Conservative Chancellor, George Osborne, whose ideas are based on balancing government expenditure by taxes – what is referred to as a 'balanced budget'. However, the continuation of the recession in Britain led to considerable doubts about the balanced budget approach that Osborne was championing.

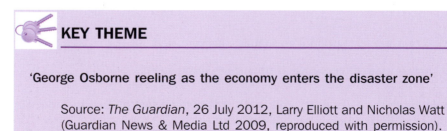

KEY THEME

'George Osborne reeling as the economy enters the disaster zone'

Source: *The Guardian*, 26 July 2012, Larry Elliott and Nicholas Watt (Guardian News & Media Ltd 2009, reproduced with permission).

George Osborne was coming under intense pressure from business, the City and the opposition on Wednesday to rethink his hardline austerity approach after news of a deepening, double dip recession dealt a severe blow to the government's deficit reduction strategy.

The Bank of England is expected to embark on further emergency measures to stimulate growth this autumn following the release of official figures showing a shock 0.7 per cent contraction in economic activity in the three months to June . . .

Evidence that the economy is now smaller than when the coalition came to power in May 2010 prompted immediate calls for a change of course.

The Liberal Democrat peer Lord Oakeshott called Osborne a 'work experience' chancellor, and urged that he be replaced at the Treasury by the business secretary, Vince Cable.

The shadow chancellor, Ed Balls, said: 'These shocking figures speak for themselves. As we warned two years ago, David Cameron and George Osborne's ill-judged plans has turned Britain's recovery into a flat-lining economy and now a deep and deepening recession.'

Sterling fell sharply on the foreign exchanges as dealers took fright at the possibility that the credit rating agencies might strip Britain of its prized AAA status, as a result of a growth performance that has seen activity decline in five of the past seven quarters and made Britain the worst performing country in the G8 group of industrialised countries, apart from Italy.

After a slower recovery than following the Great Depression of the 1930s, UK output is 4.5 per cent lower than it was when the economy peaked in early 2008.

The British Chambers of Commerce and the Institute of Directors both called on the government to show 'leadership', urging Osborne to take advantage of low interest rates to borrow for public investment.

The chancellor said the GDP figures were 'disappointing', but that 800,000 private sector jobs had been created while the government had been reducing its inherited budget deficit by 25 per cent.

- **What major change in government policy relating to macro-economic management is highlighted in the article above?**

- **What appears to have been the impact on the economy?**

- **How do the suggestions of the British Chambers of Commerce and Institute of Directors appear to tally with some of the suggestions made by Keynes?**

- **Why do you think that George Osborne might have been seeking to cut government expenditure rather than to raise it during a recession?**

8.5 The government's role in encouraging competitive markets

In the previous chapter we outlined aspects of the role that the government can play in enabling more effective markets. In Chapter 5 we looked at different types of markets and illustrated a perfectly competitive market situation. Competition is seen to provide a number of benefits including:

- Lower prices;

- Better quality goods and services;

- Greater choice for consumers; and

- A strong incentive for firms to be more efficient.

If these benefits can be captured then businesses, consumers and society as a whole can benefit.

Competition – rivalry between firms to win business.

The Office of Fair Trading (2009) has identified the following benefits of competition in markets. That competition:

1. Drives firms to improve their internal efficiency and reduce costs. Through lower costs firms are able to offer the same goods and services as rivals but at lower cost.

2. Provides incentives to firms to adopt new technologies. By adopting new technologies before rivals and more effectively than rivals a business can obtain competitive advantage.

3. Provides incentives to firms to invest in innovation. Investment in innovations enables firms to provide better quality existing products and to develop new products that are market focused.

4. Reduces managerial inefficiency. As a result of competition managers will need to adopt more advanced and effective business models in order to stay in the game and to outsmart rivals.

Competitive markets are ones in which there is freedom of entry to new enterprises to join a market and win market share by being more competitive than existing ones. Existing firms will need to adapt their products and processes in order to respond and to retain market share.

On a national scale, healthy competitive markets provide an incentive for new firms to enter a market, enabling innovation and resulting in long-term growth in productivity and the economy as a whole.

A key role of government therefore is to support markets to become more competitive (as outlined in the previous chapter). Increased competition in UK markets also helps British firms to be more competitive in international markets. The drive to be competitive acts as a spur for British firms to reduce their costs, adopt new processes, develop new products, employ better managers and so on, which enable the economy to thrive in the longer term.

8.6 The government's role in combating market failure

Market economies work in situations where competition ensures efficient production and rewards to members of society. The market system is based on a number of assumptions:

- That markets are competitive.

- That individual members of society are free to pursue their own self-interests.

- That as individuals gain from furthering their own self interests this leads to higher levels of individual well-being.

However, an examination of the real world shows us that these assumptions don't always hold up – so there are some situations in which the market 'fails'. In situations where the market fails there is then a role for government to step in.

Examples of market failure, and steps that the government can take to deal with this failure, are shown in Table 8.1.

Reflective questions

1 What do you see as being the major causes of market failure?

2 Where markets fail do you believe that it is the responsibility of government to take action to combat these failures?

3 What actions would you recommend to tackle specific examples of market failure that you are familiar with?

8.7 The government's international role

The government plays a key role in managing economic relations between the country it governs, other specific countries, blocs of countries and the global economy as a whole.

The Prime Minister, Foreign Secretary and Chancellor of the Exchequer of the UK will have regular meetings with their international counterparts as will the Chair of the Bank of England and other senior officials.

TABLE 8.1 Examples of market failure

Example of market failure	What the government can do to tackle market failure
Monopolists exist in some markets. Monopolists can carry out restrictive practices – they can charge a price above the market rate or they can restrict supply.	The government can ban certain restrictive and monopoly practices. Through its agencies (e.g. the OFT and Competition Commission) it can investigate these restrictive practices and take action against offending businesses.
In carrying out business activities firms can create externalities (e.g. in the form of waste and pollution). Negative externalities are often the result of market individualism. A firm carries out actions without taking into consideration the impact on other individuals (e.g. those negatively impacted by the pollution).	The government can take a range of measures to tackle negative externalities. For example, it can impose fines or taxes on pollution (e.g. a landfill tax for industrial waste production). It can make the production of certain harmful substances illegal (e.g. toxic chemicals in paints requiring them to be replaced by water-based chemicals). The government can provide subsidies to producers to adopt technologies which have a lower environmental impact – and hence create fewer negative externalities.
Some goods will not be provided by private businesses because there is no way of dealing with the 'free rider' problem associated with the production of them. For example, if a company provides street lights then everyone will benefit from the street lights, not just the person that has ordered and paid for the street lighting.	The government may need to provide some public goods directly. These public goods could be paid for out of taxation which is levied on all users of the public good to find a solution to the 'free rider' problem. Examples of public goods include the police service, court system and national defence.
In some markets it is difficult for consumers to obtain enough information to make rational decisions. For example, they may not have enough information about the quality of a good before they purchase it. In extreme circumstances the consumers may feel that they have so little useful information that they decide not to purchase anything.	The government can ensure that sufficient information is provided to enable consumers to make an informed judgement (e.g. by requiring food labelling about the salt, sugar or fat content of foodstuffs, or the energy efficiency of double glazing, insulation or electrical products).
Markets where there is a monopoly element. For example, some markets may contain some element of natural monopoly.	The government can limit the power of monopolists in the interests of consumers (e.g. through price controls).

Key areas for discussion and for government management will be:

1. Developing trade relations with other countries. For the UK trade relations within the European Union are particularly important as well as relations with other major trading partners and potential new partners. Regular meetings will take place with partners in the G5 (group of five leading economies), G8 (group of eight leading industrial nations) and G20 (twenty nations). Developing an international order for trading relationships will be carried out through the World Trade Organization as well as by direct negotiations with trading partners.

G5 – the group of five leading (market-focused) industrial economies, the United States, Japan, Germany, France and the United Kingdom.

WORLD TRADE ORGANIZATION – international body set up to broker trading agreements between groups and to arbitrate in international trade disputes.

KEY TERMS

2. Contributing to discussions and helping to formulate policy in relation to the development of international means of payment and for the settlement of debts between countries (e.g. through meetings with officials from the International Monetary Fund and World Bank).

International Monetary Fund – an international financial institution which will lend participant nations international currencies so that they can maintain the stability of their own currencies and address any short-term issues associated with loss of confidence in their currency.

World Bank – an international financial institution that will lend money to countries for development projects.

KEY TERMS

3. Taking action to support the exchange rate between the pound and other currencies. The value of the pound depends on the competitiveness of the UK economy which is dependent on the effectiveness of the government's management of the macro-economy. The value of the pound in international exchange depends on the popularity of British exports and the extent to which foreigners want to invest in the UK economy. When UK interest rates increase this will encourage a greater demand for the pound attracted by a relatively higher rate of return.

The British and other governments therefore have a very important role to play in ensuring a well-functioning international system as well as furthering their own national interests.

CASE STUDY International risks to the UK economy

Research carried out by the risk analysis company Maplecroft and published at the end of July 2012 revealed that Britain is the country most at risk from the worsening of the crisis in the Eurozone. The research identified differential levels of risk in 169 countries.

The study showed why Britain is (July 2012) so exposed to international risk. The main reasons for this are:

- The poor performance of the UK domestic economy – experiencing a double dip recession at the time; and
- The UK's high level of interaction with and dependence on the Eurozone countries.

As a major European and global financial centre the UK has strong trading and banking links with the Eurozone. About 50 per cent of the UK's trade is with countries in the Eurozone and a collapse in key economies such as Spain and Italy could lead to a 7 per cent drop in UK trade and losses of about £95 billion in Britain's banking sector.

- **What challenges does the information provided in this research pose for the UK government?**

- **What are the implications in terms of the relationships that the UK needs to build with other countries and international financial institutions?**

- **What are the wider implications for the UK's management of the economy?**

8.8 The government as debt manager

The national debt of a country is the debt of the central government. Most governments run up a debt at one stage or another just as businesses and households do. The important thing is to keep the scale of the debt at a manageable proportion (i.e. at a level that the government can pay back at a future date).

Table 8.2 shows how the national debt will increase in a situation in which a government runs a budget deficit each year.

In the table:

- The term ND refers to the national debt;

- The term BD refers to the budget deficit;

- The term GR refers to government revenue;

- The term GE refers to government expenditure; and

- 1, 2, 3 and 4 refer to successive periods of time.

TABLE 8.2 How a government builds up debt

Year 1	$BD1 = GR1 - GE1$	$ND = BD1$
Year 2	$BD2 = GR2 - GE2$	$ND = BD1 + BD2$
Year 3	$BD3 = GR3 - GE3$	$ND = BD1 + BD2 + BD3$
Year 4	$BD4 = GR4 - GE4$	$ND = BD1 + BD2 + BD3 + BD4$

Budget deficit – the amount that government expenditure exceeds government revenue by.

KEY TERM

The national debt is financed both through domestic borrowing and by international borrowing. Another key ingredient of national debt is the amount of interest that a country has to pay on the debts that it builds up. As a general rule the more debt that it builds up as a percentage of the GDP of the country the greater the risk that lenders will be taking in relation to lending to that country. Credit risk agencies rate the riskiness of countries in terms of their ability to repay debts – for example a Triple A (AAA) rating indicates that it is safe to lend to a country. The better the credit rating the lower the interest that a country will have to pay on money borrowed on international markets. The worse the credit rating the higher the interest repayments will be.

It is not difficult therefore to understand how the recent Eurozone crisis has developed. Countries such as Greece have consistently run government deficits based on high government expenditures relative to tax revenues. As a result the credit ratings of Greece, Portugal, Spain, Ireland and other countries have tumbled, and so it becomes increasingly difficult to finance debt through the market.

The result is that these governments have had to go to the European Central Bank and the International Monetary Fund as lenders of last resort to request a bailout. The European Central Bank and the International Monetary Fund then have to build support from stronger economies to provide a financial package for the bailout. This is when governments, including that of the UK, have to provide leadership in terms of providing the support, ideas and political and financial will to make the bailout work.

Ideally a country should raise as much of the national debt internally as possible. When the national debt is raised internally this simply involves a transfer of resources within a country. When the debt is financed externally then lenders are far more likely to impose conditions on the borrowing nation.

Debt to GDP ratio – the national debt to GDP ratio is an indicator of the health of an economy. It is calculated as a percentage (i.e. national debt as a percentage of GDP). A sustainable debt to GDP ratio is one where the government is able to service that debt (progressively repay it with interest payments) without having to restructure that debt or have recourse to more borrowing (at a higher rate of interest) to pay off the debt.

KEY TERM

CASE STUDY The Spanish government's response to the debt crisis

In July 2012 the Spanish economy required a bailout from the European Central Bank and from stronger European economies – particularly Germany. The Spanish economy was suffering from the wider crisis in the Eurozone and more specifically because most Spanish banks had taken a hit as a result of the credit they had extended to borrowers in the Spanish property market, which had crashed with many firms going bankrupt.

As unemployment increased in Spain to dramatic proportions (24 per cent by July 2012) the Spanish government had had to pay out more and more money on social security while its tax revenues continued to fall. The net effect was that the national debt increased as government revenues fell well short of government expenditure.

The issues for central government were mirrored in the finances of regional governments in Spain. By July 2012 the Spanish government was having to pay a record interest rate of 6.459 per cent to sell five-year bonds, while rates on ten-year bonds had risen to 7 per cent. (By comparison France was only paying 1 per cent on five-year bonds.)

The Spanish government's response to the debt crisis was to introduce an austerity package of government cutbacks in public spending. This was not a popular measure with many people in Spain, with mass protests in cities across the country.

- What was the cause of the debt crisis in Spain?

- What actions has the Spanish government taken to reduce its national debt?

- What problems have resulted from the size of the national debt in Spain?

- To what extent is the Spanish debt crisis an international problem rather than merely a national one?

ACTIVITY

Carry out some online research to find out the current size of the UK national debt in comparison with GDP. Using statistics from the Office for National Statistics first, find out the most recent figures for GDP and the most recent figures for National Debt.

- How does this ratio compare with that of Germany, France, Spain and Greece? Does this raise any issues? What is the current credit rating of these countries? Is the credit rating related to the scale of the national debt?

- Set out your findings in a table, using three columns: (1) country; (2) national debt/GDP ratio; and (3) credit rating.

8.9 The government and inequality

In all economies there are people with fewer goods and services than others (in relative poverty), with some not receiving enough to meet even basic needs (in absolute poverty). This inequality between rich and poor in many countries can mean, for some, high levels of infant mortality, malnutrition, starvation, ill health and low life expectancy. A key government policy in all countries is to redistribute income more equally through society.

However, in most countries across the globe inequality persists and in some it becomes more extreme over time. For example, a study published in the US in 2007 by the economist Emmanuel Saez showed that inequality in the US had achieved an all-time high. The top 0.01 per cent of income earners in the country were taking home 6 per cent of US wages, and the top 10 per cent of wage earners received almost half the wages. The remaining half of wages was earned by the bottom 90 per cent of wage earners.

Redistributing income

Governments can redistribute income through government spending, through subsidies and through taxation:

- **Government spending**. The government can use the money that it receives from taxes and other revenues to spend on goods and services that benefit the poor more than the rich. Examples include roads to remote rural communities, and public education and health systems.

- **Subsidies**. This is where the government pays a sum of money to a consumer or a producer. For example, in India the poorest members of the community receive a ration card enabling them to buy food at below cost price from public distribution shops. Alternatively the government could pay a subsidy to a producer so that they can supply it to the market at a lower price – for example, subsidies to farmers in the European Union.

- **Taxation**. The government can tax the rich and redistribute this income – for example, through spending on public goods.

8.10 Industrial and regional policy

Industrial policy

Industrial policies – policies with the purpose of influencing the development of particular industries.

KEY TERM

In a market economy constant change will take place in the structure of industries within the economy as a result of changing patterns of consumer demand and because of the development and adoption of new technologies. Some industries and businesses will be expanding while others are contracting.

TABLE 8.3 Accelerative and decelerative strategies

Accelerative strategies	Decelerative strategies
Designed to speed up the growth of new 'sunrise industries'	Designed to slow down the decline of 'sunset industries'
Achieved through the instruments of government grants, soft loans and subsidies	Achieved through providing grants and subsidies to declining businesses and to soften the blow of their decline

As some industries decline there will be adjustment costs associated with unemployment. At the same time as new industries develop they may be held back by the lack of expansion capital and labour shortages resulting from people not having the right skills.

The government can play a role where appropriate in slowing down the decline of certain industries – a decelerative strategy. It can also employ an accelerative strategy to encourage the development of potential growth industries (see Table 8.3).

KEY TERMS

Accelerative strategy – a government industrial strategy designed to support the development of new growth industries ('sunrise' industries).

Decelerative strategy – a government industrial strategy designed to slow down the decline of 'sunset' industries.

The success of the strategies outlined above depends fundamentally on:

- The government's ability to identify those sectors of the economy that are most likely to grow. In recent years, this has involved providing some 'seedcorn' capital to businesses in industries such as biotechnology, alternative energy and new areas of information technology such as computer gaming.

- Not channelling too many resources into supporting 'lame duck' industries that are in terminal decline. Some critics argue that a major weakness of UK industrial policy in the 1970s was that too many resources were channelled into supporting the 'lame ducks' of coal, iron and steel, and shipbuilding, which were a legacy of Britain's industrial past. Others argue that such subsidies were essential to support declining regions of the UK.

Since the late 1970s government industrial policy has switched more towards making industry more effective through enabling market forces to determine industrial restructuring. Key elements of such policy have included:

- Encouraging greater competition in markets. For example, allowing new firms to set up as opticians rather than restricting the number in the industry. Also opening up bus services to competition between private firms. Another example is allowing solicitors to advertise their services.

- Privatization of the nationalized industries.

- Reducing government subsidies to industry.

- Public/private partnerships involving the government working with private sector partners to develop new infrastructure projects such as the Docklands Light Railway in London.

- Competitive tendering for government contracts. Rather than the government running services it contracts these out to private businesses.

Successive governments have therefore liberalized markets in Britain in the belief that the market may be the most effective way of ensuring an effective industrial policy. However, it is important to recognize that this doesn't always work. For example, for the Olympic Games in 2012 the security service at Olympic venues was contracted out to a private company. In the week before the games it came to light that the recruitment of security personnel by the company had been a shambles and the government had to step in to ask the army to take a substantial role in policing the games.

In spite of the move in industrial policy towards market forces it is clear that the government still intervenes substantially in industrial policy as revealed by the following case study.

CASE STUDY Differential intervention in the energy industry

In July 2012 John Sauven, the executive director of Greenpeace, made the damning statement that:

> Osborne [the Conservative Chancellor] is becoming a threat to the climate, to energy customers and the economy. He has declared war on one of Britain's only growth sectors, actively plotting to destroy green jobs and industries. His meddling is driving up bills, locking us in to decades of dirty fossil fuel use and making energy policy unworkable.

Sauven made this statement at a time when it came to light that Treasury ministers had held meetings with representatives from energy-intensive sectors seven times more than with representatives from the green energy sector. The Chancellor of the Exchequer had not had a single meeting with green energy representatives.

This was against a background of the Chancellor trying to make a deal with the Energy Minister whereby subsidies to the onshore wind industry would only be cut by 10 per cent by the Treasury (as opposed to the 25 per cent previously planned) if in return the Energy Minister would agree to scrapping 2030 targets for carbon emissions and renewable energy in the UK. The 2030 targets act as a real spur to stimulate investment to make the UK a green economy.

- **What example is provided in the case study that shows the UK has had an accelerative strategy for the development of green energy? What form did this accelerative strategy take?**

- **How is George Osborne seeking to derail this accelerative strategy? What form does his derailing take?**

Regional policy

Regional policy – government policy that is deliberately designed to enable the development of selected regions. Often the purpose of regional policy is to counteract imbalance in the development of the regions.

Regional development in the UK provides a complex picture. At a simple level there is a disparity between core and peripheral regions of the UK. Core regions are centres of economic activity – for example, London and the South East, Birmingham and the West Midlands, and Newcastle, Sunderland and Durham in the Tyne and Wear areas of the North East. Peripheral areas are ones that are geographically distant from centres of population – for example, parts of the Highlands of Scotland and parts of East Anglia. However, when examined more closely research indicates that the picture is more blurred and that what often exists across the UK is pockets of poverty and prosperity often quite close together.

Regions tend to thrive when they contain:

- Dynamic growing industries or established industries producing popular products.

- A skilled and highly educated labour force.

- Excellent communication networks – particularly transport and information technology hubs.

- Ready access to large and growing markets.

- Attractive housing stock, leisure and recreational facilities, and green space.

- Good schools, hospitals and other welfare facilities.

Conversely, where regions lack the above facilities they tend to move in a downward spiral.

The challenge then to government policy is to support the creation of conditions that encourage regional growth. A key aspect of regional growth is to create 'growth poles' – specific regional centres that attract inward investment and dynamism (e.g. Newcastle in the North East has experienced substantial urban regeneration funding in recent years enabling it to become one of the UK's leading cities). The government can stimulate urban regeneration by moving government departments and government employment to particular areas – for example, moving parts of the BBC to Manchester has had a tremendous multiplier effect.

Regional policy has also been important within the European Union context. In creating the Single Market, involving the free movement of goods between member states, it was recognized that this would benefit stronger nations and regions (e.g. Germany and France). To compensate for this regional funds were created to support weaker regions of Europe to adjust their structures.

KEY TERM

Structural Adjustment Funds – funds provided by the European Union to enable the restructuring of weaker economies in the Union following the creation of the Single Market in 1992.

Examples of the targets of EU regional funding include:

- Youth training schemes. Training schemes for the long-term unemployed.

- Funding for rural areas to diversify their economies.

- Funding for regions with a heavy concentration of 'sunset' industries (e.g. coal mining and steel areas).

- Investment in infrastructure to open up some areas of the EU (e.g. through the construction of motorways).

8.11 Macro-economic policy tools

The Chancellor of the Exchequer and other government ministers with responsibilities for economic affairs have a range of macro-economic policy tools available to them (see Table 8.4).

KEY TERM

Macro-economic policy tools – economic instruments that can be manipulated to achieve desired goals in the wider economy.

These tools are explored individually in greater detail in other chapters. However, it is important to identify them collectively as a basket of tools that the government can use to manipulate the economy.

The current Coalition government has effectively established an income policy by setting increases in public sector pay at a very low level. The longer this income policy is maintained the more it distorts the difference between public and private sector pay levels – which can lead to an inefficient allocation of resources in the economy. On the positive side, when the government imposes wage restraints in its own sector this sets an example to private industry which is also likely to take the government's lead and to hold wages down, reducing an important element of inflationary pressure in the economy.

The government has available to it a range of policy instruments which helps to manipulate the economic climate. In carrying out an analysis of the business environment in order to make key business decisions it is helpful to review government policies to identify the potential impact that they will have on the decision.

TABLE 8.4 Macro-economic policy tools

Tool	Description	Impact on business	Additional coverage in this book
Monetary policy	Managing the money supply and interest rates	Lowering interest rates reduces business costs. Raising interest rates raises costs. Expanding the money supply encourages spending, economic growth and sales by businesses.	Chapter 13
Fiscal policy	Managing government spending and taxes	Increased government spending can generate additional economic growth, encouraging business sales. Increasing business taxes raise business costs.	Chapter 14
Competition policy	Managing competition in the economy	Encouraging competition enables new firms to enter markets, reduces market restrictions and encourages business efficiency.	Chapter 7
Trade and exchange rate policy	Managing trade relations and manipulating the exchange rate	Better trading relationships encourage exports. A competitive exchange rate enables exporters to sell into foreign markets.	Chapters 11 and 12
Industrial and regional policy	Managing the growth and decline of regions and industries	Stimulates growing industries and regions, supports existing industries and regions, and cushions the decline of 'sunset' industries and regions.	Chapter 8
Environmental policy	Managing the sustainability of the economy	Encourages businesses to take on more environmental responsibility. Encourages new 'green' industries.	Chapter 15
Incomes policy	Where the government directly controls or intervenes in the setting of wages and other incomes in the economy. It could do this for the whole economy or for the part of the economy that it controls (i.e. public sector incomes).	An incomes policy tends to have a downward impact on wage costs which can be helpful for businesses. The problem is that if an incomes policy is maintained for too long then it prevents market forces from operating to attract labour to the most productive industry and products. It creates inflexibility in the labour market.	Chapter 8

KEY THEME

Christine Lagarde's criticism of George Osborne's public sector cutbacks in Britain

In 2012 George Osborne was the British Chancellor of the Exchequer. Christine Lagarde was the managing director of the International Monetary Fund, the organization that seeks to make the international payments system between countries work more effectively and which seeks to encourage the growth of the world economy as a whole.

FIGURE 8.4

Christine Lagarde – Managing Director of the IMF

Source: Paul Mendoza/ Alamy.

When the Liberal Democrat–Conservative Coalition government came to power in 2010 in Britain, their response to a general fall in economic confidence in the wider world, and particularly in Western economies, included cutting back on government spending. We can refer to this as Plan A.

Whereas other countries such as the US sought to spend their way out of a period of falling global demand, George Osborne believed that it was important for the British government to restore confidence in the UK government's ability to meet its national debt by bringing debt down rather than increasing it. Plan A involved seeking to make sure that international investors had confidence in Britain as a country in which the government does not allow public spending to become too large. However, the problem with government cutbacks is that this leads to a wider fall in demand in the economy as a whole – a downward ripple effect of falling spending (see Chapter 1).

In her advice to George Osborne, which was widely published in the media in the middle of 2012, Christine Lagarde set out clearly that Britain should adopt an economic 'Plan B' and slow the pace of public spending cuts if the British economy remained weak. Christine Lagarde met George Osborne at the Treasury to deliver the message: that the government should consider slowing spending cuts if economic recovery stalls.

She also called on the Bank of England to do more to support the economy – presently in the grip of a double dip recession – by printing more money (a policy referred to as quantitative easing). Quantitative easing involves the central bank of a country increasing the quantity of money that the government makes available in the economy. It is a stimulus measure that has frequently been used by governments in times of recession, but the term quantitative easing only really entered public discussion during the financial crisis from 2008.

In setting out the IMF's annual verdict on the British economy, Ms Lagarde said that Mr Osborne's 2010 Budget had successfully steered Britain away from a potential financial crisis two years ago. 'When I look back to 2010 and what could have happened without fiscal consolidation I shiver', she said.

This case is very interesting in identifying some aspects of the way in which the UK government had been using macro-economic tools between 2010 and 2012.

In 2010 the British economy had a very large public sector deficit because of high levels of government spending compared with tax revenues. The impact of this was to create a substantial and growing national debt. Government fiscal policy prior to 2010 therefore was all about stimulating the economy through government spending.

However, the new Coalition government in 2010 recognized that Britain's debt position could lead to a loss of confidence in the pound and a downgrading of Britain's credit rating. The new fiscal policy therefore was to reduce government spending substantially. However, coupled with an existing Eurozone crisis and recession the UK economy was moving into an extended period of recession. The warning from the IMF therefore was that the government in 2012 should start to stimulate the economy. Their suggestion was that the government should pump more money into the economy. This is a form of monetary policy known as 'quantitative easing'. At the same time the government could increase its own expenditure (a form of fiscal policy).

- Why was Christine Lagarde praising the UK's fiscal policy in 2010?

- What monetary policy recommendations was Christine Lagarde recommending for 2012?

- How does this case show that UK government policy is partly framed by its international responsibilities?

- What do you think George Osborne's view would have been about the advice being provided by the IMF?

 ## 8.12 Summary

Government plays a major role in the economy. Decisions made by the government and the economic policies that it pursues frequently impact on business. It is important to understand the thinking behind government policy and the implications of different policy decisions for business. The government has available to it a range of tools and techniques that cover many different areas of business activity. A key role of the government is in creating a competitive market environment both nationally and internationally. In addition the government needs to manage the overall economic climate through fiscal and monetary policies that should be designed to secure economic growth. In addition the government has a range of other policies which are dealt with in greater detail in specific chapters of this book.

KEY IDEAS

The roles of government in the economy

- The government has a number of roles in a market economy. These roles enable it to influence the nature and scope of the environment in which businesses operate.

The government as producer and employer

- The government plays a smaller role than in the period leading up to the 1970s in terms of overseeing the direct production of goods. However, it is still a substantial employer of public service workers (e.g. civil servants, teachers, health service workers, etc.).

The government as stabilizer of the economy

- The government can run a deficit budget in order to pump additional demand into the economy during a period of recession.
- Alternatively the government may seek to make markets work more efficiently in order to increase the supply of goods in the economy in a time of recession.

The government's role in creating competitive markets

- The government can seek, through legislation and government agencies, to create a competitive economy in which new firms are free to enter the market. Competition is most likely to be effective when restraints to trade and other restrictive practices are forbidden.

The government and market failure

- Market failure stems from failure to account for negative externalities, the existence of monopolies and other factors.
- Government can counteract market failures by using a range of tools including subsidies and grants, as well as taxes and fines to promote positive externalities and to discourage negative externalities.

The government's international role

- Government ministers and senior civil servants meet regularly with their international counterparts.
- The government can encourage trade to support exporting businesses.
- The government can work with international partners to create confidence in the international financial system – for example, by supporting its own currency and the currencies of trading partners.
- The government can seek to influence the exchange rate in such a way as to make UK exports competitive.

The government and equality in society

- As well as creating efficient markets the government should seek to foster fair markets including the reduction in inequality in society.

The government's industrial and regional policy

- Industrial policy typically focuses on accelerating the development of sunrise industries and softening the decline of sunset industries.
- Regional policy is concerned with seeking to create a balance in the growth and development of the various regions through targeted support.
- Some neoliberal economists argue that the best way of supporting industry and regions is by allowing competitive markets to flourish.
- The EU provides subsidies and grants for peripheral regions that have suffered most as a result of the integration of EU countries into a single market.

Macro-economic tools

- The government has available to it a range of tools to manage the macro-economy. These tools are dealt with in greater detail in other chapters.
- Fiscal policy is concerned with the relationship between government spending and taxes. It is also concerned with using specific aspects of government spending and taxes to target particular strategic objectives.
- Monetary policy is concerned with alterations in the supply of money and the interest rate on money as a means of causing changes in the macro-economy in line with government objectives.
- Other macro-economic tools include competition policy, industrial and regional policy, incomes policy, environmental policy and exchange rate and trade policy.

REVIEW QUESTIONS

1. Rank what you consider to be the government's top ten economic roles in order of importance. Explain your order of ranking.

2. How can the government seek to stabilize economic fluctuations resulting from the trade cycle? Is it appropriate to seek to stabilize the economy in this way?

3. How might the government's industrial or regional policy clash with its competition policy?

4. How can markets be said to fail? What actions can the government take to combat market failure?

5. How does the government operate as a producer and as an employer? To what extent has this role changed over time?

6. What is the national debt? Explain how the size of the national debt can change over time? What are the implications for the credit rating of a country?

7. Explain how and when the government might use: (a) accelerative and (b) decelerative industrial policies.

8. What actions can the government take to support regions where economic performance is relatively weak?

9. What is the difference between monetary and fiscal policy? How can the government use monetary and fiscal policy to stimulate the economy?

10. What is environmental policy? How can the government encourage the growth of new green industries?

RECOMMENDED READING

Elliott, L. and Watt, N. (2012) 'George Osborne Reeling as the Economy Enters the Disaster Zone', *The Guardian*, 26 July.

Office of Fair Trading (2009) *Making Markets Work Better in the Public Sector*, London, Office of Fair Trading.

Patel, R. (2011) *The Value of Nothing*, Portobello Books, London.

Read Chapter 5 of this book for an interesting overview of the role of government in economic society. Patel presents the view that the interests of government in the modern world are tied up largely with those of big business.

REFERENCES

Galbraith, J.K. (1987) *A History of Economics: The Past as the Present*, Harmondsworth, Penguin.

Keynes, J.M. (1936) *The General Theory of Employment, Interest and Money*, London, Macmillan.

USEFUL WEBSITES

www.gov.uk/government/policies – the site gov.uk provides an insight (from a government perspective) into all current government policies including economic ones.

9 Economic ideas and policy

CHAPTER OBJECTIVES

After carefully reading and engaging with the tasks and activities outlined in this chapter you should have a better understanding of:

- Some of the key strands of thinking that have influenced economics

- The central beliefs of classical economics

- Major developments in neoclassical economics

- Alternative Marxist perspectives

- How Keynes revolutionized economic thinking and policy-making

- The nature of the neoclassical consensus

- New ideas that have influenced economic thinking

9.1 Introduction

The economist John Maynard Keynes stated that today's economic policies and ideas are often shaped by some long dead economist. Economic ideas are influential long after they are first set out and strands of economic thinking which lose popularity in one period are frequently revived in another. Many of the ideas of current day supporters of the free market were first set out in a coherent structure by Adam Smith who was writing in the second half of the eighteenth century.

Keynes' own ideas were championed by Gordon Brown (the Labour Prime Minister) in the first decade of this century – including the idea of increasing the role of government spending during the economic crisis. In the United States the Federal Reserve (the central bank) engaged in successive phases of quantitative easing (i.e. the government making more finance available to the economy throughout much of the financial crisis). Keynes had recommended that one cure for a recession would be to bury money under the ground and then dig it up during periods of recession.

This chapter focuses on one of the key themes of this book – the economic ideas that underpin different views about how a market economy should be structured. In particular, economic ideas focus on the appropriate role for government – how much should the government intervene in the workings of the economy?

Business students need to have a clear understanding of the ideas that have shaped economics. Economic ideas are not neutral – they are based in some measure on points of view. You will see in this chapter that the classical and neoclassical economists are firm believers in the power of the market. The world in which they developed their ideas was one of growing prosperity, trade and specialization which they attributed to the workings of the market. In contrast, other contributors to economic thinking, including Keynes and Marx, were able to identify some of the weaknesses of reliance on the market. Keynes' and Marx's ideas were shaped in some measure by the evidence of widespread unemployment and inequality in the periods when their ideas were shaped.

At the end of this chapter we focus on some key strands of 'green' economics – ideas that have been developed in a period when environmental issues are all too obvious. Businesses are impacted by decisions that are made by policy-makers. The policy-makers' perspectives are substantially influenced by their take on what is significant in economic ideas.

9.2 The development of economic thinking

In the UK and US the development of modern economic thinking is usually traced back to the work of Adam Smith. Adam Smith was a Scottish economist whose most famous work has the title *An Enquiry into the Nature and Causes of the Wealth of Nations*. This work was published in 1776 during the period of the Industrial Revolution in this country and in a period of expanding international trade. Smith's text provided an explanation and justification of the growth of capitalist economies – resulting in the wealth of nations. To carry out his work Smith read extensively about new developments in trade and industry as well as visiting sites of industrial activity and commerce to get a better understanding of the processes taking place.

Smith's work established some of the key questions which economists today investigate in their research, particularly with regard to the role of government in the economy, problems associated with restrictions to free trade, and the supporting systems and frameworks required to enable the economy to grow.

It is essential for all business students to have a sound understanding of economic ideas. Economic ideas influence policy-makers and thus help to shape the policies they make. These policies then shape the macro- and micro-environments in which business decisions are made. The economic environment in Britain, Germany, Russia, Brazil, India, China and in every other country is different because governments and other decision makers have responded differently to economic ideas.

9.3 The classical economists

Karl Marx coined the term 'classical economics' to refer to the early economists Adam Smith, David Ricardo and John Stuart Mill who saw the market as providing the best way of coordinating the use of resources in society. Smith believed that if individuals pursued their own self-interest this would lead to the best solutions for society as a whole.

Classical economists – early economists who outlined a set of economic principles to support and describe the workings of the free market.

KEY TERM

Smith's work referred to an 'invisible hand' that guides the economy to arrive at appropriate decisions. Consumers are able to express their choices through the money that they are willing to spend on buying goods. For example, when you go to the supermarket to purchase £50 worth of groceries you will make personal calculations about which basket of goods will give you the greatest satisfaction. Thousands of other shoppers are making their own calculations.

Tesco, Sainsbury's and other supermarkets are able to analyse the data from millions of customers at their stores across the country to see what is selling well. These suppliers then make sure they provide customers with those items that sell well and generate most profit. The main aim of the supermarket chains will be to maximize profits. In seeking a profit they will provide customers with what they want. This market system (driven by what Smith regarded as an 'invisible hand') is a wonderfully efficient way of channelling resources in ways that meet customers' needs.

Smith's studies led him to demonstrate also how the economy benefits from specialization and the 'division of labour'. For example, he showed how specialization in a pin factory enabled the employees to produce large quantities of pins by each specializing in a particular process. They were able to produce far more than an individual producing pins on his or her own.

David Ricardo extended Smith's ideas to focus on the benefits to economies of international trade. He developed the 'law of comparative advantage' showing that the principle of specialization can be extended to trading between nations. Countries should focus

on those products where they have the greatest comparative advantage – for example, today Scotland concentrates on alternative energy (e.g. wave and wind power), whisky and water, whereas China concentrates on textiles and a range of manufactured goods.

Comparative advantage – a situation in which an individual, company, region or country can produce a good at a lower opportunity cost than a competitor.

John Stuart Mill developed the concept that individuals should be able to pursue their own particular aims and goals provided they did not harm or prevent others from pursuing their own interests.

From the brief outline set out above you should be able to appreciate the overall areas that the classical economists were justifying:

- The right of individuals to carry out economic activities for themselves in order to generate profit and other rewards;

- The importance of specialization and trade; and

- Emphasis on economic freedom rather than government control. This means that individuals in society are free to make decisions – for example, about what to spend their money on, whether to set up an enterprise, and how to run that enterprise – rather than having the government make these decisions on the behalf of citizens.

Reflective questions

Adam Smith (1776: 14) wrote the following:

> It is not from the benevolence of the butcher, the brewer, or the baker that we expect our dinner, but from regard to their own self-interest. We address ourselves, not to their humanity but to their self love, and never talk to them of our necessities, but of their advantage . . . Every individual is continually exerting himself to find out the most advantageous employment for whatever capital he can command. It is his own advantage, indeed and not that of society which he has in view . . . He intends only his own gain, and he is in this, as in many other cases, led by an invisible hand to promote an end which was no part of his intention. By pursuing his own interest he frequently promotes that of the society more effectually than when he really intends to promote it.

1 What do you think Smith meant by this? What are the implications for the way in which modern day business is conducted?

These ideas are very important because they continue to underpin some of the thinking of some modern day politicians and decision makers including the Conservative Chancellor George Osborne and Prime Minister David Cameron.

9.4 The Marxist economists

In the 1960s and 1970s the ideas of Karl Marx and other socialist writers such as Vladimir Lenin and Mao Tse-Tung were seen as providing a radical alternative way of thinking about the allocation of resources in society. Today, these thinkers are rarely mentioned in mainstream economics textbooks. However, it is still important to understand the significance of this body of work.

Those writers who were influenced by Karl Marx pointed to a fundamental flaw in capitalist models of development as outlined by Smith and the classical economists. Marx believed that there was a fundamental difference between the wage-earning class (the proletariat) and the capitalist owners of industrial capital (the bourgeoisie). The capitalist system was fundamentally based on the exploitation of the proletariat. Eventually this fundamental division in society would lead to a communist revolution after which resources would be placed in the hands of the people.

This theory seemed particularly apt during the first three quarters of the twentieth century when there were communist revolutions in Russia, China, Cuba and other countries. This led to the collectivization of resources, with most of the important economic decisions being made by government planning authorities. Other countries also adopted a similar socialist model – for example, in parts of Africa, South East Asia and to a certain extent in India.

However, in the 1970s such ideas were partially discredited as a result of the relatively slow growth of many economies that adopted such models, so that rather than the proletariat moving forward it seemed as if they were being economically disadvantaged (although their position in society as equal citizens might be seen to have advanced). Marxist economics provides a polar extreme to classical economics in that it is based on the centralization of economic decision making rather than being based on free markets.

9.5 The neoclassical economists

In the West (e.g. Western Europe, and the United States), from the 1870s onwards, economics came to be dominated by the neoclassical school of economists – William Stanley Jevons and Alfred Marshall in England, Leon Walras in Switzerland, John Bates Clark in America, Carl Menger in Austria and Hermann H. Gossen in Germany. The emphasis of these writers was very much on the micro-economy, examining ways in which individual markets, industries and consumers operate.

The neoclassical economists drew up an idealized picture of a rational economic individual making deliberate choices. They built up a theory of value based on decisions at the margin (the extra bit) of consumption.

Writing to his brother on 1 June 1860, Jevons wrote:

> as the quantity of any commodity, for instance plain food, which a
> man has to consume, increases, or the utility or benefit derived
> from the last portion used decreases in degree. The decrease of
> enjoyment between the beginning and end of the meal may be
> taken as an example. (Jevons, 1886: 51)

KEY TERM

Marginal utility – the additional benefit gained from the consumption of one additional unit of a commodity.

The neoclassical model is based on individualism, with the key economic actor being the individual rather than groups. Individual actions are determined (according to this approach) by rational deliberation (although there are boundaries to that rationality) with individuals seeking to maximize personal utility (well-being).

KEY TERM

Rationality – the belief that individuals make rational calculations, in this context in order to support economic decisions.

The sum of all of these individual actions, in an environment that is based on incentives (according to the neoclassical economists), can then be examined on an economy-wide basis. Incentives are based on relative prices, with individuals (producers and consumers) seeking to maximize benefits relative to outlays. Relative prices play a central role in making sure that there is no overproduction (wastage) of goods or undersupply (causing scarcity) through the process of supply and demand in the market place. In order to remain competitive firms are pressurized by the market system into being efficient.

The neoclassical economists argued that the rational consumer would consume extra units of a product until the value (marginal utility) of the marginal unit consumed was equal to its price (to consume more would lead to a loss of satisfaction because the income spent could be better spent on units of items yielding higher marginal utilities). The rational producer would produce extra units only so long as the marginal (extra) revenue from doing so was greater than the marginal cost.

The marginal revolution was applied widely across economics – for example, marginal productivity describing additional units produced by additional quantities of factors of production. Marginal productivity was also used to describe how wage levels were determined, the quantities of output that manufacturers would want to produce and so on.

In 1874 Leon Walras published his *Elements of Pure Economics* in French, which involved the development of the idea of general economic equilibrium set out in the form of a system of simultaneous equations. In his work he set out to link the various markets that make up the economy. The system that Walras built was based on a number of assumptions, including perfect competition between firms, freedom of entry of firms into the market, mobility of factors of production and price flexibility. In such a competitive system firms' revenues would be matched by their costs and consumers' incomes by their outlay on goods.

Neoclassical economists such as Walras were therefore building a model to illustrate the working of an efficient market system. It is important to understand that this system relies on the market being allowed to work smoothly, free from restrictions resulting from monopoly practices by businesses or needless restrictions imposed by governments.

Alfred Marshall, the Cambridge economist, provided some of the clearest explanations of neoclassical economics in his best selling text *Principles of Economics* (1890), which went through eight editions. One of his most important contributions was in creating the Marshallian Cross, what we today refer to as the demand and supply diagram showing how market prices are determined.

KEY TERM

The Marshallian Cross – a new way of looking at markets, created by Alfred Marshall. The Cross contains two elements: (1) supply – the quantity of a good that suppliers will bring to market at different prices; and (2) demand – the quantity of a good that consumers will want and be able to buy at different prices.

CASE STUDY A simplified explanation of Say's Law

Paul Davidson (1994: 14) sets out a simplified version of Say's Law in the following way:

> The sole explanation of why people produce, that is supply things to the market, is to earn income. Engaging in income-earning productive activities is presumed to be disagreeable. People will work only if they can earn sufficient income to buy the products of others that can provide them with sufficient pleasure to compensate for the unpleasantness of the income earning activity. If people are rational utility maximisers, then all income earned in the market by the selling of goods and services is spent to buy (demand) things produced by others. Say's Law implies that a recession or depression will never occur. The very act of production generates enough income, and demand, to produce everything produced. Businessmen seeking profits are always able to find sufficient demand for any output produced by workers.

- **Does the outline of Say's law set out above match your common sense understanding of how the world works?**

- **Are there any deficiencies that you can see in the above outline of Say's Law?**

- **If people work in order to earn to spend on goods produced in the market why might lack of demand occur leading to recession?**

While the neoclassical economists tended to focus on what we refer to today as micro-economic issues, and general equilibrium within and between markets, they also assumed that the macro-economy would tend towards full employment. This assumption was based on a piece of economic logic referred to as Say's Law, stemming from the work of the French economist Jean-Baptiste Say (1767–1832). Say argued that the process of supplying goods creates a demand for goods, 'The creation of one product immediately opened up a vent for other products' (Say, 2001: 57).

Using Say's simple piece of logic it appears that the economy will always be close to the full employment point because owners of factors of production (e.g. workers, capitalists, etc.) make their factor services available in order to spend their income on other products. In the short run a particular commodity might be oversupplied, but this will lead to a reduction in its price. While there may be some temporary unemployment in the economy, this will soon disappear as production adjusts towards goods that are in greater demand.

Neoclassical economics thus became the conventional orthodoxy up until the Second World War. As a discipline it became increasingly mathematics-bound although Alfred Marshall (a mathematician by training) had argued against this tendency, making the case for plain speaking and good communication in the presentation of economic ideas.

KEY THEME

The political dimension of classical and neoclassical economics

Neoclassical economists often developed a political dimension to their writing. For example, in 1944 the Austrian economist Friedrich Hayek published a famous short book with the title *The Road to Serfdom*. The road to serfdom that he was criticizing was government intervention in the free market.

Hayek, who had fled from persecution by the Nazis, saw the centralizing state as taking away individual freedom and liberty. Later on Margaret Thatcher was to become a keen supporter of Hayek's ideas. She is famously reported to have criticized a member of her government during a cabinet meeting. She banged a copy of Hayek's book on the table saying 'That is not what we believe in – this is what we believe in' (i.e. free market principles).

- An 'ideology' is a set of ideas that shapes a person's thinking about the world or key elements of the world about them. To what extent can belief in the free market be seen as an ideology?

- Why do you think that some people believe in a free market ideology?

- How is free market ideology likely to shape policy-making by governments that believe in this ideology?

- What are the implications for business of governments and other key decision makers having a free market ideology?

9.6 Keynesian economics

However, not everyone was happy with neoclassical economics. While it dominated conventional Western economics there were a number of dissenting voices. A major critique of Western development came from the influential figure of Mohandas K. Gandhi, who was deeply opposed to the pattern of exploitative resource use and ecological irresponsibility of capitalist economies. He painted an alternative approach to economics based on localization, and the meeting of people's needs at grassroots level, rather than the domination of the globe by huge multinationals. The path which he advocated struck a chord in India in the 1940s and continues to provide a focus for the green movement and for environmental economics.

The economist Knut Wicksell (1851–1926), while developing a broadly neoclassical analysis, was highly critical of assumptions that the market was fair and presented the case for government interference to address issues of inequality. Essentially he criticized the 'reality' of justifications for the neoclassical model, stating:

> As a matter of fact all argument in favour of free competition rests on one tacit assumption, which, however, corresponds but little to reality, namely that from the beginning all men are equal. If that were so, everyone would be equipped with the same working power, the same education and, above all, the same economic assets and much could then be said in favour of free, unhampered competition; each person would have only himself to blame if he did not succeed.
>
> But if all conditions are basically unequal, if some people have goods hands from the beginning and others hold only low cards, free competition does nothing to stop the former from winning every trick while the later pay the table. (Wicksell, 1953)

A major critique of Western economics stemmed from the Russian Revolution and the establishment of socialist planning in Eastern bloc economies in the early part of the twentieth century. The problem for Lenin (the revolutionary leader) and the new socialist system builders was that while Marx had provided them with a critique of capitalist society, he had not developed a model for a socialist state. The two major problems facing Lenin were those of accelerating economic growth and of planning. Adopting Marx's view that interest on capital represented exploitation, Soviet planners had no clear mechanism for allocating capital in a developing society. The socialist critique of capitalism was based on a belief that a 'just and equitable society' is the only appropriate means of building economic relations.

The most significant critique of neoclassical economics was mounted by John Maynard Keynes in his *General Theory of Employment, Interest and Money*. In his short first chapter to the book, Keynes wrote (1936: 3):

> I have called this book the General Theory of Employment, Interest and Money, placing the emphasis on the prefix general. The object

of such a title is to contrast the character of my arguments and conclusions with those of the classical theory of the subject, upon which I was brought up and which dominates the economic thought, both practical and theoretical, of the governing and academic classes of this generation, as it has for a hundred years past. I shall argue that the postulates of the classical theory are applicable to a special case only and not to the general case, the situation which it assumes being a limiting point of the possible position of equilibrium. Moreover, the characteristics of the special case assumed by the classical theory happens not to be those of the economic society in which we actually live, with the result that its teaching is misleading and disastrous if we attempt to apply it to the facts of experience.

Keynes' assertion was that the market clearing at the full employment level (as suggested by Say and the classical economists) was only one possibility among a range of other possibilities. He had lived through the 1920s and 1930s and the assertion that full employment was a natural state of affairs, as suggested by Say, appeared clearly at odds with the evidence in front of his eyes.

Keynes' view was that the level of national income and output was determined by aggregate demand in the economy, and that this fluctuated over time. The economy could therefore be at equilibrium with full employment, 1 million unemployed or 10 million people unemployed. Aggregate demand was determined by its components including consumer demand (which is a function of income), investment demand (determined by the marginal efficiency of capital and the rate of interest), government expenditure (determined by government policy) and the level of exports (determined among other things by the competitiveness of exports).

KEY TERMS

Aggregate demand – the total level of macro-economic demand (i.e. total demand by consumers) + total demand for investment purposes + government demand + (exports – imports).

Consumption – the total level of macro-economic demand by consumers (e.g. for immediately consumable goods such as food, as well as for consumer durable goods such as fridge/freezers and television sets).

Investment demand – the total level of macro-economic demand by firms for machinery, equipment and other items that add to production capacity.

Government demand – the total level of spending by the government both on consumption items such as free meals in public hospitals and schools, and also on public investment (e.g. the building of roads, and schools).

Keynes was a firm believer in the powers of the market in allocating resources in the micro-economy, for example in the *General Theory* he argued that 'there is no objection to be raised against classical analysis of the manner in which private self-interest will determine what is produced, in what proportions the factors of production will be combined to produce it, and how the value of the final product will be distributed between them' (1936: 378).

However, in terms of macro-economic equilibrium he argued in his *General Theory* that it would only be by chance that the economy would clear at the full employment point and that responsible government could not stand idly by and allow the sort of widespread unemployment of the 1920s and 1930s to reoccur. He therefore advocated government demand management. Keynes' book had a tremendous impact in unsettling neoclassical complacency about how to run a capitalist economy. Keynes' ideas were to become the dominant economic orthodoxy from the Second World War until the late 1970s.

Keynes' view of aggregate demand and aggregate supply can be illustrated in the following diagrams.

Keynes' aggregate supply curve

Keynes' aggregate supply curve illustrates the relationship between business people's expected sales revenues in the future and the quantity of labour they will hire to produce these expected future sales. The aggregate supply curve (AS) starts at zero and shows that if no sales are expected nothing will be produced. If £k of sales are expected then kN of workers will be employed, if £m of sales are anticipated then mN of labour will be employed etc.

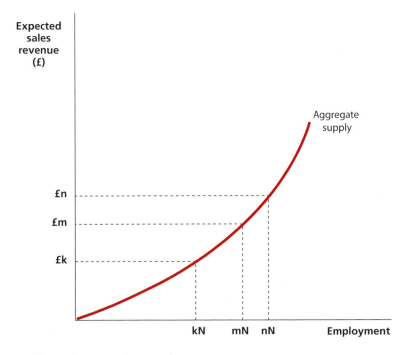

FIGURE 9.1 Keynes' aggregate supply curve

Keynes' aggregate demand curve

Keynes' aggregate demand (AD) curve shows how much spending will be carried out by all buyers at a given level of employment. Like the aggregate supply curve this is upward sloping. The higher the level of employment, the more income is earned and therefore spending on goods and services will increase.

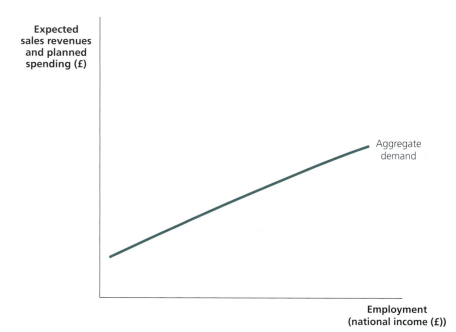

Figure 9.2 Keynes' aggregate demand curve

Combining the aggregate demand and aggregate supply curves

The aggregate demand and aggregate supply curves that Keynes envisaged are different. Where aggregate demand meets aggregate supply (i.e. at point E) we have equilibrium in the market.

However, this does not often coincide with the full employment point. Full employment is thus an exceptional case rather than a general case.

When Keynes set out his *General Theory* (in the 1930s) unemployment rates in the UK were very high in historical terms. In terms of diagrammatic representation we could illustrate this by assuming that the full employment point is at N2 whereas the current market equilibrium is at N1 (where N represents the number of workers employed). In order to close this gap planned spending (i.e. demand) needs to be higher. Where there is a general lack of demand Keynes believed that the government had to step in to raise demand levels within the economy.

The diagram below illustrates Keynes' aggregate supply and demand curves on the same diagram where equilibrium E is less than the full employment point.

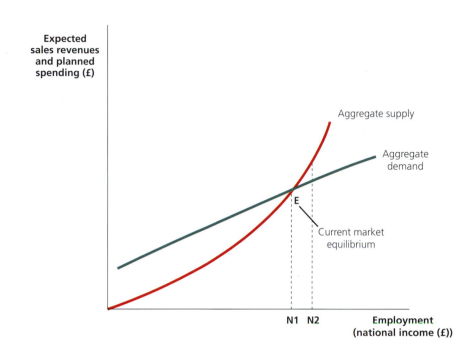

FIGURE 9.3 Combining aggregate demand and aggregate supply (showing unemployment)

Keynes' solutions to creating full employment were based on macro-economic management by the government, for example by:

- Raising government expenditure in a period of recession. The government wouldn't have to raise its own expenditure by the total shortfall. This is because, as we saw in Chapter 1, any new expenditure that takes place in an economy has a ripple effect referred to by economists as a multiplier effect. When the government spends more, for example in building a new school, then those that receive the building contracts and work on the building site will earn income which they will go on to spend.

- Lower government taxes in a period of recession. Lowering taxes leaves tax-payers with more disposable income. They will be encouraged to spend some of this income and again there will be a multiplier (ripple) effect.

9.7 The neoclassical consensus

James Tobin, one of the leading American Keynesian economists, argued the Keynesian case when he stated that:

> A strong case can be made for the success of Keynesian policies. Virtually all advanced democratic capitalist societies adopted, in varying degrees, Keynesian strategies of demand management after

World War Two. The period, certainly until 1973 was one of un-parallelled prosperity, growth, expansion of world trade, and stability. Unemployment was low, and the business cycle was tamed. (Tobin, 1997: 459)

However, hard line neoclassical economists were prepared to give little if any ground to the new Keynesian ideas. They argued that the market economy had failed to function in the inter-war period because of inflexibilities in the market. In particular they pointed to the powers of trade unions in preventing wages from adjusting in a downward direction in response to falling demand. The 1920s and 1930s were therefore explained away as a special case.

The Pigou effect was used by the neoclassical economists to explain how the economy would automatically move out of a recession. The Pigou effect (developed by Arthur Pigou) argues that when the economy goes into a recession wages and prices fall, leading to an increase in the value of purchasing power of a sum of money; if prices fall by a half, £1,000 will buy twice as much as before (i.e. what previously could have been bought for £2,000). People who hold money will therefore find that they can buy more than before with it and so will be encouraged to increase their expenditure. This will encourage businesses to produce more, helping to move the economy back to full employment.

In the United States the economists Alvin Hansen and his student Paul Samuelson popularized Keynesian ideas. Samuelson reworked a number of Keynes' ideas, such as the relationship between the multiplier and accelerator effects, and produced the best-selling economics text of all time, *Economics*, which has gone through numerous editions.

KEY TERMS

Multiplier effect – the knock-on ripple effect that results from an injection of new demand into the economy. The new spending is respent by the recipients of the extra income generated from the spending. This goes through a series of ripples, each of which is less strong than the previous one.

Accelerator effect – the impact of a change in consumer spending on firms' investments in capital goods. A relatively small change in the consumer goods industry typically has a more than proportional impact on the investment goods industry.

Samuelson used the term 'neoclassical consensus' to describe the way that he and other American economists had fused together neoclassical and Keynesian views of the market. The neoclassical consensus was based on a general belief that market-based models are the most effective way of allocating resources in the economy, but that government intervention is required at times to help the market to work more effectively.

9.8 The free market revival and monetarism

The nature of economic ideas is that they tend to reassert themselves after a period of time although in a different form. In the late 1970s and early 1980s, with the election of Margaret Thatcher as Prime Minister in Britain (1979) and President Reagan in the United States in 1980, there was a revival of classical and neoclassical economic thinking. Particularly influential in the new wave of thinking was Professor Milton Friedman from the University of Chicago. His ideas were set out in three important books: *Capitalism and Freedom* (1962); *A Monetary History of the United States, 1867–1960* (1963) (co-authored with Anna Schwartz); and *Free to Choose* (1980) (co-authored with Rose Friedman).

Friedman's ideas were particularly influential because he was adept at presenting his ideas in an understandable way to millions of people through newspapers and a television series as well as through his books.

Friedman's core belief is in economic freedom. In *Capitalism and Freedom* (1982: 10) he set out that:

> As liberals we take freedom of the individual, or perhaps the family, as our ultimate goal in judging social arrangements. Freedom as a value in this sense has to do with the interrelations among people.

Like Adam Smith, Friedman supported voluntary cooperation of individuals – the technique of the marketplace – as the best way of coordinating the economic activities of millions.

He saw this technique of coordination as being the best and only way of securing economic freedom, stating that:

> The possibility of co-ordination through voluntary co-operation rests on the elementary – yet frequently denied – proposition that both parties to an economic transaction benefit from it, provided the transaction is bi-laterally voluntary and informed. Exchange can therefore bring about co-ordination without coercion. A working model of a society organized through voluntary exchange is a free private enterprise economy – what we have been calling competitive capitalism. (1982: 14)

Friedman noted that in the 1920s and 1930s intellectuals in Europe and America were increasingly in favour of expanding the role of the state. They argued that with the development of democratic societies government could be used as an agent to make a better society. As the century moved on more and more people became convinced that economic tools such as Keynesian policies could be used to make the capitalist system work better through the benevolence of government.

However, by the 1960s Friedman was to reject this notion, and he argued the importance of weighing up the evidence for and against an increased role for the state. In his conclusion to *Capitalism and Freedom* he argued that:

> We now have several decades of experience with governmental intervention. It is no longer necessary to compare the market as it actually operates and government intervention as it ideally might operate. We can compare the actual with the actual. (1982: 199)

He argued that if this comparison is made, it is clear that government intervention has not had the desired result. While Marx and Engels had written in the *Communist Manifesto* that the 'proletarians have nothing to lose but their chains. They have a world to win', the reality was that workers in Russia had far less freedom than in any Western state. At the same time a whole host of government measures in Western countries had failed – for example, regulation of the railways to protect consumers had led to increasing monopoly powers for existing railway companies, support for farmers had led to the waste and embezzlement of funds, housing programmes had led to deteriorations in housing, social security programmes had led to rising numbers living off social security and so on.

However, Friedman did see government as playing a useful role in society. He states that:

> The existence of a free market does not of course eliminate the need for government. On the contrary, government is essential both as a forum for determining the 'rules of the game' and as an umpire to interpret and enforce the rules decided on. What the market does is to reduce greatly the range of issues that must be decided through political means, and thereby to minimize the extent to which government need participate directly in the game. (1980: 15)

Perhaps the most fundamental contribution Friedman made to economics was in his study (with Anna Schwartz) of the importance of the role of money in the economy.

Friedman and Schwartz's detailed study of the relationship between money and prices during the Great Depression provided evidence that the Federal Reserve in the US helped to increase monetary instability. Their view was that the US Federal Reserve failed to provide adequate liquidity when the demand for money increased in the US as a result of banking crises which led to a lack of confidence. The Federal Reserve had the power to increase liquidity but they failed to do so.

His study of the Great Depression shows that a contraction in the money supply by the central authorities lay at the heart of the crash. Friedman believed that the supply of money in an economy should be increased slowly in line with the growth of that economy. If the money supply is increased too slowly or held constant this leads to recession. If the money supply is allowed to increase too quickly this leads to inflation.

Friedman's simple rule therefore is that the money supply should be increased at a stable rate, regardless of the circumstances of the moment. It is based on two central principles:

1. The change in the money supply is the only key influence on the overall level of spending and economic activity; and that

2. In order for the central bank to create a climate that creates prosperity and stable prices it needs to increase the money supply in a stable and well-publicized manner at a rate related to the real rate of growth of the economy.

The period of the 1980s and 1990s saw a shift to free enterprise economics in most parts of the world. The emphasis by governments was in rolling back the influence of the state:

- Through the privatization of state companies and industry. Many of these were returned to ownership by private shareholders in the belief that this would encourage greater efficiency.

- The reduction of government regulation of business – simplifying legislation to enable more competition between business and less paperwork and restrictions.

The impact of these changes was to create a more dynamic private sector and fewer regulated economies.

 ## 9.9 The 'Third Way'

Greater economic freedom brings with it more opportunities for enterprise and individual dynamism. However, it also brings greater opportunity for corruption and malpractice. The mid 1990s were characterized by a number of political and business scandals resulting from lack of sufficient controls. In the political sphere the exposure of corruption by Members of Parliament led to an increasing loss of credibility for the Conservative Party in Britain, which at the time was championing free market economics. The stage was set for the arrival of a new form of political and economic thinking – the 'Third Way'.

In 1997, Britain elected a Labour Government with alternative views about how the economy should be run. This they labelled the Third Way. Whereas the previous Conservative government had focused on controlling the money supply in order to keep inflation down and the economy growing, the new Labour Chancellor, Gordon Brown, stressed the priority of economic policy as being that of abolishing unemployment. The watchword for the new government was on 'modernization'.

A key thrust of modernization policies was that the market must play a key part in macro- and micro-economic decision making. Firms need to operate in a competitive environment in which the state does not subsidize loss-making industries or artificially support some companies at the expense of others.

The Third Way was focused on unleashing enterprise and market forces in the economy while at the same time ensuring key social provision to support social policies, including the protection of weaker members of society. The emphasis under the Third Way was on bringing together the private and public sectors. For example, the government developed public private partnerships. Private finance initiatives (PFIs) involved enlisting the skills and expertise of the private sector in providing public services. The scheme encouraged private companies to be involved in the building and running of public services such as hospitals, colleges, railways and schools. The government would provide some of the finance with other components being provided by private companies.

Many PFI schemes were based on what is called DBFO (design, build, finance and operate). This means that the private sector partner is responsible for:

- Designing the facilities, although the requirements are initially specified by the public partner – that is the school, college or hospital, etc.;

- Building the facilities;

- Financing the capital cost (the private partner then makes a profit by taking an income from the public partner for providing the facility); and

- Operating the facilities, providing facilities management and support services.

KEY THEME

Anthony Giddens and the 'Third Way'

The concept of a Third Way as employed by the Labour Party, particularly under the leadership of Tony Blair, was articulated by Blair's teacher at university Anthony Giddens (and set out in a book *The Third Way*, 1998). *The Third Way* provided an alternative way of organizing economies, based on a belief that it was time to put an end to the 'class politics' of the past, and that it was possible to combine the market with the government's steering influence in a democratic society in which people were committed to shared community goals.

Giddens' book identified reasons why socialism and free market economics had failed, providing an opportunity for a new type of consensus. In explaining why socialism failed to have relevance he stated that:

> In hindsight, we can be fairly clear why the Soviet Union far from surpassing the US, fell dramatically behind it, and why social democracy encountered its own crises. The economic theory of socialism was always inadequate, underestimating the capacity of capitalism to innovate, adapt and generate increasing productivity. Socialism also failed to grasp the significance of markets as informational devices, providing essential data for buyers and sellers. These inadequacies only became fully realised with intensifying processes of globalisation and technological change from the early 1970s onwards. (1998: 4–5)

In explaining the failure of free market economics Giddens identified a basic tension between old-fashioned Conservatism, with its cautious and pragmatic view of the need for change, and modern free market philosophies that pin 'hopes for the future on unending economic growth produced by the liberation of market forces' (1998: 99–128). He argued that the permanent revolution of market change undermines traditional institutions and patterns within society, destroying the bonds that hold societies together.

Giddens sought to create a new agenda for social democratic states based on a framework of individual responsibility for society, and the community for the individual – this is generally characterized as the Third Way.

In the new democratic state, all members of society are expected to play a part and to take responsibility for their own actions.

TABLE 9.1 Locating the position of the Third Way

	Social democracy (old left)	Third way (centre left)	Free market economics (new right)
Political philosophy	Class politics of the left	Modernizing movement of the centre	Class politics of the right
Economic philosophy	Old mixed economy	New mixed economy	Market fundamentalism
Government philosophy	State dominating society	New democratic state	Minimal state
Welfare policy	Strong welfare state	Social investment state	Welfare safety net

Table 9.1 shows how the Third Way lies between the social democratic state of the old left, and free market economics as characterized by the Thatcher and Major years (1979–1997).

For Giddens, the modern state is a 'social investment state' which should enable the human agents to make the very best use of their skills and abilities, and to ensure that potentially able people do not become excluded but make a full and active contribution to the community. Groups that have traditionally been excluded consist of ethnic minorities, women, lesbian and gay people, the disabled, the lower working class, the over-50s and lone parents. Hence the Labour government introduced 'New Deals' for these people to give them every possible opportunity to be included in the community.

Complementing this vision is a social investment state that enables traditionally excluded groups to become included. For example, government should invest in projects to get the long-term unemployed back to work and invest in retraining traditionally excluded groups. However, there are certain lifestyles which the state may be tolerant towards, but which it is unwilling to fund. For example, people who choose not to work for a living should be allowed to do so, although they will not be allowed to make use of the social security system to fund the chosen lifestyle.

In essence, members of a society have a responsibility for each other and should rise to this responsibility rather than expecting the state or the market to provide the solutions for them.

- **How does the Third Way bridge the gap between a market ideology and the idea of a socialist state?**

- **What happens to the driving force of individual self-interest that was envisaged by Adam Smith in the social investment state?**

- **What is the role of government in the economy in the social investment state?**

9.10 New ways of thinking about the economy

The economic (and political) ideas that we have outlined so far in this chapter involve a fundamental 'big idea' about how to organize the economy:

- Classical and neoclassical economics – a belief in the free market as the driver of economic efficiency and the betterment of individual members of society.

- Keynesian economics – that the free market does not guarantee full employment, and that the government has to step in to manage investment expenditure in the economy to secure long-term growth and full employment.

- Marxist economics – that there is a fundamental division of interests between owners of capital and those that work for capitalists, which will ultimately lead to a crisis in capitalist society.

- The Third Way – a belief in a social investment state to support individual responsibility by members of society for themselves and their society.

These ideas are supported by politicians and political parties, for example:

- Margaret Thatcher (Conservative) was a free market fundamentalist.

- Gordon Brown (Labour) was a self-professed Keynesian.

- Tony Blair (Labour) was a key adherent of the Third Way.

Not surprisingly therefore, when the current Conservative group of the Conservative–Liberal Democratic Coalition presented their manifesto for election to Parliament in 2009 – they needed a 'big idea'.

There is some debate about how 'big' the ideas they chose actually were. The fundamental flagship idea presented in the manifesto was termed the 'Big Society' and was framed for David Cameron, the current Prime Minister, by Baron Nat Wei, who is a member of the House of Lords and the government Chief Advisor on Big Society. Wei is a social entrepreneur and social reformer.

Fundamentally the idea is based on a free market ideology of taking power away from politicians to give it to the people. Individual members of society are to be empowered to become free economic and political agents in society. Community groups and volunteers will be given more control in establishing priorities in relation to the provision of local services.

There are five main components to the Big Society idea:

1. To give communities more power to make decisions for themselves. Power is devolved from centralized to localized decision making.

2. People are to be encouraged to take an active role in their own communities (particularly through volunteering).

3. An ongoing transfer of powers from central to local government.

4. Support for the development of cooperative societies, mutual benefit societies, charities and social enterprises.

5. To make government decision making more open and transparent – particularly by producing a lot of information about government and its activities.

KEY TERMS

Cooperatives – organizations that are set up and run by their own members for cooperative purposes (e.g. manufacturing and retailing cooperatives, marketing cooperatives).

Mutual benefit societies – mutuals are groups who set up an organization for their joint benefit (e.g. to save money for and to build houses as a group).

Social enterprises – enterprises that are set up to achieve social and environmental needs.

However, there are a number of criticisms of the Big Society idea. One key criticism is that it is a rushed idea that hasn't been thought through clearly. While it contains some good ideas it is not a coherent set of ideas. Examples of good ideas include David Cameron's idea of creating a Big Society Bank based on drawing on funds in other banks that have lain dormant for long periods of time. The Big Society Bank will lend to charities, voluntary groups and social enterprises that can show that they will be able to repay loans from their ongoing income.

When the Big Society idea was launched it was initially to be piloted in four areas of the country including Liverpool. However, in 2011 Liverpool City Council pulled out stating that government cutbacks to the voluntary sector in this country meant that the scheme was not sustainable. Volunteers could not be expected to step in to paper over the cracks resulting from government cutbacks. Another criticism of the Big Society concept is that, coupled with current government free market ideology, it leaves members of society to 'sink or swim'.

A fundamental criticism of the Big Society is that it is based on communities taking over activities that were previously the responsibility of government. However, the government was not providing the skills and training to manage this transition. Volunteers and charities do an enormous amount of work already in society – they can't be expected to do more without the support and partnership of government.

In 2012 a new book, *Faith in the Public Square*, authored by the retiring Archbishop of Canterbury Rowan Williams, included a damning criticism of the Big Society:

> Introduced in the run up to the last election as a major political idea for the coming generation [it] has suffered from a lack of definition about the means by which such ideals can be realised. Big Society rhetoric is all too often heard by many as aspirational waffle designed to conceal a damaging withdrawal of the state from its responsibilities to the most vulnerable. (*The Observer*, 2012)

Green economics

Chapter 15 deals in greater detail with the development of 'green economics'. However, it is helpful to introduce some of the themes here as part of an important recent contribution to economic thinking.

In recent years serious attempts have been made by economists to build environmental considerations into the market mechanism. Some of the most useful work in this field has appeared in a series of books called the *Blueprint for a Green Economy* produced by a team of researchers working with David Pearce, which had a major influence on UK environmental policy.

Pearce and his co-writers asserted that a major policy objective should be to create sustainable development. But this is where the problem starts – most people agree that 'sustainable development' is a good thing but nobody is clear exactly what it means. A useful starting point was provided by the World Commission on the Environment in 1987: 'development that meets the needs of the present generation without compromising the ability of future generations to meet their own needs'.

Development is generally seen as something that is positive. It means being better off tomorrow than we are today. But what exactly is development? Measures such as GNP (gross national product) indicate the living standard of people measured in terms of quantities of goods that can be purchased, but there is a significant difference between the terms 'standard of living' and 'quality of life'.

Pearce suggests that sustainable development involves enhancing both the standard of living and the quality of life. The value of the environment is an important part of this quality of life. Pearce and his team therefore suggested that in moving forward we need to consider:

- The environment;

- The future; and

- Equity (fairness).

Pearce introduced the term 'futurity' to refer to the principle of taking a long-term view of things. If one generation leaves the next with less wealth than it inherited then it has made the future worse off.

We also need to think about the nature of this legacy. The history of recent development has often involved the conversion of 'natural wealth' (e.g. reserves of ores, oil and timber) into 'capital wealth' (e.g. factories, car parks and cinemas). Pearce suggests that it is not good enough simply to argue that growth is taking place because our 'stock of wealth' is increasing. Instead he argues that sustainable development involves leaving a legacy of capital wealth and natural wealth to future generations.

Pearce also argues that we need to address the issue of equity (fairness). This should involve tackling the issue of fairness between one generation and another (intergenerational equity) and between people living on the planet at the same time (intragenerational equity). If we fail to tackle the issue of equity we will never get agreement about how to tackle environmental problems. If some groups and countries create too much environmental pollution then this impacts on others at a global level.

Pearce argues that there is a pressing need to develop ways of valuing the environment. Many environmental resources do not have prices attached to them. It is therefore important that we should develop an idea of what the environment is worth – to place a proper value on the environment.

Much of Pearce's work therefore has been concerned with developing ways of giving a monetary value to the environment. This then enables decisions to be made which do not ignore the environment. For example, if we can accurately place a value on an environmental resource (e.g. an area of natural beauty) then it is possible to calculate the impact of spoiling that resource (e.g. by building a motorway across it).

Pearce argues that monetary measures of environmental values can be used to reflect the strength of support for an environmental asset (e.g. by asking people how much they would be willing to pay to protect an environmental asset such as a blue whale or a beauty spot). Provided that the support in monetary terms is big enough, this presents a strong case for preserving the environmental quality.

Of course, there are strong criticisms of this approach. Many critics argue that it is nonsense to place a value on the environment. For example, some critics suggest that we can't treat the environment as a good that can be broken up into separate parcels and traded off. However, if we don't put a price on the environment there is a very real danger that we will continue to destroy it as we did in the twentieth century.

A major difficulty in valuing the environment is that different people will place different values on it according to their perspective. There has always been a split between those concerned with the environment and those pushing for fast economic growth, and the environment may be given a low priority by those who see other needs as being more pressing – for example, there may be business concerns from those worried about losing competitive advantage when environmental controls are tougher where they are producing compared to where competitors are producing. Governments of developing countries may argue that their priorities are to put food into the mouths of starving people rather than to focus on global environmental demands.

The problem with valuing the environment through the marketplace is that those in favour of the approach are seen as apologists for the market system and that they continually downgrade the value of the environment. Those that place a high value on the environment are opposed to conventional ways of placing a monetary value on the environment because some of them are philosophically opposed to treating the environment as a commodity that can be bought and sold.

In a market economy it is likely that the only way that the environment will be accounted for is by attaching a price to environmental degradation and impacts. In a market economy the government can use taxes and subsidies to place valuations on the impact of environmental effect – for example, by making polluters pay for the quantity of pollution they create and by taking environmental costs into account in new building projects.

Increasingly the environment is being accounted for and businesses are increasingly accountable for the impact they have on the environment. In company reporting large businesses are expected to include a business review. For most large companies the business review will include a section in which they recount their corporate responsibility policies and programmes. A corporate social responsibility (CSR) report involves a business setting out in a transparent way the impact that it is having on the environment as well as other aspects of CSR such as ethical sourcing of products and what the business is doing in the communities that it serves.

We return to examine the nature of sustainable business and green economics in Chapter 15.

 ## 9.11 Summary

This chapter has provided you with an overview of many of the key themes that underpin economic thinking. The chapter has focused on the works of some of the key thinkers in the field to show how economic ideas have developed over time. Many of the key ideas focus on the issue of the effectiveness of the market system as a way of organizing economic relations between firms, household and government. The chapter shows how the ideas of economists have been applied by politicians to create the organizing principles around which economic relations were structured in particular periods of time.

The classical and neoclassical economists focused on explaining and validating the market system. Keynes and other writers have sought to identify ways of modifying the market system so as to make it more sustainable. Understanding economic theory is essential to all business students because it helps to provide a clearer picture of how economic decisions impact on business.

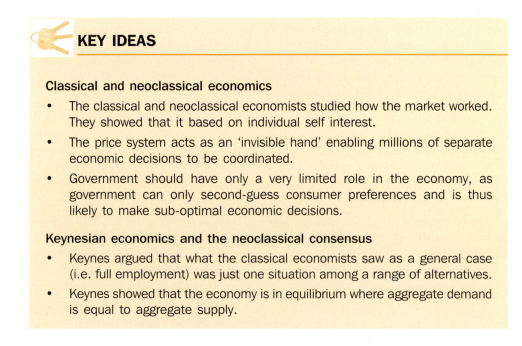

KEY IDEAS

Classical and neoclassical economics

- The classical and neoclassical economists studied how the market worked. They showed that it based on individual self interest.
- The price system acts as an 'invisible hand' enabling millions of separate economic decisions to be coordinated.
- Government should have only a very limited role in the economy, as government can only second-guess consumer preferences and is thus likely to make sub-optimal economic decisions.

Keynesian economics and the neoclassical consensus

- Keynes argued that what the classical economists saw as a general case (i.e. full employment) was just one situation among a range of alternatives.
- Keynes showed that the economy is in equilibrium where aggregate demand is equal to aggregate supply.

- In order to achieve full employment and a growing economy it is necessary for the government to intervene in the market to secure sufficient investment to act as a motor for long-term growth. The government should compensate when private sector investment is insufficient to secure full employment.

- Keynes saw fiscal policy as being a vital economic tool.

Monetarist economics

- Monetarists believe that management of the money supply is the most effective tool for controlling the economy.

- Friedman showed that the money supply should increase by a small and predictable rate in line with the growth of the economy.

- Monetarists believe that government intervention in the economy goes against the principles of allowing consumers freedom of choice and leads to inefficiency.

The Third Way and the Big Society

- Third Way policies were implemented by Tony Blair's Labour government in line with the teaching of Anthony Giddens.

- The Third Way is a middle route between the market economy and a socialist economy.

- The Third Way is based on individual responsibility supported by a social investment state.

- The Big Society is the approach that has been adopted by the Conservative–Liberal Democratic Coalition government.

- The Big Society involves the reduction in the role of government and the increase in decision making by community groups and volunteers.

- Big Society ideas have been criticized for combining the idea of greater voluntary responsibility but coupled with less support from government.

Green economics

- Green economics involves incorporating environmental considerations into economic decision making.

- David Pearce has proposed economic policies that place a value on the environment.

- By placing values on environmental resources they are likely to be used more effectively and efficiently in the market economy.

REVIEW QUESTIONS

1. What is a free market? What did Adam Smith see as being the role of the free market in society?

2. What were the key developments in neoclassical economics that built on the earlier work of the classical economists?

3. Contrast the roles of monetary policy and fiscal policy in Keynesian and classical economic theory.

4. How did Keynes' view of full employment differ from that of the classical economists?

5. What was Keynes' view of the role of the state in the management of the economy?

6. What is the relationship between economic ideas and economic policy-making? How then are economic ideas likely to impact on business?

7. Contrast the views of the role of individuals in the Third Way social investment society and in the Big Society.

8. To what extent is the concept of Big Society congruent with that of free market capitalism?

9. How is the Third Way consistent with: (a) free markets; and (b) government intervention in the economy?

10. How can the market take account of environmental degradation and pollution?

RECOMMENDED READING

Friedman, M. and Friedman, R. (1980) *Free to Choose*, Chicago, University of Chicago Press and Penguin Books.

> This book gives a very clear outline of free market economic thinking. The text is based on a series of television programmes produced by Friedman for a public audience.

Dransfield, R. and Dransfield, D. (2008) *Key Ideas in Economics*, Cheltenham, Nelson Thornes.

> This book is designed to introduce readers to the development of economic ideas from Adam Smith to the present day. It introduces the writings of the economists whose works are outlined in this chapter.

Skidelsky, R. (2009) *Keynes, The Return of the Master*, London, Penguin.

> This book outlines the work of John Maynard Keynes and shows how it is relevant in a world of financial crisis.

REFERENCES

Davidson, P. (1994) *Post Keynesian Macroeconomic Theory: A Foundation for Successful Economic Policies for the Twenty-first Century*, Cheltenham, Edward Elgar.

Friedman, M. (1982) *Capitalism and Freedom*, Chicago, University of Chicago Press, (first edition 1962).

Friedman, M. and Friedman, R. (1980) *Free to Choose*, Chicago, University of Chicago Press and Penguin Books.

Friedman, M. and Schwartz A.J. (1963) *A Monetary History of the United States, 1867–1960*, Princeton, Princeton University Press.

Giddens, A. (1998) *The Third Way: The Renewal of Social Democracy*, Cambridge, Polity Press.

Hayek, F. (1944) *The Road to Serfdom*, London, Routledge.

Jevons, H.A. (ed.) (1886) *Letters and Journals of W. Stanley Jevons*, London, Macmillan.

Keynes, J.M. (1936) *The General Theory of Employment, Interest and Money*, London, Macmillan.

Marshall, A. (1890 [1920]) *Principles of Economics, An Introductory Volume*, 8th edition, reprinted 1961, London, Macmillan and Co. Ltd.

Marx, K. and Engels, F. (1998) *Communist Manifesto*, New York, Penguin.

Observer, The (2012) 'Rowan Williams Pours Scorn on David Cameron's "big society"', *The Observer*, 24 June.

Pearce, D., Markandya, A. and Barbier, E. (1989) *Blueprint for a Green Economy*, London, Earthscan.

Say, J.B. (2001) *A Treatise on Political Economy: Or the Production and Distribution of Wealth*, translated from the 4th edition, Kitchener, Batoche Books.

Smith, A. (1776) *An Inquiry into the Nature and Causes of the Wealth of Nations*, republished (1976), edited by R.H. Campbell and A.S. Skinner, Oxford, Clarendon Press.

Tobin, J. (1997) 'How Dead is Keynes?', *Economic Inquiry*, 15 (4): 459–68.

Walras, L. (1874) *Elements of Pure Economics, or the Principles of Social Wealth*, 1954 translation of 1926 edition, Homewood Illinois, Richard Irwin.

Wicksell (1953) *Value, Capital and Rent*, translated by S.A. Frowein, London, London School of Economics.

Williams, R. (2012) *Faith in the Public Square*, London, Continuum.

USEFUL WEBSITES

You can watch two excellent videos online outlining the ideas of Keynes and Friedman.

www.youtube.com/watch?v=D3N2sNnGwa4 – Friedman 'Free to Choose' video.

sms.cam.ac.uk/media/761745 – 'John Maynard Keynes: Life – Ideas – Legacy'.

10 Economic indicators

CHAPTER OBJECTIVES

After carefully reading and engaging with the tasks and activities outlined in this chapter you should have a better understanding of:

- The importance of economic indicators for economists and business analysts
- Measurements that are used to record the growth of the economy
- Key measures of employment and unemployment and what they tell us about economic efficiency
- How inflation can be measured through the consumer price index
- The significance of the dependency ratio for a growing economy
- The importance to business of interest rates
- How the exchange rate affects an economy and businesses
- The importance of other economic indicators

10.1 Introduction

Macro-economic analysis involves working with economic indicators to find out what changes are taking place in important economic variables and to get a better understanding of the relationship between these variables. Some of the most useful economic indicators are constructed from data collected by the Office for National Statistics.

This chapter outlines the nature of some of the key indicators and shows what they measure. For example, changes in gross domestic product (GDP) can be used to measure economic growth and changes in the consumer price index can be used to measure inflation. Studying changes in key economic indicators will give you a much better grasp of fundamental changes taking place in the economy. Business analysts should regularly monitor economic indicators to get a better understanding of changes taking place in the economic environment.

10.2 What are economic indicators?

Economic indicators are things that can be measured that tell us something about what is happening in the wider economy. Just as in a car you have gauges showing the amount of petrol in the petrol tank, the oil level and the engine temperature, so too we have indicators which show the overall growth of the economy, the level of inflation, the unemployment level and so on. These indicators are very helpful to economists and to analysts planning the strategy of a business.

Many of the statistics that are used to construct economic indicators are collected by the Office for National Statistics (e.g. changes in employment and jobs, and changes in prices of goods). Other statistics are collected and recorded by the Bank of England, other banks, and the Treasury.

On 12 July 2012 the opening page of the UK Office for National Statistics website revealed the following key statistics:

- GDP –0.3 per cent

- Consumer price index (CPI) 2.8 per cent

- Unemployment rate 8.2 per cent

Reflective question

1   What do you think the three economic indicators set out above indicate? Note that the first one shows a minus figure.

In the sections that follow we will outline the significance of these three indicators which relate to the growth of the economy (changes in GDP), changes in average prices (changes in the CPI), and the rate of unemployment in the economy.

KEY TERMS

The Office for National Statistics – the UK's largest independent producer of official statistics and the recognized national statistical institute in the UK. The mission statement of this organization is 'Trusted statistics – understanding the UK'.

Bank of England statistics – (available at www.bankofengland.co.uk/statistics) The Bank of England compiles and publishes a range of monetary (e.g. the interest rate) and fiscal (e.g. details of government taxes and spending) statistics. These include domestic banking statistics, external financial statistics and international banking statistics.

Economic indicators are particularly important to business, for the following reasons:

- When the economy is growing (increasing GDP) then there is more demand for the outputs of business as a whole.

- When prices are rising by small and steady amounts then business can make plans for the future and anticipate rising revenues.

- When unemployment rates are at levels where there is some surplus labour then businesses know that they will be able to recruit at least some types of labour without having to bid up wages.

The student of business knows that a key tool for business planning is the PEST analysis. A PEST analysis involves a business carrying out a detailed analysis of how changes in the political and legal environment, the economic environment, in social trends, and in the development of new technologies impact on the business. A key part of the tool is the 'E' part – the economic analysis. Economic analysis typically involves identifying changes and trends in economic variables that are set out in economic indicators. Therefore all business students need to have an understanding of economic indicators and what they represent.

10.3 Indicators that show the growth of the economy

In broad terms when an economy is growing this is good for business as the population will be spending more money. The economic indicator that is used to measure the growth of the economy is GDP.

An important part of the work of some economists involves the study of changes in the economy over time. We can measure whether the economy is growing and the pace of growth of the economy. One of the most widely used methods of doing this is to plot changes in GDP over time. GDP is a measure of the total output produced in an economy in a particular period, such as a year or quarter. It is the most common measure of national income and indicates how an economy is growing. Rises in GDP indicate that the value of goods being produced is increasing.

Comparisons of GDP can be made over time. Table 10.1 uses statistics based on the World Factbook to compare GDP in Nigeria in 2011 with 2009.

TABLE 10.1 Illustrating growth of GDP in Nigeria

	2009	2010	2011
GDP (US$ billions) purchasing power parity	356.7	387.8	414.5

Purchasing power parity – the purchasing power parity (PPP) approach is a way of making comparisons between standards of living in different countries. In simple terms this is calculated by working out what each item in a country would cost if sold in the US in US dollars.

There are several ways of measuring GDP. The important thing is to use a method that yields accurate results.

The output method

This involves adding up the output produced by the various industries in the economy. In Nigeria:

- Agricultural output makes up about 35 per cent of GDP;

- Industry makes up about 33 per cent of GDP; and

- Services make up about 31 per cent of GDP.

It is important not to double-count outputs. For example, some agricultural crops will be processed into packaged and tinned food. To avoid double counting, statisticians only count the value added by each industry (and not inputs that have already been counted once).

Double counting – when a figure is counted more than once (e.g. the value of part of the output of a final goods industry also being counted when it was produced and sold by an intermediate industry such as a producer of raw materials).

The expenditure method

Add together the final spending on outputs produced by a country. There are four types of spending:

1. Consumer spending (by households on goods and services);

2. Investment spending (by businesses on premises, machinery and equipment);

3. Government spending (on goods, services and investment); and

4. Net exports (the difference between exports and imports).

Nigerian GDP is the output of the Nigerian economy, including exports to other countries. Spending by Nigerians on imports is deducted from GDP because the spending leaves Nigeria to be spent on the output of foreign countries. Nigeria typically runs a trade surplus – it exports more goods than it imports largely as a result of its extensive oil revenues.

The income method

This involves adding together the incomes earned for producing all the goods that year. Only incomes earned for producing outputs are included. Therefore, 'transfer payments' such as pensions and unemployment benefit are not included because no work was produced to earn those incomes. The main type of income in Nigeria (and other countries) comes in the form of wages and salaries, although other incomes such as profits, interest and rent are also important.

GDP per head

The figure for GDP per head of population is probably more informative than the total value of GDP, but it does not take account of the way income is spread out or distributed between the different income groups in the population.

Nigeria has Africa's highest population, with about 150 million people. The GDP per head is $2,600 (2011 estimate). This is one of the lowest figures for GDP per head on an international scale (148 out of 195 countries). In Nigeria there is considerable inequality on a regional, and individual, basis. In a business context it is important to understand figures for GDP per head because they provide us with important information about household income and the likely disposable income which will translate into consumer spending power.

> **GDP per head/per capita** – GDP calculation which involves dividing the national income (GDP) by the number of people in a particular country. It shows average income per head.

KEY TERM

Growth in GDP

Economists have identified cycles of economic activity – periods of faster growth, followed by periods of slower growth, as well as some time when the economy is contracting. When the economy contracts, we term this a recession (a period in which GDP falls for two successive quarters).

The illustration below identifies the growth of the UK economy from 1970 to recent times. Since the 1980s Britain has typically experienced growth of the economy when making comparisons with earlier time periods. You can see that in many years the economy was growing at a rate of between 1 and 2 percentage points per year.

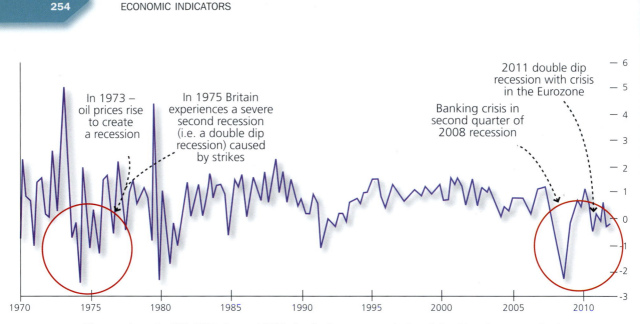

FIGURE 10.1 Fluctuations in UK GDP from 1970 (including two periods of double dip recession)

Growth is good for business. In a period of growth spending increases, this encourages people to build their businesses, expand capacity and produce more goods. However, during periods of recession we experience falling levels of output, incomes and expenditure.

A good example of a recession is that which occurred between 1973 and 1976. This was a period of shock for the world economic system. This was fundamentally caused by an increase in oil prices. Oil producing exporting countries (OPEC) grouped together to restrict the quantity of oil supplied to international markets (in order to raise prices). They were successful in raising prices but this led to a worldwide recession. It is not difficult to understand why.

Energy is a central cost for most businesses. A rapid rise in oil prices led quickly to rising business costs. Businesses responded by raising their prices but the knock-on effect was a fall in demand for the products that businesses were supplying. They were forced to cut back production and employ fewer workers – leading to a recession. As prices rose workers demanded higher wages and in cases where their demands were thwarted many took strike action. In 1975 the UK was faced by a second 'double dip' recession. Output fell month by month for almost a year in 1973 and also fell consistently in 1975–1976.

In 1980, when Margaret Thatcher's government came into power cutting back government spending, Britain narrowly avoided another double dip recession.

Most recently we have experienced a double dip recession in 2008–2009 and at the end of 2011–2012 resulting firstly from a financial crisis and then from the prolonged crisis in Eurozone countries such as Greece, Spain, Ireland and Portugal (countries that Britain exports to).

The cause of the most recent economic crisis has been explained in the following way:

> The immediate cause of the great unravelling was the so-called 'sub-prime' market, which was in itself nothing new. It was one aspect of the market that lent money to poorer people, at higher risk of default, in return for higher rates of interest. It had previously been a whole industry carved out between door-to-door loan sharks, shunned by the mainstream lenders. The big banks had been criticised on both sides of the Atlantic for failing the third of the population they considered unworthy for credit. But instead of expanding their own operations to cover them, they invested in 'sub prime' companies to mop up the marginally bankable instead, and foremost among these was HSBC.
>
> So it was hardly surprising that it was HSBC that revealed, in February 2007, that they were setting aside extra funds to cover bad debts in their American sub-prime lending portfolios. On the same day, one of the biggest sub-prime lenders in the USA, New Century in California, experienced a catastrophic loss of confidence after revealing a quarterly loss. . . .
>
> What had happened was that the investment banks believed they had discovered a way for mortgage lenders to lend money to poorer people at high rates of interest, but at negligible risk. What they did was to bundle the loans they had made together with a range of other loans from other markets, with varying degrees of risk, and sell them as safe investment. Then they could lend money from the sale to more investors and so on. (Boyle and Simms, 2009: 5)

Just as in the mid-1970s the economic crisis of 2008–2009 was caused by a shock to the economic system. The impact of the shock has led to a fall in spending, income and output.

The impact of recession

For many countries the impact of recession has, among other things, been an increase in government debt.

Recession – a period when there is a fall in GDP for at least two quarters.

KEY TERM

During the good years of economic boom governments are able to increase spending on a range of projects (e.g. better roads, hospitals and schools). For example, in the period immediately leading up to 2008–2009 the government had set money aside for school regeneration – some new 'super schools' with a huge building investment.

An important part of government spending is based on borrowing. If lenders believe that government will pay them back they will lend to governments at relatively low rates of interest. Each week the government issues government bonds to cover borrowing. The financial markets are pleased to lend the government money because governments are usually seen as being reliable repayers of loans.

However, once the shock to the system materialized then governments like other borrowers were in trouble. With the economy moving into recession government taxes started to fall, leading to bigger and bigger government deficits (the gap between what a government spends and what it receives in taxes). Financial institutions therefore became more reluctant to lend governments money, and governments found it more difficult to pay back what they had borrowed.

As a result credit agencies have increasingly downgraded the credit rating of governments. The most desired credit rating a government wants is Triple AAA status. If you are a Triple AAA borrower then you can borrow for a lower rate of interest. The lower your rating the higher the rate of interest you will have to pay.

CASE STUDY The impact of business on the economy

This section has focused on the impact of changes in GDP on business. In a boom businesses as a whole stand to benefit. In a recession the business sector tends to suffer. However, it is also important to appreciate that businesses themselves make a significant contribution to the growth of the economy. Efficient business operations making popular products help an economy to grow. This point is illustrated clearly through the development of the Apple iPhone 5 in late 2012.

At the time of its launch a number of economists pointed to the potential of the product (the iPhone 5) and the company (Apple) to provide a real boost to the US economy and help to pull the economy out of recession. For example, the Chief economist for JP Morgan, Miahael Feroli, predicted that the iPhone 5 might add between a quarter and a half percentage point to the country's GDP. Writing to JP Morgan's clients Feroli asserted that: 'Sales of iPhone 5 could boost annualized GDP growth by $3.2 billion, or $12.8 billion at an annual rate.'

His calculations were based on previous successes of the Apple iPhone, and industry specialist predictions for sales. In making the calculations he counted the value of the sales and subtracted any costs of buying in imported components to produce the phones. (It is important to note that some economists were more cynical, suggesting that any increases in sales of iPhones would at least in part lead to falling sales of other products.)

- Why is a company such as Apple so important for the US economy?

- Can you think of a UK-based company whose sales are likely to have a significant impact on GDP for the UK?

- How does an increase in GDP from the activity of a single business lead to a ripple effect across the economy as a whole?

- How might business activity collectively help to stimulate GDP?

Triple AAA rating – international credit rating agencies such as Moody's and Standard and Poor's attach a rating to national governments (in the same ways as credit ratings are given to businesses and individuals). A Triple AAA rating is the highest level of financial security showing that the government of that country is financially secure and likely to be able to repay all borrowing. Once countries become less stable they can be downgraded (e.g. to A– or lower).

Comparisons of living standards

While GDP may be helpful for measuring some aspects of the growth of the economy it is not necessarily an effective measure for making comparisons of living standards.

GDP measures the total value of goods produced in an economy in a given period of time. Until the 1970s, GDP was widely regarded to be a good measure of living standards. The argument was that if an economy produced more goods then people in that country would become better off. GDP and GDP per head were regarded as good ways of measuring the economic growth of a country.

It might be claimed therefore that the economic indicator GDP would be a good way of:

- Measuring the growth of economies over time; and
- Making a comparison between the levels of production, income and spending between countries.

CASE STUDY Comparing countries

The World Economic Outlook Database, April 2012, provided the following ranking (see Table 10.2) of the top ten countries in the world in terms of GDP (purchasing power parity) $ million.

- Why is the US top of the world GDP indicators table?

- What would a country need to do to move up the GDP indicators table?

- Why might the GDP indicators table not give a clear picture of how well off individual people are in the countries listed?

- Is measuring GDP a good way of measuring economic growth and comparing standards of living in different countries? Give reasons for your answer.

TABLE 10.2 Top ten countries in the world in terms of GDP

Rank	Country	GDP ($m)
1	United States	15,094,025
2	China	11,299,967
3	India	4,457,784
4	Japan	4,440,376
5	Germany	3,099,080
6	Russia	2,383,402
7	Brazil	2,294,243
8	United Kingdom	2,260,803
9	France	2,217,900
10	Italy	1,846,950

Criticisms of using GDP as an economic indicator

Since the 1970s there has been a lot of criticism of linking GDP with standards of living:

- It does not take into account inequality in society. For example, the Brazilian economy grew rapidly in the first decade of the twenty-first century compared with other smaller countries. However, Brazil has one of the highest levels of income inequality in the world. The richest 10 per cent of Brazilians receive 50 per cent of GDP while the poorest 10 per cent receive less than 1 per cent. Most countries around the world have not been very successful in reducing inequality in recent years. For example, a report published by Oxfam in Britain in 2012 reported a sharp increase in inequality in recent years. In 2011, while the earnings of FTSE 100 executives went up by 49 per cent the annual pay of waiters and waitresses fell by 11 per cent. The average director of one of Britain's top 100 companies was earning 145 times more than their average worker. So although GDP per head in a country might rise over time, prosperity does not necessarily make much difference to the living standards of poorer people.

- GDP simply measures the value of goods produced. GDP calculations do not take into account the harmful effects of growth, such as pollution and waste. A country that produces more food does not necessarily produce healthy food. Cigarettes are counted as 'goods' even though they create lung cancer and other illnesses.

- GDP calculations are not very good at making comparisons between countries. This is because GDP is usually calculated within a country using the currency of that country. For example, GDP in South Africa is measured using the South African Rand (ZAR), but the value of the Rand may change over time against other currencies.

- Standard of living is not the same as quality of life. People may have more goods but they are not necessarily better off or happier. In recent years, economists have suggested that a person's quality of life depends on a range of factors, including being healthy, being free from stress and worry or living in a pleasant climate – all factors that are not measured by simple GDP calculations.

A happiness indicator

Many economists are coming round to the belief that a good way of measuring well-being in society is through a happiness indicator. As part of a process of collecting statistics in the UK the Office for National Statistics now asks respondents to rank between 1 and 10 how satisfied they are with life, how happy did they feel yesterday, how anxious did you feel yesterday and to what extent do you feel that the things you do in your life are worthwhile?

This happiness survey is part of a survey of 200,000 people. Statisticians use these findings coupled with 'objective' measurements, such as life expectancy and wealth to measure the well-being of the population and to assess the impact of government policies on well-being.

Using this approach is thought to have advantages over simply measuring GDP because how well off people feel depends on such things as their health and whether they have a job (things not traditionally measured by GDP). Studies by the Office for National Statistics in Britain showed that things that matter most to people are health, relationships, work and the environment.

An important finding from research into well-being was the beneficial effect of 'altruism' on people giving their time to volunteer.

Altruism – unselfish concern for the welfare of others.

A happiness or well-being index is not just useful as a measuring tool. It is also helpful in that it is indicative of the sorts of policies that can increase well-being. For example:

- Improving the mental health of the long-term unemployed could help them find work;
- Protecting parks and green spaces raised people's wellbeing; and
- Reducing pressure on families would help increase children's happiness.

Other indicators have been used as alternatives to measure well-being. For example, the 'popsicle index' was developed in the United States to measure the number of people in a particular neighbourhood who believe that it is safe for a child in that area to go and buy an ice lollipop from a local shop unaccompanied by an adult.

The human development index

The human development index (HDI) is a broader method of measuring quality of life. The well-known economists Mahbub ul Haq and Amartya Sen led a team of economists that developed this for the United Nations Development Programme.

The HDI contains three elements:

1. Standard of living, as measured by GDP per head.

2. Life expectancy at birth.

3. Education as measured by: (a) adult literacy (given a weighting of two thirds); and (b) primary, secondary and tertiary enrolment in education (given a weighting of one third).

Achievement in each of these three areas is measured by how far a country has gone in attaining the following goals:

- Real GDP per head of US$40,000. Real GDP is the value of goods produced in a given period when we have taken out the effects of price rises caused by inflation.
- Life expectancy of 85 years.
- Adult literacy and enrolments of 100 per cent.

KEY THEME

The UK's happiness index

The current Liberal Democrat–Conservative Coalition government has encouraged the development by the Office for National Statistics of a happiness index in the UK. The first results were published in July 2012. The results are based on a survey of 165,000 people as part of the annual population survey. People were asked to reveal their rating of 'life satisfaction'. The study found that the average rating in Britain is 7.4 out of 10. 80 per cent of people gave a rating of seven or more when asked the question 'Are things that you do worthwhile?' Anxiety was seen as a negative indicator – again anxiety levels were scored out of 10.

Survey results indicated that satisfaction is highest among 16–19 year olds and 65–69 year olds.

The results of the survey suggest that relationships are important in life satisfaction. 82 per cent of people in marriages or civil partnerships gave high or medium life satisfaction ratings, 71 per cent of single people and 60 per cent of divorced people. Women rated slightly higher than men on both the 'life satisfaction' and 'worthwhile' questions but reported an average of 3.3 for anxiety compared with 3 for men.

● **Do you think that measuring happiness is a more reliable or less reliable way of measuring well-being than GDP?**

● **Do you think that using a happiness index would make it possible to measure changes in well-being over time?**

● **Do you think that measuring 'happiness' should be considered an appropriate economic indicator?**

These goals have not yet been fully attained by any country, so the actual indicators are expressed as decimal shares of the ideal. Therefore, 0.5 represents halfway towards the goal. The HDI score for any country is measured between 0 and 1. The highest score is 1.

Using human development indices, countries are ranked into four categories: very high, high, medium and low. Table 10.3 shows some of the countries in the very high, medium and low categories, with their ranking in brackets and the HDI score as a decimal.

For example, Norway consistently ranks number one in the HDI, with an index of 0.943 in 2011. This figure is derived from statistics which show that, for example on:

• Health – Norwegians have a life expectancy at birth of 81.1 years (2011).

• Income – the GNI per capita in international dollars (2011) was 47,557.

• Gender inequality – the gender equality is high (with a difference of only 0.075 in 2011).

TABLE 10.3 Human development indices for some countries

Very high	HDI	High	HDI	Medium	HDI	Low	HDI
Norway (1)	0.943	United Kingdom (28)	0.863	Barbados (47)	0.709	Malawi (160)	0.493
Australia (2)	0.929	United Arab Emirates (30)	0.846	Iran (88)	0.782	Senegal (166)	0.464
New Zealand (3)	0.910	Poland (39)	0.813	Maldives (95)	0.773	Burundi (174)	0.394
Germany (9)	0.905	Lithuania (40)	0.810	Jamaica (100)	0.766	Chad (175)	0.392
Japan (12)	0.901	Portugal (41)	0.809	Algeria (104)	0.754	Niger (182)	0.340

Source: United Nations Human Development Indicators, 2011.

Reflective questions

2   Countries with an HDI of more than 0.9 are classified as very high, those between 0.8 and 0.89 as high, between 0.5 and 0.79 as medium and under 0.5 as low. Is it possible for a country to experience economic growth while at the same time experiencing a fall in its HDI?

3   The Chinese government has recently reduced its economic growth targets so as to focus more on reducing the environmental impact of growth. What is likely to be the impact on the HDI in China?

ACTIVITY

Do some research to find where the following countries are ranked and what their HDI score is: Greece, Argentina, Cuba, Zambia, Brazil, Sri Lanka, Malaysia, Kuwait, the United States and Mexico.

Criticisms of HDI are that it fails to take into account the impact of economic growth on the environment. The economist Bryan Caplan has criticized HDI as concentrating on too narrow a range of indicators. He says that HDI is a measure of how Scandinavian your economy is because it focuses on areas such as education and health care, which countries like Norway and Sweden do particularly well.

In some countries HDI is also measured in areas of the country. In India HDI is measured for each of the country's states, and even for different districts within the states. This enables national and regional government to identify areas of great hardship and to use this as a basis for providing support. The Indian government also places particular emphasis on measuring infant mortality and this, rather than life expectancy at birth, is sometimes used as an indicator.

An alternative way of looking at development is the human poverty index (HPI). This was created by the United Nations, which regards it as a useful way of measuring human deprivation. It includes indicators such as the proportion of the population living below the poverty line and the rate of unemployment.

HPI is often regarded as a more accurate measure of deprivation than HDI in highly developed countries because it takes account of those living below the poverty line. For the purpose of the index, these are people whose incomes fall below half the average (median) disposable income in the country.

10.4 Employment indicators

Another important type of indicator that is helpful to economists are figures relating to employment, unemployment and the breakdown of employment. This indicator is particularly important because it tells us something about the productivity of the economy. Where people are employed they are contributing to GDP and the welfare of the nation. Where they are not working they are dependent on those in work. Generally speaking an economy will be efficient where there is a high proportion of people in work and the economy will be less efficient where there is a higher proportion of people who are unemployed. There are a number of useful definitions used as indicators of the impact of employment on the economy.

KEY TERMS

Claimant count – the number of people who are claiming Jobseeker's Allowance (a form of unemployment benefit).

Employment rate – percentage of those of working age in work. In Britain this relates to the percentage of the population aged 16 to 64 who are available for work.

Employment – measures the number of people in paid work and differs from the number of jobs because some people have more than one job.

Unemployment rate – those without a job who want a job.

Numbers in full-time employment – number of people in full-time jobs.

Numbers in part-time employment – number of people doing part-time jobs.

In the UK information about employment figures can be easily accessed online from the Office for National Statistics' 'Labour Market Statistics'. This publication is updated every month to reveal important trends. For example, statistics are published for the employment rate among 16 to 64 year olds, the number of people in employment, the unemployment rate and the number of unemployed people. Other indicators include comparisons of figures for public and private sector employment. The bulletin also shows changes in average earnings of people in work and labour productivity. Other statistics make comparisons between males and females in employment and regional differences in employment and unemployment rates.

Recent trends in employment indicators in the UK

An increase in the proportion of part-time jobs at the expense of full-time jobs

As the economy grows over time you would expect an ongoing increase in the numbers of full-time jobs as well as part-time jobs. In fact over time there has been an ongoing increase in the number of part-time jobs at the expense of full-time work. This is illustrated in Table 10.4.

TABLE 10.4 Illustrating the growth of part-time employment in the UK in recent years

	Employees working full-time (000s)	Employees working part-time (000s)
Jan–Mar 2010	18,127	6,557
Jan–Mar 2011	18,385	6,672
Apr–Jun 2011	18,415	6,678
Jul–Sep 2011	18,269	6,520
Oct–Dec 2011	18,243	6,610
Jan–Mar 2012	18,199	6,685

Disproportionate numbers of female workers in part-time jobs

Further analysis of the figures also reveals that full-time work is more typically carried out by male employees, whereas part-time work tends to be dominated by female employment.

For example, in the period January–March 2012 the employment figures could be broken down as follows:

- Males in employment: full time 11,071; part time 1,427.

- Females in employment: full time 7,077; part time 5,138.

However, to get a clearer picture of how effective the economy is in utilizing human resources it is often more helpful to look at unemployment rates. The claimant count measures the numbers of people seeking Jobseeker's Allowance on the second Thursday of each month. The claimant count for April 2012 was 1.616 million, which was 4.9 per cent of the population.

Further calculations are made to find out unemployment by age and duration. This can be a particularly damning indicator – for example, when it can be shown that a relatively high percentage of people aged between 25 and 49 have been out of work for a relatively long time.

ACTIVITY

Investigate Table (2) unemployment by age and duration from the latest version of 'Labour Market Statistics' (available online) to find out what groups of the population are typically unemployed for the longest periods of time.

Changes in the relative proportion of public and private sector workers

Another area that is of interest to economists is the relative scale of employment in the private and public sectors of the economy.

There is an ongoing debate about the suitable scale of the private and public sectors:

- Supporters of the free market (including many members of the Conservative Party in Britain and the Republican Party in the US) believe that the government sector should be as small as possible. The belief is that public sector workers are less productive and that the economy is more efficient with a larger private sector.

- Supporters of the important social and economic role of government (more closely associated with the Labour Party in Britain and the Democratic Party in the US) believe that government employment provides a group of public servants who provide essential economic, welfare and administrative benefits for society as a whole.

Table 10.5 illustrates the relative size of the public and private sectors in the UK during a recent time period.

The figures in Table 10.5 coincide with a period of deliberate manipulation of employment in the economy by the Coalition government. The Liberal Democrat–Conservative Coalition cut back government spending and hence employment in national and local government. Part of the argument for doing so was a belief that the private sector would be able to absorb job losses from the public sector.

TABLE 10.5 Changes in the relative size of public and private sector employment between 2009 and December 2011

	Public sector		Private sector	
	(000s)	%	(000s)	%
Dec 2009	6,352	22.0	22,490	78.0
Mar 2010	6,323	21.9	22,539	78.1
Jun 2010	6,292	21.6	22,853	78.4
Sep 2010	6,263	21.5	22,858	78.5
Dec 2010	6,212	21.3	22,947	78.7
Mar 2011	6,180	21.1	23,059	78.9
Jun 2011	6,054	20.8	23,115	79.2
Sep 2011	5,979	20.5	23,128	79.5
Dec 2011	5,942	20.4	23,173	79.6

CASE STUDY The 2010 spending review

The 2010 spending review was a significant landmark in setting out the Coalition government's perspective on reducing the size of the public sector. In a period of looming double dip recession the Conservative Chancellor George Osborne set out one of the most substantial programmes of government spending cuts for decades, including cuts in welfare spending, local council spending and police budgets. The government also raised the pension age and reduced benefits to poorer households. The Chancellor justified the cuts as encouraging fairness, reform and growth.

The spending review involved cutbacks to government departments of an average 20 per cent. The Chancellor justified the cuts by making the claim that the previous Labour government had been spending too much and the country could not afford to have such extensive welfare programmes and such a large public sector at a time of international economic hardship. In his statement he made the claim that: 'Today is the day when Britain steps back from the brink, when we confront the bills from a decade of debt. . . . It is a hard road but it leads to a better future' (HM Treasury, 2010).

The cutbacks were designed to involve the reduction of 500,000 public sector jobs by 2014–2015. The government argued that the private sector would step in to create new jobs to take up the slack in the public sector. The cutbacks would enable tax reductions to businesses and to households that would encourage the growth of the economy. George Osborne also claimed they would help to reduce government debt and restore international confidence in the British economy.

- Identify two economic indicators mentioned in the case study that would be significant for businesses. How might changes in these economic indicators impact on businesses?

- Why do you think that the Chancellor introduced the cutbacks? To what extent do you think they are based on 'economic thinking' and to what extent are they based on 'ideology' – and what do you think is the 'ideology' on which the decisions might have been taken?

- Can you see any potential drawbacks that might result from the 'cutbacks'?

Participation rates

The number of people available to work in an economy depends on:

- The number of people within the working age range; and
- The number of people within that age range who are prepared to participate in work.

This is the participation rate:

$$\text{Participation rate} = \frac{\text{Number who are prepared to work}}{\text{Number within working age range}}$$

The participation rate is important because it is indicative of the size of the available labour force in an economy.

The industrial structure

Another way of examining patterns of employment is to look at the industrial structure of an economy. Table 10.6 gives some statistics for the UK, from December 2011 (source ONS). In examining the table please compare the total number of jobs with the number employed in total in service industries. This shows that the UK is primarily a service sector employer, although manufacturing industries are also highly important (as are primary industries such as agriculture).

From the table it is possible to contrast primary activities (e.g. agriculture, forestry, fishing, mining and quarrying – items A–E) with secondary activities (e.g. manufacturing and construction – C–F) and services (G–S):

TABLE 10.6 Numbers employed in different UK industries December 2011

Standard industrial classification	Numbers employed (000s)
All jobs (A–S)	31,537
A. Agriculture, forestry and fishing	420
B. Mining and quarrying	62
C. Manufacturing	2,514
D. Electricity, gas, steam and air conditioning supply	135
E. Water supply, sewerage, waste and remediation services	192
F. Construction	2,055
G. Wholesale and retail trade; repair of motor vehicles and motorcycles	4,778
H. Transport and storage	1,483
I. Accommodation and food service activities	2,047
J. Information and communication	1,235
K. Financial and insurance activities	1,111
L. Real estate activities	422
M. Professional, scientific and technical activities	2,468
N. Administrative and support service activities	2,492
O. Public administration and defence; compulsory social security	1,618
P. Education	2,698
Q. Human health and social work activities	4,022
R. Arts, entertainment and recreation	874
S. Other service activities	914
G–S Total services	26,160

- Extractive/primary industries use natural resources.

- Secondary industries use raw materials from the extractive industries to produce finished goods.

- Services provide services to people, to other businesses and to government.

As a modern advanced economy the UK is primarily a service provider.

10.5 Inflation indicators

Average prices are measured by governments using the CPI and the retail price index (RPI). The indices measure changes in average prices over a year. Measurements are made by recording prices of goods and services that most people will be expected to buy, or put in an imaginary shopping basket. Government statisticians decide what goods to include in this basket. The list should be updated to take account of changing spending patterns.

Price index – a measure of the average level of prices of a selected set of goods and services compared to the prices of the same goods and services in a particular base year.

Consumer price index (CPI) – an indicator that measures the change in the cost of a fixed basket of goods and services including housing, food and transport. It is collected and calculated on a monthly basis. Can also be referred to as a cost of living index.

Retail price index (RPI) – an indicator measuring changes in prices but does not include housing costs.

A basket of goods

The imaginary shopping basket for a typical family in the UK contains about 650 items from the categories listed in Table 10.7. The percentage figure shows the broad weight attached to a specific category based on the percentage of income a typical household will spend on items in this category (figures are for 2010).

The typical basket of goods for the UK shows the consumption pattern in a sophisticated modern economy. The item at the top of the table is transport, which not only includes car purchase, maintenance and fuel but also expenditure on rail, bus and other forms of transport. Spending on recreation and culture will include gym memberships, spending on watching sports fixtures and purchasing theatre and

TABLE 10.7 Weighting attached to goods in the UK price index

Sector	Weighting (%)
Transport	16.4
Recreation and culture	15.0
Housing and household services	12.9
Restaurants and hotels	12.6
Food and non-alcoholic beverages	10.8
Furniture and household goods	6.4
Clothing and footwear	5.6
Alcohol and tobacco	4.0
Communication	2.5
Health	2.2
Education	1.9
Miscellaneous	9.7

cinema tickets. Over time some of the weights attached to particular categories and products will alter. For example, in the recession people are spending less on restaurant meals and more on cooking at home.

KEY TERM

Weighting – the weighting is a figure given to a category of goods according to the percentage of a typical household's income that is spent on it.

A price index

A price index uses a single number to indicate changes in prices of a number of different goods. This is calculated by comparing the price of buying the basket of goods with a starting period, called the base year. The base year is given a figure of 100. So if the average price of goods in the basket today is 10 per cent higher than the base year, the price index will be 110. Changes in average prices (the cost of the basket of goods) can be measured on a monthly, quarterly or annual basis.

Inflation

Inflation is a persistent or sustained rise in the general level of prices over a period of time. So not every price will rise, but average prices will. The effect of this rise on ordinary people will vary depending on what they buy.

Price inflation in the UK is calculated by the Office for National Statistics once every month. One of the responsibilities of the Office for National Statistics is to decide on the 650 goods and services to be included in the price index, or 'basket'. The selection is made after carrying out a survey of spending patterns – what typical families in the UK are buying. From time to time new items will enter the basket and old items (that are now less commonly bought) will be taken out of the index. Price movements are measured in around 150 randomly selected areas throughout the UK. Around 180,000 separate price quotations are used every month to compile the indices. The outlets in which the prices are collected are selected randomly (the weights are held constant for one year at a time).

Statistics covering the prices of all items in the CPI are carefully gathered across the UK.

KEY TERMS

Average annual rate of inflation – computed as a percentage change of a 12-month average of the CPI.

Year-on-year inflation rate – calculated as a percentage change of the CPI between the current month (e.g. November 2012) and the same month a year ago (e.g. November 2011).

The Office for National Statistics carries out some detailed analysis of changes in inflation rates to pick out trends. For example, take a look at the figures in Table 10.8 showing changes in the CPI from July 2010 to July 2011. Note that comparisons are being made over one month, over 12 months and with the base year (2005).

TABLE 10.8 Consumer price index (CPI) – United Kingdom

		Index (UK, 2005 = 100)	% change over 1 month	% change over 12 months
2010	Jul	114.3	−0.2	3.1
	Aug	114.9	0.5	3.1
	Sep	114.9	0.0	3.1
	Oct	115.2	0.3	3.2
	Nov	115.6	0.4	3.3
	Dec	116.8	1.0	3.7
2011	Jan	116.9	0.1	4.0
	Feb	117.8	0.7	4.4
	Mar	118.1	0.3	4.0
	Apr	119.3	1.0	4.5
	May	119.5	0.2	4.5
	Jun	119.4	−0.1	4.2
	Jul	119.4	0.0	4.4

Source: Office for National Statistics.

Looking at the figures it is clear that comparing the end of the period with the start there has been a steady increase in the rate of inflation from 3.1 per cent to 4.4 per cent.

The Office for National Statistics also carries out more detailed analysis of specific categories to find out which ones are rising and which are falling and why – and whether this is based on expected seasonal trends or is unusual.

KEY TERM

Harmonized index of consumer prices (HICPs) – how the CPI is known internationally. HICPs are calculated in each member state of the European Union. HICPs are used to compare inflation rates across the European Union. The European Central Bank (ECB) uses the HICP as the measure of price stability across the euro area.

Calculating average price changes

Calculating average price changes will give the rate of inflation. The calculation involves two sets of data:

1. The price data (collected each month); and

2. The weights (representing patterns of spending, updated each year).

With this data it is possible to construct a weighted price index.

Price index – shows how much the price of a given item has risen compared with a base year of 100. The weighted price index shows the price index times the weight attached to the product category.

A consumer spending survey has been carried out that shows the percentage spend of typical households in an imaginary country. Table 10.9 shows how the percentage spend forms the basis of the weighting given to the categories. Note that the weighting for food is twice that for clothing because typical households spend twice as much on food as on clothes.

TABLE 10.9 A weighted table

Category	Percentage spend	Weight
Food	40	4
Clothing	20	2
Transport	10	1
Other household goods	30	3
Total	100	10

The next stage is to identify price changes in each of these product categories. Let us suppose that surveys carried out in supermarkets, shops and other retail outlets across the country show the following changes since the base year:

- Food prices have increased by 20 per cent;

- Clothing prices have increased by 10 per cent;

- Transport prices have fallen by 10 per cent; and

- Other household good prices have increased by 30 per cent.

To find out the average change in price we need to take account of each of these price changes in terms of how much consumers spend on that item (the weight). For example, the increase in food prices of 20 per cent will have a major impact on average prices

TABLE 10.10 A weighted price index

Product category	Weight × Price index	Weighted price index
Food	4 × 120	= 480
Clothing	2 × 110	= 220
Transport	1 × 90	= 90
Other goods	3 × 130	= 390
Total		1,180

because 40 per cent of household income is spent on food. In contrast, even though transport prices have fallen by 10 per cent, this will have a smaller impact on average prices because consumers only spend a tenth of their income on transport.

To create a weighted price index we need to multiply the weight for each item by the price index for that item, shown in Table 10.10.

Finally, divide the weighted price index by the total number of weights:

$$\frac{1180}{10} = 118$$

This shows that prices have risen on average by 18 per cent (i.e. from the base year figure of 100 to 118 in the new year).

Problems involved in using a price index

The price index is designed to show general increases in prices and how they affect consumers. There can be problems, however, with its use as an indicator:

- The index does not necessarily show how price changes affect some groups of consumers. For example, in Kenya food is allocated a weighting of 40 per cent. However, there are a substantial number of people who spend 80 per cent or more of their income on food.

- The index makes comparisons with a base year. However, if prices were low at the base year the comparison may exaggerate the price rise. If prices were high at the base year the index comparison may suggest that subsequent price changes have been low (especially if the base year is at the top or bottom of the trade cycle fluctuation).

- Some items, for example fuel and food, are subject to quite a lot of variation.

For indicators to provide useful information it is essential that the statistics gathered are accurate.

Track the inflation rate by regularly checking (each month) figures provided by the Office for National Statistics on their website, or alternatively by tracking reports about inflation in the newspapers.

ACTIVITY

Reflective questions

4   Why do businesses need to monitor the inflation rate in an economy?

5   Why should businesses factor inflation rates into business calculations?

The impact of inflation on business

Inflation is regarded by economists as one of the main factors distorting the economy and creating uncertainty. This section identifies some of the consequences of inflation for business and for groups that make up the economy.

Mild inflation of 1 or 2 per cent is not particularly harmful because it encourages producers to supply more to the market. When inflation rises more quickly it can disrupt economic decision making because it becomes difficult for businesses, governments and ordinary people to make plans. Inflation results in a loss of value of units of currency. The reverse of inflation is deflation, when prices start to fall. Deflation (negative inflation) discourages businesses, which may restrict supply to markets.

CASE STUDY Deflation in the summer of 2012

In the UK, June and July 2012 were characterized by some very bad summer weather with weeks of rain. The Queen's Diamond Jubilee was expected to create additional sales for retailers but the rain acted as a dampener. Figures produced by the Office for National Statistics showed that sales grew by just 0.1 per cent in June – they had been forecasted to rise by 0.6 per cent. This occurred at a time when the UK was already in recession. The four-day Jubilee weekend had no significant impact on sales.

A number of retailers reported falling sales. For example, Halfords blamed the bad weather for a 10.5 per cent fall in sales (compared with the previous period a year earlier) in bicycles, camping and leisure products in the quarter leading up to June.

The Office for National Statistics stated that retailers were forced to cut prices to tempt shoppers. Clothing sales increased by 2.5 per cent but retailers had been forced to cut the price of clothes by an estimated 3.5 per cent.

- How might deflation be as big a problem for an economy as inflation?

- Why might deflation coupled with recession be a particularly worrying trend?

- Use the concept of elasticity of demand to explain why clothes retailers will have suffered in the summer of 2012.

Businesses may suffer in a period of inflation. A lot of business activity involves supplying goods on credit, perhaps to other businesses. Payment may be required one month, three months or six months later. When money starts to lose value quickly, businesses become reluctant to supply on credit. Therefore, inflation is very harmful to business activity.

Ideally business requires stability and gently rising prices to encourage growth and investment. The American economist Milton Friedman (Friedman, 1968, also see Chapter 13) believed strongly that inflation distorts and disturbs the way markets work. His empirical studies of inflation revealed that as the rate of inflation increases so too do fluctuations in changes in the rate. This creates great uncertainty for those seeking to make rational economic decisions. The market works best when buyers and sellers are able to make price comparisons. When it is not clear what prices are and how they are likely to change in the future this causes real uncertainty in the minds of economic agents. They may defer making some of the decisions that they would make if there was greater certainty and they may make errors in the decisions that they make. The net result is that markets become less efficient – often leading to falling output and rising unemployment.

Other groups in the economy also lose out in a period of inflation:

- Savers. Many people like to save money each month for future needs. Their savings may be deposited in a bank or kept in a safe place. However, during a period of inflation savings lose their value. When the money comes to be spent it is not worth as much as when it was first saved. Similarly, money saved in a pension scheme can lose value by the time the saver becomes old enough to draw on it. The net effect is that during a period of inflation people may cut back on savings, choking off a supply of funds to business.

- Low-income households. Low-income households are also likely to suffer in a period of inflation. They may be poorly paid workers who are not in a trade union. Workers who are unskilled and so have less bargaining power, such as office cleaners and car park attendants, also suffer in times of inflation. Skilled workers in well-paid jobs may be able to bargain with their employers to receive wage increases. This is often the case for people who work for the government, civil servants, teachers, the police and armed forces.

The competitiveness of the economy can also suffer. An economy that suffers from relatively high levels of inflation compared with its competitors will become less competitive. The price of the country's exports will rise faster than substitute goods in international markets. For the countries with higher rates of inflation their balance of trade in goods and services will deteriorate.

10.6 Population indicators

Demography is the study of population. Demographers are interested in the relative sizes of populations in different countries, how population compares with available resources and the distribution of populations (e.g. into male and female or by age category).

The population of England and Wales increased by 3.7 million between 2001 and 2011 according to the 2011 census.

Census – the counting of the population and the characteristics of the population. A full census is carried out every ten years (e.g. 2001, 2011, 2021, etc.).

KEY TERM

Key reasons for the latest increase in population are:

- Increased life expectancy;

- Sustained immigration; and

- Robust fertility levels.

The population of England and Wales in 2011 stood at 56.1 million. Coupled with the population of other parts of Britain the total population was about 63 million. England is one of the fastest growing countries in Europe and London in particular has grown so that now over 8 million people live there, a rise of 850,000 from the previous census.

The 2011 census also revealed the extent of the ageing population. One in six people in England and Wales is over 65. One of the most rapidly growing sections of the population is the over-90s, which will soon be over half a million. The under-5s have also increased substantially in numbers by 400,000 since 2001 to 3.5 million.

The optimum population

For economists the optimum population –the ideal or best population size – has the 'best' ratio of people to other resources. The optimum population depends on the availability of other resources. Some countries are underpopulated – they do not have enough people to use existing land, capital and other resources efficiently.

An ageing population occurs when the average age in a region or country increases. This is currently happening in many countries across the globe including the UK. Key economic problems associated with ageing populations include:

- An increase in the dependency ratio – there are fewer people working and paying taxes, and they must support more older people who may be receiving state pensions, so there is increased government spending on health care and pensions.

- Higher taxes for those in work, which could discourage them from working so hard.

- A shortage of workers, which could push up wages leading to wage inflation.

In Germany in 2010 there were four workers supporting each retired person. By 2020 the ratio could be down to 2:1.

KEY TERM

Dependency ratio – a measure of the proportion of the population which is composed of dependants (e.g. those too old to work and those too young to work) compared with those in the working population. A rough indicator (in the UK) might be: Population under 16 + Population over 64 / Population aged 16–64.

Of course this is blurred by factors such as changes to working ages by recent legislation.

KEY THEME

Dependency in London?

The 2011 census showed that the population of London had grown by 850,000 in a decade. Does this mean that London has a greater problem of dependency (i.e. a higher dependency ratio) than the rest of the UK? Actually this is not the case. A population pyramid compares the numbers of males and females in different age categories in a country or territory. Each bar in the pyramid represents five years and the length shows the population in that age category: the age distribution. The structure of the pyramid is determined by births, deaths and migration.

The shape of the population pyramid in England and Wales is typical of that for a developed country (see Figure 10.2):

- Low death rate
- Lower birth rate
- Long life expectancy

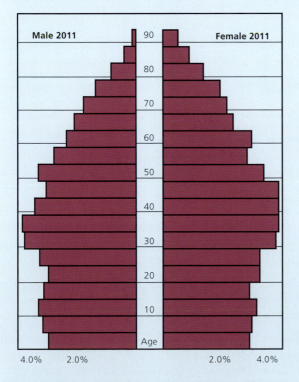

FIGURE 10.2 Population pyramid for England and Wales (2011)

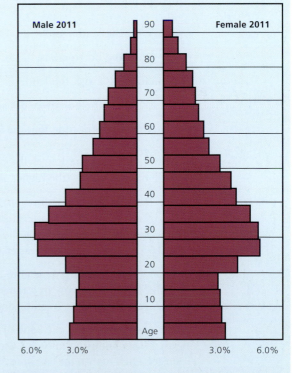

FIGURE 10.3 Population pyramid for London (2011)

However, if we examine the population pyramid for London in 2011 we see a different picture (see Figure 10.3).

● **How does London's population pyramid differ from that for England and Wales?**

● **How would you explain the reasons for the differences in the two pyramids?**

● **What does this tell us about the dependency ratio in London compared with England and Wales?**

● **What are the implications of the population pyramid in London for employers seeking labour and employees looking for work?**

10.7 The interest rate

More detail is provided about interest rates in Chapter 13. The interest rate is the price that businesses pay for borrowing money. There is not just one interest rate but many depending on:

* Who the lender is;

* Who the borrower is;

* How big a risk the lender is taking;

* Whether the borrower has some form of security to put up against the loan; and

* The length of time that the loan is taken out for.

In simple terms the longer the period the loan is taken out for, and the bigger the risk the lender is taking, the higher the rate of interest will be.

The Bank of England is in charge of the government's monetary policy. In recent years the interest rate has been used as a weapon to combat inflation or to encourage macro-economic expansion. During the recession the interest rate has been kept at a record low of 0.5 per cent to make it easier for business and consumers to borrow.

The rate of interest is crucial to businesses because most of them borrow to finance the business. They borrow in a range of ways – for example, in the form of bank loans and overdrafts, and most small businesses use their credit cards as a major source of funds.

The government sets the Bank of England an inflation target (e.g. 2 per cent). The interest rate is then adjusted in such a way as to keep the economy operating within this inflation target. Each month the base rate the Bank of England charges is decided by the independent Monetary Policy Committee that is chaired by the governor of the Bank of England. If inflation is increasing above the target rate the Monetary Policy Committee will be inclined to raise interest rates (to choke off spending). If growth of the economy is too slow then interest rates will be lowered.

Find out the current base rate charged by the Bank of England. How has this changed over the last six months? What is the government's current inflation target? How is monetary policy being used to achieve this target?

The base rate is the rate that the Bank of England charges other financial institutions. It is not the rate that businesses pay for loans. The interest rate that ordinary customers and businesses pay will be higher than this, depending on their credit rating and the risk that banks and other lenders are taking in lending to them.

 10.8 The exchange rate

The exchange rate is the rate at which one international currency such as the pound will exchange against other international currencies such as the euro, the US dollar, the Indian rupee, etc. The exchange rate is determined in international foreign exchange markets and involves millions of trades every day.

The exchange rate is of key importance to businesses that trade in international markets. For example, when the UK pound depreciates (loses value against other currencies) it will become easier for British businesses to sell goods abroad. However, as we shall see in Chapter 11, it is not as simple as that because we also need to consider the elasticity of demand for UK exports.

The interest rate and the exchange rate as a general rule are connected. A fall in the interest rate is likely to lead to a fall in the exchange rate. This is because when interest rates fall in the UK foreign investors are discouraged from investing in the UK because UK interest rates are relatively less attractive than interest rates elsewhere.

10.9 Summary

In this chapter we have introduced a number of key economic indicators that are relevant to business decision making. It is important for you to understand what these economic indicators are and what they measure. You should be able to explain indicators associated with GDP, alternative measures of economic welfare, employment figures, the CPI, key demographic indicators, the interest rate and the exchange rate.

KEY IDEAS

Indicators showing the growth of the economy

- Figures for GDP (gross domestic product) enable economists to study changes in the economy over time and to compare growth rates of national economies.
- GDP can be calculated through the output, income or expenditure method.
- However, if we want to examine changes in living standards then we need to broaden the scope of our indicators.
- Happiness indicators and the human development index provide a much broader picture of what is meant by well-being.

Employment indicators

- Employment indicators provide an insight into the changing shape of the labour market in the UK.
- Typical employment indicators relate to the relative importance of part-time and full-time jobs, and the relative importance of the public and private sectors.

Inflation indicators

- Inflation measures the general increase in the level of prices over time.
- Like other indicators the data for the construction of this index are collected by the Office for National Statistics.
- Prices are collected from many different sales outlets across the country. Weights in the index are allocated according to the percentage of a household budget spent on different categories of items. A base year is used to make comparisons of general price changes over time.
- Mild inflation can be beneficial to an economy provided it is at a steady and predictable rate. Inflation become problematic when it rises at an unacceptably high rate creating instability and making it difficult to make rational economic calculations.

Population indicators

- Demography is the study of population. A census is taken at regular intervals (in the UK every ten years) to identify the size and structure of a country's population.
- The population of the UK is growing at one of the fastest rates in Europe.
- During the last ten years we have seen particularly strong growth of population in London.
- Britain has an ageing population and the size of the dependent population is increasing (i.e. the percentage of the population dependent on the working population).

Interest rates

- The interest rate is the price of money.
- Interest rates in the UK are related to the Bank of England's base rate.
- Interest rates charged to businesses vary according to the risk the lender is taking and the amount of time that the loan is for.
- Interest rates are used to manage inflation in line with the government's inflation targets.

Exchange rates

- The exchange rate is the rate at which one country's currency will exchange for other international currencies.
- The exchange rate and the interest rate tend to move in the same direction.
- A depreciation in a country's exchange rate will make it easier for exporters to export goods and services.

REVIEW QUESTIONS

1. What are economic indicators? Which economic indicators are particularly significant for business and why?

2. Explain the following terms: GDP measured using purchasing power parity; and GDP per capita. Why might a country have a relatively high GDP and a relatively low GDP per capita?

3. Why might GDP per capita not be a particularly effective measure of human welfare. What alternative indicators might be used to measure well-being?

4. What is the interest rate? Who sets the interest rate and what changes have taken place in UK interest rates in recent times?

5. How would you measure the dependency ratio? Why is this a significant economic indicator?

6. What are headline indicators? Why are they significant for business?

7. What key changes have taken place in employment patterns in the UK economy in recent times?

8. What does the consumer price index measure? What is the rate of inflation?

9. How can rapidly rising inflation make it difficult for businesses to make plans?

10. What would an 'ideal' set of economic indicators look like for business?

REFERENCES

Boyle, D. and Simms, A. (2009) *The New Economics: A Bigger Picture*, London, Earthscan.

Friedman, M. (1968) 'The Role of Monetary Policy', *American Economic Review*, 58 (1): 1–17.

HM Treasury (2010) *Spending Review Statement*. Available at: http://www.hm-treasury.gov.uk/spend_sr2010_speech.htm (accessed January 2013).

USEFUL WEBSITES

Examine up-to-date statistics related to the following economic indicators:

www.ons.gov.uk/ons/index.html – consumer price indices available on the Office for National Statistics website, Consumer Price Index.

www.statistics.gov.uk/hub/labour-market/index.html– labour market statistics available from the Office for National Statistics, Labour Market Statistics.

hdr.undp.org/en/statistics – human development indicators available from United Nations Human Development Indicators.

www.imf.org/external/pubs/ft/weo/2011/02/weodata/index.aspx – comparisons of GDP in different countries, the World Economic Outlook Database.

11 The international economy

CHAPTER OBJECTIVES

After carefully reading this chapter you should be able to:

- Explain the benefits of international trade for consumers, producers and countries

- Differentiate between absolute and comparative advantage

- Outline the significance of international trade to the UK economy

- Explain the key components of a balance of payments account

- Identify the UK's main trading partners

- Explain the main benefits of trading blocs

- Analyse some of the impacts to the UK of being a member of the European Union

- Evaluate different exchange rate systems

- Analyse issues associated with the euro as an international currency

- Define terms of trade and their implications for international exchange

11.1 Introduction

This chapter starts out by outlining the theory of international trade, with particular focus on the benefits of specialization. It explains the nature of the theory of comparative advantage which provides a justification for economies to focus on what they do best. The chapter then shows various ways in which a business organization can enter a foreign market. It then goes on to examine ways in which the UK benefits from trade and to show that our major trading partners (apart from the US and China) consist primarily of countries in the European Union (EU).

We show how the EU was originally set up and how it has expanded to cover economic, political and social objectives. In addition, as well as the geographical spread the depth of integration within the EU has increased with successive periods of expansion. The chapter also outlines the nature of international exchange and exchange rates. We show that the euro is the currency of the Eurozone which does not include Britain. The Eurozone has been subject to extensive crises requiring bailouts from the core countries at the heart of the EU – particularly Germany. The EU continues to be in crisis and this impacts on the UK because our EU neighbours are our closest trading partners and because we have a number of political, social and economic ties with these countries.

11.2 Advantages of international trade

There are many advantages in trading internationally – some of them are advantages to consumers, some for producers and most benefit the economy as a whole.

- **Choice**. If you go to buy a product today there is plenty of choice. Take mobile phones, for example. The choice is bewildering. While the number of products to decide between is large, the variety of choice enables a buyer to purchase a phone that has just the right sets of applications and features to meet their individual requirements. One can choose from the products of many different firms from many different countries (e.g. Nokia from Finland, China Mobile from China, Samsung from South Korea, iPhone from the United States and so on).

- **Quality**. Why do people in Britain like buying BMW cars? Or Japanese hi-fi systems? Trade not only gives us lots of choice, but also gives us quality that is not available from British manufacturers. It is trade that gives us these opportunities.

- **Price**. Some countries can produce products more cheaply than we can in the UK, so buying them in from abroad means that our consumers can get these items more cheaply. This not only benefits them, but it also helps to keep inflation down.

- **We can buy things we cannot produce at home**. Why do we buy bananas from the Windward Islands in the Caribbean? Because it is difficult to grow bananas in the cold and wet conditions of Britain. Trade allows us to buy things that are uneconomical to produce at home because of natural disadvantages that we may have in producing them.

- **Wider markets**. There is a limit to how much we can sell in our home market. With a limit of roughly 57 million people (2011 census figure) to sell to, a company can only expand to a certain extent. However, if it trades globally sales expansion potential is almost limitless. Trade therefore allows firms to grow and earn more wealth.

- **Less unemployment**. Because firms can grow more easily output expands and therefore more employees are needed. More employment injects money into the economy through wages, which helps to increase growth in the economy.

- **Wealth earned for the nation**. When we sell abroad there is a flow of foreign currency into the country. This earns wealth for the nation and the economy grows.

Trade therefore helps the economy to grow and as a result contributes to higher standards of living for all of the citizens in our country. Good international trade relations actually boost all the economies of all of the countries taking part.

Ways in which firms can enter foreign markets

Ways in which firms enter foreign markets are described as 'market entry strategies'. These methods are outlined below and then revisited in greater detail in Section 12.6. There are three main types of market entry strategy:

1. Exporting;

2. Joint venturing; and

3. Foreign direct investment (FDI).

Exporting

This is the simplest way to enter a foreign market. The company produces all of its goods in the domestic economy and then has them transported to the export market. The products may be modified for distinct regional markets.

When entering foreign markets firms may initially test the water through a low-cost method such as selling through an intermediary. This type of indirect exporting is relatively cheap and involves little investment – however, it involves sharing profit with the distributor.

The next step therefore may be direct exporting. A firm can:

- Set up a domestic export department.

- Set up an overseas branch that deals with sales, distribution and perhaps promotion.

- Send a home-based sales representative abroad to find business.

- Work with overseas sales agents.

Joint venturing

This involves joining with an overseas company to set up a new independent company (joint venture) jointly owned by the two businesses. Joint venturing is a particularly attractive way of entering new markets where political and commercial connections need to be made, and language and cultural differences may require expertise on the ground. Varieties of joint ventures include:

- Licencing arrangements whereby a company enters into an arrangement with a licensee in a foreign market. For a fee or royalty the licensee earns the right to produce the company's product or use their manufacturing processes. A company can use licencing to enter a foreign market with little risk. However, if it gives the licensee access to intellectual property rights there is the danger of them being copied.

- Contract manufacturing enables the company that takes out a contract to produce a product or service.

- Joint ownership ventures involving two companies joining forces to set up a separate company that is distinct in its own right. Sometimes foreign governments insist on a certain proportion of a business being in the hands of local business people (e.g. 51 per cent). In this case it is necessary to set up a joint venture to operate in an overseas market. Another situation in which a firm may choose to set up a joint ownership venture would be when it lacks the financial, physical or managerial resources to undertake the venture alone.

Disadvantages of joint ownership ventures are that disagreements might arise between partners. For example, one partner may want to take profits out of the business whereas the other might seek reinvestment and growth. There may also be differences in preferred styles of managing and running the business.

Direct investment

The most significant form of involvement in foreign markets involves direct investment, including the ownership of foreign-based manufacturing and the assembly of manufacturing facilities. Foreign direct investment (FDI) can take the form of takeover of foreign companies by share purchase or simply setting up and investing in a business offshoot from scratch. FDI gives an international company the greatest amount of control of international businesses. It is the most expensive form of investment. In directly investing in a foreign country a firm needs to build strong relationships with government officials and trading partners including suppliers, customers and employees. The firm would be able to develop its own manufacturing, marketing and human resource policies.

Risks involved in FDI include change of government, lack of understanding of local cultures, conditions and tastes, and other ways in which the firm would be disadvantaged by lack of knowledge of overseas markets (although this can be addressed by employing nationals of the country).

11.3 Comparative and absolute advantage

In order to understand the benefits of international trade on an international scale it is necessary to understand the law of comparative advantage. David Ricardo (see Chapter 9), writing nearly 200 years ago, devised a theory about trade called the theory of absolute and comparative advantage.

CASE STUDY Ford develops the Ford Figo for the Indian market

Ford is a huge US-based multinational. In the early part of the twentieth century it had invested in the Indian market, but by the 1950s had withdrawn because it was making losses. However, with the recent growth of the Indian market Ford saw this as a fresh opportunity. In 1995 it developed a joint venture (50:50) with Mahindra & Mahindra, a large Indian company.

Ford India Private Ltd was set up and focused mainly on selling American-designed models in India. However, it was clear that the Indian market had real potential and in 1998 Ford increased its investment to 72 per cent of the company and invested large sums of money in developing production in India. Recently they have developed a new car designed specifically for the Indian market based on detailed research in India. The car is called the Ford Figo and is designed specifically for a target customer – named 'Sandeep'.

Sandeep is defined by Ford India's marketers as an individual with his head in the clouds but feet on the ground. Sandeep is young, just married and lives at home with his parents. Sandeep is aspirational and reasonably well educated. He is looking to move from a two-wheeler motorbike to a four-wheeler car. The Ford Figo is targeted at the small cars segment of the car market (a segment which accounts for 70 per cent of all car sales in India). In the first month that the car came on the market 10,000 were ordered and sales growth has gone from strength to strength with 100,000 being produced within the first 15 months. The Ford Figo is now exported to five countries and is expected to be marketed further afield.

- **What would have been the benefits to Ford of re-entering India by starting a joint venture?**
- **Why do you think that Ford expanded its investment in the Indian market?**
- **How has Ford's marketing changed to take account of the new realities of the growing Indian market and what have been the benefits of doing so?**

KEY TERMS

Comparative advantage – a situation where an individual, company, region or country can produce a good at a lower opportunity cost than a rival.

Absolute advantage – a situation where an individual, company, region or country can produce a good more efficiently than a rival.

Ricardo identified the key role international trade has to play in creating economic growth and boosting living standards. The basis of his theory is actually very simple: if each nation specializes in what it is good at producing more will be produced globally. If the country trades internationally with other specializing nations then they can all benefit from exchanging products.

We probably could grow bananas in the United Kingdom if we invested enough resources in capital equipment to produce an artificial environment, but we could not produce many and it would be terribly wasteful of our factors of production. So specialization increases global output. If we then trade with each other, all countries can get the products that they need and more needs and wants can be satisfied around the world. Thus international trade can contribute to solving that basic economic problem of scarcity.

The following simple example illustrates this principle. Here we have two countries, Germany and China, both producing high-quality industrial machines and bicycles. To make the illustration clear we will assume that each country has ten workers divided equally between the production of machines and bicycles. The production levels relate to a specific period of time (e.g. one month).

TABLE 11.1 Germany and China using half of their resources to produce machines and bicycles

	Production	
	Industrial machines	Bicycles
Germany	40	40
China	5	250
Totals	45	290

We can see from Table 11.1 that five workers in Germany can produce 40 high-quality machines (eight per employee) whereas China can only produce five similar machines (one per worker). Germany therefore has as absolute advantage in the production of machines and Ricardo's theory suggests that it should specialize in the production of machines. China, however, has an absolute advantage in the production of bicycles – it should therefore specialize in manufacturing bicycles. Total production should therefore increase. We can now illustrate the position if each country specializes solely in what it does best (see Table 11.2).

TABLE 11.2 Germany and China using their resources only on the best lines

	Production	
	Industrial machines	Bicycles
Germany	80	0
China	0	500
Totals	80	500

If you compare Table 11.1 with Table 11.2 you can see that the world total has increased from 45 to 80 for industrial machines and from 290 to 500 for bicycles. As long as Germany sells industrial machines to China and China sells bicycles to Germany more needs and wants can be satisfied in both countries. (However, please note that trade will only be beneficial if trading takes place on terms that are beneficial to both countries.)

However, Ricardo took his trade theory one step further. He showed that trade could still be advantageous when one country has an absolute advantage in both products, as long as there is a difference in their relative efficiencies (comparative advantage). The following example illustrates the principle of comparative advantage.

A country will have a comparative advantage when, through trade, it is able to lower the opportunity cost of goods compared with the opportunity cost from just producing and trading goods in the domestic economy. Table 11.3 shows that Japan is better at producing both television sets and chemicals than Nigeria.

TABLE 11.3 Output per worker per day in Japan and Nigeria

	Television sets	Chemicals (units)
Japan	8	800
Nigeria	2	400

Japan can make four times as many television sets as Nigeria but only twice as many units of chemicals. The opportunity cost of producing one television set is lower in Japan than in Nigeria. It is 100 chemicals in Japan whereas in Nigeria it is 200 chemicals. Japan's comparative advantage therefore is in the production of television sets.

Although Nigeria has an absolute disadvantage in producing both products, it has a comparative advantage in making chemicals. Its opportunity cost of making one unit of chemicals is 1/200th of a television set. In Japan it is 1/100th of a television set.

The logic of comparative advantage therefore is that Japan should concentrate on what it does 'most best' and Nigeria should concentrate on what it does 'least worst'.

Reflective questions

1 In what circumstances is a country likely to focus its resources on producing those goods in which it has a comparative advantage?

2 Are there any situations where this might not occur?

In the course of time comparative advantage is likely to alter with changes in technology and other factors that impact on supply in a country. Where the country becomes more efficient at producing specific goods then its comparative advantage in producing these goods will be enhanced and its relative costs of production will improve. For example, in recent years China has improved its performance in producing a wide range of advanced technological goods.

11.4 The UK as a trading nation

One of the key features of the UK economy is that it is a trading economy. Exporting and importing make a significant contribution to the economy.

Exports – the value of goods and services that domestic producers provide to foreign consumers. They represent goods and services sold to other countries.

Imports – the value of goods and services that domestic consumers buy from overseas suppliers.

The UK is one of the world's largest trading nations. It is the sixth biggest exporter of goods after China, the US, Germany, Japan and France.

Just as significantly, the UK is the second biggest exporter of services after the US largely because of the contribution of the City of London with its international banking, insurance and financial services.

Balance of trade – the balance of trade of any country combines its trade in visible goods with its trade in services in a single account.

Figure 11.1 (which is derived from a range of official UK statistics) shows the balance of trade set out in chart form. The key detail to pick out is that the UK typically runs a deficit in its trade in goods and a surplus in its trade in services. However, the deficit in goods is significantly more than the surplus in services so that the line illustrating total trade is typically a negative figure.

One of the key issues of the financial crisis that started in 2007 is that it has shaken confidence in the UK financial sector. Millions of jobs in Britain are reliant on the country continuing to be seen as a strong and reliable centre for financial services.

11.5 The balance of payments

The balance of payments – a record of all the transactions between one country and all other countries during a specific time period. From a business point of view this should be seen as an accounting record.

The balance of payments should be seen as a summary setting out the sources of funds for a country and the uses of funds (see Table 11.4).

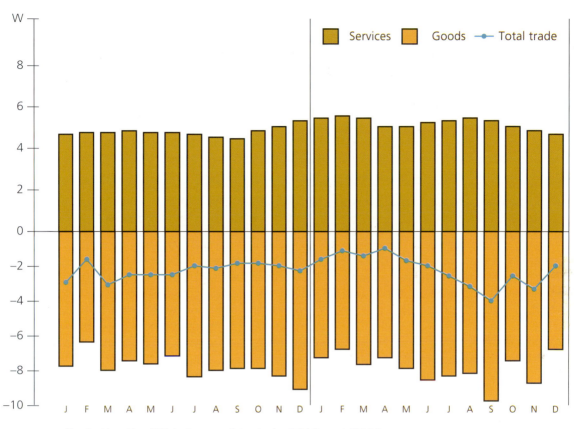

FIGURE 11.1 Illustrating the UK balance of trade in 2010 and 2011

There are two main components of the balance of payments account:

1. The current account showing the exports and imports of goods and services for a particular period of time; and

2. Financial and capital flows that take place over a specific time period.

Business students will be familiar with the concept that all accounts balance. This principle applies to the balance of payments account. In simple terms:

Current account (balance) + Capital and financial flows (balance) +
   Balancing item = 0

The balancing item – an accounting adjustment that needs to be made such that the account balances at zero (i.e. the net figure after all errors and omissions have been accounted for).

KEY TERM

CASE STUDY The impact of falling international trade on a company – Burberry

Burberry is an iconic British brand. Its bags, suitcases, scarves and other items are distinctive and easy to recognize (characterized by camel, red and black check patterned items) by consumers seeking to purchase a luxury brand. Burberry sales seemed to be recession proof in the period 2008–2009 largely as a result of growth in exports to China and affluent parts of South East Asia. Burberry's largest markets are in Britain, France, Germany and China.

In terms of luxury goods the US is the biggest luxury goods market (valued in 2012 at $77 billion with Japan second at about $32 billion). However, it is China that is the fastest growing market and by 2017 China is expected to be the second biggest luxury market followed by Japan, Italy and France.

During the recession in 2008 and 2009 companies like Burberry operating in the luxury segment benefitted from the continued growth of the Chinese market with GDP rising at about 10 per cent a year. However, by 2012 the growth of the Chinese economy had begun to slow down. As a result, by late 2012 the sale of Burberry products in China and other parts of the globe had started to fall. In mid-September 2012 Burberry revised its expected profit figures downwards and this immediately led to a fall in the total value of Burberry shares by £1 billion. In a review of the market for shareholders, the Chief Executive of Burberry stated that the company was facing a more 'difficult external environment' – including a slowdown in the increase in sales in China, the rest of Asia, Europe and America.

- Why is international trade important for a company like Burberry?

- What sorts of factors are likely to impact on the sales of Burberry products in China and other key markets?

- To what extent is a company like Burberry able to isolate itself from falling sales in some countries by focusing on markets in other countries?

TABLE 11.4 Sources and use of funds in international payments

Sources of funds	Uses of funds
Funds earned by a country from exports of goods and services.	Funds spent on purchasing imports from other countries.
Funds earned by a country from foreigners investing in that country.	Funds used by a country's citizens to invest in foreign companies.

Figure 11.2 demonstrates how the balance of payments is structured.

The balance of payments account can thus be summarised as:

Current account balance + Capital balance + Financial balance +
Net errors and omissions = 0

11.6 The UK's main trading partners

An analysis of the UK's main trading partners (exports and imports) shows that apart from the United States, most of our other main trading partners are major countries in the European Union. If you look at Tables 11.5 and 11.6 it is immediately obvious how significant these trading partners are to the UK (e.g. Germany, Spain, Ireland, Italy, the Netherlands and France).

Why is this the case?

- These countries are producers of the sophisticated high-end industrial goods and services that consumers in this country can afford (e.g. expensive perfume and clothes, high-quality motors cars and engineering products, and sophisticated pharmaceutical products).

- These countries are made up of consumers with above average spending power and thus able to afford to buy the sophisticated products produced in the UK. They also are the home to many major multinational companies that seek sophisticated industrial products. Currently the major manufactured exports of the UK are telecommunications equipment, automobiles, medical and pharmaceutical products, automatic data processing equipment and aircraft.

Similarly, the European Union provides an excellent market for sophisticated financial products, and the specialist services provided by the UK's world-class financial services sector.

Using the figures in Tables 11.5 and 11.6 below combine the latest figures for UK trade to European countries. Calculate what percentage of UK imports and exports goes to its top 25 trading partners.

ACTIVITY

11.7 The importance of trading blocs

The world today is organized into a number of major trading blocs. Most significantly, from the UK's point of view, was the development of what is now known as the European Union, which has experienced successive waves of integration since it was set up by the Treaty of Rome in 1965. An area of free trade between members can be described as a trade bloc.

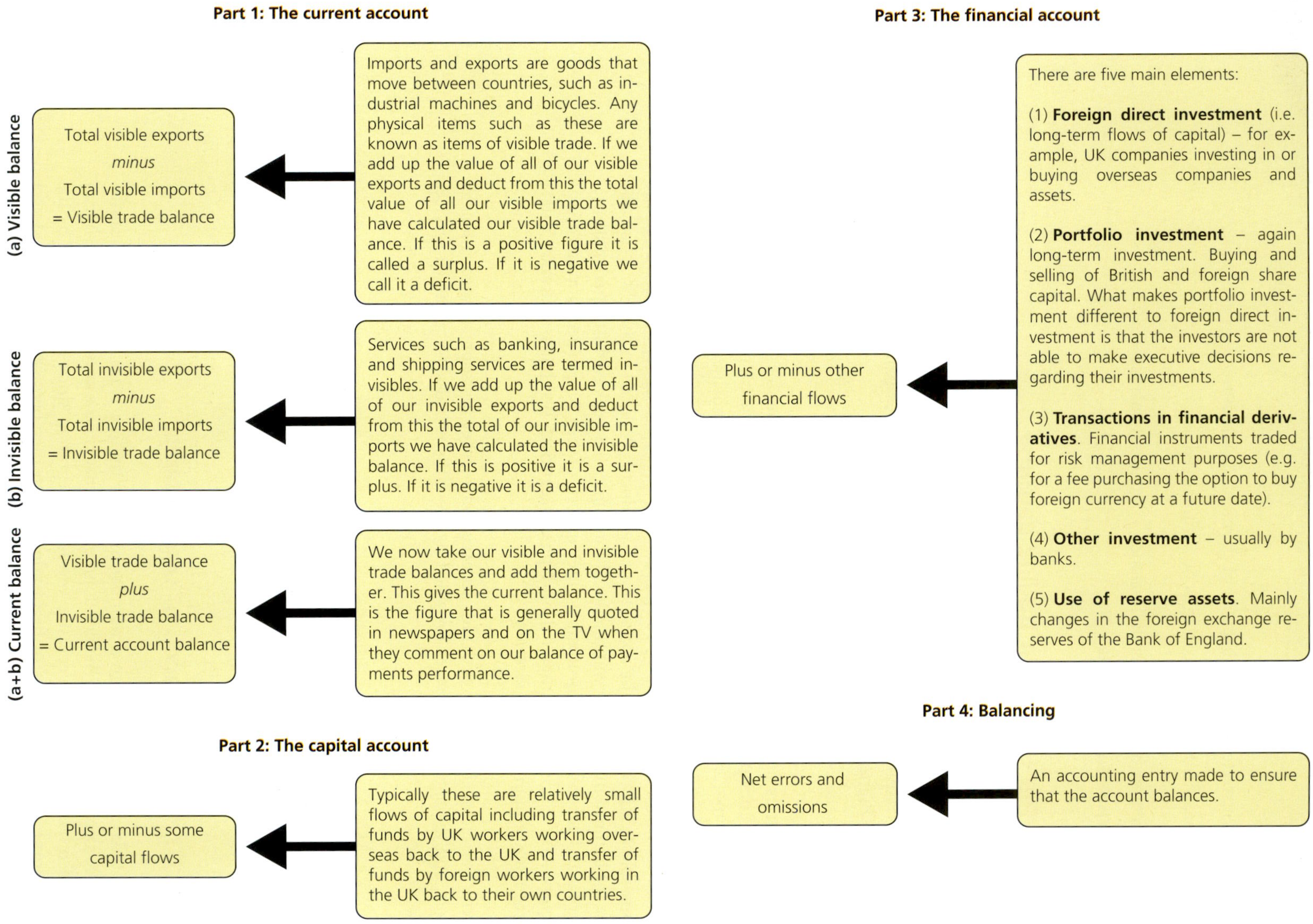

Part 3: The financial account

There are five main elements:

(1) **Foreign direct investment** (i.e. long-term flows of capital) – for example, UK companies investing in or buying overseas companies and assets.

(2) **Portfolio investment** – again long-term investment. Buying and selling of British and foreign share capital. What makes portfolio investment different to foreign direct investment is that the investors are not able to make executive decisions regarding their investments.

(3) **Transactions in financial derivatives.** Financial instruments traded for risk management purposes (e.g. for a fee purchasing the option to buy foreign currency at a future date).

(4) **Other investment** – usually by banks.

(5) **Use of reserve assets.** Mainly changes in the foreign exchange reserves of the Bank of England.

↓

Plus or minus other financial flows

Part 4: Balancing

An accounting entry made to ensure that the account balances.

↓

Net errors and omissions

Part 1: The current account

Imports and exports are goods that move between countries, such as industrial items such as industrial machines and bicycles. Any physical items such as these are known as items of visible trade. If we add up the value of all of our visible exports and deduct from this the total value of all our visible imports we have calculated our visible trade balance. If this is a positive figure it is called a surplus. If it is negative we call it a deficit.

↓

Total visible exports
minus
Total visible imports
= Visible trade balance

(a) Visible balance

Services such as banking, insurance and shipping services are termed invisibles. If we add up the value of all of our invisible exports and deduct from this the total of our invisible imports we have calculated the invisible balance. If this is positive it is a surplus. If it is negative it is a deficit.

↓

Total invisible exports
minus
Total invisible imports
= Invisible trade balance

(b) Invisible balance

We now take our visible and invisible trade balances and add them together. This gives the current balance. This is the figure that is generally quoted in newspapers and on the TV when they comment on our balance of payments performance.

↓

Visible trade balance
plus
Invisible trade balance
= Current account balance

(a+b) Current balance

Part 2: The capital account

Typically these are relatively small flows of capital including transfer of funds by UK workers working overseas back to the UK and transfer of funds by foreign workers working in the UK back to their own countries.

↓

Plus or minus some capital flows

FIGURE 11.2 The basic structure of the balance of payments

TABLE 11.5 Top UK export countries

Rank	Country	Year to date 2011 (£m)	Year to date 2010 (£m)	% Change
1	United States	31,712	30,894	2.7
2	Germany	27,539	23,502	17.2
3	France	18,905	16,542	14.3
4	Netherlands	18,823	17,189	9.5
5	Irish Republic	14,063	13,307	5.7
6	Belgium	12,949	10,835	19.5
7	Italy	8,287	7,193	15.2
8	Spain	7,946	8,065	−1.5
9	China	7,055	5,839	20.8
10	Sweden	5,103	4,504	13.3
11	India	4,597	3,172	44.9
12	Switzerland	4,400	4,063	8.3
13	Canada	4,126	3,445	19.8
14	Hong Kong	4,120	3,464	18.9
15	Russia	3,853	2,692	43.1
16	UAE	3,844	3,101	23.9
17	Japan	3,667	3,443	6.5
18	Poland	3,655	2,999	21.9
19	Australia	3,380	2,609	29.5
20	Turkey	3,115	2,452	27.1
21	Singapore	2,929	2,704	8.3
22	South Africa	2,836	2,201	28.9
23	Norway	2,732	2,390	14.3
24	Saudi Arabia	2,554	2,440	4.7
25	Denmark	2,477	2,242	10.5

Source: *The Guardian*. Available online at: www.guardian.co.uk/news/datablog/2010/feb/24/uk-trade-exports-imports (accessed January 2013).

KEY TERMS

Free trade – exists where goods and services can flow freely between countries with no barriers to trade such as tariffs.

Customs union – where a bloc of countries establish a common external tariff with common restrictions such as the same tariffs on imports from outside the customs union.

TABLE 11.6 Top UK import countries

Rank	Country	Year to date 2011 (£m)	Year to date 2010 (£m)	% Change
1	Germany	41,107	37,812	8.7
2	United States	25,076	25,574	–2
3	China	24,828	23,172	7.1
4	Netherlands	23,019	21,390	7.6
5	Norway	20,014	15,359	30.3
6	France	19,138	18,133	5.5
7	Belgium	15,729	14,054	11.9
8	Italy	11,629	11,720	–0.8
9	Irish Republic	10,436	10,421	0.1
10	Spain	9,094	8,350	8.9
11	Japan	6,998	6,220	12.5
12	Switzerland	6,525	7,018	–7
13	Russia	6,326	4,290	47.5
14	Sweden	6,289	5,282	19.1
15	Hong Kong	6,119	6,141	–0.4
16	Poland	5,843	4,957	17.9
17	Canada	5,208	5,483	–5
18	Denmark	5,017	3,306	51.8
19	India	4,954	4,560	8.7
20	Turkey	4,498	4,141	8.6
21	Qatar	4,185	1,756	138.3
22	Czech Republic	3,510	3,279	7.1
23	Singapore	3,194	3,205	–0.3
24	Taiwan	2,831	2,387	18.6
25	Hungary	2,516	2,593	–2.9

Source: *The Guardian*. Available online at: www.guardian.co.uk/news/datablog/2010/feb/24/uk-trade-exports-imports (accessed January 2013).

Trading blocs are set up for the mutual benefit of members. For example, the UK benefits from being able to treat all 27 member states of the European Union as a single market for our goods. Tariffs and complicated paperwork are removed enabling us to sell our goods freely across the EU. This is of tremendous benefit to UK businesses as the majority of our trade is with the EU. This is of great benefit to producers of sophisticated upmarket goods and services. Trading blocs enable large-scale production and marketing. A key disadvantage of belonging to a trading bloc is that it exposes domestic companies to greater competition.

Other examples of trading blocs include the North American Free Trade Agreement (NAFTA) between the US, Canada and Mexico covering the liberalization of trade between these countries, and the Association of Southeast Asian Nations (ASEAN).

Progressively, steps have been made to integrate the world economy on a global scale (see Chapter 12). However, often there are major trade disputes between trading blocs (e.g. between NAFTA and the EU). Trade disputes often lead to tit-for-tat retaliation where one group of countries levies a tax on certain items from a rival trading bloc leading to retaliation.

Reflective question

3 To what extent do you believe that the creation of trading blocs furthers the possibility for international specialization based on the law of comparative advantage?

11.8 The UK and the European Union

The UK's membership of the European Union (EU) is undoubtedly one of the major influences on the UK economy today. The turbulence which has recently hit the Eurozone has impacted substantially on the UK economy and has been one of the factors blamed by the Conservative Prime Minister for Britain's poor economic performance.

In examining the EU it is important to understand it as:

1. An economic union

2. A social union

3. A political union

Each of these elements are important in their own right, but they are also closely related. Economic decisions typically will have political and social effects as well as economic ones.

The structure of the EU

An economic union

Key features of the EU are that it involves:

- A free trade area of 27 countries.

- A common external tariff.

- A monetary union involving 16 of the members, with the euro as a common currency. The Eurozone's monetary policy is determined by the European Central Bank (ECB).

A political union

The EU has its own political institutions including:

- The European Parliament of elected Euro MPs.

- A Council of Ministers, which involves regular meetings between Ministers from the various member states.

- The European Commission, which is a permanent body responsible for drafting regulations and directives that are EU-wide rules governing many aspects of life and business within the Union.

- The European Court of Justice, which settles disputes between members states, businesses and individuals within the EU.

A social union

The social union is based on what is described as the Social Chapter to the treaties governing the EU. The Social Chapter is designed to secure common levels of social provision for citizens in members states, including limitations on the hours that can be worked and important aspects of welfare and health provision.

Development of the EU

The idea of developing a strong EU was proposed at the end of the Second World War as an initiative to create stronger political ties and to end the tensions of two world wars. If people could share common ideals and goals then this would hopefully lead to greater collaboration.

The European Coal and Steel Community

The starting point was the development of the European Coal and Steel Community in 1951. The idea was to 'pool' German and French coal and steel resources under a common authority. Coal and steel were key resources for these economies. Shortly after, Italy, Belgium, the Netherlands and Luxembourg joined this community.

The European Economic Community

The next step took place in 1956. This was the creation of a free trade area among the six countries. It was a customs union with a common external tariff. It was felt that such an initiative would yield substantial economic benefits to all parties.

The Single Market

By 1992 the UK and most of the other Western European states had joined the EU. The next major step forward took place with the Single European Act which came into force in 1992.

The Single Market involved what was referred to as the four freedoms – the freedom of movement within the Union of:

- Goods
- Services

- People

- Capital

This was a substantial economic move towards greater integration. In addition to the existing free trade area, people could now move freely to seek work and there were to be free capital flows within the Union.

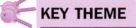

KEY THEME

The Cecchini Report (1992)

The Cecchini Report identified four main consequences of a well-organized single market which would be of benefit to business:

1. Cost reductions. Because companies would produce on a larger scale in a new mass market this should lead to falling costs for each unit of production.
2. Improved efficiency. Industries would need to reorganize to serve mass markets. This reorganization, coupled with competition, should increase efficiency.
3. New patterns of competition. Those industries and areas with the most effective resources would make the biggest gains.
4. New innovations, processes and products. These would flow from the larger, more competitive market.

- **The Cecchini Report identified a range of benefits for members of the EU. In your view would these benefits be shared equally by the member states?**

- **How might some of the 'benefits' of creating the Single Market have led to some of the problems for European Union economies today?**

The Maastricht Treaty and the Social Chapter

The European Union has been created and developed through a series of treaties between member states. Renegotiation and ratification of these treaties over time has led to shifts in the structure and working of the union. 1993 marked a significant date with the ratification of the Maastricht Treaty.

The Maastricht Treaty created what are referred to as the 'three pillars' that support the European Union. These are:

1. Revised national treaties that are supranational in nature. Supranational means that they are binding on all member countries. Any member of the EU is now a EU citizen and can live, reside and move freely within the EU.

KEY THEME

The impact of EU regulations

The Working Time Regulations were introduced in the European Union in 1998. The Conservative government of the time was resistant to accepting these regulations. They felt that they act as a restriction to the flexibility of labour markets and would lead to economic inefficiency. Eventually, under the next Labour government which was more in favour of social protection, Britain agreed to abide by these regulations.

The Working Time Regulations included introducing a 48-hour maximum working week. The Regulations gave rise to wholly new rights and obligations relating to work and rest. The principle provisions are:

- A limit on the average working week to 48 hours (though individuals can choose to work longer).
- A limit on night workers' average normal daily working time to 8 hours.
- A requirement to offer health assessments to night workers.
- Minimum daily and weekly rest periods.
- Rest breaks at work.
- Paid annual leave.

The Regulations define a worker as someone for whom an employer has a duty to provide work, who controls when and how it is done, supplies the tools and other equipment and pays tax and National Insurance contributions. However, these are indicators rather than exhaustive or exclusive criteria. The majority of agency workers and freelancers are likely to be workers in the context of the Regulations.

- **From a business point of view, what do you consider to be the main arguments for and against the adoption of a 48-hour maximum working week?**

- **From a social point of view, what do you consider to be the main arguments for and against the adoption of a 48-hour working week?**

- **Can you think of any organizational or procedural problems that might arise through the implementation of the 48-hour ruling?**

- **Which kinds of business organizations will benefit from the 48-hour ruling and which will not?**

2. Cooperation in justice and home affairs. This includes cooperation in relation to crime, law and order and immigration.

3. Cooperation in common foreign and security policy.

In addition, a Social Chapter was created in the Treaty. Initially the UK did not sign up to the Social Chapter. One of the main objectives behind the Social Chapter was to guard against 'social dumping'. As part of the attempt to run a fair single market, the member states wanted to prevent countries with poorer social standards from reaping benefits over those with tougher standards. The Social Chapter would therefore create the basis for common standards in terms of minimum pay, holiday entitlement, maternity leave, health and safety at work, etc.

There are three key economic impacts of the Social Chapter:

1. It creates a level playing field in terms of competition between countries. They each are required to implement the same set of social standards.

2. It creates greater protection for workers and citizens.

3. It raises the costs of production resulting from implementing better social provision.

Enlargement of the EU

Over the years there have been successive enlargements of the EU as new members have joined:

- 1956   Germany, France, Belgium, Luxembourg, the Netherlands, Italy
- 1973   Denmark, Ireland, the UK
- 1981   Greece
- 1986   Portugal and Spain
- 1995   Austria, Finland, Sweden
- 2004   Cyprus, the Czech Republic, Estonia, Hungary, Latvia, Lithuania, Malta, Poland, Slovakia, Slovenia

The most recent expansion of the EU involved integration with some very small states such as Malta and Cyprus, and Eastern European states that had formerly been part of a socialist bloc centred around Russia. The 2004 integration process was thus both a political and economic step based on increasing the sphere of influence of the EU.

In order for member states to join the EU they had to meet what were referred to as the Copenhagen Criteria, which stated that they must:

- Be a stable democracy, respecting human rights, the rule of law and the protection of minorities;
- Have a functioning market economy; and
- Adopt the common rules, standards and policies that make up the body of EU law.

CASE STUDY Cameron calls for a reappraisal of Britain's position in the European Union

In a speech on 23 January 2013 David Cameron suggested that new thinking is required about the nature of the EU and Britain's position within it. He argued that while the European Union was effective in creating lasting peace in Europe, this is not the purpose today – rather, it is to 'secure prosperity'. He argued that developments in emerging markets such as India and China have a profound impact for EU economies. He argued that there is a fundamental change in the environment in which businesses operate:

- As a result of fundamental problems in the Eurozone; and
- Because of a crisis of European competitiveness, as other nations across the world soar ahead. He states that 'taken as a whole, Europe's share of world output is projected to fall by almost a third in the next two decades'.

He argued that in the twenty-first century the new EU should focus on five key aspects:

1. Competitiveness – including securing transformative trade deals with the US, Japan and India as drivers towards global free trade.
2. Flexibility – operating with the flexibility of a network of different types of countries rather than as a cumbersome bloc.
3. Power should flow back to member states. Rather than expecting everything to be harmonized countries should be allowed to make individual choices.
4. Democratic accountability – with a bigger and more significant role for national parliaments.
5. Fairness – so that arrangements in the EU are fair to all participants.

Cameron then went on to make a case for being able to renegotiate the way that the EU is structured. He argued that what is required is for European member states to reconsider what the structures and agreements governing the nature of the EU should look like, particularly in the light of the Eurozone crisis and increasing competition on a global scale. Once this discussion has taken place and changes are made then, if returned to power, the Conservative government will oversee a referendum to establish whether people in this country still want to remain in the EU. This would be likely to occur in 2017.

Source: Cameron, D. (2013) 'EU Speech', 23 January.

Key benefits to the most recent members of the EU have been:

- Access to a large, established and growing market.
- Access to greater inflows of capital from existing EU members. For example, many joint ventures have been established between companies in France, Germany and the UK and their partners in Poland, the Czech Republic, etc.

- The ability for citizens to live and work elsewhere in the EU and to transmit part of their earnings back to their home country.

- Access to new technologies to update the economy arising from partnerships with existing EU countries and companies.

Key benefits to existing members resulting from the enlargement include:

- Access to a pool of skilled and unskilled migrant labour who may be willing to work at a lower wage than current market rates.

- Access to wider markets for goods and services.

- An opportunity to invest capital at good rates of return in potentially growing economies.

 11.9 Exchange rates

When you buy t-shirts or other items of clothing produced in China you will want to pay for them in the currency of your own country (unless of course you live in China). The t-shirts will most likely have been imported into your country by a specialist importer or by a large retailer. The Chinese manufacturer that made the t-shirts may not want to be paid by the importer in the currency of your country. This is because the Chinese manufacturer will need to pay their own workers and suppliers of cotton in the currency of China, the yuan. The importer will therefore need to purchase yuan to pay the Chinese manufacturer. Foreign currency can be bought and sold in the foreign exchange market (or forex). This market specializes in exchanging dollars, yuan, rupees and other currencies.

The exchange rate between two currencies is determined by demand and supply. If the demand for US dollars by Indians (to buy American goods) rises quickly while the demand for rupees by American (to buy Indian goods) remains steady, then the value of the dollar will rise against the rupee – for example, from US$1 = 45 rupees to US$1 = 47 rupees.

You can see from this analysis that a major determinant of the value of a currency is how popular the currency is – that is, the strength of the demand for it. One of the major factors influencing demand is the extent to which foreigners want to buy goods from that country. For example, the Singapore dollar tends to be a relatively strong currency because many foreigners buy goods from Singaporean companies.

Another factor strengthening a currency is its use for international trading. For example, the US dollar has for many years been used by countries for trading because it tends to keep its value over time. It is therefore both a means of exchange and a store of value.

There in not just one exchange rate for a currency: it can often be exchanged for the currencies of many other countries – for example the yuan against the dollar, the yuan against the euro, the yuan against the rupee. This means that there are multiple exchange rates.

ACTIVITY

Find out the current exchange rate of the pound against the euro, the US dollar, the yuan and the Indian rupee. After two weeks, check the exchange rates again. How have they altered? What explanations can you provide for this? Produce a graph or chart that shows the rates over six weeks.

Exchange rate systems

A country's government and central bank must decide how to manage (influence) the exchange rate. There are two main approaches:

1. Fixed exchange rates: the value of a currency is fixed against another currency or group of currencies. This fixed rate is maintained by the government and central bank. For example, the government could set the exchange rate such that two dollars' worth of a particular currency might be exchanged for one US dollar (this is actually the case with the Barbados dollar). This helps to make the currency that is fixed against the US dollar stable.

   However, it may make it difficult for the country to sell its goods on international markets if the exchange rate is set at too high a level for exporters to be competitive. A disadvantage of having a fixed rate is that the government has to support the existing rate even when the rate makes it difficult for exporters to sell their goods competitively.

2. Floating exchange rates: The value of your currency changes from day to day according to the demand and supply for it. If we are finding it difficult to sell exports the currency will fall in price (as demand falls). Lowering the price of the exports makes them more competitive and hopefully sales will improve.

Exchange rate fluctuations

Another way of looking at the exchange rate is as the price of buying the currency of one country with that of another country. Like other prices, the exchange rate will then be determined by the demand for and supply of it.

If more people in India want to buy US dollars, the demand curve will shift to the right and the price of dollars will increase when bought with rupees. This may be because more Indians want to import goods from the US. Figure 11.4 shows this change. It is referred to as an appreciation in the price of the dollar.

In contrast, if Indians want to buy fewer goods from the US this leads to a fall in demand for dollars and a fall in value – that is, a depreciation of the dollar. The price of a currency may fall as a result of an increase in the supply of that currency – for example, as a result of citizens of that country using their domestic currency to buy more imports. An example of this is that the US dollar is accepted widely as an international trading currency and more and more dollars have been entering the international exchange market. The increase in the supply of dollars over time (see Figure 11.3) leads to its depreciation against other currencies, such as the EU's euro.

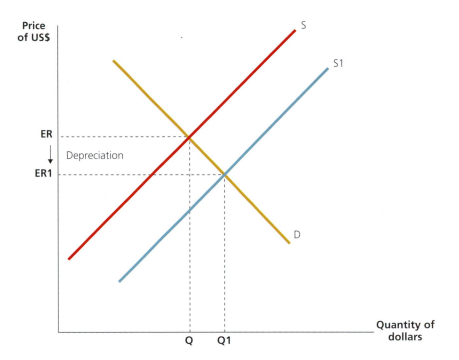

FIGURE 11.3 A depreciation of the dollar against the euro

For the last 20 years the US has been running large current account deficits with the rest of the world. This has helped the world economy because US dollars are widely accepted as a means of international exchange.

Under a system of freely floating exchange rates the value of currencies will appreciate and depreciate continually, in line with changes in demand for and supply of currencies for international exchange. Foreign exchange is bought and sold for trading purposes and also for investment, such as buying shares in companies in other countries. Some people also buy currency in order to speculate – for example, to buy at a low price and sell when prices rise.

A destabilizing effect on currencies can be caused by speculators – people who make money from trading in currencies. Sometimes they will sell a country's currency and others rush to do the same. The speculator might then buy the currency back at a much lower price and gamble that it will rise again.

Currency price can also be affected by the interest rate in one country compared with interest rates in other countries. Investors want to invest where interest rates are higher and raising the rates can encourage in inflow of capital, increasing demand for the currency and leading to a rise in its exchange rate.

TABLE 11.7 Indian rupees (INR) to 1 US dollar (USD)

Date		Exchange rate
Friday	29 March 2013	54.25541
Sunday	31 March 2013	54.30411
Monday	1 April 2013	54.30525
Tuesday	2 April 2013	54.42497
Wednesday	3 April 2013	54.43550
Thursday	4 April 2013	54.89050
Friday	5 April 2013	55.101214

Appreciation of the US dollar against the Indian rupee

The US dollar depreciates against the Indian rupee when there is a fall in the demand for dollars to exchange for rupees.

The US dollar appreciates against the Indian rupee when there is an increase in the demand for dollars to exchange for rupees.

Table 11.7 illustrates an appreciation in the value of the dollar. The table shows historical exchange rates between the Indian rupee (INR) and the US dollar (USD) between Friday 29 March 2013 and Friday 5 April 2013.

We can illustrate this appreciation in the form of Figure 11.4.

Key implications of this chart are that:

- American tourists visiting India exchanging their money on 5 April would receive more rupees in exchange for dollars than those exchanging money on 29 March.

- Whilst the value of the dollar has appreciated against the rupee, the rupee has depreciated against the dollar.

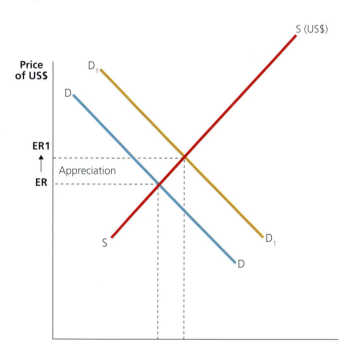

FIGURE 11.4 Appreciation or the US dollar against the Indian rupee

- Indian exporters would find it easier to export goods to the US if this trend continued because it would lead to a falling price of Indian goods in the US.

- US exporters would find it more difficult to export goods to India if this trend continued.

Devaluation and revaluation

Revaluation of a currency occurs when its value is adjusted. For example, the rate of exchange between a country's currency and the US dollar was previously 10 units to one US dollar. Now the government has changed the rate to 5 units equal to one US dollar. This would make the dollars half as expensive to people wanting to buy them with the revalued currency.

In a system where exchange rates are fixed against other currencies they may become overvalued over time. For example, a country might find that at the existing exchange rate it is difficult for exporters to compete with cheaper (or better quality) products from rival countries. The government may then have to act and devalue the currency – that is, force the exchange rate down. The central bank would be instructed to supply an increased quantity of the currency onto international markets. This would reduce its price and bring about devaluation (see Figure 11.5), and at the same time make imports more expensive. These two effects would help to improve the current account balance.

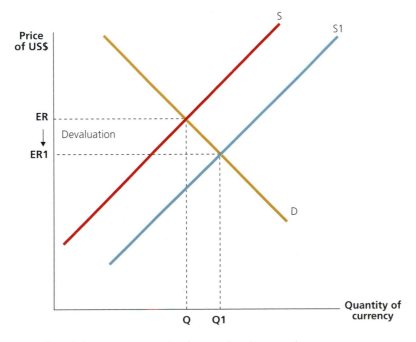

FIGURE 11.5 Devaluing a currency by increasing its supply

Consequences of exchange rate fluctuations

Changing exchange rates affect those most concerned with the trading process – exporters and importers. They also have knock-on impacts on the economy – for example, price changes for consumers (of imported goods) and for producers whose inputs have an imported component, such as the cost of raw materials, including energy costs.

Table 11.8 shows the effect of rises and falls in the value of a currency.

TABLE 11.8 Illustrating the effects of appreciation and depreciation of a currency

Home currency appreciates (gets stronger); external value of the currency goes up.	Exports from home country become more expensive to customers from other countries, therefore more difficult to sell. Exporters will sell less/make less profit. Value of exports decreases.	Imports from other countries become cheaper, including raw materials and finished goods. Importers will find goods from other countries cheaper to buy, so they can sell more in the home country, enabling them to make more profit. Value of imports increases.
Home currency depreciates (gets weaker); external value of the currency goes down.	Exports from home country become less expensive to customers from other countries, therefore easier to sell. Exporters will sell more/make more profit. Value of exports increases.	Imports from other countries become more expensive, including raw materials and finished goods. Importers will find goods from other countries more expensive to buy, so they can sell less in the home country/make less profit. Value of imports increases.

TABLE 11.9 Consequences of exchange rate fluctuations (depending on elasticity)

Australian exporters	Exporting goods with an inelastic demand benefitted from higher sales revenues (other exporters selling good with elastic demand were not able to benefit and may have lost out).
Australian importers	Were able to import goods more cheaply, leading to increasing profit margins. Benefitted from cheaper fuel, raw materials and part-finished goods.
Australian consumers	Benefitted from cheaper prices of imported goods.
Australian government	Benefitted from a healthy economy with a strong foreign trade sector.

Price elasticity of demand for exports and imports

The consequences of exchange rate fluctuations depend on the price elasticity of demand for traded goods. In 2010 the Australian dollar appreciated because more people wanted to buy Australian goods. Demand for these goods was relatively inelastic. The demand for Australian dollars was also relatively inelastic. Table 11.9 shows the effect of this.

The consequences of a depreciating currency

There are also advantages to the depreciation of a country's currency. In 2010 the British pound depreciated against the euro because of the weakness of the UK economy in the 2008–2009 recession. This fall in the value of the pound sterling was a major factor in helping Britain pull out of recession in 2010. In 2010 UK manufacturing reported increases in exports, particularly of modern engineering products, because their goods were less expensive for foreign buyers.

The effect of a depreciating currency depends on the price elasticity of demand for exports and imports. If demand for exports is elastic, a fall in the currency will lead to a greater than proportional increase in sales of exports. If the demand for imports is also elastic, a depreciating currency could lead to a more than proportional fall in imports.

11.10 The euro

One section of the Maastricht Treaty related to the setting up of a monetary union (the European Monetary Union, or EMU).

There are considerable benefits from having a single currency (the euro). For UK citizens (if we were to join the euro) this would mean that they could spend the money they earned in any other Eurozone country. People could move their financial assets such as bank balances freely within the Eurozone. Financial transactions with citizens and businesses within the Eurozone would be carried out in exactly the same way as transactions made in our home economy.

> **Transaction costs** – the costs of making a financial transaction. Creation of the euro as a single currency eliminates the transaction cost of changing money from one currency to another.

KEY TERM

Another benefit of having the euro is that it eliminates exchange rate risks within the Eurozone. Because all 17 countries that use the euro use the same currency there are no exchange rate movements against each other's currencies.

Another key advantage is that it creates clear price transparency. Because there are no exchange rate calculations required it is a straightforward process to make price comparisons involving prices in different countries.

KEY THEME

The benefit of a common currency for business

For large companies the development of a single currency would be particularly beneficial. International trade does not consist of large numbers of 'one-off' transactions. It consists of well-established patterns of trading between individuals and companies.

Many international transactions involve trades within the same company. For example, Unilever (the detergents and home products company) in the UK trading with Unilever in the Netherlands. Very many of these relationships are based on contracts which specify products, prices and conditions of supply months, and sometimes years, ahead. Such arrangements offer security of service and a guarantee of essential components some way into the future. The production process is planned some time in advance of intended delivery dates. Clearly it is advantageous to companies if prices are also negotiated in advance, in order to secure future supplies of components or finished goods at predetermined prices.

Where the trade is conducted within a single country with a single currency this presents little problem. An agricultural cooperative in the Paris basin would not think twice about agreeing to purchase a Renault tractor from a local supplier in three months' time at a fixed price. They may, however, have cause to ponder about importing a tractor from a supplier in the UK at a fixed price in three months' time. For instance, between 2010 and 2012 the value of the euro fell between 15 and 20 per cent against the pound. If the French cooperative had ordered a British tractor it might have found that it was paying substantially more for the tractor as a result of the fall in the value of the euro.

In these situations fluctuations in the value of international currencies can detract in a substantial way from international trade because currency fluctuation confuses commercial calculations. If Britain was part of the Eurozone then commercial exchanges would be a lot simpler and a lot more attractive.

- **Why might a business be reluctant to import from a country with which it does not share the same currency?**

- **What are the benefits of having a common currency with your major trading partners?**

The birth of the euro

On 1 January 1999, 11 sovereign nations finally handed over control of their currencies to a committee of bankers. The euro was launched at a value of just over $1, just over 70 pence at the time. At the time Britain was the only EU member not to join. The currencies of the member states were exchanged for euro notes and coins. The ECB based in Frankfurt took responsibility for monetary policy including interest rates and monetary flows. It was hoped that the credibility and strength of the euro would make it an international reserve currency like the US dollar.

In preparing for the launch of the euro, member states were expected to meet certain 'convergence criteria'. These criteria related to demonstrating sound financial policies within countries. Important criteria included limits to the size of the national debt, public sector borrowing requirements and control over inflation.

In the zeal to create the euro some of the member countries were allowed to join the Eurozone even though they had not fully met the expected criteria. Critics at the time suggested that this was storing up problems for the future.

When the euro was first launched it started to lose value against the dollar and other exchange currencies. In the first two years after its launch the euro continued to lose value and the ECB was forced to intervene to stop the value of the currency from falling even further.

The ECB's actions included:

- Buying euros with its own reserve funds in order to try and pull up the value through increased demand.

- Raising interest rates within the Eurozone to encourage investors to invest, attracted by higher interest rates. Between 5 November 1999 and 6 October 2000 the ECB raised interest rates seven times.

Finally in 2003, with growth in the Eurozone countries sufficient, confidence was placed in the euro and its value continued to rise against the dollar and sterling. The euro had established itself as a credible international exchange currency.

The Eurozone – the Eurozone consists (in 2012) of 17 countries. These are: Austria, Belgium, Finland, France, Germany, Ireland, Italy, Luxembourg, Netherlands, Portugal, Spain, Greece, Cyprus, Malta, Slovenia, Slovakia and Estonia.

KEY TERM

11.11 Crisis in the Eurozone

Any financial system is reliant on users having confidence in that system. Users of a financial system are borrowers, lenders and individuals who use the currency that the system employs. Confidence in the Euro is illustrated in Table 11.10.

TABLE 11.10 Changing confidence in the euro over time

Euro launched in 1999 until 2003	Will the euro work as an international exchange currency? Users are not sure and therefore have limited confidence in the system. Value of the euro falls.
Confidence builds in the euro, 2003–2008	Eurozone countries experience steady growth in trade and GDP. Users become confident in the effectiveness of the euro. Value of the euro rises.
The global financial crisis impacts on weaker members of the Eurozone, 2008 and beyond	The financial crisis exposes countries that had done particularly well in the previous five years – leading to a liquidity crisis in those countries. Value of euro falls.

During the period 2003–2008 there was steady economic growth in the Eurozone countries. For example, Ireland was seen as a 'tiger economy' attracting foreign investors who were impressed by the low costs of setting up in Ireland and low tax rates. Countries such as Greece expanded through programmes of public sector expenditure and social provision.

However, the financial crisis quickly exposed some of the problems associated with being a member of the euro. There is a single value for the euro in international exchange markets based on the average strength of the economies within the Eurozone. For a strong economy such as Germany this can have real positive benefits. Germany produces, among other goods and services, advanced industrial products (e.g. BMW and Audi cars) and complex pharmaceutical products and machine tools. These are products that consumers are willing to pay premium prices for across the globe. Because Germany has adopted the euro it is relatively easy to sell these products in global markets.

However, there are more problems for Greece in being part of what is for them a relatively strong currency group. The euro is stronger than what was previously the Greek currency (the drachma). It therefore became more difficult for Greece to compete internationally. As the Greek private sector became relatively less effective the state stepped in by spending more money through the public sector.

During the financial crisis these problems were really exposed. Whereas Germany, Luxembourg and to a lesser extent Belgium and the Netherlands were relatively well placed because of their stronger economies, the weaker economies of Greece, Portugal, Spain, Ireland and Italy became exposed. Many companies in these countries were driven out of business and the government had to cut back its own expenditure. Governments in countries such as Greece found that they did not have enough money to continue to support their economies and had to turn to the ECB, to the International Monetary Fund (IMF) and to other countries to borrow money in order to survive.

CASE STUDY The Greek bailout

During 2012 the Greek economy was constantly in the news. The Greek government ran out of funds to service the public sector of the economy at a time in which the private sector had crashed. One problem was that everyone had someone else to blame. The IMF, ECB and ultra-conservative politicians in Greece blamed successive Greek governments for wasteful public expenditure, while socialists in Greece blamed international bankers, the German government and the IMF for allowing a crisis to develop resulting from greed in the world financial sector.

In order to receive ongoing bailout funds, in the summer of 2012 Greece's new government had to agree to draconian cutbacks in public expenditure as highlighted in the following article which appeared in *The Economist* (21 July 2012):

> Tempers frayed this week, as Greece's new coalition government tried, and failed, to find 11.5 billion euros of spending cuts demanded by the EU and IMF in 2013 and 2014 as part of the country's second international bail-out. 'Some ministers didn't seem to realise their budgets need to be slashed, not trimmed', fumed a finance ministry official.

Yet one culprit, Antonis Roupatkiotis, the justice minister, noted that his ministry's allocation of increasingly scarce funds had already shrunk from 950 million dollars in 2009 to 550 million this year. He claimed that fresh cuts would result in a near-collapse of the judicial process. It was already plagued by inadequate court facilities and long delays in reaching judgements – especially in cases involving alleged corruption and tax evasion.

After a week of number crunching, the team led by Yannis Stournaras, the technocratic finance minister, was able to present only about 7.5 billion euros of cuts for approval by the coalition government's three political leaders. About 4 billion of the cuts would come from reductions in social spending and from imposing a ceiling on public-sector pension payments of 2,400 euros a month, as well as barring Greeks from drawing two separate pensions.

The health care system would also take a hit: spending on drugs and medical equipment, which health ministry officials say is still among the highest per person in southern Europe, would be cut by 2.1 billion euros.

- Why has the Greek economy been hit particularly hard by the financial crisis?

- How is the Greek government responding to this crisis? Do you think that it is appropriate that the Greeks should be required to make such cutbacks in order to receive bailout funds from the EU?

Because Britain is not part of the Eurozone it has not suffered as directly as the Eurozone countries from issues associated with bailouts for Eurozone countries. However, there are ways in which Britain is directly impacted by the Eurozone crisis:

- Because the Eurozone is our major trading partner then the collapse of this area immediately impacts on UK exporting.

- The weakening of the Eurozone has been complemented by a rise in the value of the pound against the euro making it more difficult for exporters to sell into the Eurozone. At the same time imports from the Eurozone have become more competitive and cheaper in Britain.

- Although Britain is not part of the Eurozone it has committed government funds to help to bail out the Eurozone (although they are smaller than those contributed by similar size economies such as France and Germany).

- Because the UK government has not been as committed to bailing out the Eurozone as many other European companies it has lost some friends who see Britain as not being fully committed to the concepts of political, economic and social union.

The problem with the Eurozone crisis is that it seems to be self-perpetuating. Some commentators would like Greece to leave the Eurozone and go back to the drachma. However, it is argued that if Greece leaves then who is next. There will simply be a run on the next weakest economy. Already (July 2012) the Spanish government has had to go to the ECB and the IMF to secure bailout funds.

Key issues associated with the euro, include:

- The initial cost of setting up the euro (i.e. the initial adjustment from national currencies to the euro). There was also some criticism that the creation of the euro had an inflationary impact (i.e that sellers raised their prices at the time that the euro was launched).

  The loss of control over macro-economic policy by member states. The ECB sets its interest rates in line with economic circumstances in the Eurozone as a whole rather than being able to cater for individual needs of separate states.

The issues associated with handing over powers to the ECB have been highlighted by the recent Eurozone crisis. Once a country is part of the Eurozone and is suffering an economic crisis:

- It is unable to alter its interest rates (it is only the ECB that can do that).

- It is unable to devalue its currency against those of its trading partners because they all share the same currency.

- It can't pump more money into its national financial system – only the ECB can do that.

- It can't increase public sector spending because the ECB and the IMF will not allow the country to do that as a condition of receiving a bailout.

11.12 Terms of trade

Earlier in this chapter we explored the law of comparative advantage to help you understand the economic reasons for specialization. It is important to recognize that countries will only benefit from trade if they do so on terms that benefit both parties. It is a similar situation to when an accountant completes the accounts for their window cleaner. Both may have a comparative advantage in their chosen area and they can benefit from exchanging services for a price. However, if the window cleaner or the accountant decide to charge each other what are considered unreasonable prices then they might not carry out an exchange. If businesses in Country A put up their prices by too much then consumers in Country B may not be inclined to make an exchange.

The terms of trade are simply the average price of exports divided by the average price of imports. When the average price of exports relative to the price of imports increases then the terms of trade improve. This is because a country only has to exchange a smaller basket of goods (exports) to receive the same sized basket of imports as before. The terms of trade are usually set out as an index.

$$\text{Terms of trade} = \frac{\text{Index of export prices}}{\text{Index of import prices}} \times \frac{100}{1}$$

A terms of trade index will start out as 100 in a given year. When the index goes up above 100 then the terms of trade have improved compared with the base year. When they go below 100 they have deteriorated compared with the base year.

Remember though, that when the terms of trade improve this does not necessarily mean that the balance of payments will improve. It all depends on the elasticity of demand for exports compared with the elasticity of demand for imports.

When the terms of trade improve and demand for exports is relatively inelastic compared with the demand for imports then the balance of payments will improve.

When exchange rates change this will also alter the terms of trade, so there are a number of things we need to consider when examining the impact of changes in the exchange rate for our currency:

1. Has the exchange rate appreciated or depreciated?

2. What is the impact on the terms of trade?

3. Have the terms of trade improved or deteriorated?

4. What is the elasticity of demand for exports and for imports?

5. What is the impact of these changes on the balance of payments?

Reflective questions

4   Under what circumstances would an appreciation in the currency lead to an improvement in the balance of payments of a country?

5   Under what circumstances would a depreciation in the currency lead to an improvement in the balance of payments of a country?

11.13 Summary

In this chapter we have examined the nature of the international economy in which businesses operate. Most large companies (and many smaller ones) engage in international trade – buying and selling raw materials, and semi-finished and final goods. Key influences affecting business are the rate of exchange between currencies and the trading relations that a country has with exchange partners. Increasingly the world is organizing around regional trade blocs, so a significant external environmental factor for UK business is our relationship with trading partners in the EU.

KEY IDEAS

The theory of international trade

- International trade is based on specialization, which is based on comparative advantage.

- Comparative advantage involves a country being able to produce with a lower opportunity cost than a rival and trading items in which it has the lowest opportunity cost.

UK trade specialization

- The UK exports goods in which it has the greatest comparative advantage.

- Examples of UK exports include manufactured goods such as telecommunications equipment and automobiles and services based in the City of London such as banking and insurance.

- The UK's main trading partners are the United States, the EU and China. The majority of UK trade is with EU countries.

The balance of payments

- The balance of payments is an account showing sources of funds and uses of funds. The account will always balance.

- The current account shows trade in goods and services. Typically the UK runs a deficit in visible trade and a surplus in invisible trade. The overall current account shows a negative balance.

- Other parts of the balance of payments principally consist of capital flows.

The European Union (EU)

- The EU is the UK's main trading partner. It was originally set up as the European Coal and Steel Community before becoming the European Economic Community and later the European Union.

- The EU is based on economic, social and political integration.

- The EU is a free trade area, has a common external tariff, and 11 member countries are part of a currency union based on the Euro.

- Key advantages of being a member of the EU relate to access to markets, the ability to benefit from economies of scale and the reduction in costs of doing business.

Exchange rates

- An exchange rate is the rate at which the currency of one country will exchange against one or more international currencies.

- A fixed exchange rate is one where the rate of exchange between two currencies is maintained at an agreed level (e.g. US$1 = 2 Barbados dollars).

- A floating or free exchange rate is where the exchange rate between two currencies is determined on a day-to-day basis by the demand and supply of that currency.

- Fixed rates create greater stability and clearer expectations but can cause problems when the rate is set too low or too high. A floating/free exchange rate adjusts to the relative strength of an economy in international trading and enables the value of the currency to reflect the current strength of that country's economy.

The euro

- The euro is the common currency of the EU.

- Monetary policy within the Eurozone is managed by the European Central Bank (ECB).

- After an initial period of difficulty the euro grew in strength but has been badly hit by the financial crisis leading to a loss in value.

REVIEW QUESTIONS

1. Differentiate between absolute and comparative advantage. How does comparative advantage provide a basis for international trade specialization?

2. What are the main benefits to a country from engaging in international trade?

3. Outline the structure of the balance of payments accounts.

4. Describe the typical pattern of the UK's balance of payments on current account.

5. How is a floating exchange rate different from a fixed one?

6. In what ways has the development of the EU involved a deepening process (i.e. greater integration) and in what ways has a widening process (expansion) occurred?

7. What are the key economic features of the EU?

8. What are the benefits and costs of having a single economic currency?

9. Which features of the EU has the UK been slow to sign up to and why?

10. What are the 'terms of trade'?

RECOMMENDED READING

Charter, D. (2012) *Au Revoir Europe: What if Britain left the European Union?* London, Bitetback Publishing.

REFERENCES

Cameron, D. (2013) 'EU Speech', 23 January. Available at: http://www.number10. gov.uk/news/david-cameron-eu-speech/ (accessed January 2013).

Cecchini Report (1992) 'Europe 1992: The Overall Challenge (Summary of the Cecchini Report)'. Available at: http://aei.pitt.edu/3813/ (accessed January 2013).

Economist, The (2012) 'The Greek Bailout', *The Economist*, 21 July 2012: 34.

USEFUL WEBSITES

www.uktradeinfo.com – the most useful figures for UK trade can be found at this government site.

12 The economics of globalization

CHAPTER OBJECTIVES

After carefully reading the content of this chapter you should be able to:

- Discuss what is meant by globalization in a business and economics context

- Identify the roles played by the main actors in the economic processes associated with globalization

- Analyse the roles of the World Trade Organization (WTO), International Monetary Fund (IMF) and World Bank

- Explain common forms of protectionism that are used to limit trade

- Outline the nature of foreign direct investment and its impact on the global economy

- Suggest ways in which firms can enter global markets

12.1 Introduction

This chapter introduces one of the most important aspects of the modern macro-economy, the nature of globalization. Business operates in an external environment in which economic forces are particularly significant. Key economic drivers of globalization have been the growth of international markets and the expansion of international trade. The growth of the global economy has been supported by the spread of free market economics across the globe which has encouraged specialization and trade. The development of international means of exchange (i.e. reserve trading currencies such as the dollar) and the influence of international bodies such as the World Trade Organization (WTO) have enabled a process of globalization.

However, the concept of 'globalization' (whatever it signifies) is by no means universally accepted as a good thing and for some the recent financial crisis is seen as a symbol of the wider crisis of globalization. This chapter also looks at different forms of protectionism, which is one approach that countries take to defend their home markets against more aggressive international competitors. The chapter concludes by defining and describing foreign direct investment (FDI) and looks at some of the ways that business organizations can enter new markets.

12.2 What is globalization?

No economics text would be complete without a chapter on the economics of globalization. Recent economic events have increased our awareness that all of us are dependent upon or impacted by what is happening in the global economy. It is not just car workers in France, or construction workers in Poland, that have felt the impact of the financial crisis but also taxi drivers in Greece and bankers in London.

In 2012, most people were aware that there has been a rapid slowdown in the growth of economic activity not just in Europe and the United States but in emerging economies, particularly India and China. Globalization is often cited as one of the major culprits for the financial crisis.

KEY THEME

The crisis of globalization

Robert Skidelsky (2010) argues that the 'financial crisis' was fundamentally a crisis of globalization and the thought processes that underpinned it. Skidelsky identifies three kinds of failure that led to the financial crisis:

1. Institutional – 'banks mutated from utilities into casinos'. Skidelsky argues that regulators and policy-makers had come to believe in an 'efficient market theory' – a view that financial markets would not consistently mis-price financial assets and therefore needed little regulation. In the event

what actually happened was that many assets were overpriced for a substantial period of time.

2. Intellectual – that thinkers had failed to understand that the market could fail to allocate resources in an efficient way. Skidelsky quotes Alan Greenspan, the Federal Reserve Chairman, who stated in the autumn of 2008 that the Fed's monetary management had been based on a flaw. Greenspan stated that the 'whole intellectual edifice . . . collapsed in the summer of [2007]'. The failure was that the majority of economists believed in the neoclassical economic view of markets as being self-correcting.

3. Moral – the flawed belief in economic growth for its own sake – based on a worship of money as a means to 'achieve a good life'.

● **What did the financial crisis have to do with globalization?**

● **Which of the failures that Skidelsky outlines do you think would have been the most likely culprit for creating the financial crisis?**

● **What other aspects do you think could have triggered the crisis?**

Globalization has been blamed in recent times for many different problems – for example, climate change and environmental pollution, crop failures and famines in Sub-Saharan Africa, job insecurity and unemployment across the world just to name a few.

But what exactly is globalization? There are two polar opposite views on this (see Figure 12.1).

The development of a world society fuelled by greed, in which there is increasing inequality between the haves and the have nots, and in which resource depletion and pollution are creating catastrophic global problems from which no one is immune. Population continues to rise at alarming rates over and beyond the carrying capacity of the planet.

The development of a world society based on growth, expanding markets and trade between nations; the growth of the global economy provides the opportunity for better living standards for all, resulting from the development of new technologies, markets and products. Market economics provides a rational way of allocating resources to their best uses.

FIGURE 12.1 Opposite views of globalization

TABLE 12.1 Evidence to support opposite views of globalization

Negative evidence	Positive evidence
Rising numbers living in poverty	Rising world GDP per head
Climate change	Improving global science
Loss of biodiversity	New technologies
Financial crisis	New products
Deteriorating corporate governance	Improving corporate governance
Ineffectiveness of economic tools	Strength of economic tools

Both of these perspectives of globalization are well supported and both sides can point to evidence to support their case (see Table 12.1).

For many economists the reality of globalization lies somewhere between these two polar extremes. Economists recognize the benefits of globalization and the drawbacks. Economists study both the negative evidence and the positive evidence in order to get a better understanding of what is taking place and the contribution that they can make.

KEY TERM

Globalization – globalization is a slippery concept. It is one that can be interpreted in different ways according to a person's view of whether globalization is desirable or undesirable. The processes described by the term globalization relate to the increasing integration of different parts of world systems including communications, transport/travel, finance and trade, as well as cooperation. It is a complex concept because it also deals with issues such as individual identity – for example, do we see ourselves as global citizens?

From an economic perspective globalization can be conceptualized in the following way. Globalization can be defined as the increasing integration of markets for goods, services, capital and people. Globalization involves an acceleration in the expansion of international production, distribution, marketing and selling of goods into more worldwide geographical locations in response to changing demands in the marketplace.

It is all very well to attribute globalization to some external globalizer outside of ourselves. However, much of the pressure for change comes from consumers. Today many of us expect our local supermarkets to supply us with exotic food products from all over the world throughout the year, and we accept it as the norm that we can buy consumer durables such as cars, televisions, DVD players and mobile phones which may have been produced in Brazil or South East Asia.

The UK and other countries' companies respond to this globalization process by developing global strategies based on sensitivity to events and forces that are reshaping the business environment. An organization must respond to its external environment and adjust its corporate strategy accordingly. For example, technological advances are opening up world markets to an organization's competitors. If the organization does not respond to this challenge then its own business will get left behind.

As businesses become more involved with the global economy, they will need to constantly review the appropriateness of their current mission and objectives. Long-term planning has to be adjusted to take into account the changes involved in the global economy. Missions, objectives and strategies need to be adjusted to build a global dimension.

KEY THEME

Three or more waves of globalization

A very useful analysis of the development of thinking about globalization was presented by Luke Martell in 2007. He identified three waves of thinking about globalization based on prevailing ideas. These were:

1. First wave – globalist thinking.
2. Second wave – sceptical thinking (about globalization)
3. Post-sceptical or transformationalist thinking (about globalization)

First-wave thinkers

Martell traces early thinking about globalization as a theme to the 1980s. During the late 1980s and the 1990s writers such as Kenichi Ohmae (1990, 1995) advanced third-wave thinking about the power of globalization in sweeping away national boundaries, economies and cultures. National economies were seen as losing their significance as multinational corporations became more powerful, as capital flowed more freely around the globe and large companies were able to transfer technology and money seemingly at will to new locations.

The literature at the time was full of examples of multinationals whose sales revenues were greater than those of some substantial European economies (i.e. GDP figures). Martell cites the examples of Coca-Cola and McDonalds as examples of companies with multinational ownership, distributed production facilities, workforces and consumers. Other examples that were frequently cited as exemplars were Unilever and Shell. Both the supporters of globalization (e.g. neoliberal economists) and those in opposition (e.g. neo-Marxists) could agree that the world economy had opened up.

Martell argues that the first wave was typically seen as being 'economistic' in nature – a period in which business interests took centre stage as a driving force relative to the powers of governments. National cultures were seen as becoming more 'homogenized' (similar). (The development of the Internet and globalized television broadcasting helped to accelerate this trend.)

Second-wave thinkers

Martell identifies the second wave of thinkers as being sceptical about globalization. A good example of this was the writing of Hirst and Thompson

(1998). Hirst and Thompson carried out detailed analysis which showed that earlier periods of history (e.g. during the late nineteenth and early twentieth centuries) had been periods of extensive global trade and liberalization, which had been then put on the back foot by two world wars – and it was only in the late twentieth century that the process of trade liberalization was catching up on previous periods of economic liberalization.

The sceptics argued that the evidence for globalization was actually quite thin. They argued that nation states continued to be powerful, particularly the US and in Europe. They pointed to evidence of nationalism being strong (and actually strengthening) in key areas of the world.

Rather than a global economy developing there was strong evidence that the globe was actually dominated by uneven development and differentiation in the spread of globalization – a continuation in the division between the rich world and the poor world. Countries at the core of the world economy (e.g. the US, Germany and the 'tiger economies' such as South Korea) were moving forward while peripheral countries (e.g. Sub-Saharan Africa) was less integrated into the world economy.

Questions were raised by a number of sceptics about whether globalization would bring with it benefits such as the alleviation of poverty. Even in terms of products there was still an emphasis on differentiation. Martell cites the example of McDonalds which was tailoring its products to local rather than global requirements (e.g. shrimp burgers in Japan and kosher burgers for Jewish customers).

Post-sceptical/transformational thinking

The third wave consists of groups of thinkers (e.g. Held and McGrew, 2003) who cite available evidence to demonstrate that the process of globalization is clearly evident before our eyes.

Third-wave thinkers synthesize (bring together) the ideas of the first two waves. They present a more complex picture of globalization 'in which globalisation is seen as occurring but without just sweeping all away before it' (Martell, 2007). In the economic sphere national government and national economic institutions sit alongside global players and impacts such as the movement of capital by international finance and multinational companies. Economic problems such as inequality should not be seen just as a difference between core and peripheral nations because problems like poverty are a feature within the core areas too (e.g. within poorer areas of major cities), and affluence exists in substantial measures in poorer countries (e.g. within affluent suburbs of major cities).

Third-wave thinkers do not see globalization as being an inevitable process that pushes all existing institutions aside – rather, we as global citizens can shape the process of globalization. Third wavers recognize that globalization is leading to significant changes but it is far more complex than the views set out by first-wave thinkers.

The economic dimensions of the 'three waves' can be set out in the following way (see Figure 12.2).

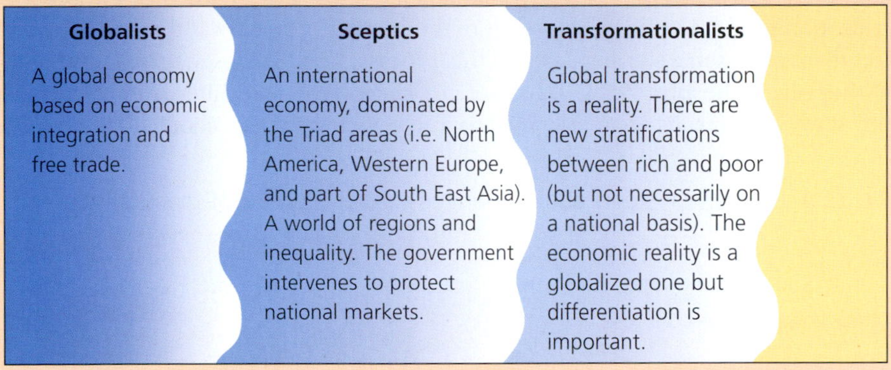

Globalists	Sceptics	Transformationalists
A global economy based on economic integration and free trade.	An international economy, dominated by the Triad areas (i.e. North America, Western Europe, and part of South East Asia). A world of regions and inequality. The government intervenes to protect national markets.	Global transformation is a reality. There are new stratifications between rich and poor (but not necessarily on a national basis). The economic reality is a globalized one but differentiation is important.

FIGURE 12.2 Economic images of the three waves

Source: Based on Martell (2007).

- **Which of these waves of thinking matches the evidence of your wider reading, the information that you receive through the media and your own experience of living in the modern world?**

- **What are the implications for business of this process of globalization?**

- **Do you think that we have moved beyond third-wave thinking to a fourth wave? If so what are the features of fourth-wave thinking?**

The recent financial crisis has thrown the issue of globalization into sharp perspective. In the period leading up to 2007 the world economy had been growing, particularly in the so-called emerging economies such as China and India which had been growing by close to 10 per cent (GDP growth). However, the financial crisis put the brakes on the growth of the world economy and plunged North America and Europe into recession with a knock-on effect for global trade.

For a number of thinkers this signalled a fundamental weakness in a globalization process underpinned by market thinking. A number of writers identify the financial crisis as representing a fundamental flaw in the dynamics of globalization. In an increasingly connected world shocks to one part of the system can lead to a fundamental crisis with a range of knock-on effects for more and more parts of that system. Failures in the financial system spill over into the industrial system, and national governments do not have the economic strength or finance to save their domestic economies.

Initially relatively small economies have to seek bailouts from the international financial system and then this triggers problems in progressively larger economies (e.g. Spain and Italy). What are required are an international financial system and governance structures to prevent the negative impacts stemming from a globalized financial economy from spreading further.

What is clear is that the recent financial crisis is forcing thinkers to reappraise the process of globalization, which can only be a good thing.

In 2009, the American consultancy company McKinsey carried out a survey of global trends. They asked business executives what their view was of whether the process to globalization would slow down as a result of the crisis. The result was that most executives expect there to be some slowing down in this process. The McKinsey survey was based on what they saw as the most visible aspects of globalization – trade, international capital and labour flows. The results are represented in Table 12.2 (based on about 1,000 responses).

TABLE 12.2 Executives' views about changes in the process of globalization

	Slowed	No change	Accelerated
Commitment to free market economics	72	19	10
Capital flows across countries	64	16	20
Trade	64	20	16
Movement of labour	56	16	27
Extent of companies' global operations	51	17	33
Integration of financial markets	48	17	35
Influence of international organizations	41	21	38

Note: Expected conditions 3–5 year from now (table adapted from McKinsey findings).

One area of interest that the table reveals is that it is what many see as the intellectual driving force behind globalization that the executives were seeing as most likely to slow down – and the development of financial markets and the influence of international organizations as least likely to slow down.

Some views on the idea of the development of globalization are much more critical and deep seated, as illustrated by the following key theme which explores an anti-global perspective.

KEY THEME

The world is not for sale

José Bové is one of the most widely recognized members of the anti-globalization protest movement in the world today. He came to the attention of the world's media when he led some Farmers' Confederation followers on an attack on a McDonald's under construction in the southern French town of Millau in August 1999.

Initially Bové was involved in local issues protesting against the powers of the state in France, particularly in relation to the local economy. This then developed into a fight against globalization in the form of the American multinational

McDonald's. Bové has increasingly fought the issue of globalization through the world's media, acting as an anti-globalization spokesman in protests against the WTO. He led an invasion by 1,300 Brazilian farmers of plantations run by the American biotechnology firm Monsanto.

Bové's finest hour came with the dismantling of the McDonald's in the French town of Millau in response to a tariff placed on French cheese by the United States because the French had refused to allow hormone-treated beef to be imported from the US. For Bové it was a form of natural justice to strike back at McDonald's as a symbol of *malbouffe* (bad food).

Bové described the protest in the following way in 2002:

> We wanted to do this protest in broad daylight, with a large group of people, a non-violent action, but symbolically very strong, and up front with the authorities. We were careful to explain ahead of time to the police that our objective was to dismantle the McDonald's. They informed their superiors and the police chief. Then an officer from the police department called us to say that he was going to ask the manager at McDonald's for a sign of some kind so we could destroy that, that it be more symbolic. We told him: 'Are you kidding? That's nuts. We're going to dismantle the doors and windows.' . . . The protest went along and everybody, including the kids, helped dismantle the interior of the building; partitions, some doors, electrical outlets, and sheet metal on the roof that was nailed down but which came up easily, because it was part of a kit, decorative stuff. It was really a light-weight piece of construction the whole place. Everything was put into two tractor wagons, while some people repainted the roof of the restaurant . . . we took off in a parade to police headquarters in Millau . . . We unloaded the wagons in front of the police station.

After the action McDonald's filed a complaint and Bové and four others were placed in jail. During the period of imprisonment the campaign received letters of support and money from all over the world, including the United States.

- **In what ways can Bové's protest be seen as a campaign for local rights in the face of a globalization process?**

- **Why did Bové see it as important to engage in direct action?**

- **In what way was Bové able to use globalization to fight globalization?**

- **Do you see Bové's actions as forming a coherent critique or protest against globalization?**

- **What do you think would have been McDonald's perspective in relation to their right to set up and operate in Millau?**

Reflective questions

1   Do you feel that the anti-globalizers have a valid case?

2   Is globalization a process that should be encouraged or held in check?

12.3 Who is involved in the globalization process?

Having established that there are different ways of viewing and interpreting the process of globalization and that globalization raises heated debate and conflict (and in some cases direct action), it is next important to identify the groups involved in the globalization process.

The key groups that are introduced in this section are:

1.   Multinational and transnational companies

2.   International consumers

3.   International governments

4.   International financial institutions

5.   International institutions including the WTO, World Bank and IMF

6.   Trading blocs

Multinational and transnational companies

A multinational company (MNC) is one that operates (produces, sells or provides a service) in more than one country. Typically when we refer to multinationals we are talking about large companies operating in several countries and sometimes with a global reach. The most obvious example of a global corporation is Coca-Cola whose marketing slogan is to provide its drinks 'within an arms reach of desire' and who have set out to make Coca-Cola as popular as tea.

There are many other examples of MNCs including giant oil companies such as Shell and BP, telecommunications companies such as Vodafone and a range of computer-related companies such as Intel (microchips) and Microsoft (operating systems). Clearly an important part of the strategic agenda of these companies is global domination. Multinational strategies are examined in greater detail in Section 12.6.

KEY TERM

Transnationality index – the term transnational refers to the extent to which a firm carries out business in markets other than its home market. The United Nations Conference on Trade and Development has created a 'transnationality index' which measures the percentage of a company's business that takes place outside its home market.

TABLE 12.3 Transnationality indexes for selected companies

Company	Principal sector	Index (%)
Nestlé	Food and well-being	95
Vodafone	Mobile telecommunications	82
Exxon Mobile	Oil and gas	65
McDonald's	Fast food	61
General Motors	Automobiles	59
Sony	Electrical goods	58
Unilever	Household products	58

The transnationality index is based on three components:

1. Foreign sales compared with total sales of the firm.

2. Number of foreign workers compared with total workers in the firm.

3. The value of foreign assets compared with the total assets of the firm.

UNCTAD figures reveal firms with a transnationality index of more than 50 per cent in 2012 (see Table 12.3).

Each of the companies listed has a very clear brand image that is widely recognized across the globe. These companies provide standardized products that can be produced to scale using standard manufacturing procedures. The standard production and marketing systems of these companies can readily be applied to new markets across the globe. All of these companies have a major presence in the world's largest markets: the US, Europe, India and China.

International consumers

International consumers are ones that purchase goods and services that are provided by international companies, as opposed to local products. More and more consumers fit into this category. For 50 years or more large numbers of consumers from across the globe have made the occasional purchase from international companies (e.g. soap from Unilever and Procter and Gamble, and canned foods from Heinz). However, since the opening up of global markets from the 1980s onwards billions of global customers have started to consistently purchase a range of branded goods.

It is important to recognize that the world's biggest markets for consumer goods (by population numbers) today are not the North American markets but China, India and Africa which are geographical regions each consisting of more than 1 billion potential customers. Large multinationals recognize that once a consumer's income in a developing market rises above a certain threshold level they start to purchase Marlboro cigarettes, Sunlight soap or Lipton ice tea rather than local varieties.

International governments

International governments have a highly active role in the globalization process. Governments recognize the potential benefits as well as the dangers of globalization. Governments recognize that multinational companies bring with them jobs and technology transfer. They bring with them the potential to earn much needed foreign currency and 'sweeteners' for being allowed to operate in a particular territory.

The state therefore tends to build relationships with favoured multinationals (e.g. the Nigerian government works closely with Shell to exploit oil resources, and the UK government works with Nissan and other Japanese car makers to develop a car industry in this country). Multinationals help to contribute dynamism to an economy – helping to provide jobs and tax revenues. On the negative side multinationals can create aspects of 'dependency'. The host government may be required to make political and economic concessions to win partnership with the multinational. Some multinationals contribute to corruption in a country by lining the pockets of corrupt officials, helping to create a culture of corruption.

International governments also work closely with the private financial sector – including international banks and international institutional lenders such as the World Bank and the IMF. This is an area that has proved problematic for many countries in the past (and today). Countries have borrowed from lenders for development purposes and to finance the government sector. This has led to increased levels of debt, particularly in countries where economic growth has not been at the levels expected. The knock-on effect has been one of 'dependency'. Borrowing governments have had to accept requirements set out by the lenders, resulting in the loss of the government's autonomy to set its own policies.

International financial institutions

The development of the global economy has been fuelled by finance from international capital markets. Investors continually seek the investment opportunities that yield the highest rate of return. It is possible to invest in the 'sovereign debt' of almost every country on the globe and the shares of most large multinationals can easily be bought on international stock markets. Investors seek to maximize returns on (what may be risky) investments in order to achieve the most desirable incomes. Investment usually involves an element of risk particularly in an international context.

International investors typically consist of large financial institutions that pool investment from a variety of sources (e.g. pension funds consisting of the pension contributions of many future pensioners and investment trusts pooling the contributions of many small investors). In addition investors include high net-worth individuals looking for a return on their investment. Other sources of funds include the investment arms of major commercial banks such as HBOS and Barclays. Risk capital in search of high returns from these sources became a major source of international capital in the period leading up to and after the financial crisis.

International institutions including the WTO, World Bank and IMF

Since the Second World War there has been a substantial growth in the power and influence of international economic institutions – the WTO, the World Bank and the IMF. These institutions are examined in more detail in Section 12.4. Their significance in terms of globalization processes is that they have enabled countries to gain access to liquid and long-term capital that have facilitated the development process, helped countries through short-term (and long-term) debt crises and promoted the expansion of global trade.

Trading blocs

Trading blocs such as the North American Free Trade Areas and the European Union (EU) have helped to accelerate trade within large regional groupings, and also provided an impetus to wider trade liberalization through the WTO.

In the creation of trading blocs there are different levels of integration, as set out in Table 12.4.

If you study Table 12.4 you can see that as we move from left to right we have increased integration within a trading bloc. For example, the EU lies somewhere between a complete economic and political union but has still a long way to go (e.g. lack of common currency, only some shared political institutions).

It is important to understand the linkages between the global players and the dynamics of these inter-relationships in order to understand the power of globalization as a concept and as a reality (see Table 12.5).

While Table 12.5 shows that there is an extensive dynamic for globalization in many parts of the world there is resistance, often to protect local interests including business interests. This is illustrated in the case study below relating to the oil industry in Brazil.

TABLE 12.4 Different levels of economic and political integration

Free trade area	Customs union	Common market	Economic union	Political and economic union
Removal of tariffs between countries	Removal of tariffs between countries	Removal of tariffs between countries	Removal of tariffs between countries	Removal of tariffs between countries
	Common external tariff	Common external tariff	Common external tariff	Common external tariff
		Capital and labour mobility between countries	Capital and labour mobility between countries	Capital and labour mobility between countries
			Common economic policy and shared currency	Common economic policy and shared currency
				One government

TABLE 12.5 Linkages between the global players

Global players	Why they want to get involved	Impact of involvement
Multinationals	To access larger markets (generate more sales and revenues).	Supplying global products, global employers and global partners (e.g. with national governments).
Consumers	To access global products such as internationally recognized brands.	Providing global demand for goods and services.
Governments	To manage the process of 'globalization' within their boundaries, and to secure 'benefits' from partnership with multinationals, financial institutions and international economic institutions.	Legitimizes the role of multinationals, strengthens the power of multinationals and acts as a check on the activities of multinationals.
Financial institutions	To provide capital in order to yield a return for investors.	Provides the capital that enables business expansion and government borrowing. Potential to destabilize markets.
International economic institutions	To encourage liberalization of trade and to provide liquid and long-term capital for economic growth.	Establishes some of the rules that govern international exchange, development policies and relationships. Often seen to have strong pro-market focus.
Trading blocs	To further the trading interests and other collaborative benefits to members.	Creates a momentum for wider trade liberalization but can also trigger trade wars between large blocs.

12.4 The economic institutions of globalization

The period between the two world wars was one of economic crisis largely as a result of the failure of governments to set in place a workable international financial system. There was a lot of mistrust between countries resulting in nations pursuing their own self-interest at the expense of the development of an effectively functioning trade system. Because the world economic system was in crisis countries tended to impose restrictions on imports rather than to engage in free trade.

Key problems that were exposed were:

- A reduction in world trade resulting from trade restrictions.

- Weak development of international exchange currencies that would generally be accepted in trade by all countries (before the First World War gold had been the international exchange currency).

- Lack of international financial institutions for supporting world trade and development.

CASE STUDY Local content rules in Brazil

Offshore oil reserves were discovered in Brazil in 2007. This was a huge find comparable to the discovery of oil in the North Sea off the coast of Britain. Brazil has sought to ensure that the exploitation of these oil reserves is largely carried out by Brazilian companies.

Brazil introduced local content rules. Legislation was passed which has ensured that up to 65 per cent of deep-water drilling and 85 per cent of onshore blocks are controlled by Brazilians. In addition there are caps on the foreign provision of equipment and services so that 85 per cent of these are provided by Brazilian companies.

The oil industry in Brazil is dominated by the state-controlled oil company Petrobas. The problem for the exploitation of the oilfields is that Petrobas and the other oil companies in Brazil may not have the capacity to fully exploit this scarce resource. Petrobas has regularly had to reduce its forecasts of how much oil it will be able to produce and this has led to regular falls in the value of the company's shares.

The government in Brazil has also capped the price of fuel in Brazil at a low figure, making it difficult for Petrobas to generate the level of profits required to grow at the rate required for efficient production. The company is lacking in sufficient oil rigs and supply boats to effectively manage its operations. In a developing economy raising fuel prices is a particularly sensitive issue because low fuel costs are a major driver of growth.

- To what extent is Brazil's policy of price controls on fuel prices and local content rules a process of resistance to forces of globalization?
- What are the benefits of pursuing this policy?
- What are the potential drawbacks?

Immediately after the Second World War a meeting was held at Bretton Woods in the US which created the foundations for a new world economic order. The Bretton Woods Agreement (1945) created the two major institutions which have been fundamental in the international economy ever since. Bretton Woods established the World Bank and the International Monetary Fund (IMF).

The World Bank

The main purpose of the World Bank is to provide assistance to nations to support them in the process of development. Most countries in the world today are members of the World Bank. When the World Bank was set up it was called the International Bank for Reconstruction and Development and its funds were used to help reconstruct war-ravaged European economies. Today the Bank lends mainly to developing countries.

In the 1960s and 1970s much of the lending of the World Bank was to countries for major infrastructure projects (e.g. the building of dams, railways and bridges). The emphasis has today shifted so that in addition to infrastructure support the World Bank also lends for welfare development (e.g. expenditure on education and health services). The World Bank sees itself as a partner with a borrower nation – it doesn't lend the total amount of the sum required, expecting the host nation to provide some funds itself. The World Bank also provides technical support and advice to developing nations.

Loans provided by the World Bank are often tied to expectations of structural reform in the borrowing nation. Countries will be expected to put in place 'structural adjustment plans'.

KEY TERM

Structural adjustment – structural adjustment typically requires a borrower nation to put in place 'robust' economic institutions – for example, to reduce government spending and public debt as a percentage of GDP, to engage in privatization and market liberalization, to show progress towards democracy and so on. Critics of structural adjustment see this as including a process of political manipulation, particularly as a way of imposing free market economics on developing nations.

The International Monetary Fund (IMF)

The creation of the IMF was a major step and should be seen as an important enabler of globalization. Again, most nations in the world are members of the IMF. Member countries contribute to a central pool of currencies. The size of the contribution depends on the size of the member state's GDP and the extent of their foreign trade. The central pool of currencies provides the basis for the IMF to lend to nations requiring funds.

The IMF has contributed in two major ways to globalization:

1. By enabling the convertibility of currencies. The currencies of all member nations are convertible (at various exchange rates) into other members' currencies. This enables the expansion of trade.

2. Helping to create more stable exchange rates. Today most countries have floating exchange rates that fluctuate depending on the demand and supply of these currencies. The IMF has created rules that manage the relationship between these currencies. The IMF also provides short-term funds that help the monetary authorities of countries (typically a central bank) to maintain rates at relatively stable levels. This means that when there is a crisis of confidence in a country (and hence in its currency) there is some back-up provided by the IMF preventing the value of a currency from collapsing to unmanageable levels.

The significance of the IMF in creating the financial conditions for the growth of international trade since the Second World Ward cannot be underestimated. However, like the World Bank, the IMF will place conditions on providing loans to countries – for example, that they reduce the size of the public sector and engage in monetary and fiscal policy actions that are acceptable to the IMF. The IMF played a major role in providing back-up lending to economies in the wake of the recent financial crisis.

The World Trade Organization (WTO)

The WTO was formed in the wake of a series of international trade conferences which produced the General Agreement on Tariffs and Trade (GATT). The WTO is financed by its member states.

The WTO has had a significant impact on globalization processes. Since 1 January 1995 it has been a permanent body with two main functions:

1. To facilitate the settlement of trade disputes between countries; and

2. To oversee multilateral trade agreements between countries in relation to trade in goods and services and in relation to trade-related aspects of intellectual property rights disputes.

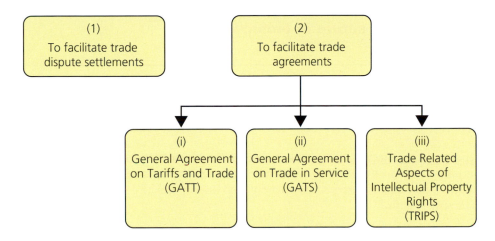

FIGURE 12.3 Key functions of the WTO

Becoming a member of the WTO is a significant step towards a country being able to fully enjoy the benefits of globalized world trade. For example, becoming a member of the WTO was a significant step that has enabled China to dominate world manufacturing and the export of manufactured goods in recent years.

The WTO has overseen major discussions and agreements on a global scale involving countries reducing or eliminating tariff restrictions on a range of products. In addition, the dispute resolution process enables countries to ask the WTO to step in and resolve issues with a binding judgement if they feel that they have a disadvantage resulting from some trade agreement.

However, it is important to appreciate that there has been and continues to be considerable dissatisfaction with some of the agreements forged by the WTO. In particular, agreements relating to the removal of barriers to trade in services (the General Agreement on Trade in Services, or GATS) and trade-related intellectual property rights (TRIPS) have been seen to benefit the richer nations with less being done for poorer nations. Many developing countries feel that they have not been granted enough access to agricultural markets – for example, EU and US agricultural markets for some crops continue to be highly protected with extensive subsidies to farmers.

The Doha rounds of talks which have taken place during the first years of the twenty-first century have sought to tackle issues such as agricultural subsidies that handicap poorer nations, but progress has been very slow.

ACTIVITY

Carry out some Internet-based research to find out the latest outcomes of the Doha round of talks. Are these moving forward to giving greater access for developing countries to the agricultural markets of developed countries?

12.5 The nature of protectionism

KEY TERM

Protectionism – involves countries protecting their domestic industries by carrying out anti-competitive practices that provide domestic industries with a greater advantage (than would exist without the protection).

A country can protect its domestic industries by levying a tariff or alternatively using a non-tariff method of protecting industries. Tariffs are the most widely used method of protecting domestic industries. Tariffs are placed on imports of goods. They may be *ad valorem* or specific.

KEY TERMS

Ad valorem tariffs – tariffs that are a percentage of the monetary value of an import (e.g. 10 per cent).

Specific tariffs – taxes on the weight or physical quantity imported.

Non-tariff measures

Non-tariff measures include:

- Quotas
- Import licences
- Administrative complexity
- Subsidies
- Exchange control
- Exchange rate manipulation

- Embargo
- Product standard regulations

Quotas

Quotas are limits on the amount of goods that can enter a country. They may restrict the number or value of imports. For example, there may be a limit imposed on the number of pairs of shoes from China entering the EU market in a given year. Alternatively they could take the form of a limit on the value of inputs (e.g. 50 million euros' worth of shoes imported from China). A quota has the impact of reducing supply to a market which will usually result in a rise in domestic prices (relative to the situation without a quota).

> Carry out some online research to find examples of goods with restrictions on their entry into Britain in the form of trade quotas. In each case try to think out the rationale for imposing a quota.

ACTIVITY

Import licences

Governments can grant licences for the import of certain goods. Not granting a licence is a type of protection.

Administrative complexity

The government may require importers to fill in time-consuming paperwork.

Subsidies

Subsidies are payments to a domestic producer. The effect is to make domestic goods cheaper to produce, often enabling them to be sold at lower prices than imports. The subsidy may take the form of a lump sum or a cheap loan to a domestic business.

Export subsidies have the opposite economic effect to tariffs. They involve a direct payment to an exporter (for example the US and EU governments provide a number of agricultural subsidies including those to cotton farmers).

Exchange control

Exchange controls occur when government prevents or limits the amount of foreign exchange to which importers have access – for example, if Indian importers are not allowed to buy dollars they many not be able to buy goods from the US.

Exchange rate manipulation

The government can buy or sell its own currency in order to alter the exchange rate – for example, it could sell its own currency in order to reduce the exchange rate and make exports cheaper.

Embargo

An embargo is a complete ban on the importation of certain types of goods or goods from specified countries.

Product standard regulations

A country may require all goods to meet certain technical or other standards. Imported goods may not meet these standards because they are primarily produced for a different market with different standards.

Arguments used to justify protection

Supporters of protectionism may justify it on the following grounds:

- To protect infant industries. New producers and new product developments in a domestic economy may need, in the first instance, to be protected from existing multinational producers who may be producing products at low cost. The infant industry only needs to be protected for a limited period of time until it can stand on its own feet and compete on equal terms (hopefully comparatively better ones).

- To protect employment. Protectionism is often justified in that it preserves jobs in the domestic market. However, it could be argued that in the longer term countries should not protect industries in which they are comparatively less efficient because they are not making best use of their resources.

- Security of key industries. Some industries may be crucial to an economy (e.g. energy and food). Should an economy become dependent on other countries for these essential resources then it could place itself in a strategically weak position.

12.6 Foreign direct investment

Foreign direct investment (FDI) consists of all of the capital transactions that are made in order to acquire a long-term interest in a company that operates in a country other than the investor's country. There are different definitions of how substantial the investment needs to be to be defined as FDI. It is reasonable to accept a figure of 10 per cent or more as constituting serious FDI.

The important thing about FDI is that of involving a long-term relationship between the investor and the country (or company) that is being invested in.

FDI is unevenly spread across the globe. The United States and Europe continue to be the biggest recipients of FDI, although increasingly capital is searching new growth opportunities across the world and huge economies such as China and India are increasingly becoming important as recipients of FDI because of the investment opportunities there.

Why the BRICs succeeded

Although growth has slowed in the BRIC economies (by 2012, as a result of the impact of the global recession) it is helpful to identify the reasons why the BRIC economies have flourished so much in an era of globalization.

KEY THEME

The growth map – economic opportunities in the BRICs and beyond

In 2001, Jim O'Neill introduced the concept of the powerful BRIC economies in a paper in Goldman Sachs' Global Economic Series.

The BRICs are Brazil, Russia, India and China. Based on an analysis of global GDP, O'Neill wrote that these countries, which then controlled 8 per cent of the world GDP, would see their share of the world economy grow substantially during the next decade. He predicted the increasing importance of these countries to the global economy – particularly China.

In his 2011 book, *The Growth Map*, O'Neill showed how his expectations had been exceeded. He showed that in early 2011 the size of Brazil's economy had exceeded that of Italy and that China had overtaken Japan as the world's second largest economy. While the world's economy doubled between 2001 and 2011 a third of this growth was accountable to the BRICs. In China it was exporting that was the major driver of growth. In contrast, in India it was domestic consumption as average incomes increased.

In 2005, O'Neill and some of his colleagues at Goldman Sachs set out to identify some of the new major growth economies. They called these the N-11 (the Next 11). They are: Bangladesh, Egypt, Indonesia, Iran, South Korea, Mexico, Nigeria, Pakistan, the Philippines, Turkey and Vietnam. They predicted that Mexico and South Korea could be almost as influential as the BRICs.

Part of O'Neill's work was to show that the BRICs and the N-11 provide really sound opportunities for FDI. O'Neill identified eight particularly strong investment opportunities: Brazil, Russia, China, India, Indonesia, Korea, Mexico and Turkey.

His work showed that what distinguishes these economies in the global market place are:

- Rapid growth
- Largely sound government debt
- Robust trading networks
- Huge numbers of people moving up the economic ladder

You can see from this list that these are countries whose features make them particularly effective players in a global market-oriented economy. O'Neill called these eight countries 'growth markets'.

- **What sorts of businesses are most likely to be interested in the growth opportunities outlined above?**

- **Which of the factors listed do you think are most significant in making the so-called 'growth markets' attractive?**

- **Why are investors likely to see these 'growth markets' as long-term opportunities?**

Key drivers for growth have been that:

- The BRIC countries are home to nearly 3 billion people (about half of the world's population). China and India each have over 1 billion people. Brazil has 180 million and Russia 140 million. More people produce more output. Collectively they earn more wages and other forms of income, and this is the basis for high levels of total consumption.

- Productivity. The more that a given set of workers can produce with available resources the quicker the economy grows. Because emerging economies are coming from further behind (compared with highly advanced economies) then there are much greater opportunities for productivity growth. These countries also have young and expanding labour forces.

- In China in particular there has been a move from rural areas to the cities. The mass urbanization in China today has acted as a real stimulus to the growth of consumption (in the same way as it did in Britain during the Industrial Revolution).

In contrast to the BRICs those countries with ageing populations and low fertility rates such as Japan and some of the larger continental (European) countries have tended to experience slow growth.

The importance of economic indicators

O'Neill and his co-researchers (2011) have developed what they refer to as a growth environment score (GES) to identify variables that are good indicators of the likely growth of an economy. Interestingly, they identify these indicators as being: (1) macro-economic indicators; and (2) micro-economic indicators. They are shown in Table 12.6.

The findings are very interesting in terms of a range of points that we have made in this book. In terms of macro-economics, economies tend to prosper where: inflation is pre- dictable and at a very low rate; the government deficit is manageable given expected tax revenues; investment spending is available to secure improvements in production capacity; the country has a manageable level of external debt so that it is not dependent on others outside its borders to any great measure; and the economy is open for trade, for the flow

TABLE 12.6 The growth environment score index (GES index)

Macro-economic indicators	Micro-economic indicators
Inflation	Use of mobile telephones
Government deficit	Use of the Internet
Investment spending	Use of computers
External debt	Life expectancy
Degree of openness	Education
	Rule of law
	Corruption
	Stability of government

TABLE 12.7 Illustrating strengths in terms of growth potential of different economies

	Performed well	*Performed poorly*
China	Macro-economic stability Openness to trade Education	Technology Corruption
Brazil	Political stability Life expectancy	Education Government deficit
Russia	Investment spending	Political stability Corruption Inflation
India	Rule of law	Education Technology adoption Fiscal position Openness

of capital, labour, new technologies, etc. On the micro-economic side we need to have the right supporting technologies and infrastructure for business (computers, access to the Internet, etc.), and we need a stable government with little or no corruption. One of the greatest drivers of growth in any society is education. There are so many good economic effects that come from having an excellent primary, secondary and tertiary education system – for example, motivated citizens, able and flexible workers, innovators and entrepreneurs, and the ability to work with complex technologies.

O'Neill's GES index is calculated from 1 to 10. In 2005, China's GES ranked highest among the BRICs followed by Russia, Brazil and India. China performed best on macro-economic stability, openness to trade and education but less well on technology and corruption.

12.7 Strategies for entering global markets

In concluding this chapter it is helpful to examine some of the strategies that UK businesses might employ when entering the global market. There are a number of ways they can do this depending on the level of commitment they want to make to the global sphere.

Exporting

At a base level companies may simply export products overseas using channels that are available (e.g. exporting through an overseas export house that arranges all or most of the arrangements for the distribution and sale of products in the overseas market). Alternatively they may agree to directly supply overseas retailers or manufacturers (in the case of capital goods).

In the case of exporting, the exporter may not need to modify their product for the overseas market. So exporting is a relatively low-cost strategy for entering international markets.

Licencing or franchising

Licensing involves allowing a foreign company to produce one or a number of your products under licence in return for a royalty fee on sales. Franchising takes this one step further. The franchisor grants the franchisee the right to make, sell or distribute their product within a given geographical area. Typically the franchisor will provide the know-how and training, the brand name, and perhaps the equipment and marketing materials required to operate the franchise. On an international scale the franchisor must carefully monitor the franchise operation to make sure that it matches the specified standards expected. Franchising is widely used in international fast-food operations.

Franchise – a business partnership between a franchisor who provides a brand image, equipment and training to a franchisee who contributes some of the start-up capital for the business and their time and hard work to run the business. The profits are shared between the franchisor and franchisee in line with an initial franchise agreement. The franchisor benefits from having local people with local knowledge committing their enterprise and efforts to selling goods and providing services that enhance the reputation of the franchisor in a new international market.

Global strategic alliances (GSAs)

A GSA involves a deeper commitment to the international economy. Shenkar and Yadong state that GSAs provide a particularly effective strategy for expanding globally. They define a GSA as:

> cross border partnerships between two or more firms from different countries with an attempt to pursue mutual interests through sharing their resources and capabilities. (2004: 314)

They identify two main types of GSA:

1. Equity joint ventures (EJVs). This is where two companies from different countries set up a new legal entity such as a company in which they both hold shares. They may have an equal partnership in the EJV (holding the shares on a 50/50 basis) or alternatively one could be a major shareholder.

2. A cooperative joint venture. Here the two parties (companies) would set out an agreement covering cooperation on specific aspects. For example, they may cooperate specifically for exploration purposes (e.g. joint exploration for oil). Alternatively they may cooperate for research and development purposes. They could then determine independently how they use the results of the research. Similarly they could cooperate in the marketing of goods and services.

Joint venture – a new venture which is set up by two separate companies each of which maintains a stake in the new venture.

Shenkar and Luo (2008) identify a number of reasons for building a GSA. Important reasons include: the synergy resulting from cooperation. Synergies are benefits resulting from cooperation that are greater than the individual benefits to the two parties involved in joint relationships. Synergies are sometimes described as the 2 + 2 = 5 effect. Examples of synergies identified by Shenkar and Luo are that:

- Companies can carry out investment projects that would be too costly for a single firm to conduct.
- Access to the knowledge and technological know-how of the partner.
- The two companies by operating together are able to build a big enough scale of operations to compete with a larger competitor.

A further important reason for building a GSA, according to Shenkar and Luo, is that this 'allows a firm to boost local acceptance as perceived by foreign consumers' (2008: 317).

Many European companies have opted for the joint venture format when entering the Chinese and Indian markets in order to be able to learn from local marketing knowledge and connections in these complex economies.

Foreign direct investment (FDI)

FDI provides a more intense way for companies to commit to other parts of the international economy. For example, this may take the form of a takeover of other companies on an international scale. For example, the UK confectionery industry has been subjected to successive waves of multinational expansion with many major UK businesses operating in the confectionery industry being taken over.

In the late 1980s one of Britain's best known confectionery companies, Rowntree Macintosh (manufacturers of Quality Street, Smarties and many other well-known brands) was the subject of a 'midnight raid' by Swiss firm Nestlé. This involved the rapid purchase of shares by Nestlé to the point at which they had a majority stake in the company (through a process which is now illegal). However, more recently (2010) another major British confectionery company, Cadburys, was subject to a successful takeover by US-based company Kraft. This time Kraft had offered successively higher bids to shareholders who eventually sold on a company with a long British heritage based on social as well as economic values (e.g. a commitment to their employees, originally by building workers' houses and amenities at Bournville near Birmingham).

The reasons for the FDI in each of these examples was to capture globally branded products that were distinctive and iconic and to drive synergies with existing product ranges at Nestlé and Kraft. You can see that this type of takeover activity involves the company carrying out the takeover gaining far more control than is the case in exporting or a joint venture arrangement.

Direct operations

Finally a large multinational may set up its own factories and operations directly in an overseas country. Some large multinationals (e.g. oil companies such as Shell and BP,

CASE STUDY Tesco in China

FIGURE 12.4 Tesco Legou shop

Tesco has been one of the most successful UK businesses in forging partnerships in China. Tesco quickly realized the value of the Chinese market as part of their strategy of international expansion. China has large numbers of potential customers seeking high-quality supermarket produce in urban areas.

Tesco's original strategy involved working in a joint venture with a local partner that already had a number of supermarkets in China. Tesco targeted China's most rapidly growing cities as target markets. Learning from working with its local partner Tesco was able to realize the benefit of not just selling the range of foodstuffs and household goods that can be purchased in a typical UK supermarket but also the importance of meeting the expectations of Chinese customers in terms of having live produce (e.g. fresh fish and poultry) so that parts of the supermarket would look more like a street market.

Chinese shoppers in urban areas typically prefer to arrive at the shops on foot rather than parking their cars and so a shopping mall format was an ideal way to attract large numbers of customers. Tesco also changed their name to meet local norms – calling the supermarket chain Tesco Legou (which translates as Happy Shopper) that has proved to be popular and instantly recognizable. Tesco has increasingly bought out its local partner so that it now has a 90 per cent stake in the business and feels confident that it has an excellent understanding of doing business in China.

- Why do you think that Tesco originally set up as a joint venture in China?
- What benefits would Tesco have gained from the joint venture format?
- Why do you think that Tesco has now taken on board a greater responsibility for running the operation itself?

household goods firms such as Unilever or Procter and Gamble, car manufacturers such as Honda and Toyota) may have the confidence and expertise to do this.

The advantage to the multinational is that it is totally in control of all operations and is able to take all of the profit for themselves. Disadvantages include the costs of setting up and operating the plants and the risks that are taken in a foreign country. However, prior to engaging in full-scale manufacturing in a new country a major company will carry out a detailed risk analysis and will engage in a thorough market research review of the new market.

12.8 Summary

Global economics is a complex area which is subject to different interpretations. Some economists and business people are in favour of globalization not just because it provides more business opportunities but because it enables the market economy to reach into more people's lives across the globe and to bestow more benefits on larger numbers of people. However, for the critics of globalization this trend is problematic, leading to rising inequality and dependence rather than independence. As the world economy becomes increasingly more entwined then problems can become magnified and take on global proportions, as witnessed in the recent financial crisis.

There are a number of key players in the global economy and the interaction between consumers, producers, financiers, governments and international institutions tends to nudge the world towards greater levels of interdependence so that globalization is a growing reality. The growth of FDI means that investors are increasingly taking a longer-term interest in the economies of other nations. A key characteristic of the global economy is that today it isn't just dominated by the United States and Europe, but that there are newly emerging markets that are playing a substantially more significant part in the global economy – particularly the BRIC economies. From a business perspective there are a number of stages of involvement in a global economy each based on an increased commitment, ranging from exporting and licencing to large-scale ownership of factories and other units of operations.

KEY IDEAS

The nature of globalization

- Economic globalization involves increased levels of trade, the flow of capital and the movement of people as well as the development of international means of exchange.
- Globalization has been viewed in different ways ranging from:
  - (1) first wave – a move to growing integration driven by multinational enterprises and rising living standards;
  - (2) second wave – a sceptical perspective, that globalization isn't actually as extensive as claimed, that national governments are still important

and influential, and that globalization brings with it problems as well as benefits; and

(3)   third wave – that the evidence does point to globalization as a real process that is taking place, but that we need to study the downsides as well as the benefits.

The participants in globalization

- Globalization is made up of a cast of billions – including global consumers and producers as well as providers of finance, governments and international institutions.

- Transnationality indexes reveal that a number of major multinationals carry out substantial parts of their operations globally with often only a relatively small concentration in their home markets.

- The WTO, World Bank and IMF have been key drivers of globalization, encouraging trade and providing liquidity but also creating stipulations that actually make some countries more dependent on market mechanisms.

Foreign direct investment (FDI)

- FDI involves investors developing longer-term interests in the economies of other countries.

Growing markets

- The BRICs (Brazil, Russia, China and India) have been identified as major new contributors to the global economy.

- Another four economies have been identified as 'growing economies'. They are characterized by features that lend themselves to integration in a global market economy.

- Macro- and micro-economic factors contribute to whether a particular country or market is ready for relatively fast economic growth.

- There are a number of ways for a business to enter the international/global economy ranging from exporting to direct involvement (e.g. by takeover).

REVIEW QUESTIONS

1. Define the following: (a) multinational company; (b) transnationality index; and (c) foreign direct investment.

2. To what extent does the recent financial crisis support a 'first wave' view of globalization? Or does it coincide more with a 'second wave' or 'third wave' view?

3. Which do you think has contributed most towards the development of a global economy – the WTO or the IMF?

4. Is globalization a process that increasingly gains momentum over time or is this an inaccurate representation of views about the globalization process?

5. What is the difference between a quota and a tariff? What part do these restrictions have to play in the globalization process?

6. How can GSAs help UK-based companies to engage in more global business activity?

7. What are the disadvantages of FDI to a host country? Why might it welcome FDI despite these disadvantages?

8. What level of market involvement would you recommend for a UK-based business entering a relatively unstable but potentially lucrative overseas market?

9. What are the characteristics of the BRICs? Identify one other country that shares similar characteristics with the BRICs – and explain how.

10. What is the relationship between market models of economic growth and globalization?

RECOMMENDED READING

Martell, L. (2007) 'The Third Wave in Globalization Theory', *International Studies Review*, 9 (2): 173–96.

A detailed analysis of the three waves of thinking about globalization.

O'Neill, J. (2011) *The Growth Map, Economic Opportunity in the BRICs and Beyond*, London, Penguin.

O'Neill's highly readable account of how a number of new economies are prospering and transforming the way that the global economy is shaped is an excellent outline of new economic opportunities in terms of markets, growth of emerging economies and opportunities for FDI.

REFERENCES

Bové, J. and Dufour, F. (2006) *The World is Not for Sale*, London, Verso.

Held, D. and McGrew, A. (2003) *The Global Transformations Reader*, London, John Wiley.

Hirst, P. and Thompson, G. (1998) *Globalisation in Question*, Cambridge, Polity Press.

McKinsey and Company (2009) 'How Executives View Globalization', *McKinsey Quarterly Review*, Spring.

Martell, L. (2007) 'The Third Wave in Globalization Theory', *International Studies Review*, 9 (2): 173–96.

Ohmae, K. (1990) *The End of the Nation State, the Rise of Regional Economies*, New York, Simon and Schuster.

Ohmae, K. (1995) *The Borderless World: Power and Strategy in the International Economy*, London, Harper Collins.

O'Neill, J. (2011) *The Growth Map, Economic Opportunity in the BRICs and Beyond*, London, Penguin.

Shenkar, O. and Luo, Y. (2008) *International Business*, 2nd edition, London, Sage.

Shenkar, O. and Yadong, L. (2004) *International Business*, Hoboken, NJ, John Wiley.

Skidelsky, R. (2010) *Keynes: The Return of the Master*, London, Penguin.

USEFUL WEBSITES

www.wto.org – this is the site of the World Trade Organization. The WTO deals with the global rules of trade between nations. Its main function is to ensure that trade flows smoothly and predictably, and that trading disputes are resolved in an orderly way.

www.worldbank.org – this is the site of the World Bank. The bank offers loans, advice and an array of customized resources to more than 100 developing countries in transition.

www.imf.org – this is the site of the International Monetary Fund (IMF) with links to news about the IMF, Fund Rates and IMF publications.

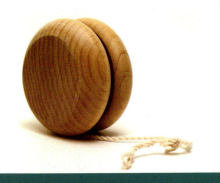

13 Money, banking and finance

CHAPTER OBJECTIVES

After carefully reading this chapter you should be able to:

- Identify ways in which the financial crisis has impacted on changes in the financial sector

- Describe the functions of money

- Outline the main activities of commercial banks

- Explain the role of the central bank in the economy

- Understand how banks create credit

- Analyse and evaluate definitions of the supply of money

- Explain how monetary policy can be used to control inflation

13.1 Introduction

This chapter sets out the very important role that money and banking play in the economy. The financial services sector is one of the most important sectors of the UK economy and the City of London is one of the world's leading financial centres.

The significance of this sector to the UK economy has been highlighted by the recent financial crisis. Failures in the banking industry have spread to other sectors of the economy leading to the most significant economic crisis in most people's living memory.

This chapter outlines how banks create credit and shows how the credit creating process is based on confidence in the banking sector. If this confidence starts to erode it can have dramatic repercussions in every area of economic life. The chapter shows that the functions of money include acting as a store of value. When the credibility and functioning of money is called into question, as it recently has been in countries badly hit by the recession such as Greece, then the fabric of society can crumble leading to civil disturbance and loss of life.

13.2 The significance of the financial crisis

The recent financial crisis highlighted the important role that money, banking and finance play at the heart of the economy. In the wake of the crisis bankers (particularly investment bankers) became a widespread target for criticism. A criticism levelled at investment bankers was that they had taken careless risks with other people's money while at the same time paying themselves huge bonuses. The type of criticism levelled at bankers is illustrated by an article that Vince Cable (the government's Business Secretary) wrote in the *Daily Mail* on 9 February 2009, in which he stated that 'The bonus-hunting bankers ... stand charged with destroying wealth on an epic scale. Foolish, greedy, irresponsible behaviour and excessive risk-taking led to massive losses ... which (are) now costing millions their jobs and many their homes.'

Some of the targets for criticism following the financial crisis include:

* Governments for failing to keep a check on the financial sector of the economy.

* The Bank of England for failing to effectively regulate the financial sector.

* Heads of commercial and investment banks and their boards of directors for allowing risk-taking to reach unmanageable levels.

* The investment banking industry for creating financial products which, rather than providing financial stability, created unnecessary levels of risk.

* The banking industry for failing to separate its 'high street' banking operations from speculative investment banking products.

In Britain in the period leading up to the financial crisis the nature of banking had changed substantially. Traditionally banking had been a cautious industry. Caution had become part of the banking industry as a result of some of the spectacular failures of early banks in the seventeenth and eighteenth centuries that had become bankrupt as a result of lending too much and not being able to pay back depositors.

For much of the twentieth century, banks in this country were carefully regulated by the Bank of England. Heads of commercial banks met on a regular basis with the Chair of the Bank of England who gently made suggestions about lending policies for the industry as a whole. The Bank of England set down carefully prescribed ratios setting out how much banks were able to keep in a liquid form to meet potential withdrawals from depositors.

However, from the late 1970s, onwards, banks were encouraged to become more competitive. New banks were created from former building societies (that lend for house purchases). A number of building societies changed their status from 'mutual benefit societies' to 'public limited companies' (PLCs). In simple terms mutual benefit societies are owned by their members, including depositors and borrowers. In contrast PLCs are owned by shareholders.

In 1986 the City of London went through a process of deregulation termed the Big Bang introduced by Margaret Thatcher's Conservative government. The aim of this was to encourage greater competition between financial institutions by enabling these institutions to sell a much wider range of products. Building societies such as the Halifax were able to enter the banking market. Existing banks became multi-product firms, selling shares in companies in addition to their traditional business of selling insurance and mortgages.

The 1990s and early years of the twenty-first century were a period of prosperity and economic growth in this country. The banking sector flourished in this period and many well-known banks such as HBOS and Barclays increased their prosperity and ranked among the top twenty UK businesses in terms of stock market value (referred to as market capitalization).

KEY TERMS

Big Bang – term used to describe the deregulation of many activities in the City of London enabling new 'banks' to develop, existing ones to engage in new financial activities, and banks to start trading in stocks and shares.

Market capitalization – the total value of all of the shares in a company at a particular moment in time.

A criticism that has been levelled at the banking sector is that it encouraged a 'culture' of risk taking. In business we use the term culture to describe 'the way we do things around here'. What had happened in banking was that a culture of caution had changed into a culture of risk taking. In addition to taking more risks as a result of the process of deregulation financial institutions became more inclined to take bigger risks in order to compete with rivals.

It now appears that major decision makers in the economy had become over optimistic. For example, the Prime Minister went on record as saying that 'the era of boom and boost is over' – suggesting that politicians and economists had learned how to ensure long-term prosperity. What they hadn't anticipated was the suddenness and extent of the global financial crisis.

In the period leading up to the financial crisis financial institutions had increasingly exposed themselves to riskier positions. For example, many of the major banks in Britain, Europe and the US had invested in what proved to be 'toxic assets'. For example, Sir Fred Goodwin's Royal Bank of Scotland had invested heavily in the United States in financial institutions that had lent in the sub-prime market. The sub-prime market consists of financial institutions that lend to individuals with a poor credit record (e.g. to purchase houses, cars, etc.). When the sub-prime market collapsed in 2008 this led to a rapid decline in the assets of RBS, HSBC and many other banks.

The response to the financial crisis has taken a number of forms:

- The recommendation that large banks will be required to separate their investment banking and high street banking operations. The belief here is that when households put their money into a bank they do so in order to keep their money safe, and perhaps to make a modest return on their deposits. They do not expect the high street bank to speculate with their money. If banks want to speculate through the investment banking arm they can do so but not with the money that they receive from ordinary customers.

- The recommendation that banks and other financial institutions (BOFIs) should separate their risk committees and audit committees. The Walker Report (2009) was set up in the wake of the financial crisis. Audit and risk committees are committees made up principally of independent directors of a PLC. The audit committee principally is backward facing. It seeks to make sure that the financial reports of companies and their systems of internal control comply with requirements and are fit for purpose. In contrast, risk management is forward looking.

Prior to the Walker Review many companies' risk management was the responsibility of the audit committee. What is now expected is that the risk committee of an organization will:

- Identify the principal risks and uncertainties that face the business and are likely to impact on strategic objectives;

- Prioritize these risks and uncertainties;

- Identify mitigation to keep risks and uncertainties within the bounds of the risk appetite of the organization; and

- Identify accountabilities for risk – who is responsible for managing the risks and uncertainties that are recorded.

Another important recommendation of the Walker Review in relation to BOFIs was that corporate governance structures should be improved to encourage constructive challenge in the boardroom. A major failing in banks was that there had been too much 'groupthink' in boardrooms. There was not enough challenge. The Walker Review therefore focused on boardroom behaviour.

The Corporate Governance Code in the UK expects that at least half of the directors of companies should be independent non-executive directors. It is essential that these non-executive directors should bring to the boardroom independent judgement and the willingness to ask awkward questions when they believe that questions need to be asked.

> ### Reflective question
>
> 1   One of the criticisms of boards of directors of BOFIs in the period leading up to the financial crisis is that they were characterized by 'groupthink' rather than constructive challenge. Why do you think that this might have been the case, and what changes need to be made in order to counteract this situation?

ACTIVITY

Access the Walker Report online. Read through the introduction to the report and the conclusion. What are the main points that are being made there about changes that need to be made in the governance of BOFIs?

Another response has been the requirement that banks and other financial institutions restore their liquidity positions in line with potential risks. In the wake of the financial crisis it became clear that certain financial institutions had overexposed themselves by lending too much. This threatened the collapse of the whole financial system, not only in the UK but on an international basis. In the UK the government, acting through the Bank of England, required banks to restore their liquidity positions. Initially this involved reducing their lending – in particular more risky lending.

On an international scale the financial crisis has had wider implications. A number of countries in the Eurozone have been hit particularly hard. These countries are Portugal, Italy, Greece, Ireland and Cyprus.

The problem for these five countries is that not only were their banks exposed by high levels of risky borrowing – but so too were their governments. Another Eurozone country that has suffered is Spain but for different reasons. In Spain a key issue has been the high level of personal debt built up by individuals in the previous period of economic prosperity. This debt has not been sustainable in a period of recession when banks are seeking to rebuild their liquid reserves of cash.

Greece, Ireland, Portugal, Italy and Cyprus are characterized by high public debt (whereas in Spain government debt is much lower).

KEY TERMS

Public sector deficit – a situation where the government of a country spends more than it takes in taxes and has to balance the difference through borrowing.

Eurozone – term used to describe a monetary union based on a common currency: the euro. Eurozone countries (17 in total) include Germany, France, Italy, Portugal, Ireland, Spain, Greece, Holland, Luxembourg, Belgium, Finland, Cyprus, Malta, Slovenia, Slovakia and the Netherlands.

In normal times international financial institutions will lend to governments. The government deficit is met by an issue of government bonds. A government bond is a paper claim that the treasury of a country produces promising to repay the bond at some date in the future. In order to borrow, however, the government must pay interest on the loan. The amount of interest that the government pays is dependent on the risk that the lender is taking. The greater the risk the higher the rate of interest.

During the financial crisis it became increasingly likely that the governments of Portugal, Italy, Greece, Spain and Ireland might not be able to repay all of their loans. As a result credit rating agencies lowered the credit rating of these governments.

KEY TERM

Credit rating agencies – these are firms that specialize in rating (evaluating) the creditworthiness of a customer based on records of how much they have borrowed and how much income they are earning to repay the loan. On an international scale the key ratings agencies are Fitch Ratings, Moody's Investor Services and Standard & Poor's.

When a credit rating agency lowers its credit rating then the borrower will only be able to borrow at higher and higher rates of interest.

The financial crisis has therefore exposed the financial system to unprecedented levels of risk and resulting losses, not only in Britain but also in many other countries. This has led to unemployment for large numbers of financial sector workers, and a ripple downward multiplier effect in national economies and at the international level.

The UK Business Secretary Vince Cable, in July 2012, described the investment banking industry as being rotten to the core. He described it as having a culture of greed which had led to poor judgement.

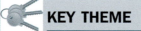

KEY THEME

Appointing a new Governor for the Bank of England

In 2013 Mark Carney will become the first non-British Governor of the Bank of England. His previous post was as Governor of the Bank of Canada (a country with a strong reputation for financial probity and safe financial practice). The governor of the Bank is also the Chair of the Monetary Policy Committee. Up until now the Governor of the Bank of England has always been British.

In July 2012 the economist Danny Blanchflower, who was part of the Monetary Policy Committee of the Bank between 2006 and 2009, stated that 'no British banker is fit to take over the Bank of England'. He made this statement because so many British banks had been involved in serious scandals. The most recent at the time were the interest rate fixing on inter-bank lending rates which a number of commentators have referred to as fraud.

The Financial Service Authority's top banking regulator had referred to Barclays as having a 'culture of gaming' and it was revealed that staff at HSBC had laundered billions of dollars for drugs cartels, terrorists and pariah states. HSBC transported billions of dollars of cash in armoured vehicles, cleared suspicious travellers' cheques worth billions, and allowed Mexican drug lords to buy planes with money laundered through Cayman Island accounts.

- Why do you think that Danny Blanchflower was suggesting that the next Governor of the Bank of England should not be British?

- Why is it so important for the integrity of the banking system to be upheld?

Against this background it is important to gain a good understanding of the role of money and banking in the economy.

13.3 The functions of money

Money is anything that is widely accepted or used to exchange for goods. Today when we think about money we are typically referring to notes and coins. However, households and businesses also use many other ways of making payments, such as credit and debit cards.

Before money was used people would barter – that is, exchange goods (say a goat for several chickens) – and this requires the two people who make the trade to want what the other has to offer (a double coincidence of wants). The obvious disadvantage is that one partner may not have enough goods to make the exchange fair, or they might not want a whole goat for example. People realized that small but valuable items, such as cowrie shells, could be used instead.

Why were cowrie shells used as money so widely? Look at this list of the characteristics of the shells:

- Scarcity – shells were valuable because they were relatively scarce.

- Acceptability – people were prepared to accept the shells as payment.

- Portability – the shells could easily be carried for long distances.

- Durability – the shells were hard wearing and long lasting.

- Divisible – shells could be supplied in various quantities, to buy purchases of different sizes. Purchases would be possible using a few or, for the wealthy, hundreds of shells. In modern terms a car can be priced at thousands or millions of dollars. Dollars can be divided into cents for small items like a packet of chewing gum or piece of fruit.

The functions of money are as follows:

- As a medium of exchange – money is generally accepted as a means of payment for goods.

- As a unit of account – the price of an item can be measured in terms of how many units of currency it is worth. For example, whereas a low-quality top may cost £10, a high-quality one may be valued at £100 or more.

- As a store of value – you can save money because it keeps its value. Saving enables use of the money in the future.

- As a standard for deferred payments – borrowers are able to borrow money and pay it back at a future date.

13.4 Commercial banks

Commercial banks are owned by shareholders. The profits that these businesses make are either ploughed back into the business or are distributed to shareholders in the form of dividends. The profits of commercial banks (apart from during the financial crisis) are very high compared with most other businesses. It is because of this that shareholders in these companies have been willing to accept the high levels of remuneration paid to executive directors and key employees in these organizations. Shareholders that receive high dividends are more likely to accept high rewards paid to directors.

Commercial banks provide a safe place to keep money and will also lend money. Sometimes they are called retail banks because their lending to business and households is relatively small compared with some investment banks which provide large sums of capital to business. In Section 13.2, however, we saw that in recent times the distinction between commercial and investment banks has sometimes become blurred. The UK government is seeking to differentiate these two components of a financial intermediary in order to safeguard the customers of retail banks.

The main functions of a bank are:

- Keeping money safe. A bank's vaults are more secure than a safe deposit box in a private house. Individuals and businesses can open bank accounts. They deposit money in the account. Savings accounts pay the depositor a set rate of interest on sums saved. Current accounts are for keeping money safe, but sums can be withdrawn to make payments. A current account may pay some interest, but this will be lower than on a savings account. Banks also keep documents and other valuable items in safe deposit boxes.

- Lending. Many people and businesses need to borrow money – for example, for expensive purchases such as a car. Businesses may borrow from banks when they want to grow.

Borrowing methods include:

- Loans – borrowing a fixed sum (e.g. £1,000) for a set period of time (e.g. two years). The business will need to pay back the sum borrowed (£1,000) plus the agreed rate of interest. For example, if the interest rate is 10 per cent, then over the two years the borrower will pay back £1,100 (£1000 + £100 interest).

- An overdraft – that is, taking out more than has been put into the account. The borrower has an agreed overdraft limit and will pay interest to the bank if the account is overdrawn.

- Credit cards. This enables users to buy goods and pay for them later. Every month users receive a statement showing how much they owe the bank. If they pay the bill by a given date they will not have to pay interest. Many businesses use credit cards to finance short-term cash-flow needs. A debit card is a means of payment using funds in your own bank account rather than through borrowing.

- Mortgages. Banks lend to firms and households to buy homes, office buildings and factories. The legal deed of ownership of the property are kept by the bank until the mortgage has been repaid. Mortgages are usually for long periods of time, such as 25 years.

Commercial banks act as financial intermediaries in the way outlined in Figure 13.1.

Commercial banks also perform a number of other important services that benefit the economy:

- They provide means of making payment, such as cheques and banker's drafts. A banker's draft is a slip of paper printed with the name, address and logo of the bank, on which the customer writes the name of the person and the amount they wish to pay. The bank then transfers money to the recipient. Banks can also make regular payments in the form of standing orders (set payments of regular sums) into a named account. Banks process payments through automatic electronic payments as well as Internet banking. In some countries (e.g. in 2018 in the UK) banks will stop the use of cheques because cards are much easier to use.

- They provide foreign currency. If you visit another country that uses different currency, your local bank may be able to provide you with the currency. However, ATMs (automated teller machines) make it easy for a customer to withdraw money in most urban areas worldwide.

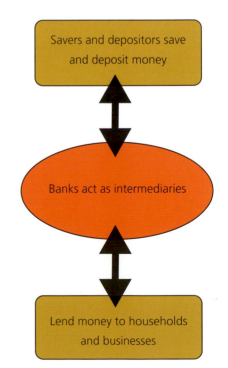

FIGURE 13.1
Banks as intermediaries

13.5 Central banks

Every country has a central bank whose job it is to supervise the banking system in the domestic economy. In Britain the central bank is the Bank of England, in Germany it is the Deutsche Bundesbank, in the United States it is the Federal Reserve.

The central bank influences the economy in the following ways. The head of the central bank holds regular meeting with senior officials from the other banks to outline policy for lending. If there is too much spending in an economy leading to rising prices, the head of the central bank may request that banks reduce lending. If there is too little spending in the economy leading to recession banks will be requested to lend more. The central bank also creates rules (financial regulations) that affect things such as how other banks can be set up and how much they can safely lend.

As well as supervising the financial system, the central bank has additional functions:

- Printing the notes and minting the coins that are legal tender (notes and coins that should be accepted as payment). It also destroys torn notes and worn-out coins.

- The central bank acts as a lender of last resort. If another bank needs cash in a hurry (perhaps because depositors are withdrawing unusually large sums of money) it can borrow from the central bank. In this situation, the central bank may decide to penalize other banks for lending too much and charge them a high rate of interest. Other banks set their interest rates at levels just above the central bank's base rate – that is, the rate set by the central bank on which all other interest rates are based.

- Supervising monetary policy. This determines the quantity of money in the economy and the interest rate. The central bank helps the government to create and manage monetary policy.

- Acting as banker for the commercial banks and for the government. By acting as the bankers' bank, debts between the commercial banks can be settled through their accounts at the central bank.

- Government tax revenue and major spending is carried out through accounts with the central bank.

- The central bank helps the government to borrow money by issuing government bills and bonds. The total amount the government owes to lenders is called the national debt. The bonds are official promises to repay money in the future with interest in return for the loan. Wealthy investors and other financial institutions are happy to lend governments money because in many countries it is a very safe investment.

- Helping to manage the international financial system. On a worldwide scale there need to be generally acceptable methods of making payments for international transactions. This requires confidence in the international financial system. The International Monetary Fund (IMF) was set up to provide supervision for the world's banking system. One of its functions is to lend money to governments to help them in times of financial crisis when investors may have lost confidence in the banking systems of those countries. Central banks work closely with the IMF to create financial

TABLE 13.1 Change in interest rates

Reduction in interest rates	Borrowers find borrowing cheaper, borrow more, increase spending
Increase in interest rates	Savers save more, borrowers borrow less, spending falls

stability. Countries deposit gold and their own currency with the IMF. This can then be lent to countries in crisis. Leading central bankers will meet regularly with important government officials and members of the IMF to create better systems of international financial management.

- The central bank plays a major role in setting interest rates. The interest rate is the price paid for borrowing money. Setting interest rates gives the central bank considerable power in the economy. Changing interest rates helps the central bank to control lending by other banks (see Table 13.1).

13.6 The creation of credit

While commercial banks are owned by shareholders the vast proportion of their capital comes from depositors. This is one of the major criticisms levelled at banks and their responsibility for the financial crisis. They have been poor stewards of other people's money.

The traditional way in which banks operate is through the creation of credit. Depositors place their money with the banks and the banks look after it for the depositor.

It did not take the early bankers long to realize that not all of the money that is deposited with them will be withdrawn in the short period. Banks are thus in a position to make loans over and above the money that is deposited with them. This is referred to as the creation of credit.

For the sake of simplicity let us assume that depositors will only want to withdraw 10 per cent of their deposits in the near future. What happens then when a depositor places £100 in their bank account? Working on the figure of 10 per cent withdrawals, the bank will keep £10 in cash and then relend the remaining £90 to borrowers.

Assuming there is only one bank and the borrowers spend the money they have borrowed then the £90 will feed its way back into the banking system. Working on the 10 per cent basis the bank will now hold on to £9 and relend £81. This is referred to as the banking multiplier.

Assuming that the bank will continue to relend 90 per cent of deposits made with it and retain 10 per cent in reserves, then eventually the £100 that was deposited with the bank will be able to support £1,000 of loans.

$$\text{Money base} = £100$$

$$\text{Loans} = £1,000$$

What applies in the case of a single bank, can be extended to the banking system as a whole. If all of the banks work on a 10 per cent cash to loans basis then £100 of money deposited in the banking system will lead to loans made by all of the banks of £1,000.

It is very important to understand how banks create credit. What should be clear from this is that the banking system will only work effectively if depositors are happy to leave the majority of their money deposited with the banks rather than wanting to withdraw it. The banking system will only work provided that the banks are able to accurately calculate the size of the banking multiplier and how much they need to keep in their reserves to finance withdrawals.

CASE STUDY The collapse of Northern Rock

Northern Rock was a very successful bank in the early part of the first decade of the twenty-first century. It was able to benefit from the deregulation of banking in the UK, which enabled financial institutions to provide a range of different types of financial products to customers. It benefitted from being located in the North East of England where staff wages were relatively low compared with banks whose Head Offices were in London. As a result it was able to offer highly competitive mortgages and to win an increasing share of the mortgage market. It was able to lend for longer periods of time at higher rates of interest and borrow for shorter periods of time at lower rates of interest.

At the time the financial crisis hit the United Kingdom at the end of 2007 it was offering home loans of up to 125 per cent of the values of the properties being purchased. 60 per cent of the finance of Northern Rock was raised from short-term borrowing. When the financial crisis rolled into Britain from the United States, suddenly financial institutions found that they could no longer borrow. Northern Rock quickly ran out of cash and on 13 September 2007 Northern Rock applied to the government for emergency funding.

In February 2008 Northern Rock was nationalized by the British government at a cost of £100 billion. The key problem facing Northern Rock was that it was borrowing money in the money markets in order to lend that money out to customers in the form of mortgages. Northern Rock was then reselling those mortgages on international capital markets to investors. However, when the financial crisis set in in 2007 international investors were no longer willing to buy these mortgages, leaving Northern Rock with a shortfall.

- What does the Northern Rock case tell us about how banks create credit?

- What dangers are revealed by this case about the creation of credit?

- How might Northern Rock have been able to survive the financial crisis?

The quantity theory of money

One of the most important elements of economic theory is the 'quantity theory of money'. The development of the quantity theory of money is originally associated with the New Zealand economist Irving Fisher. In simple terms the theory sets out that the rate of growth of the money supply determines the rate of inflation. More recently this idea has been adapted by Milton Friedman and referred to as 'monetarism' (see below).

The traditional quantity theory of money is typically set out in the following way:

$$MV = PY$$

Where:

M = the quantity of money
V = the velocity of circulation of money (i.e. the average number of times money changes hand in the economy in exchange for final output of goods)
P = the average price of final outputs of goods
Y = the real quantity of final output produced in the economy in a given time period

This is true by definition. If you think about it logically you will be able to see that the money in the economy multiplied by the number of times it changes hands will be the same as the value of the goods produced in the economy multiplied by their average prices.

This theory was a key part of classical economic thinking. These economists believed (based on empirical research) that V and Y remain relatively constant over time. In the long run, therefore, P is determined by the supply of money in the economy (M). The challenge then for monetary authorities such as the Bank of England is to carefully control the money supply.

In the 1950s Milton Friedman reworked the quantity theory. Friedman's studies revealed that V and Y are stable and easy to predict in the long run. He therefore altered the money equation slightly to state that:

$$P = M - Y$$

So the rate of inflation is determined by the growth of the money supply minus the rate of growth of the real quantity of final output.

Friedman made a strong case for increasing the money supply at a slow and steady rate in line with the growth of the economy. He was opposed to tinkering with the money supply by the monetary authorities. Changes in the money supply should be predictable. Friedman believed strongly that short-term measures to alter the supply of money in the economy have a destabilizing effect. A major reason for this is the lagged effect of changes in the money supply. For example, if the central bank increases the money supply during a depression this will take time to have an effect on economic activity and prices. By the time the policy had an impact, it might be inappropriate (perhaps a contraction in the money supply would be required). Friedman was thus strongly opposed to short-term tinkering with the money supply. He was also highly critical of the inability of central banking authorities to define and measure the supply of money.

13.7 The supply of money

There are a number of ways of defining money, varying from narrow definitions to much broader definitions.

It is important to be able to define money. If you can define money then it is possible to measure the impact of changes in the quantity of money on prices. However, defining money is very slippery. There is an economic law termed 'Goodhart's Law' (Charles Goodhart is a former Chairman of the Bank of England). His law was that as soon as you have come up with a good definition of money for analytical purposes it will no longer prove to be useful.

Definitions of money range from 'Little M0' to 'Big M4'. M0 includes all of the cash in circulation + all cash held within banks + all cash balances held at the central bank by commercial banks. M4, as well as money included in the M0 definition, also includes money held in savings accounts at banks that can be easily withdrawn, and money in deposit accounts at banks and building societies.

M4 is thus a much wider definition of money than is M0.

13.8 Monetary policy and inflation

Monetary policies have been used extensively in the UK since 1979 when Margaret Thatcher came to power. She decided a new approach was required and the methods she adopted were very successful in controlling inflation – so much so that they are still actively used today.

Monetarist policies are based on the assumption that the economy can be regulated by measuring and manipulating the levels of money supply in the economy. You might like to think of the money supply as being the total amount of purchasing power within the country. The government and Bank of England expend much effort in attempting to calculate the money supply accurately, and as we have seen there are a number of definitions of the money supply ranging from M0 to M4. Monetary policy and exchange rate policy are the UK government's main tools for controlling inflation.

If resources are being used efficiently in the economy this may lead to increases in demand in the country. Excessive demand, over and above our ability to expand production, can lead to price rises as shown in Figure 13.2.

This explanation of the roots of inflation has become increasingly important, as the government's strategy for controlling inflation for the last 25 years has been largely based on tackling this cause.

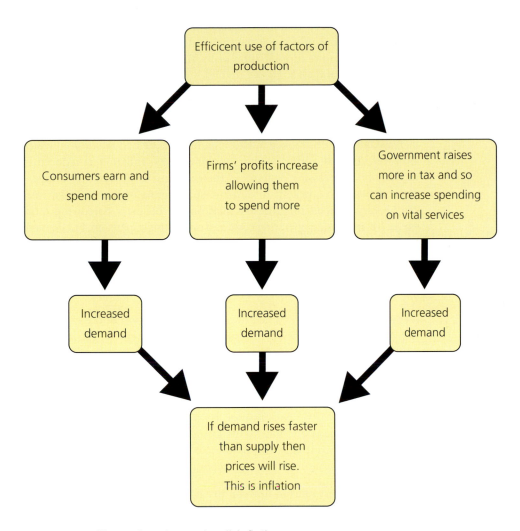

FIGURE 13.2 Illustrating demand pull inflation

The monetarist theory on inflation assumes that there is a direct link between bank lending, the money supply and ultimately inflation, and it works in the way set out in Figure 13.3.

This theory therefore draws a direct link between bank lending and the rate of inflation. If there is indeed a causal relationship between these two then controlling bank lending should control levels of inflation. If we reduce bank lending this should reduce purchasing power (money supply), which in turn should reduce demand and therefore reduce or eliminate demand pull inflation. Monetarists assume that the key factor determining the amount of bank lending taking place is the rate of interest charged: if rates are high this discourages lending (as the repayments are so high) and if rates are low lending is likely to increase.

Increased bank and building

society lending

Increased money supply

Increased demand for

goods and services

Eventually demand may

exceed supply

Demand pull inflation

FIGURE 13.3
Monetarist view of demand
pull inflation

The government can therefore regulate the economy by altering interest rates to suit their objectives at the time. Interest rate policy can be used in two main ways: to reduce inflation or to stimulate the economy, as shown in Figures 13.4 and 13.5.

The two policies may be used at different times when priorities change.

In 1979, when the main priority was to reduce inflation, interest rates were increased in order to reduce inflation and this tactic had the desired effect. However, there is a price to pay for this success. Inflation is reduced in this way by suppressing demand in the economy. Unfortunately industry needs demand to enable it to develop, so a regime of high interest rates can be very difficult for industry. Not only is business borrowing more expensive, increasing operating costs and preventing expansion, but demand is also low. High costs and low demand is a bad recipe for business, and it is therefore not surprising that many businesses found it difficult to survive under high interest rates. However, it did achieve its objective and inflation fell dramatically.

As the UK attempted to come out of the deep recession of the early 1990s the government was aware that industry needed help to get it moving again, and this was provided by using interest rate policy in the opposite way: to stimulate the economy. Interest rates were reduced, thus reducing business costs and stimulating demand: a fine recipe for business success. This was one of the key factors that helped the UK out of the recessionary problems of the early 1990s. Interest rates fell as the UK chose to free the currency from the restrictions of the European Exchange Rate Mechanism (ERM) – this meant that the pound no longer needed to shadow the Deutschmark so that high rates of interest were no longer necessary.

Since 2008 interest rates in this country have been at a historic low of 0.5 per cent in an attempt to lower business costs and to stimulate borrowing in the economy. In theory the demand for money will increase when interest rates are low. However, in a period of chronic recession businesses will be reluctant to invest and households will save rather than spend. Figure 13.6 illustrates the potential impact of low interest rates.

However, what happens in the real world isn't as simple and straightforward as outlined in Figure 13.6.

In 2012 interest rates were very low, but this didn't stimulate demand as required. Banks in the UK were reluctant to lend money to business (particularly small businesses) in the fear that should the recession continue then they might end up with more toxic assets at a time when they were seeking to restore more liquidity to their balance sheets.

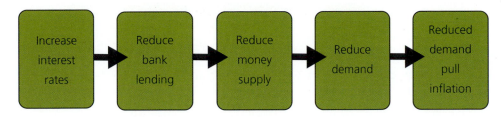

FIGURE 13.4 Using interest rates to reduce inflation

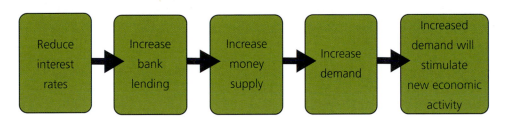

FIGURE 13.5 Using interest rates to stimulate the economy

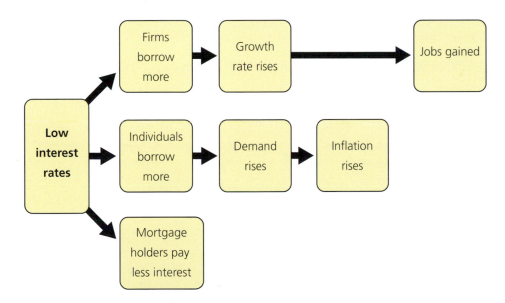

FIGURE 13.6 The potential impact of low interest rates

CASE STUDY The Monetary Policy Committee

Until May 1997 all UK monetary policy decisions were taken by the UK government through the Chancellor of the Exchequer, who made the decisions and announced any changes. In May 1997 the New Labour government decided to alter this.

There had been accusations that some interest rate changes were made not at times that suited the economy best, but at times that suited the government best. So interest rates might be reduced just before an election to make the government more popular and give them a greater chance of re-election.

To avoid this possibility of bias in the future, the Chancellor of the Exchequer, Gordon Brown, announced that in the future all interest rate decisions would be made by the Bank of England. He appointed a Monetary Policy Committee (MPC), chaired by the Governor of the Bank of England, and instructed them to meet monthly to decide on interest rates for the next month, with the specific objective of achieving the government's underlying inflation target of no higher than 2.5 per cent.

While the Chancellor retained the right to overrule the committee's decisions in 'extreme economic circumstances', the committee is now free to independently make decisions that it believes are right for the country, without fear of bias. The process has been operating for some time now and appears to be working smoothly. Although not everyone agrees with all of the decisions taken, we can be sure that they are made without the influence of political pressure.

You can obtain more detail on the role of the MPC at the Bank of England MPC website.

- Visit the Bank of England website at www.bankofengland.co.uk and check the latest decisions on interest rate changes that have taken place.

- What do you think are the reasons behind the latest decisions taken by the MPC (look at the last two decisions)?

- What effect will those decisions have had on the following groups?

    (a)   Mortgage payers

    (b)   Businesses

    (c)   Companies looking to expand

    (d)   Consumers

🗝 KEY THEME

Barclays had a 'culture of gaming – and of gaming us', says chief banking regulator

In an article in *The Guardian* (17 July 2012) the authors Jill Treanor, Nicholas Watt and Dominic Rushe made the following points (Guardian News & Media Ltd 2012, reproduced with permission). Note that this was in the light of revelations that a number of banks had been manipulating the inter-bank interest rates that they charged each other – a form of collusion:

> The top banking regulator at the Financial Services Authority yesterday accused Barclays of having a 'culture of gaming' in testimony to MPs that laid bare the difficult relationship between the bank and its regulator.
>
> Andrew Bailey described this month's evidence of former Barclays boss Bob Diamond to the Treasury select committee of MPs as 'highly selective' and said there was 'a problem with the institution and that came from the "tone at the top"'.
>
> As the FSA revealed it was investigating another seven institutions for attempting to manipulate interest rates, Lord Turner, the regulator's chairman, also indicated that he had dropped broad hints two days after Barclays was fined for Libor rigging that Diamond should leave the bank.

- What do you understand by the term the 'tone at the top'? How can the tone at the top impact on the culture of an organization?

- What sort of tone at the top should be set in a leading financial institution like Barclays?

- Why is it so important to the UK economy to have creditable financial institutions?

Financial Services Authority (FSA) – the FSA is the regulator for all financial services in the UK, including banking, insurance, mortgages and other financial products. Since 1 April 2013 it has been replaced by the Prudential Regulation Authority and the Financial Conduct Authority. The Bank of England has overall responsibility for risks to the financial system as a whole (systemic risk).

KEY TERM

13.9 Summary

This chapter has shown how money and banks are at the heart of modern economies. Money is a store of value, a means of exchange and a unit of account. When the value of money falls and confidence is shaken in banking systems this can have deep-seated impacts on the wider economy. Banks create credit and the bedrock on which the financial system and economic system are based. It is essential to maintain the credibility of financial institutions. The chapter goes on to explore the quantity theory of money, an understanding of which is central to forming effective monetary policy.

Businesses need access to money and credit at interest rates that are affordable. They also need to rest secure that the financial system is secure and that the Bank of England, Prudential Regulation Authority, Financial Conduct Authority and others responsible for the financial system are carrying out their business in an effective way.

KEY IDEAS

The financial crisis

- The financial crisis starting from 2008–2009 resulted from a crisis in the US sub-prime market which rapidly spread to high street banks and other financial institutions.
- The financial crisis seems in part to have been due to insufficient monitoring of risks in the financial sector.
- The Walker review was set up to review the financial crisis and has recommended the separation of the risk and audit committees in BOFIs, the establishment of an appropriate 'tone from the top', and the encouragement of greater critical challenge in boardrooms.
- There continues to be a lack of confidence in the probity of some of the UK's major financial institutions.

Money and banking

- The main functions of money are as a medium of exchange, a store of value, a standard for deferred payments, and as a unit of account.
- The commercial banks provide a variety of services to customers including keeping money safe and lending through a variety of credit instruments.
- Banks act as financial intermediaries.
- There is strong pressure for banks to separate ordinary banking activities from investment banking.
- The Bank of England is the government's bank and the bankers' bank.
- The Bank of England has overall responsibility for monitoring systemic risk to the financial system of this country.

- The independent Monetary Policy Committee recommends the Bank of England base rate which is the base for all other interest rates.

- The Bank of England manages the government's monetary policy.

- The two main weapons of monetary policy are interest rates and the quantity of money.

The quantity theory of money

- The quantity theory of money essentially sets out the relationship between the quantity of money and price levels.

- There are various definitions of money ranging from narrow money (M0) and widening out into broad money (M4).

- Friedman and the monetarists believe that the money supply should increase by a steady and well-publicized rate each year to stimulate growth. There should be no rapid changes in the money supply.

REVIEW QUESTIONS

1. What is money? Can banks create money?

2. What is meant by the creation of credit? How does the financial system depend on customers having confidence in the banks?

3. In what ways are ordinary high street banking operations different from investment banking?

4. What important recommendations did the Walker Report make in relation to corporate governance of BOFIs?

5. What are the main functions of the Bank of England?

6. What is the Monetary Policy Committee? What decisions does it make? What actions could the monetary policy take in a period of rising inflation?

7. Explain the way in which Milton Friedman adjusted the original quantity theory of money.

8. What was Milton Friedman's view about appropriate changes in the quantity of money in an economy over time?

9. What do you understand by the term 'quantitative easing'? How might quantitative easing help an economy in a period of recession? Who would be responsible for quantitative easing?

10. What are the key functions of money and which of these functions are threatened in a period of inflation?

RECOMMENDED READING

Cable, V. (2009) *The Storm: The World Economic Crisis and What It Means*, London, Atlantic Books.

> The Business Secretary provides a highly readable and challenging overview of the causes of the world economic crisis and sets out some ideas for moving forward.

Skidelsky, R. (2009) *Keynes: The Return of the Master*, Chapter 1, London, Penguin Books.

> Provides an overview of the background to the financial crisis and the key players in the crisis.

Walker, D. (2009) *A Review of Corporate Governance in Banks and Other Financial Institutions*, London, HM Treasury.

> In the wake of the financial crisis Sir David Walker and a team of reviewers set out a report into corporate governance in BOFIs.

REFERENCES

Cable, V. (2009) *The Storm: The World Economic Crisis and What It Means*, London, Atlantic Books.

Treanor, J., Watt, N. and Rushe, D. (2012) 'Barclays had "a culture of gaming – and of gaming us", says chief banking regulator', *The Guardian*, 17 July 2012: 20.

USEFUL WEBSITES

www.bankofengland.co.uk – the Bank of England's website provides useful information about key financial indicators. The Monetary Policy Committee page provides details of the latest and previous decisions made by the Committee in relation to setting interest rates.

http://webarchive.nationalarchives.gov.uk/
http://www.hm-treasury.gov.uk/d/walker_review_261109.pdf – The Walker Report.

14 Government fiscal policy

CHAPTER OBJECTIVES

After carefully reading this chapter you should be able to:

- Define and explain the term fiscal policy

- Outline the main types of government spending, taxes and borrowing in the UK

- Differentiate between discretionary fiscal policy and automatic stabilizers

- Understand key reasons for taxation and common types of tax

- Contrast direct and indirect taxes and illustrate the impact of levying an indirect tax

- Illustrate and evaluate the impact of government subsidies

14.1 What is fiscal policy?

Fiscal policy – government policy designed to deliberately alter the amount of government spending or taxation to help achieve 'desirable' macro-economic objectives by changing the level and composition of aggregate demand.

Fiscal policy involves:

- Changing the relationship between the relative size of spending and taxes. For example, this might involve raising government spending while holding taxes constant.

- Structural changes in government spending and taxes. For example, the government may alter the emphasis in its taxation and spending patterns (e.g. spending more on investment in infrastructure and less on welfare spending).

It was Keynes that changed economists' thinking about the importance of fiscal policy. Keynes felt that monetary policy on its own is not sufficient to achieve a growing economy with full employment. Keynes believed that a desired state of affairs for the economy is one in which interest rates are permanently low and fiscal policy is used to achieve a continuously high level of public or semi-public investment.

Keynes' studies showed that private investment (i.e. by businesses) tends to fluctuate depending on whether we are in a period of boom (high investment) or recession (low investment). In periods when the private sector fails to invest then the government can step in to secure steady and growing investment in the economy over time.

Public investment – investment by central and local government in capital projects (e.g. the building of roads, hospitals and schools).

This is the main point of difference between Keynesian ideas and classical and neoclassical economics (including monetarism) (see Table 14.1).

TABLE 14.1 The difference between classical and Keynesian ideas

The classical/monetarist view	The Keynesian view
Monetary policy should aim to secure stable prices	Monetary policy should aim to secure low interest rates that encourage business investment
Fiscal policy should aim to secure a balanced budget (i.e. government spending = government taxes)	Fiscal policy should be based on providing growing investment in the economy over time. Where there is a shortfall of private investment in a recession then the government should step in with a deficit budget (government spending > government taxes)

There are thus three broad-brush approaches to fiscal policy:

1. The balanced budget (government spending = government taxes).

2. The deficit budget (government spending > government taxes).

3. The surplus budget (government spending < government taxes).

14.2 Government spending, taxes and borrowing

The UK government announces its fiscal policy in its annual budget which is presented by the Chancellor of Exchequer to Parliament and to the country. The Liberal Democrat–Conservative Coalition government that was elected in 2010 created the Office of Budget Responsibility (OBR), which it sees as providing fiscal responsibility in government. The OBR supports the Chancellor in providing a managed set of accounts for government expenditure, taxes and borrowing.

In the 2012 budget the OBR and the Chancellor outlined what were referred to as a 'total managed expenditure' target of £683 billion for 2012–2013. This establishes departmental expenditure limits for each government department. The figures set out in the 2012 budget are listed in Table 14.2.

What is clear from these figures is that much of government expenditure is on social welfare provision (e.g. pensions, health and education). As such it can be seen as social investment in a better society. Welfare provision helps to provide healthier and more educated citizens who are able to make a more impactful contribution to society. The figures outlined below include expenditures by both national and local government.

TABLE 14.2 Government spending targets (2012–2013)

	Target (£bn)
Social protection	207
Health	130
Education	91
Debt interest	46
Other	43
Defence	39
Personal social services	33
Public order and safety	32
Transport	22
Housing and environment	21
Industry, agriculture and employment	19
Total	683

Source: Office for Budget Responsibility.

TABLE 14.3 Public sector current receipts (2012–2013)

	Receipts (£bn)
Income tax	155
National insurance	106
Excise duties	48
Corporation tax	45
VAT	102
Business rates	26
Local tax	26
Other	64
Total	592

Source: Office for Budget Responsibility.

If we now look at public sector current receipts for 2012–2013 we see the picture illustrated in Table 14.3.

Descriptions of these different types of taxes and the impact that they have on business are provided below. The headings include items that are collected nationally by Her Majesty's Revenue and Customs (HMRC) such as income tax and corporation tax, as well as local taxes collected by local authorities such as business rates.

The figures shown in Tables 14.2 and 14.3 illustrate the fact that in 2012–2013 the expected budget deficit was £91 billion.

£683 billion – £592 billion = £91 billion.

In the budget speech that was made to Parliament the Coalition Chancellor of the Exchequer, George Osborne, made the statement that: 'Public Sector Net Borrowing will fall from its post war peak of 11.1% of GDP in 2009–10 to 4.3% in 2014–15 and to 1.1% in 2016–17' (HM Treasury, 2012).

This was a calculated statement of economic policy. During the recession in 2008–2009 the Labour Government had deliberately engaged in Keynesian budget deficits to stimulate the economy, including more expenditure on the public sector of the economy. Osborne's recipe was more in line with classical/monetarist thinking (i.e. restoring the economy towards a balanced budget).

You should be able to see that fiscal policy is both an economic and a political policy. Those who support Keynesian demand management fiscal policies see the government as having a role in stepping in to spend money when the economy is in recession. For example, the Labour Party's response to the recession in 2008–2009 was to engage in a process of quantitative easing.

KEY TERM

Quantitative easing – involves the government creating credit in the economy by printing more money. This creates additional demand in the economy at a time when consumers and the government are cutting back their expenditures. In contrast, those who support classical/neoclassical and monetarist ideas see the ideal budget as being a balanced budget.

The difference between government spending and taxes is referred to as the public sector borrowing requirement (PSBR). When there is a fiscal deficit (taxes are less than government spending) the government will need to borrow by selling long-term government bonds or short-term bills.

KEY TERM

Government bonds – long-term securities that pay a fixed rate of return. They have a long period (e.g. ten years or longer) before they mature (i.e. when they are repaid to the lender). Government bonds are usually bought by financial institutions seeking a safe source of investment.

KEY TERM

Treasury bills – the government regularly issues (sells) treasury bills. These are sold on the money market. They are usually sold for a period of 90 days, and are bought by discount houses. Discount houses buy the treasury bills for less than their face value (i.e. at a discount).

Local government expenditures involve payments that the council disburses for running local services – for example, to contracting companies to collect local refuse or to maintain local parks, as well as maintaining local roads and providing street lighting. The council then pays for these services through two main sources: council tax (paid by householders) and a grant from central government. Where local council expenditures are greater than revenues, the local council will need to borrow by issuing local government bonds.

KEY TERM

Public sector net cash requirement (PSCNR) – this is the total borrowing by national and local government.

KEY THEME

Reasons for public spending

The key reasons why the government spends money in the economy are set out below:

- To supply goods and services that the private sector would not provide in the normal course of events. Examples include the police and fire service, hospitals and state schools, as well as welfare payments and benefits such as unemployment pay.

- To inject extra spending into the macro-economy, so as to achieve increases in aggregate demand over time in order to stimulate economic growth and to combat unemployment.

- To improve the supply side of the economy so that the supply of goods across the economy becomes more efficient. For example, this would include expenditure on public transport schemes and roads and railways, as well as education and training.

- To reduce the negative externalities (harmful effects) of business activity (e.g. by taxing polluters for the pollution they create).

- To subsidize certain industries (e.g. new industries that might grow to make a valuable contribution to the economy in the future).

- To distribute income more fairly (equitably) – for example, by taxing those with higher incomes and giving more benefits to those on lower incomes.

- For each of the reasons for government spending try to identify a recent example that has been in the news – for example, a recent case where the government has increased its spending on the supply of goods and services.

- For each of the reasons for government spending try to identify the extent to which the reason would be supported (or not) by those in favour of free market economics.

- For each of the reasons for government spending try to identify the impact that it will have on local businesses in your area.

ACTIVITY

Rates of tax – for example, for income tax, corporation tax and value added tax (VAT) – are changed on a fairly regular basis at the time the Chancellor announces his or her budget decisions, depending on the type of fiscal policy that the government is pursuing. Search online for Business Link – taxes in the UK, to find out the latest rates of the main types of taxes.

14.3 Types of fiscal policy

In addition to distinguishing between balanced, surplus and deficit budgets it is also helpful to differentiate between discretionary fiscal policies and automatic stabilizers:

- Discretionary fiscal policies are one-off policy changes designed to achieve a specific objective. For example, business taxes may be lowered for the purposes of stimulating business enterprise. This is a one-off adjustment for a specific purpose.

- Automatic stabilizers are fiscal mechanisms designed to enable the economy to remain on an even keel. For example, when the economy moves into a recession then the proportion of taxes paid by taxpayers (particularly on low incomes) should fall so that their disposable income is maintained. Similarly, in a period of boom when inflation is looming then an automatic stabilizer would ensure that a larger proportion of income is taken in taxes than previously in order to limit the growth of disposable incomes.

In designing tax structures the government should seek to combine discretionary fiscal policies to achieve specific objectives, with long-term stabilizers to achieve the objective of steady and sustained growth of the economy.

14.4 Types of taxation

Tax – a payment made by individuals or businesses to the government.

The government imposes taxes for various reasons:

- To raise revenue. The earliest taxes were raised by governments to pay for the expenses of the rulers of a country and to finance wars. Today, taxes are levied to raise money to cover a range of government expenditures – for example, on building schools, hospitals and roads, paying for defence and a police force.

- To discourage certain activities – for example, those that some see as anti-social in terms of the damage to health and pollution that they cause, such as smoking or driving. So cigarettes, cars and fuel may be heavily taxed.

- To discourage the import of goods. Import taxes are referred to as tariffs. They can be levied as a percentage of the value of imports (an *ad valorem* tax) or a set tax on each item imported (a specific tax).

- To redistribute income from the rich to the poor.

Economists make a distinction between:

- Direct taxes, for which the burden falls on the person paying it – for example, when you pay income tax it is taken directly from your wages and paid to the government.

- Indirect taxes, which are imposed by governments on goods and services, but are eventually paid by consumers rather than by businesses that collect the tax for the government in the first instance.

The payer of a direct tax has no choice about whether they pay the tax. In contrast, consumers can decide whether or not to buy a good with a tax on it. Because of this element of choice some people believe that the government should rely more on indirect than direct taxes. For example, Conservative governments in Britain have always favoured indirect taxes such as VAT rather than direct taxes such as income tax (which it sees as a disincentive to work).

Progressive, regressive and proportional taxes

If income is going to be redistributed then the rich need to pay more in tax than the poor.

A progressive tax takes a greater proportion of income from a wealthy person than from a poor person. So someone earning £20,000 a year might pay 15 per cent tax on this income (£3,000), someone earning £50,000 a year might pay 20 per cent tax on this income (£10,000) and a person earning £100,000 a year 25 per cent tax on this income (£25,000). In each case the richer the person the more disposable income that they have after tax (see Table 14.4).

TABLE 14.4 Illustrating the impact of a progressive tax

Income (£)	Disposable income after tax (£)	Tax rate (%)
20,000	17,000	15
50,000	40,000	20
100,000	75,000	25

A regressive tax is one where the poor pay a higher percentage of their income in tax than the rich. This happens when the government imposes a tax at a set rate. For example, a person may pay £20 for a licence to fish in a river, and £100 a year to tax their car or pay some other set flat-rate tax. You can see that £20 for the fishing licence would be a higher percentage for a poor person to pay than a wealthy person.

Progressive taxes redistribute income in favour of the poor. Regressive taxes redistribute income in favour of the rich. Proportional tax refers to a situation in which tax rises in proportion to the income of the taxpayer (see Figure 14.1).

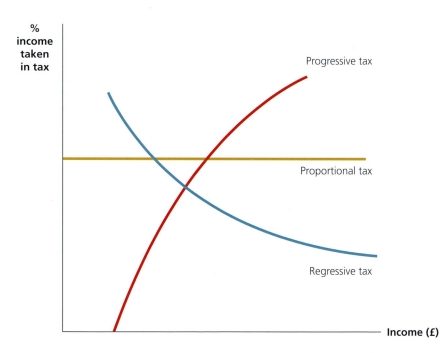

FIGURE 14.1 The relationship between income and the percentage of tax taken

Common taxes

Taxes that are common to many countries include the following:

- A tax on incomes. This will often take the form of a progressive tax. Higher-income earners pay a larger percentage of income in tax. The tax is collected directly from the taxpayer – usually being deducted from their wage or income by their employer. In Britain earners receive a tax-free allowance from the government of several thousand pounds. Income above this level is then charged at a standard rate. Once higher levels of income are earned the taxpayer will pay at successively higher rates depending on their earnings.

- National insurance. In the UK national insurance is also collected by the employer on behalf of the government. It is calculated as a percentage of income. It includes both an employer's contribution and an employee's contribution. National insurance payments help to provide the payer with a range of benefits including unemployment, sickness and accident benefit, as well as contributing towards the state pension.

- A tax on purchasing. An example of this is VAT. Producers and sellers of goods pay the tax to the government as a percentage of the value they add in the production of an item. The retailer then collects the tax from the end consumer. Consumers can choose to purchase goods with VAT charged on them or to save their money. It is only when consumers choose to buy VATable goods that they become taxpayers. Supporters of the free market tend to support emphasis on indirect taxes rather than direct taxes as a means of collecting government revenue. They believe that this fits in with the concept of freedom of choice.

- A tax on company profits. Taxes on company profits, like income taxes, are direct taxes. A company declares its annual profit in an income statement. The income statement will show 'earnings before tax'. Companies pay taxation at a very similar rate to that paid by individuals. However, there are many adjustments which must be made to the profit figure in order to calculate the company's taxable profit. These adjustments will be discussed with HMRC before the final taxation charge is agreed.

- Taxes on imports. Taxes on imports are termed tariffs. They are levied on goods that are most likely to compete against domestic goods and services. They are indirect taxes.

- Taxes on specific products – for example, cigarettes, alcohol, petrol, etc. These are indirect. They may be regressive if they hit the poor harder than the rich.

- Other taxes. There are a number of other taxes including:

  - Capital gains tax – a tax on investments that have gained in value. The taxpayer only pays the tax when they sell or resell their assets.
  - Council tax – paid to local government to pay for local services. The amount that you pay is relative to the value of your home.
  - Stamp duty – a tax charged when someone buys a new house worth more than a given value.
  - Air travel tax – a flat rate payment charged on all airline tickets.

ACTIVITY

Carry out some Internet-based research to find out current rates of:

- Stamp duty
- VAT
- Capital gains tax
- The standard rate of income tax
- Air travel tax

14.5 The impact of direct and indirect taxes

One of the key aspects of life that economists study is the impact of incentives. Incentives are rewards (or punishments) that encourage us to carry out particular actions. Taxes act as incentives and disincentives to individuals and businesses to behave or not to behave in certain ways.

CASE STUDY The impact of tax on large businesses

For all businesses tax can be seen as a cost of production. Whatever the size of the business, owners and directors are likely to argue that taxes are too high. High taxes help to make a business less competitive and eat into business profits.

Because large multinational businesses operate on an international scale an important decision for them is where to locate centres of operations and their head offices. An important consideration will be different levels of taxation in different countries.

If the government sets a tax rate too high it can discourage some desirable business activity. For example, in February 2010 Unilever, one of the world's largest producers of household goods, threatened to move its manufacturing operations away from Britain because of high tax rates. The chief executive said: 'We . . . have choices where we put research laboratories . . . manufacturing facilities and . . . where we put senior management' (Steiner, 2010). At that time Unilever employed 174,000 workers around the world, with 9,000 of these in the UK. Corporation taxes in Britain at the time were 28 per cent compared with 15 per cent in Germany and 12.5 per cent in Ireland.

- Carry out some Internet-based research to compare different levels of company taxes in three countries of your choice. Which of these countries has the lowest and which the highest level of business taxes?

- Why might a company choose to locate its operations in a country where tax rates are lower?

- Why might a country prefer to locate its operations in a country where tax rates are higher?

TABLE 14.5 Benefits and drawbacks of direct taxes

The disadvantages of direct taxes	The advantages of direct taxes
They can act as a disincentive to hard work, enterprise and saving. Some people may be discouraged from working overtime or seeking promotion because of the disincentive effect of higher tax rates. Similarly entrepreneurs may be discouraged from setting up in business or extending themselves because they feel that rates of tax on profits are too high. Taxes on savings reduce the reward from saving. This might act as a disincentive to save.	It is possible to argue that higher tax rates actually encourage some people to work harder in order to maintain their income. (Workers with fixed financial commitments such as mortgage repayments feel that they have to work harder in order to keep up the mortgage.) Direct taxes often help to redistribute income and wealth. Direct taxes also tend to work as automatic stabilizers. Direct taxes are a good way for governments to raise revenue in economies where productivity and incomes are high.

There are a number drawbacks to direct taxes, particularly when they are set too high, but there are also benefits (see Table 14.5).

There are also a number of benefits and drawbacks associated with indirect taxes (see Table 14.6).

We can now illustrate the incidence of a sales tax and how the amount of tax paid depends on the elasticity of demand for the item being taxed.

The price elasticity of demand for a product determines how much revenue the government is able to collect from indirect sales taxes. When a sales tax is increased the supply curve of a good shifts to the left. The sales tax acts as a cost to the business. The supply curve shifts upwards by the amount of the tax.

TABLE 14.6 Benefits and drawbacks of indirect taxes

Drawbacks associated with indirect taxes	Benefits associated with indirect taxes
They tend to be regressive so that they hit the poor harder than the rich. For example, in the case of VAT, poorer households are more likely to spend their income rather than to save it. Increasing indirect taxes also has an inflationary impact as they are likely to raise prices. VAT calculation involves detailed paperwork which is particularly a burden for smaller businesses.	They are relatively easy and cheap to collect (for the government) as firms do some of the work in collecting them. They are believed to create less of a disincentive to work hard and to be entrepreneurial. They can be used selectively for specific purposes (e.g. to target smoking or alcohol use). They are harder to avoid by taxpayers. They are relatively easy to adjust (e.g. by altering the rate from 17.5% to 20%). The main benefit of indirect taxes is that they give greater choice to the taxpayer about whether to buy goods on which indirect tax is levied.

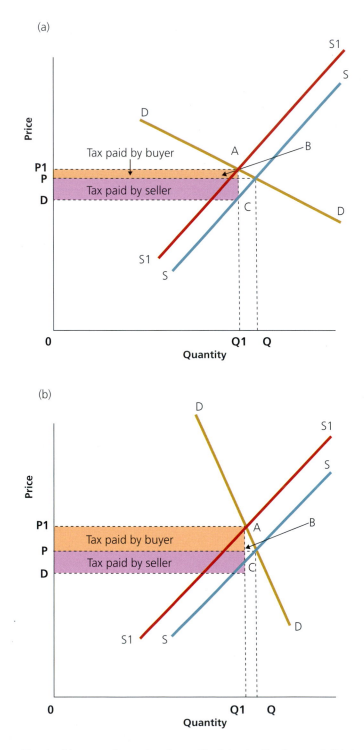

FIGURE 14.2 The incidence of a sales tax with (a) elastic demand (b) inelastic demand

Figure 14.2 compares an increase in a sales tax by the same amount for a good with an elastic demand curve, and for one with an inelastic demand curve. Figure 14.2a (product with elastic demand) shows that the increase in the sales tax leads to a relatively large fall in the quantity demanded (Q to Q1), compared with the impact of the sales tax shown in Figure 14.2b (product with inelastic demand).

Figure 14.2 also shows how much of the tax will be paid by the seller and how much by the customer. Incidence of tax refers to who pays the major part of the tax. In Figure 14.2a the incidence of the tax falls mainly on the seller. This is because the total amount of tax that will have to be paid is P1ACD. Out of this the consumer pays PP1AB – that is, the increase in price from P to P1 multiplied by the quantity now traded in the market 0Q1. The seller has to pay the rest of the tax DPBC. If demand is elastic, sellers will of course be able to raise their prices only a little.

In contrast, in Figure 14.2b, with inelastic demand the size of the rectangle DPBC (the incidence of tax to the seller) is much smaller than PP1AB (the incidence of tax to the buyer). If demand is inelastic, sellers are of course much better placed to shift the incidence of the tax to the buyer.

Where knowledge of elasticity is useful

Knowledge of elasticity and the impact on indirect taxes helps the government to set tax rates for VAT and other sales taxes. It also helps government to decide how much they can charge in terms of import taxes to discourage imports.

The government should also consider elasticity in tax levels for licences – for example, car licences, waste and pollution charges, and local business taxes.

Imposing taxes that are too high can lead to:

- Falling sales and falling incomes – and hence rising unemployment as workers are laid off and businesses close.
- An incentive for businesses and individuals to avoid paying taxes, leading to an 'undercover' economy involving tax evasion.

Effective taxes should focus on producing desirable goods and services and discourage businesses from carrying out undesirable activities. They should not discourage effort and initiative. They should also provide suitable revenues for the government. Effectively designed tax systems should create a good relationship between government and private producers. They should be simple to operate and understand, and not need excessive form-filling by taxpayers.

14.6 The impact of government subsidies

Just as the government can use taxes as a tool for fiscal manipulation of the economy it can also use subsidies. Subsidies can be used to incentivize particular activities that the government sees as being desirable.

Most subsidies are sums of money provided by the government to a producer or supplier for a specific purpose. They may be provided for several reasons:

- To encourage the production of goods of national importance. For example, the government may provide subsidies to farmers to produce essential food supplies. The subsidy guarantees an income to the farmer.

- To encourage the development of new products and industries. In the short term these products and industries may be uncompetitive, resulting in losses being made by private producers. For example, in many countries the government provides subsidies to encourage the development of new forms of energy, such as wind and solar power.

- To provide support for industries that are in decline and that are major employers of labour. If the industry did not receive a subsidy it might not make a profit. Closing the industry could have negative externalities, such as unemployment, which would result in the government having to make unemployment payments to those out of work. The subsidy is thus both socially desirable and economically sound from the government's point of view.

- To protect domestic industries against foreign competition. The subsidy has the same effect as lowering the cost to the supplier.

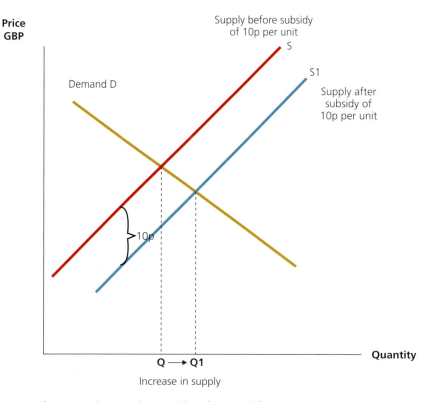

FIGURE 14.3 Increase in supply resulting from a 10 pence subsidy

The effect of a subsidy if illustrated in Figure 14.3.

When a supplier receives a subsidy it will be encouraged to produce more for the market. This leads to a shift to the right of the supply curve. When the supply curve shifts to the right this leads to an increased supply at lower prices. Figure 14.3 shows that a subsidy of 10 pence per unit supplied has led to an increase in supply from S to S1. The quantity supplied has increased from Q to Q1.

Of course, a subsidy does not always lead to an increase in supply. For example, in a loss-making industry the more likely effect will be to stop supply from falling rather than leading to its increase.

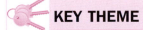

KEY THEME

The budget 2012

The article below appeared on *The Guardian* website on 21 March 2012 following the budget (Guardian News & Media Ltd 2012, reproduced with permission).

Budget 2012: A shocking budget from an unfair chancellor

George Osborne's strategy is to secure support for boosts to business and the rich by raising tax allowances – and forget about the unemployed and the lowest earners . . .

Even after the serial leaking, this was still a shocking budget. Shocking in the way it skated over the weakness of the British economy. Shocking in the way it ladled out still more pain to those dependent on welfare benefits. Shocking in the way it cut the tax burden for millionaires.

That said, this was – in its way – a skilful package of measures, which had greater intellectual coherence than the hotchpotch of measures served up by George Osborne in last November's autumn statement. The politics of the budget were immediately apparent: try to secure broad support for the big concessions to business and the rich by helping those on lower incomes through an increase in the personal tax allowance. Leave it to Labour to worry about those who are unemployed or on the lowest incomes, who will not benefit from the income tax breaks. It was the way Nigel Lawson did it back in the 1980s.

This, though, remains a gamble and a big one at that. Lawson's big tax-cutting budgets of 1987 and 1988 took place when the economy was booming, real incomes were rising rapidly, house prices were going through the roof and the exchequer was overflowing with cash. None of that applies today, and while the forecasts produced by the Office for Budget Responsibility showed no further downgrades to the outlook for 2012 and 2013, there was no improvement either. The economy will continue to chug along in first gear this year, with even the expected 0.8 per cent growth vulnerable to a fresh crisis in the Eurozone or higher oil prices.

Voters who are experiencing a third year of falling real incomes may feel less well disposed towards the coalition than Osborne expects. Indeed, their abiding memory of the budget is likely to be the largesse shown to the rich. The decision to scrap the 50p tax rate was taken on the thinnest of evidence and it remains to be seen whether the increase in stamp duty on £2m homes and the clampdown on tax avoidance raises the revenue the government expects. Previous administrations have seen their fiscal arithmetic come unstuck by over-estimating the take from stamp duty, and Osborne is now dependent on the uncertain revenues from high-end property sales to make his sums add up.

Ultimately, modern budgets are judged against three yardsticks. The first of these is whether they help or hinder the growth in the economy. Osborne was right to say that Britain borrowed its way into trouble and must earn its way out again, but it remains to be seen whether his apology for an industrial strategy can quicken the pace of activity. Thus far, the government's record has been lamentable: the economy is still 4 per cent smaller than it was before the Great Recession started in 2008.

The second function of a budget is to balance the books. Weaker growth means lower tax receipts and higher spending: Osborne has already abandoned his plan to complete the repair job on the public finances by the end of this parliament, and further slippage looks likely. Finally, in modern times there has been increasing pressure on chancellors to show that what they are doing is fair. Under Labour, budgets were fair and progressive. Osborne has chosen a different course.

The article suggests that budgets should be judged by three criteria:

- Whether they support the growth of the economy;
- Whether they help to balance the government's books; and
- Whether they are fair.

● **Using the information provided in the article, what evidence is there that the 2012 budget was likely to meet these criteria?**

● **What type of fiscal policy/ies is George Osborne pursuing and what do you think would be his rationale for doing so?**

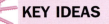

14.7 Summary

Fiscal policy is the deliberate manipulation of government expenditure and revenues in order to achieve given policy objectives. At one level this involves the relationship between total public spending and total public revenues. For example, a deficit budget can pump extra spending into the economy whereas a budget surplus would withdraw spending from the economy. Fiscal policy also involves adjusting different types of tax and spending in order to target specific objectives. For example, the government may shift the emphasis from direct to indirect taxes or from regressive to progressive taxes.

Keynesian economists believe that fiscal policies can be used by the government to stimulate the economy. In contrast neoclassical and monetarist economists believe that there should be a balanced budget.

KEY IDEAS

Fiscal policy

- Fiscal policy is government policy designed to use its own spending and the taxes that it raises in order to achieve desired policy objectives such as full employment or economic growth.
- Whereas monetarists seek to balance government revenues and taxes, Keynesian economists believe that fiscal stimulus can be used to support economic growth and to counteract unemployment.
- The balance between government spending and taxes is made up by government borrowing (or paying back debt).

Government expenditure

- The main area of government expenditure is on welfare, including health, education and social benefits.
- Government expenditure is one of the main ingredients of GDP.
- Free market supporters believe in rolling back the size of the government in the economy.
- Government spending includes central and local government spending.

Government taxes

- Progressive taxes take a greater percentage of income from the rich than the poor. Regressive taxes take the greatest proportion from the poor.
- Direct taxes are deducted directly from a taxpayer's income at source. In contrast, indirect taxes are collected by a third party on behalf of the government and citizens have a choice as to whether to buy goods with indirect taxes imposed on them.

- Direct taxes include income tax, national insurance and corporation tax. Indirect taxes include sales taxes such as VAT.

- An increase in an indirect tax can shift the supply curve for a product to the left because it has the same impact as a rise in costs of production.

- An increase in a subsidy can shift the supply curve for a product to the right because the subsidy has the same impact as a reduction in costs, acting as an incentive to a producer to supply more to the market at the same prices as before.

REVIEW QUESTIONS

1. What are the main weapons of: (a) fiscal policy; and (b) monetary policy?

2. How is the view of classical economists and monetarists different to that of Keynesian economists in relation to how fiscal policy should be used to manage the economy?

3. What are automatic stabilizers? How might income tax operate as an economic stabilizer? Relate your answer to: (a) a boom in the economy; and (b) a recession in the economy.

4. What are the main types of government spending in the UK economy?

5. What are the main sources of government revenue?

6. Why is the current government seeking to reduce the PSBR?

7. Explain the difference between progressive and regressive taxes and between direct and indirect taxes. In each case provide one or more examples.

8. What are the main arguments used to support and criticize a shift in emphasis from a focus on direct taxes to indirect taxes. Relate your answer to taxes such as income tax, corporation tax and VAT.

9. How do taxes and subsidies work as incentives?

10. Draw a diagram to illustrate the economic impact of subsidizing the production of a specific product of your choice.

RECOMMENDED READING

Taxation: Policy and Practice by Andy Lymer is a book that is updated each year and gives an up-to-date coverage of the UK's taxation system. It can be ordered online from Fiscal Publication, Accounting Education.

REFERENCES

HM Treasury (2012) *Budget 2012*. Available at: www.hm-treasury.gov.uk/budget 2012.htm (accessed January 2013).

Steiner, R. (2010) 'Unilever Threatens to Pull Out of Britain Over Rising Taxes', *Daily Mail*, 11 February. Available at: www.dailymail.co.uk/news/article-1250083/ Unilever-latest-company (accessed January 2013).

USEFUL WEBSITES

www.hm-treasury.gov.uk/budget2012.htm – read the latest edition of the budget published online at HM Treasury Budget and the most recent year.

15 Green economics

CHAPTER OBJECTIVES

After carefully reading this chapter you should have gained an understanding of:

- The challenges facing the planet and its people from economic growth

- Some simple tools for modelling environmental impacts on the economy

- The nature of sustainable development

- Alternative types of capital in addition to man-made capital

- Cost–benefit analysis

- Weak and strong sustainability

- Understand the benefits of taking a wider view than conventional economic perspectives of sustainability

- Outlining international initiatives involving wider collaboration for sustainability

- Explaining how ecological footprints can be used to measure environmental impacts of economic activity

- Analysing sustainable business models

15.1 Introduction

This chapter focuses on an area of economics that is often neglected in traditional general economic texts – the impact of the economy on the environment. As well as creating 'goods' the economy also produces 'bads' in the form of waste, pollution and other impacts. Economics as a discipline needs to take account of negative impacts of economic activity.

This chapter shows how some economists have sought to incorporate concern for the environment into market models using a cost and benefit approach. Other writers have sought to measure 'ecological footprints' of human activity in order to enable decision makers to make more rational decisions about the best use of scarce resources. Businesses are increasingly being required to report on their contributions to sustainability through corporate social responsibility (CSR). Enlightened businesses increasingly seek to develop business models focusing on a Triple Bottom Line. The chapter also looks at the impact of intergovernmental initiatives such as the Rio and Kyoto Treaties, which have sought cooperation in order to achieve wider sustainability goals.

15.2 The environmental challenge

The tension between economic growth and environmental sustainability lies at the heart of the problem of the overuse and lack of foresight that frequently applies to our use of scarce resources.

The classic representation of this problem was set out in an article by Hardin and Baden (1997). They used the example of a piece of common land for which villagers have common property rights. The land is able to provide for the needs of herdsmen who graze their animals. However, there comes a point at which eventually there are too many people using the land – and everyone suffers. One more person uses the land, and beyond this point the land can provide for no one.

This is a situation that we are increasingly becoming familiar with in modern society – for example, in the depletion of fish stocks in common fishing grounds. Recently we have seen a number of international conferences focused on a key issue of the tragedy of the commons in relation to global warming. The argument here is that as more and more people want to enjoy the sort of products enjoyed in the richer parts of the world, which are based on high energy consumption patterns, then increasingly this will limit the ability of everyone to benefit from the modern industrial economy.

KEY TERM

The commons – this term originally related to common or shared land belonging to villagers on which they could jointly graze their animals. Today the commons is used to refer to common resources that are shared by global, national and local citizens such as the air which we breathe, oceans and fisheries, and other shared resources.

15.3 Reappraising simple economic theory

In the early part of the twenty-first century we have come increasingly to recognize the impact of 'shocks' in forcing us to rethink our theories of the world. In particular we have recently been faced with a number of environmental shocks which increasingly demand our attention. For example, some cities in China that are at the heart of the push for industrialization tend to be covered in a haze or smog of chemical pollutants. A cocktail of toxins from industry and automobiles forces people to cover their faces when travelling to work. Similarly we faced the dramatic impact of climate change in the form of drought and regional flooding in the same year (the summer of 2012).

The problem with shocks is that we don't know how big a shock we need to really make key decision makers sit up, think, and take positive action. Evidence tends to indicate that this would need to be a fairly big shock – for instance, in Athens when air pollution reaches a given level only people with even letters on their number plates are allowed into the city, the next day it is the turn of the odd letters (some people have responded by buying an extra car). There seems to be clear evidence that climate change will have an impact on sea levels. Many governments argue that this presents a strong case for immediate action.

Unfortunately there are others who are dragging their heels. While the UK and much of the EU are 'believers' in the need for change, there are other countries, especially the United States, (although the Obama government has redressed much of this emphasis) who continue to be unbelievers (arguing that global warming is less of a threat than is made out, or that their own growth in carbon-dioxide output can be offset elsewhere, for example by the reforestation of the Amazon.

Reshaping economic tools

Today we know enough about some of the relationships between the feedback loops between the economy and the environment to reshape some of the economic concepts and tools that we apply to economic growth and environmental sustainability. Incorporating consideration of the environment into traditional economics can be illustrated by examining two simple economic tools: 'the production frontier' and the 'simple circular flow of income model'.

KEY TERMS

Production possibility frontier (PPF) – shows the maximum output of two goods or services that can be produced given the current level of resources available and assuming efficiency in production.

Circular flow of income – shows the flows that take place between firms and households in relation to the production process. Companies produce output by hiring factors of production. They pay factor incomes to the factors of production (a flow of income). The households then spend their income (a flow of expenditure) on the goods and services sold by firms.

Questioning the production possibility frontier

In setting out production possibility frontiers it appears that there is a trade-off between alternative quantities of 'goods' (capital or consumer goods, guns or butter, etc.) which can be produced from existing quantities and qualities of resources.

In Figure 15.1 an economy is able to use all of its existing resources to produce combinations of goods set out on a PPF. For example, assuming that the economy produces two types of goods: consumer goods and capital goods, at a given moment in time (period 1) it can produce any combination of goods along PPF1 (e.g. x of capital goods and y of consumer goods). Alternatively it might produce a different combination along PPF1.

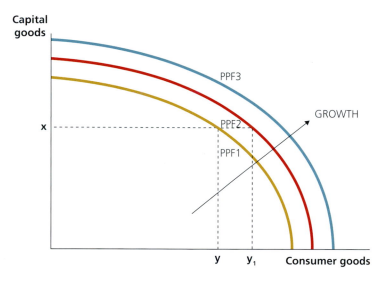

FIGURE 15.1 The production possibility frontier and economic growth

In the course of time the economy grows and is able to produce bigger baskets of combinations of capital goods and consumer goods. So for example in time period 2 the economy might be able to produce combinations of goods along the higher production possibility frontier (PPF2). We can see that PPF2 is 'better' in terms of goods production because now if the economy were to choose to produce x of capital goods, for example, it could now combine this with y1 of consumer goods (y1 is more than y).

This process of moving the production possibility frontier outwards is often referred to as economic growth. However, the traditional analysis outlined above is based on an assumption that may prove untenable. The analysis assumes that the PPF can keep moving out into clear white space. Unfortunately (or fortunately), this may not be the case. We may also need to take account of constraints pushing down on the PPF curve resulting from the negative (spillover) effects resulting from the production of 'goods' (see Figure 15.2).

Spillover effects – the secondary results of economic activity. They are often referred to as externalities. Externalities can be positive (i.e. benefits) or negative (i.e. costs). When a producer sells a good to a customer the producer traditionally focuses on the private costs and benefits related to the transaction. However, most economists believe that it is also important to consider the wider social costs and benefits – for example, that the good may cause pollution (negative spillover) and waste (negative spillover) when being disposed of.

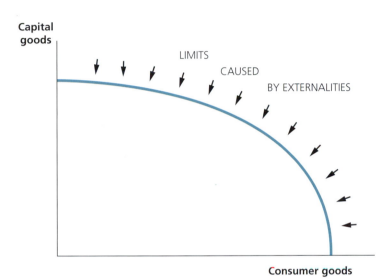

FIGURE 15.2 Constraints on the production frontier

This limit to growth is illustrated by the way in which China downgraded its growth expectations for its economy in 2011. The Chinese economy had been growing by rates of close to 10 per cent in 2007 and 2008, with a slight downturn then resulting from the impact of the wider global recession. However, in 2011 China decided to downgrade its expectations of economic growth still further by putting aside part of its expected growth to focus on measures to clean up the environment (e.g. closing down heavily polluting plants).

We can illustrate this another way by setting out a simple circular flow model of the economy (see Figure 15.3).

Figure 15.3 shows the relationship between the creation of gross national output (GNP), national income and national expenditure. Firms' outputs are in response to demand in the form of consumer expenditures. The output is in the form of 'goods' and, of course, firms employ the factor services of households to produce output, paying incomes in return. In this circular flow model, growth would take place as a result of an increase in outputs, incomes and expenditure. A rise in GNP would be represented by an increase in 'goods'.

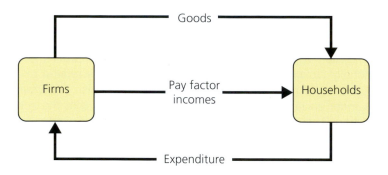

FIGURE 15.3 Simple circular flow model

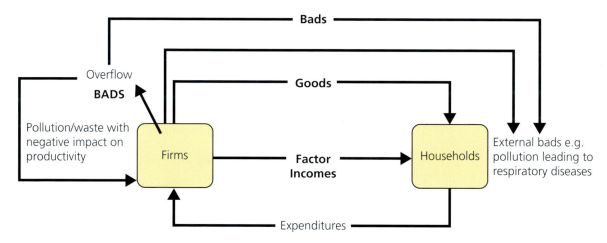

FIGURE 15.4 The creation of economic 'bads' such as pollution

However, the weakness of this model is that it does not take account of the negative spillover effects of production. Production can and often does lead to the creation of externalities such as pollution which we can refer to as 'bads' (see Figure 15.4).

In examining this broader model of the economy we realize that there is more involved than simply the formal economy, and as such environmentalists refer to the 'carrying capacity' of the planet (or a geographical area).

KEY TERM

Carrying capacity – a term borrowed from ecology that refers to the maximum or equilibrium number of organisms of a particular species that can be supported indefinitely in a given environment.

Of course, we can argue that bads can be dealt with – they can be recycled, removed from the system, or stored in waste sinks. Unfortunately, the nature of sinks is that unless they are effectively treated they can spill out, and form a loop back into the system with a negative effect on production.

The 'haze' situation in parts of South East Asia, where a cloud of pollution forces government officials to close down industrial activities for periods of time when pollution gets too bad, illustrates this feedback loop.

In the harmful effects of pollution we see a potential 'doomsday scenario'. The doomsday scenario is not a new one. Thomas Malthus (1798) was one of the earliest political economists to raise issues about the limits to growth. He was writing at a time when population had started to increase rapidly. He talked about absolute scarcity, where the earth would not be able to sustain rising levels of population. 'Natural checks' would then lead to human disasters that prevented further increases in population. He predicted this by applying the principle of diminishing returns in production.

However, David Ricardo (1817) highlighted a more optimistic scenario in which the limits to growth could be staved off through technological progress and the ability of the market to limit the overexploitation of resources through the price mechanism. Ricardo's followers base their views on the idea of relative scarcity and propose that markets have the ability to effectively channel scarce resources into the most appropriate lines. As population rises the quality of resources used will decrease, costs of production will increase, and hence product prices will rise, reflecting the relative scarcity of resources. Rising prices thus act as the check which prevents society from depleting resources too quickly. Modern day Ricardians also tend to have confident belief in the abilities of technology to create solutions and new products (spurred on by the rewards of the pricing system generated through higher profits).

Reflective question

1   Taking into account the evidence around you, including information you have read in books, seen in television newspaper reports and from your own personal experience, are you inclined towards a pessimistic Malthusian view or a more optimistic Ricardian view?

Some writers believe that continued economic growth is bad. It is bad because our economic activity is a very large subsystem within planet Earth. This planet is finite, non-growing and materially closed. Macro-economics fails to take into account the size of the economy relative to the ecosystem. The entire foundation of micro-economics is built on the concept of finding the optimal point, yet economists abandon this concept of optimal scale when it comes to the macro-economy – more is assumed to be better.

The economist Kenneth Boulding raised the worrying image of spaceship Earth. He contrasted a 'cowboy economy' and a 'spaceship economy'. In his view, historically we

CASE STUDY Environments are not constraints

This case study is based on an article by Erle Ellis in a feature on Rio+20, in *This is Africa*, June/July 2012. The article starts off by showing that Malthusian ideas remain the core message behind efforts of many of those concerned with conserving the environment. The article goes on:

The current human situation is certainly riskier than ever. Our populations have never been larger, nor have our consumption of resources or impact on nature. There is growing scientific consensus that human alteration of Earth's climate, biosphere and indeed the entire Earth system has gone so far that it has forced the entire planet into a new geological epoch, the Anthropocene. Yet there are multiple reasons why the conventional environmental message – that 'humanity must halt its transgression of environmental limits or face catastrophe' – will not move us towards a more sustainable approach.

The most important reason is that this hypothesis is not supported by scientific evidence. The consensus from archaeology, anthropology, demographers and others who study human–environment relationships over the long-term, is that there is no simple relationship between human populations and the environment. Popular portrayals of societal collapse in the face of environmental limits are anecdotal. The consensus of archaeologists – those most expert in the science of long-term human–environment relationships – is that the story relates more closely to the capability of social systems to adapt, innovate, and sustain themselves in the face of social and environmental stressors than of catastrophic failures in the face of biophysical limits.

Ever since Paleolithic humans developed social learning and the use of fire, it has been the strength of human systems, our social structures and dynamics, not the productivity of environments, that has enabled us to become the single most powerful species in the history of the planet. The transformative power of human systems has increased and developed over the long-term, with our agricultural and industrial powers growing as the cumulative product of increasingly greater scales of social and environmental interaction and experience, technical and social innovation and learning, and the accumulation of social and material capitals.

The current rate and intensity of human alteration of the Earth system has no precedent. Yet overwhelming evidence demonstrates that socially powerful human systems confronted with potent environmental challenges and apparent limits will adapt, innovate and transform themselves and their environment rather than collapse and fail. As a result, human populations have grown and been sustained far beyond their 'natural limits' for millennia. In the Anthropocene, the Earth systems that sustain humanity are primarily those sustained by human systems themselves by our social interactions and our environmental engineering. The boundaries to humanity are no longer environmental but social.

- **Is the overall message set out in this article a pessimistic one or an optimistic one?**

- **What does Ellis see as being the broad-brush solution to environmental issues?**

- **In your view what contribution can economists make to developing effective social systems?**

could operate on the basis of the cowboy analogy. The lone cowboy working his way across the plains of America could make a fire from brushwood at night on which he cooked a mess of beans and in the morning kick out the fire that he had made and move on. However, in a world of huge populations and industrial production we can't continue to act as if we are individual cowboys. A more realistic image is of us all living inside an enclosed space capsule in which resources are finite. When we use resources we create waste and pollution and it stays within the capsule with us. We have to learn to live within the capsule more effectively.

The reality is that many environmental resources have not been priced through the market. This is particularly true in the case of waste and pollution, which have only recently been taken into 'serious' consideration in economic analysis.

Reflective question

2 How accurate do you think Boulding's analysis of 'spaceship earth' is?

15.4 Sustainable development

In recent years serious attempts have been made by economists to build environmental considerations into the market mechanism.

Pearce *et al.* (1989) have asserted that a major policy objective should be to create sustainable development. But this is where the problem starts – most people agree that 'sustainable development' is a good thing but nobody is clear exactly what it means. A useful starting definition was provided in 1987: 'development that meets the needs of the present generation without compromising the ability of future generations to meet their own needs' (World Commission on Environment and Development, 1987).

World Commission on Environment and Development – this is also referred to as the Brundtland Commission as it was chaired by the Norwegian Prime Minister Gro Harlem Brundtland. It was concerned with identifying how countries of the world could secure lasting development. A key innovation in its thinking was also to take into consideration the environmental impacts of growth.

KEY TERM

Development is generally seen as something that is positive. It means being better off tomorrow than we are today. But what exactly is development? Measures such as GNP indicate the living standards of people measured in terms of quantities of goods that can be purchased, but there is a significant difference between the terms 'standard of living' and 'quality of life'. Pearce suggest that sustainable development involves enhancing both standard of living and quality of life. The value of the environment is an important part of this quality of life and we need to consider:

- The environment

- The future

- Equity

Futurity – Pearce introduces the term 'futurity' to refer to the principle of taking a long-term view of things. If one generation leaves the next with less wealth than it inherited then it has made the future worse off.

We also need to think about the nature of this legacy. The history of recent development has often involved the conversion of 'natural wealth' (e.g. reserves of ores, oil and timber) into 'capital wealth' (e.g. factories, car parks, cinemas). Pearce suggests that it is not good enough simply to argue that growth is taking place because our stock of 'wealth' is increasing. Instead he argues that sustainable development involves leaving a legacy of capital wealth and natural wealth to future generations.

He suggests that we need to tackle the issue of fairness between one generation and another (intergenerational equity) and between people living on the planet at the same time (intragenerational equity).

Equity – fairness (which is different from equality).

Intergenerational equity – fairness between one generation and generations that follow it.

Intragenerational equity – fairness between people living at the same time (e.g. between people in rich Western economies and developing economies).

If we fail to tackle the issue of equity we will never get to an agreement about how to tackle the 'tragedy of the commons'. If, for example, the United States says that 'because we are a developed nation we deserve to graze 100 sheep on the common land' and then tells a developing country that it should not increase the number of sheep it has from one to two then the representative of the developing country will argue that this is patently unjust.

15.5 Different forms of capital

One of the key innovations of Pearce's economics was that he differentiated between different forms of capital. Traditional economics focuses on capital in the form of physical capital (i.e. machinery and equipment). Pearce sees this as forming just one type of capital: Km. In addition Pearce identified three other forms of capital: Kn, Kh and Ks.

Kn is natural capital consisting of all the gifts of nature: lakes, parks, the sea, the animal kingdom, etc. This is the most important aspect of capital in terms of preservation of environmental resources. Much of Pearce's work therefore relates to Kn.

Kh is human capital. Human capital resides in human beings and their ability to generate wealth. Obvious ways of developing human capital are through education and training, but in addition we need to consider aspects such as healthcare and diet.

Ks is social capital. Social capital is the capital that resides in society and enables social groups to transform well-being over time. Social capital can easily be destroyed (e.g. in the breakdown of families and communities).

Sustainable development as envisaged by Pearce involves a much broader perspective of capital development than that outlined by more traditional economics. Pearce's view provides a basis for policy-making involving real 'economic growth'.

Pearce points out that society frequently make choices (e.g. a piece of green land may be transformed into a car park or a housing estate). In order to make this choice it is necessary for society to understand and to take account of the decisions it is making.

True sustainability can only be achieved when there is development in capital as a whole. For example, in time period 2:

Km + Kn + Kh + Ks is greater than Km + Kn + Kh + Ks in period 1

We are entitled if we so wish to make trade-offs between the different types of capital. However, rational economic choices can only be made when appropriate values are attached to nature and other capitals. Currently many decisions involving the environment fail to attach an appropriate value to natural resources. This leads to poor economic decision making and welfare losses to society.

15.6 Cost–benefit analysis

Many environmental resources do not have prices attached to them. Where goods are treated as 'free goods' they tend to be overused and exploited. It is thus vitally important that we should develop an idea of what the environment is worth.

A frequently used approach to taking account of environmental concerns in policy making is to employ cost–benefit analysis techniques. Preferences for the environment, which show up as gains in welfare to human beings, need to be measured.

Benefit – any gain in welfare. A private benefit is a benefit to a particular individual or group. A social benefit is a benefit to society as a whole. Net social benefit is calculated by taking away all private and social costs from private and social benefits.

Cost – any loss in welfare. A private cost is a cost to a particular individual or group. A social cost is a cost to society as a whole.

We are concerned then with the measurement of the benefits from improvement in, or the costs of reductions in, environmental quality. If we prefer clean air we should place a value on it, but since clean air is not bought and sold in the marketplace, at least not directly, money is not directly involved. Nonetheless, the benefit of clean air is an economic benefit – it improves the welfare of people.

In benefit estimation, money is used as a way of measuring preferences. There will be some immeasurable gains and losses. In other words money is a good measuring rod but not a perfect one.

Monetary measures of environmental gains and losses can then be used to reflect the strength of support for an environmental asset. Provided the support in monetary terms is big enough then this presents a strong case for preserving environmental quality. Expressing benefits in monetary terms also makes it possible to make comparisons with other monetary benefits arising from alternative uses of funds or other resources.

David Pearce believed that effective environmental policy required rigorous analysis in order to make best use of the environment. One of his key beliefs was that 'environmental policy matters not just for the quality of life in general, not just because natural environments have values "in themselves", but because environments and economies are not distinct' (1989: xv).

The approach outlined by Pearce is essentially a market solution involving pricing. The argument is that it is important in a market economy to place monetary measures on environmental gains and losses.

The reasons for doing so are to reflect the strength of support for an environmental asset. Here we are concerned with a concept known as 'willingness to pay'. In Nottingham recently the City Council introduced a workplace parking levy. Employees of major organizations are expected to pay a parking levy that is deducted from their pay. This helps to reduce congestion and to fund part of the development of an extended tram network. Large numbers of people have shown that they are willing to pay for this initiative whereas others have opted to share lifts, to walk or cycle to work, or to use public transport. The process of monetization through willingness to pay enables consumers to reflect the depth of their support for an environmental asset.

Provided the support in monetary terms is big enough, this presents a strong case for preserving environmental quality. For example, people may be required to pay to enter a nature reserve. The resources allocated to developing the quality of the environment in the nature reserve depend on how much they are prepared to pay. The more they pay the greater the opportunity to develop the nature reserve.

CASE STUDY Calculating total economic value

David Pearce and his co-workers have established a broad view of what we mean by total economic value. Environmental resources don't just have a value because we use them but also because we value their existence. Many people value the environment and aspects of the environment that they never directly use or visit.

A distinction can be made between 'user values' and 'existence values'. For example, we use local parks and woods to walk our dogs, to run in, to walk in and for many other purposes. From this we gain economic benefit. When we directly use an environmental resource we get 'actual use value from it'.

We also value environmental resources that we have an option to use. Although we don't currently use some local environmental resources we might do so in the future and we value having the option to do so. This gives us another economic benefit: 'option value'.

Finally there are other environmental resources that we want to be there even though we will probably have no direct experience of these resources. For example, many people want blue whales to live and thrive rather than being hunted to extinction. We may also value the existence of the Amazon rain forest. We can say that we gain economic benefit in the form of 'existence value' from the protection of these resources.

We can now set out a formula for total economic value as:

Total economic value (TEV) = Actual use value + Option value + Existence value

When looking at any decision involving the environment we need to weigh up the total costs and benefits of the project. We need a formula for net economic value.

The basic rule for carrying out any project where the environment needs to be taken into consideration should be: the benefit of the development should be greater than the cost of the development.

BD – CD – BP > 0

Where BD refers to the benefits of the development; CD refers to the costs of the development; and BP refers to the benefits of preserving the environment but not developing the area.

- **What do you see as being the strengths of this approach to valuing environmental resources?**

- **Which benefits would be most difficult to measure?**

- **Do you think that cost–benefit analysis should be applied to making decisions that involve choices about the environment?**

Expressing benefits in monetary terms makes it possible to make comparisons with alternative uses that the funds or resources required to develop the environmental resource could be used for.

Criticisms of cost–benefit analysis

Supporters of cost–benefit analysis argue that it is clear, democratic and 'green'. These supposed virtues, coupled with a quantitative approach, lead its proponents to argue that it is a 'rational' way of making decisions.

Cost–benefit analysis is seen as developing a broader-based perspective for decision making, particularly because of the way in which it embraces 'externalities' – the social and environmental consequences of decisions that are not captured by the operation of the market.

CASE STUDY Lloyds of London – calculating the cost–benefit of oil exploration

According to *The Guardian* (Kollewe and Macalister, 2012: 10, Guardian News & Media Ltd 2009, reproduced with permission) Lloyds of London became the first major business organization to raise concerns about the huge potential damage from drilling for oil in the Arctic. The whole insurance business, that Lloyds lies at the heart of, is concerned with calculating the risk of activities.

The Chief Executive of Lloyds made it clear that companies should be cautious about rushing in to drilling in the Arctic – they should think carefully first. Lloyds estimated that $100 billion of new investment was heading for the Arctic. However, the cost of cleaning up an oil spill in ice-covered areas would present 'multiple obstacles, which together constitute a unique and hard to manage risk'. The report that Lloyds produced and which was written by Charles Emmerson and Glada Lahn sets out that it is highly likely that future economic activity in the Arctic will further disturb ecosystems already stressed by the consequences of climate change.

- How are the calculations that are set out in the Lloyds report a form of cost–benefit analysis?

- What is the report suggesting the outcome of this cost–benefit analysis might show?

- The report suggests that risks being taken on top of existing risks may not be acceptable. What does the report suggest might be the nature of interlinking risks?

However, as Adams (1996) has set out in a number of critiques of cost–benefit analysis, the technique is likely to increase the level of controversy over decision making because it:

- Attempts the impossible;

- Is biased; and

- Entrenches conflict.

Adams (1996) argues that:

> Whenever cost–benefit analysts encounter people who say that something is priceless, or that attempting to put a price on it is immoral, they are stuck. Their method requires that everything be reduced to cash. The information that the cost–benefit analyst requires about how people value things is locked up inside people's heads, and the only way to gain access to it is by asking them.

The form of asking is called 'contingent valuation'; people are asked how much they would be willing to pay for the things the analyst is seeking to value if they were for sale. There is now abundant evidence that people cannot, or will not, provide meaningful answers to the contingent valuer's questions. What would you be prepared to pay to prevent the extinction of, say, the blue whale?

15.7 The sustainability spectrum

There always has been a split between those concerned with the environment and those pushing for technological advancement. The differences in people's opinions of whether it is more important to carry on down a technological path causes a very deep rift. The 'sustainability spectrum' in Table 15.1, taken from Pearce and Warford (1993), shows that different approaches to sustainability are formed through different environmental ideologies.

What we see in the final row of Table 15.1 is the distinction between different levels of sustainability. This is where the heart of the debate lies. The two main types of sustainability identified here (in bold) are 'strong sustainability' and 'weak sustainability'. An interpretation of strong sustainability is that the overall stock of natural capital should not be allowed to decline, and an interpretation of weak sustainability is that to aid the future generations an aggregate capital stock, not less than the one that exists at present, should be passed on. Unlike strong sustainability this can mean that one type of capital can be substituted for another (e.g. a wilderness area for a car park).

Attempts to set out green perspectives are often little more than characterizations of 'the green position', as if there is a unifying green perspective. The reality, as shown in Table 15.1, is that there is a range of green ideas.

TABLE 15.1 The 'sustainability spectrum'

	Technocentric cornucopian	Accommodating	Ecocentric communalist	Deep ecology
Green labels	Resource-exploitative growth-oriented position	Resource conservationist and 'managerial' position	Resource preservationist position	Extreme preservationist position
Types of economy	Anti-green economy, unfettered free markets	Green economy and markets guided by economic incentive instruments	Deep green economy regulated by macro-environmental standards	Very deep green economy regulated to minimize resource take
Management strategies	Maximize economic growth (GNP)	Modified economic growth (adjusted green accounting to measure GNP)		
Ethics	Support for traditional ethical reasoning rights and interests of individual	Extension of ethical reasoning, intra-generational and intergenerational equity	Interest of the collective take over from those of the individual. Primary value of ecosystems and secondary value of components parts	Acceptance of bioethics, intrinsic value of nature in its own right regardless of human experience
Sustainability levels	Very weak sustainability	Weak sustainability	Strong sustainability	Very strong sustainability

15.8 Taking a wider view

A major problem for economic analysis has been an over-reliance on traditional tools of analysis such as cost–benefit analysis. Economists have been most comfortable with analytical tools that appeal to the 'head' rather than the 'heart'. Perhaps the nature of economics is that we prefer to 'calculate', however deficient the calculations may prove to be. Moreover, many of the modes of calculation are locked into a conventional wisdom that is based on a 'market paradigm' which inevitably produces market-led tools in an attempt to create solutions to the 'sustainable growth' problem (e.g. taxing polluters, subsidizing those that use energy efficiently, and so on).

KEY TERM

Paradigm – a distinct pattern of thinking. For example, market economics is a way of thinking about the organization of the economy. A paradigm shift involves seeing a different pattern through a process of changing thought patterns.

However, it is possible that a number of the key assumptions that traditional economics makes about the relationship between economy and environment are invalid. For example, as Daly (1996: 15) has forcefully argued 'traditional economic measures distort our perception of well being'. GNP is a measure of the throughput of the monetary value of final production. GNP does not distinguish between missiles and food. GNP does not properly count the depletion of natural resources nor the cost of waste dumped and left for others. GNP does not reveal whether we are living beyond our means.

GNP is an index of throughput not welfare. Throughput is positively correlated with welfare in a world of infinite sources and sinks, but in a finite world with fully employed carrying capacity throughput is a cost. To design national policies to maximize GNP is just not smart.

A sustainable development approach recognises that it is not just conventional measures of economic welfare that matter. Quality of life and well-being are set by many factors – for example, income, the state of people's health, their level of education, cultural diversity and quality of the environment.

The challenge facing economics is to take a full account of the relationship between the economy and wider systems. The economist has to embrace a broader range of ideas and engage in a paradigm shift in order to create wider models rather than being overly defensive.

15.9 International collaboration for the commons

Nowhere is the need to build broader perspectives more important than in developing techniques and approaches which can make a contribution to creating international understanding over the use of 'the commons'. This has not always been the case. International collaboration on the environment has experienced a chequered history. A series of conferences has taken place to discuss, and make proposals for, international collaboration on the environment:

- The World Commission on Environment and Development (also known as the Brundtland Commission) (1987) called for global cooperation and supportive actions between countries at different stages of economic development. The report that they published had the title *Our Common Future*. The Commission proposed that with global commitment a more prosperous, more secure future was possible for all. The Brundtland Report was commissioned by the United Nations to examine long-term environmental and development strategies.

- The Earth Summit (1992). This followed up the Brundtland work. The summit brought together leaders of national governments, business leaders and leaders of alternative environmental groups to create agreements and conventions on critical issues such as climate change and its impact on desertification and deforestation.

    The Earth Summit took place in Rio de Janeiro so that the agreements made as a result of the Summit are popularly known as the Rio Treaty. Members signed Agenda 21, which was an agenda of actions for the twenty-first century. 170 countries signed up in agreement that the ideas of 'sustainable development' should be a mandatory goal for developmental and environmental policy. As a result of Rio a range of regional and sectoral (industry sectors) plans were developed. This involved a variety of groups ranging from businesses to international organization. Local Agenda 21 initiatives were developed by local groups planning sustainable solutions for their communities. However, at the Earth Summit +5 held in 1997 the overall view was that progress in achieving the original targets and goals had been slow.

- The Kyoto Treaty (1997). In 1997 another important meeting took place in Kyoto in Japan to try and reach agreement relating to the creation of greenhouse gases. Article 3 of the Kyoto Treaty set out an expectation that countries would make sure that their total production of carbon dioxide equivalent emissions of greenhouse gases would be limited, with a view to reducing their overall emissions to at least 5 per cent below 1990 levels during the period from 2008 to 2012. The greenhouse gases would be reduced through reductions in emissions coupled with the creation of 'sinks' to remove harmful emissions.

- The Earth Summit (Rio+10) was held in Johannesburg in South Africa in 2007.

- The Earth Summit (Rio+20) was again held in Rio de Janeiro (in 2012) and confirmed a commitment to Agenda 21 and other important aspects of sustainable development.

CASE STUDY Article 2 of the Kyoto Treaty

Article 2 of the Kyoto Treaty outlined a range of measures and policies that countries could employ to tackle global warming and environmental pollution, these included:

1. Enhancement of energy efficiency in relevant sectors of the national economy.
2. Protection and enhancement of sinks and reservoirs of greenhouse gases not controlled by earlier agreements.
3. Promotion of sustainable forms of agriculture.
4. Research and development of new technologies exploring new forms of renewable energy and pollution control.
5. Progressive reducing or phasing out of market imperfections, fiscal incentives, tax and duty exemptions and subsidies in all greenhouse-gas emitting sectors that run counter to the aims of the Kyoto agreement.

- **From your own knowledge, do you believe that countries have been consistently seeking to apply the types of measures and policies outlined above? Can you cite examples of cases where this is true?**

- **What sorts of fiscal incentives might encourage business policy to work in a counter direction to the objectives of the Kyoto Protocol?**

- **What will be the impact on the supply of some goods as a result of the phasing out of the market imperfections suggested in point 5 above? How might this lead to a reallocation of production resources in the economy?**

As a result of the Summit a document was produced called *The Future We Want* (United Nations, 2012). The full package of agreements, actions, commitments, challenges, initiatives and announcements made at Rio+20, the UN Conference on Sustainable Development, addresses a range of global issues that includes access to clean energy, food security, water and sustainable transportation.

The impact of the Kyoto Treaty was chequered. The United States, which was the biggest single polluter in the world at the time was opposed to the Treaty because they saw it as unworkable. Some of the other major nations such as Russia did not sign up and major emerging economies such as India were exempt.

However, since Kyoto, countries have moved more into line with the objectives of the Treaty. Russia signed up to it and the Obama government in the US has been far more disposed to adopt environmental initiatives than previous governments. The Chinese government has recognized the threat that environmental degradation poses to development and is allocating substantial resources to cleaning up industrial processes. However, there is a general feeling among critics that the major industrial nations in the world have not done enough about environmental impacts and have tended to favour business at the expense of the environment.

ACTIVITY

The key intergovernmental initiatives take place every five years (1987, 1992, 1997, 2002, 2007, 2012). Carry out some research to find out what has been the most recent report and what the key findings and recommendations were.

CASE STUDY Developing new forms of undersea energy in the UK

The UK is currently considering whether to develop thousands of miles of high-voltage cables across the ocean floor to the volcanoes of Iceland. Iceland has abundant geothermal energy and the UK is one of the best-placed countries geographically to benefit from this source of energy. The cable needs to be between 1,000 and 1,500 miles long. This link to the UK would become part of a larger European super-grid combining the wind and wave power of northern Europe with solar projects such as Desertec in southern Europe and north Africa designed to deliver reliable, clean energy to meet climate change targets and reduce dependence on fossil fuel imports. The current government believes that developing the cable link to Iceland will be critical for energy security and for providing low carbon energy.

● How does the proposal outlined in the case study meet with the philosophy of the Kyoto Treaty?

● How might the proposal yield both economic and environmental benefits?

15.10 Ecological footprints

One useful new approach to providing a 'fairer' use of environmental resources is presented by Wackernagel *et al.* (2002). The authors argue that 'sustainability' involves the interplay of three key factors:

- Carrying capacity, which is a combination of resource availability and waste absorption carrying capacity.

- Population.

- Resource use per person including waste production.

Sustainable living can only be achieved if resource use per person multiplied by the total population is less than the 'carrying capacity'.

Ecological footprinting (EF) – this is a technique that has been applied to nations, regions and cities. The aim of EF is to translate the ecological impact of human activity into the spatial area required to produce the resources consumed and to assimilate the wastes generated in any given year. Land thus becomes the unit of accounting rather than money. An ecological deficit occurs when the EF is greater than the bioproductive land area available. Ecological deficits are unsustainable.

Wackernagel *et al.* have developed an approach to combining these elements in a method that determines the 'ecological footprint' of an activity, population or way of life. The calculations can be made at the macro–global level, or on a smaller scale. Their calculations involve estimates and there is much room for improving accuracy. However, their initial results show the approach to be a powerful tool, which demonstrates resource use and overuse. They acknowledge that their estimates of resource requirements are more likely to be underestimated than overestimated.

The key to their approach is that rather than use monetary measures they calculate the land area required to support specific activities sustainably. Importantly, they base their information on current levels of technology and energy sources, rather than on possible future development. This gives an indication of the present situation, which can be used to decide whether particular actions will move us towards, or away from, living sustainably. In this respect it is a powerful tool for making 'real world' comparisons and recommendations.

ACTIVITY

Go to the World Wide Fund for Nature's website and calculate your own personal ecological footprint: **http://footprint.wwf.org.uk/**

Various calculations have been made using the concept of an ecological footprint. For example, one recent calculation of the UK's average global footprint is that we are using 5.45 global hectares (gha) per head. Relatively speaking the lowest global footprint in the UK is 4.8 gha per head compared with a higher figure of 5.56 in the east of England.

Some studies have been carried out in benchmark areas. For example BedZED, a 96-home mixed-income housing area in south London, was shown to consume 3.2 gha per head as a result of such innovations as onsite renewable energy and residents engaging in car sharing for travelling to work. On a global scale there is considerable inequity in terms of ecological footprints – for example, a recent calculation for India as a whole indicated a global footprint of 0.2. However, with industrialization in India this figure is rapidly rising.

15.11 Sustainable business models

Businesses need to gain a 'licence to operate' from their stakeholders. Most stakeholders today expect their company to behave in a sustainable way, either because of self-interest or because they believe that it is the right thing to do. A sustainable approach needs to be embedded across an organization if it is to be believable.

> **Licence to operate** – a realization that businesses need to win the support of their stakeholders if they are to be able to continue and be successful. When stakeholders turn against their companies then the fortunes of that company will suffer.

KEY TERM

A useful starting point is to establish a sustainable model for business. Richard Welford (1997) argues that in seeking to make sustainability a reality they need to have some guidance about how to proceed. It is inappropriate to be overly prescriptive because businesses differ. What are required therefore are 'pictures and descriptions of the road down which businesses should tread'. Welford identified a series of models that might be appropriate.

A simple model simply involves combining Pearce's three dimensions (as illustrated in Figure 15.5) to show what a sustainable business looks like.

This model is helpful in setting out an idealized picture but it doesn't make it clear what a business needs to do in order to become more sustainable. It is fine on theory but not so good on practical application.

A model that is more widely used by businesses in the real world is a 'three Ps' approach – people, planet and profit. The nature of such a model is that it identifies the dimensions that are important to a business. John Elkington (1997) coined the term 'Triple Bottom Line' to identify such an approach.

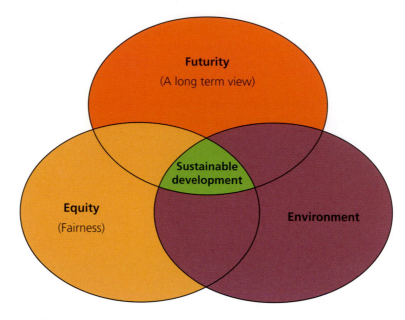

FIGURE 15.5 A simple model of sustainable development

Triple Bottom Line – the three areas on which a business should focus: social performance, economic performance and environmental performance. The success of the business is measured according to how well it does in each of these areas. A business earns a licence to operate when the various stakeholder groups with which it works (e.g. employees, the local community, regulators, government, suppliers, the environment and above all the customers) are happy with the way that it does business.

The three dimensions are:

1. Economic performance – the traditional business approach based on securing higher sales and profits, more efficient use of capital, etc.

2. Social performance – earning the commitment of employees, customers and communities based on the contribution a business makes to the community.

3. Environmental performance – based on setting the benchmark in terms of environmental standards, waste minimization and recycling.

A Triple Bottom Line approach involves creating a business system that values and shows respect for the environment, and one way of illustrating this is presented in Figure 15.6.

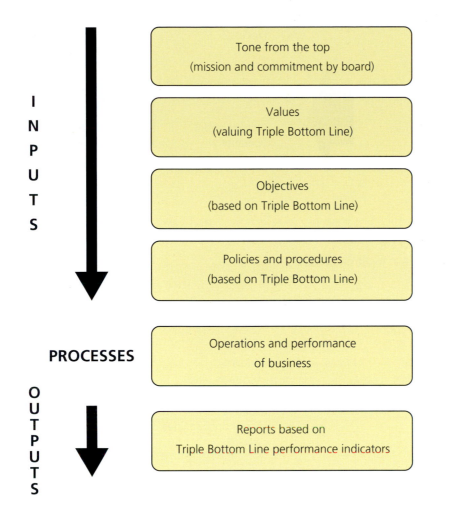

FIGURE 15.6 A Triple Bottom Line approach

Figure 15.7 shows a different way of illustrating the Triple Bottom Line, as an input/ processes/output diagram.

In terms of the Triple Bottom Line we can represent a suitable business model as involving the elements included in Table 15.2.

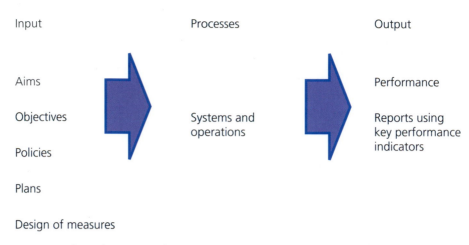

FIGURE 15.7 Input/processes/output

TABLE 15.2 The Triple Bottom Line

Triple Bottom Line model	3 Ps model	Exemplar inputs	Exemplar outputs
Economic bottom line	Profits	Budgets Business plans	Operating profit figures Sales figures
Social bottom line	People	Employee engagement policies Equal opportunities policies Community policies	Staff turnover statistics Successful community engagement programmes achieved
Environmental bottom line	Planet	Environmental management systems	Reduced pollution and waste

Environmental management system (EMS)

The Triple Bottom Line approach enables a business to operationalize a corporate social responsibility (CSR) approach securing a win–win–win result for the business, society and the wider environment. Most large organizations today employ an EMS, which may be part of a wider quality system designed to achieve organizational excellence and the minimization of waste throughout the organization.

There are a number of ingredients to an EMS that are set out below, some of which are contextualized using the example of Innocent Smoothies:

The importance of mission, values and objectives

The mission and values of an organization establish top-level aims and objectives, giving it a sense of purpose and direction. For example, Innocent, a company that produces smoothies, was set up to provide healthy products which would be good for people while at the same time making a profit for the company.

The importance of strategy

The strategy of an organization is the means by which it achieves its stated aims and objectives. The plan (which was executed) was for Innocent Smoothies to be made of 100 per cent natural fruit juices, with limited packaging and marketing activity.

The importance of policies and programmes

Policies are statements of intent about key issues. Programmes are activities designed to achieve certain objectives – often with a definite end date. Innocent's policies include purchasing only from ethical suppliers, and its programmes include staff training to familiarize them with the honest and transparent values of the organization.

The importance of key performance indicators (KPIs)

KPIs are the key measurements of the success of the business. Innocent's KPIs relate to making an economic profit, creating a social profit (e.g. through donations to good causes) and creating an environmental benefit by using resources in a sustainable way.

The importance of reporting

Innocent produce an annual report which is clear and straight to the point, using a minimum of paper and other resources and setting out the key messages of the company's Triple Bottom Line success.

The importance of reports

The Companies Act (2006) requires public listed companies to produce an annual business review. Part of this review will contain a CSR report and perhaps a separate environmental report. These reports provide some of the clearest evidence about the commitment of a company to the Triple Bottom Line. Where they are well structured and detailed this is indicative of the understanding that the company has of the Triple Bottom Line.

A report is an output from a system designed to achieve particular objectives. A company that sets out sustainability aims, policies and procedures will want to report on how effective these have been. Typically, reporting on sustainability will involve identifying Triple Bottom Line performance indicators and reporting on how effectively these have been achieved. Sustainability reporting typically takes the form of environmental, social and/or CSR reports.

Gray and Milne (2004) suggest that until recently there has been very little systematic social and/or environmental reporting. They suggest that 20 years ago companies were keen to prevent such issues from being discussed. They trace the development of environmental reporting as having started in the early 1990s and social reporting by the mid-1990s. From that time onwards CSR reporting rose up the agenda. Gray and Milne state that from the late 1990s onwards it became commonplace for CEOs and boards to discuss 'social responsibility, sustainability, triple bottom line sustainability and so on'.

However, Gray and Milne argue the case that there is still a long way to go. They believe that companies have successfully opposed the introduction of mandatory social and environmental reporting. Voluntary reporting is only likely to be successful if everyone volunteers. Gray and Milne also argue that not enough companies are producing effective reports and that the contents of such reports are not comprehensive enough. They state that 'poor standards of reporting mean that a reader cannot assess to what extent – if at all – an organisation has discharged its responsibilities to the environment and to society' (2004: 72).

The importance of identifying the negative effects of company activities

Businesses play an important role in the economic and social development of society. In the pursuit of economic growth, business activity often has 'negative spillover effects' which can be harmful to wider economic and social growth. This is illustrated in the very rapid growth of the Chinese economy in recent years. However, such rapid growth comes at a cost and it is important to include these harmful effects when reporting.

In December 2010 the Chinese Academy for Environmental Planning calculated that the cost of pollution spills, deteriorating soil and other impacts of economic growth in the country were in the order of 1.3 trillion yuan (£130 billion) in 2008. This was equivalent to 3.9 per cent of the country's GDP. Most of these costs do not appear on corporate balance sheets or government budgets, but they are accumulating year by year and amount to an environmental deficit that threatens the country's long-term prospects. The Chinese government should be applauded for reporting on the negative impact of economic growth in such a way.

Environmental reporting: incentives and disincentives

Soloman (2010: 263) puts forward the argument that in the UK 'most companies are still not reporting any environmental information, and where there is reporting it is mixed and inconsistent'. Soloman identifies four main categories of incentives that encourage environmental reporting. These are:

1. Markets. Pressures from the marketplace are one of the main incentives for corporate environmental reporting. For example, pressure from institutional investors (particularly those with an interest in socially responsible investment) requires this information to be provided by companies. However, Soloman also believes that information that is voluntarily disclosed will often have serious inadequacies.

2. Social. The requirement to satisfy a range of stakeholder groups provides an incentive to report on the social and environmental impacts of company activity. Companies need to legitimize their relationship with the wider society in which they operate.

3. Political pressure. Environmental issues are now part of mainstream politics, encompassing a wide variety of pressure groups (e.g. The Conservative Ecology Group, The Socialist Environmental and Resource Association and The Green Party).

4. Accountability. To meet an increased demand for environmental information.

However, Soloman (2010: 266) also identifies a number of disincentives to company environmental reporting. The existence of these disincentives is one explanation for why company ethical reporting may be lacking. These reasons include:

*   Reluctance to report sensitive information;
*   General lack of awareness of environmental issues;

- No legal requirement to report environmentally;

- Possible damage to company reputation;

- To avoid providing information to competitors;

- Cost of disclosure;

- To avoid providing incriminating information to regulators;

- Inability to gather the information; and

- Insufficient response feedback from stakeholders.

Users of environmental and ethical reports

There are many groups seeking access to ethical and environmental reports. These include:

- Legislators and regulators

- Local communities

- Employees

- Shareholders

- Customers

- Insurance companies

- Ethical investors

- Environmental groups

- Quangos

- Local government

- Potential investors

- Banks

- Media

- Suppliers

- Stock markets

- Central government

- Industry associations

In creating reporting frameworks it is important to ascertain what sort of information each of these groups is likely to seek in CSR reports.

Qualitative characteristics of ethical and environmental reports

Soloman (2010, p. 269) identifies a number of qualitative aspects that should be present in reports to stakeholders. These are:

- A true and fair view
- Understandability
- Relevance
- Faithful representation
- Reliability
- Freedom from error
- Consistency
- Valid description
- Substance over form
- Neutrality
- Completeness
- Corresponding information on the previous period
- Confirmation of information
- Timeliness
- Comparability
- Materiality
- Predictive value
- Prudence

ACTIVITY

Study the CSR report of a company of your choice. You will be able to access one of these online by entering the name of your selected company and the search term 'corporate social responsibility'. What evidence is provided in the report that the company is seriously considering CSR? For example, does it have clear KPIs for the key elements of the Triple Bottom Line?

The Global Reporting Initiative (GRI)

In preparing ethical reports it is helpful to look at best practice. A useful starting point is to look at the G3 guidelines provided by the Global Reporting Initiative (GRI).

The Global Reporting Initiative (GRI) – a network-based organization that pioneered the development of the world's most widely used sustainability reporting framework. The reporting framework involves disclosure on environmental, social and governance performance. This reporting framework has been drawn up by representatives from global business, civil society, labour, academic and professional institutions.

To find out more about the GRI, visit **www.globalreporting.org**.

Find out what the main suggestions are proposed by the GRI for effective disclosure under the headings of: (1) environmental; (2) social; and (3) corporate governance reporting. You could then access a recent company report for a major public company and identify how effective the reporting of that company appears to be in the light of the GRI recommendations.

The most significant reporting guidance provided by the GRI appears in their G3 guidelines on sustainability reporting. They also provide specific sectoral guidelines in sector supplements. The G3 consists of two main parts:

Part 1 is on reporting principles and evidence. This includes:

- Principles to define the report content: materiality, stakeholder inclusiveness, sustainability, context and completeness.

- Principles to define report quality: balance, comparability, accuracy, timeliness, reliability and clarity.

- Guidance on how to set the report boundary.

Part 2 sets out standard disclosures:

- Strategy and profile of company – this would include a statement by the senior decision maker in the organization about the short-, medium- and long-term strategy of the company in relation to social responsibility and sustainability. In addition there needs to be a statement about the key impacts of the company on society and the environment.

- Management approach.

- Performance indicators – a range of indicators would need to be reported on under the headings:
  - Environmental
  - Economic
  - Social performance (labour practices and decent working conditions)
  - Social performance (human rights)
  - Social performance (society)
  - Social performance (product responsibility)

CSR reporting

Most large companies today produce some form of CSR or corporate responsibility (CR) report. Additionally, companies produce environmental reports and reports on other ethical issues.

Typically the report will set out:

- A statement about the importance of social responsibility and the importance that the organization attaches to being a good citizen;

- Details of policies and practices for CSR adopted by the organization;

- Highlights of improved performance; and

- Details of how the performance indicators compare with previous performance.

In spite of the development of initiatives such as those promoted by the GRI there is still extensive variety in the way in which companies report their ethical activities. Non-executive and other directors play an important role in making sure that the reports produced by their company are appropriate to the needs of a variety of stakeholder groups, and that the scope and direction of these reports is continually improved.

Preparing a CSR report is a painstaking process. For example, simply to produce an environmental report might include each of the following (Solomon, 2010: 271):

> environmental statement by the company chairman; environmental policy statement; environmental strategy statement; environmental management system; management responsibilities for the environment; environmental audit; independently verified environmental disclosure; legal environmental compliance; research and development and the environment; company environmental initiatives; context of company environmental disclosure; product life cycle design; environmental reporting policy; product packaging; and product impacts.

Furthermore, following the Turnbull Report (Turnbull, 1999) social and environmental risks have come to be seen as an increasingly important constituent element of a company's system of internal control. Sudden unforeseen events in these areas can lead to significant financial losses – for example, the explosion on the BP oil platform in the Gulf of Mexico in 2010.

KEY TERM

The Turnbull Report – the result of a review aimed at providing enhanced guidance for directors of companies on good practice in keeping good internal controls in a company, including ensuring the quality of financial reporting and catching fraudulent activity.

Every three years KPMG carries out a survey of CSR reporting. The 2008 report showed that 80 per cent of the world's largest 250 companies issue CSR reports (compared with 50 per cent in 2005) and by 2013 that figure had risen to 100 per cent.

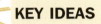

15.12 Summary

Environmental economics is a relatively new branch of economics but it is one that is of increasing importance and which has helped to shape government economic policy and business approaches to the Triple Bottom Line. David Pearce and other economists have set out to create blueprints for a green economy. The green economy that they envisage is one in which realistic values are placed on environmental resources. By establishing appropriate prices for environmental resources it becomes possible to use them in an efficient way rather than overconsuming underpriced resources. Pearce developed a model based on a wider bottom line for decision making. These ideas were adapted by John Elkington into the Triple Bottom Line, which has become an important basis for creating a people, planet and profits approach to business. Business reporting is helpful in providing evidence of the extent to which a company is taking their responsibility for the environment seriously.

KEY IDEAS

The environmental challenge
- The planet is faced by a significant environmental challenge resulting from the expansion of economic activity on a global scale.
- More and more people are making a claim to limited resources.

Reappraising simple economic theory
- Traditional economic theory doesn't fully take into account the harmful spillover effects of economic activity – for example, in the form of waste and pollution.
- It is necessary therefore to reappraise economic thinking to account for negative externalities of economic activity.
- A 'spaceship' model of the economy is more realistic than the 'cowboy economy'.

Sustainable development
- Sustainable development has been defined as 'development that meets the needs of the present generation without compromising the ability of future generations to meet their own needs'.
- The challenge to the economics profession is to contribute to providing sustainable solutions through economic analysis.

Different forms of capital
- Sustainable growth involves maintaining or improving a range of forms of capital including man-made capital, natural capital, human capital and social capital.

Cost–benefit analysis

- Cost–benefit analysis is a useful tool for comparing the costs and benefits of economic activity.
- Negative aspects are recorded as costs and positive aspects as benefits.

The sustainability spectrum

- There are different perspectives on what constitutes sustainability.
- At one end of the spectrum is 'weak' sustainability, which allows for trade-offs between different forms of capital.
- At the other end of the spectrum is strong sustainability, which requires maintenance (or preferably improvement) in all forms of capital.

Taking a wider view

- A sustainable development approach recognizes that real development goes beyond conventional measures of economic welfare to include wider sets of goals such as quality of life, including the state of people's health, their education and the quality of the environment.

International collaboration for the commons

- A number of international initiatives have involved collaboration between governments, business, NGOs and other stakeholders to create shared solutions to common development and environmental problems, including the Earth Summits in 1992, 2002 and 2012.

Ecological footprints

- Ecological footprinting (EF) is a technique that has been applied to nations, regions and cities.
- The aim of EF is to translate the ecological impact of human activity into the spatial area required to produce the resources consumed and to assimilate the wastes generated in any given year.

Sustainable business models

- A sustainable business model is a business approach designed to incorporate growth objectives based on a Triple Bottom Line focusing on economic, social and environmental impacts.

REVIEW QUESTIONS

1. How can the 'tragedy of the commons' be applied to the growth of modern economies?

2. How can cost–benefit analysis help to conserve environmental assets?

3. Identify four policies and measures that countries could adopt that were recommended by the Kyoto Protocol.

4. How does the Triple Bottom Line model enable a business to formulate plans, policies and performance indicators?

5. What is meant by the net economic value of a project? Explain how this would be calculated?

6. Explain how 'technocentric' and 'ecocentric' views of sustainability differ. How might government policy-making differ depending on which of these approaches is applied? Do you think that businesses are most likely to apply a 'technocentric' or an 'ecocentric' approach?

7. Explain the concept of the 'total economic value' of projects and plans. How does the total economic value differ from the net benefit of a project?

8. Study the Brundtland definition of sustainable development. Explain how it encapsulates the concepts of futurity, intergenerational equity and intragenerational equity.

9. Why do you think environmental economics has been neglected until recently? Is it possible to combine environmental economics with classical and neoclassical economics?

10. Why is the Triple Bottom Line so important? What does clear and transparent CSR reporting tell you about a company?

RECOMMENDED READING

Henriques, A. and Richardson, J. (eds) (2004) *The Triple Bottom Line: Does it All Add Up?* London, Earthscan.

Chapter 7 of this book is by Rob Gray and Markus Milne and examines 'Towards Reporting on the Triple Bottom Line: Mirages, Methods and Myths'. For a critical view of ethical reporting you may also want to look at Chapter 8 by Deborah Doane – 'Good Intentions – Bad Outcomes? The Broken Promise of CSR Reporting'.

Solomon, J. (2010) *Corporate Governance and Accountability*, 3rd edition, Chichester, John Wiley and Sons.

Chapter 9 of this book looks at 'Discharging a Broader Corporate Accountability'. In this chapter you can read more about the issues related to ethical and CSR reporting. It also provides a useful historical overview about the development of wider company accountability to society and the environment.

REFERENCES

Adams, J. (1996) 'Cost Benefit Analysis, the Problem, Not the Solution', *The Ecologist*, Volume 26 (1): 2.

Daly, H.E. (1996) *Beyond Growth: The Economics of Sustainable Development*, Boston, Beacon Press.

Elkington, J. (1997) *Cannibals With Forks*, Oxford, Capstone Paperback.

Ellis, E. (2012) 'Rio+20', *This is Africa*, June/July.

Gray, R.H. and Milne, M.J. (2004) 'Towards Reporting on the Triple Bottom Line: Mirages, Methods and Myths', in A. Henriques and J. Richardson (eds.) *The Triple Bottom Line: Does it All Add Up?* (pp. 70–80), London, Earthscan.

Hardin, G. and Baden, J. (1997) *Managing of the Commons*, San Francisco, W.H. Freeman.

Kollewe, M. and Macalister, T. (2012) 'Lloyds of London raises concerns about damage resulting from drilling for oil in the Arctic', *The Guardian*, 12 April.

Malthus, R. (1798 [1973]) *Principle of Population*, London, Dent.

Pearce, D. (1989) *Blueprint for a Green Economy*, London, Earthscan.

Pearce, D. and Warford, J. (1993) *World Without End, Economy, Environment and Sustainable Development*, Oxford, Oxford University Press.

Ricardo, D. (1817) *On the Principles of Political Economy*, London, John Murray.

Soloman, J. (2010) *Corporate Governance and Accountability*, Chichester, John Wiley and Son.

Turnbull, N. (2009) *Internal Control: Guidance for Directors on the Combined Code*, London, Financial Reporting Council.

Wackernagel, M., Schulz, N.B., Deumling, D., Linares, A.C., Jenkins, M., Kapos, V., Monfreda, C., Loh, J., Myers, N., Norgaard, R. and Randers, J. (2002) 'Tracking the Ecological Overshoot of the Human Economy', *Proceedings of the National Academy of Sciences*, 99 (14): 9266–71.

Welford, R. (1997) *Hijacking Environmentalism: Corporate Responses to Sustainable Development*, London, Earthscan.

World Commission on Environment and Development (1987) *Report of the World Commission on Environment and Development: Our Common Future*. Also referred to as the Brundtland Report. Available at: www.un-documents.net/wced-ocf.htm (accessed January 2013).

United Nations (2012) *The Future We Want: Outcome Document Adopted at Rio+20*. Available at: www.un.org/en/sustainablefuture/ (accessed January 2013).

USEFUL WEBSITES

Two useful Internet-based sources that will support your reading are:

www.kpmg.com/Global/en/IssuesAndInsights/ArticlesPublications/corporate-responsibility/Pages/2011-survey.aspx – the KPMG Survey of CSR Reporting for 2011.

www.globalreporting.org – here you can find out about the Global Reporting Initiative.

16 Business in the economy

CHAPTER OBJECTIVES

After carefully reading this chapter and responding to the tasks and activities in it you should be able to:

- Explain with examples how a business can match its strategic capability with the economic and wider environment

- Understand why uncertainty exists in a market economy

- Value the part that 'institutional economics' can play in developing a better understanding of how economies work (and can be helped to work more effectively)

- Provide examples of how major businesses have been able to achieve competitive advantage

- Explain the reasons for the existence of large and small firms

- Explain and analyse ways in which businesses grow

16.1 Introduction

This chapter pulls together the strands of economic analysis developed earlier in the book and builds on them. It also introduces a number of contemporary themes and case examples. The chapter starts out by showing that business strategy needs to be informed by analysis and understanding of the economic environment. Scanning the economic environment is a key element in a SWOT analysis. The chapter goes on to show that the economic environment is constantly evolving. Ideas that were bandied around about a 'Great Moderation' in economic fluctuations were crushed by the economic crisis that started in 2007 and led to an ongoing crisis, particularly in the Eurozone countries. Britain is particularly exposed to fluctuations in the Eurozone because of our trading and financial links with countries in it. This chapter draws on a key theme developed in this book: that effective risk management is required if businesses are going to safely chart their way through an environment that is full of risk.

The chapter then goes on to identify an important strand of economic thinking in the form of 'institutional economics', which is particularly concerned with the study of change. Institutional economics challenges the neoclassical perspective of focusing on free market solutions without taking into consideration institutional aspects of society (many of which are deeply ingrained).

The chapter examines the nature of a business's competitive advantage and how it can be enhanced. It shows that there is scope for small and large firms in a market economy and examines how firms can grow to a large scale in order to attain competitive advantage.

16.2 Matching business strategy with the organizational environment

A fundamental aspect of business strategy is to match the organization's strengths and weaknesses with opportunities and threats in the external environment. Chapter 6 examined the importance of business strategy. This is now built on in this opening section to Chapter 16, which outlines the importance of matching an organization's capabilities (what it can achieve) to the economic (and wider) environment in which the business operates.

A SWOT analysis is the simplest and perhaps most effective way of assessing the relationship between an organization and its external environment. SWOT is an acronym used to describe the particular 'strengths, weaknesses, opportunities and threats' that are strategic factors for a specific business. It has been suggested that this could be called a WOTS-UP analysis (see Figure 16.1).

The **strengths** and **weaknesses** of an organization are internal and relate to:

- The resources of the organization. How effective are these resources, including management, employees, capital equipment and knowledge?

- The technologies employed by the organization. Do they enable the organization to use its resources well and to be competitive?

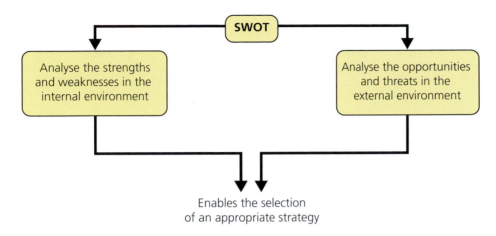

FIGURE 16.1 Elements of the WOTS-UP analysis

- The products that the organization produces. Are they in line with what customers want and need?

- The marketing carried out by the organization. Does the marketing that the organization carries out enable it to be familiar with customer expectations?

- The understanding that the organization has of its opportunities and threats. This last factor is very important. Unless the organization understands its external environment then it will be poorly placed to respond to changes outside itself.

The **opportunities** and **threats** relate to the external environment – for example, the threat of a downturn in the economy, or the threat from competition in a competitive market. Opportunities often relate to the development of new customers and new markets.

Changes in the wider economy constitute key opportunities and threats alongside changes in legal requirements, changes in social trends and buying patterns, changes in technology, and changes in environmental expectations.

It is important to recognize that changes in the business environment are typically transmitted to the business in terms of economic mechanisms. This can be illustrated by examining the business analyst's SLEPT tool and looking at the economic transmission of changes in SLEPT factors to the business (see Table 16.1).

Economists play a key role in working for large business organizations. Their work will involve 'scanning' the external environment, particularly the economic environment, to identify changes that are likely to impact on business.

Scanning the environment – carrying out a detailed analysis of changes that are external to a business, which are affecting it and are likely to continue doing so.

KEY TERM

TABLE 16.1 Applying a SLEPT analysis

SLEPT factors	Economic transmission to firms
Social change (e.g. purchasing patterns, demographic change)	Changes in demand patterns resulting from changes in fashion and buyer behaviour. Changes in supply resulting from demographic change.
Legal changes (e.g. changes in employment law, health and safety changes, product safety rules)	Changes in costs of supply resulting from changes in the law relating to how production can take place. Changes in buying patterns (e.g. as some products are prohibited).
Economic changes (e.g. in the growth of the economy, in interest rates, in exchange rates etc.)	Automatically transmitted as economic impacts (e.g. a growing economy results in increased aggregate demand and supply, etc.).
Political changes (e.g. a change in government, and hence in government policy)	Impacts on the economy in a variety of ways (e.g. through changes in subsidies and taxes to firms, and changes in demand and supply patterns resulting from a range of government policies).
Technological change (e.g. new ways of manufacturing and supplying goods and services)	Impacts through changes in the conditions of supply – some goods become a lot cheaper to make or technology alters demand patterns as consumers switch their preferences to new high-tech products.

Some of the most important economic factors that should be scanned include:

- What are the growth prospects for the economy?

- What are the growth prospects for our industry?

- What are the growth prospects in the parts of the international economy where we trade?

- What is likely to happen to exchange rates – and how will this impact on our sales?

- What monetary policy is the government pursuing and how will this impact on our business?

- What is likely to happen to interest rates – and how will this impact on our costs?

- What fiscal actions is the government likely to take in the near future and how will these impact on sales of our product and on our business costs?

- How will government taxes and subsidies impact on our products and our business?

- What action is government taking to stimulate competition in our industry and how should we respond to this?

Armed with detailed findings from a SWOT analysis an organization is then able to assess the strategic gap between what it is doing now and what it needs to do to keep up with the external environment.

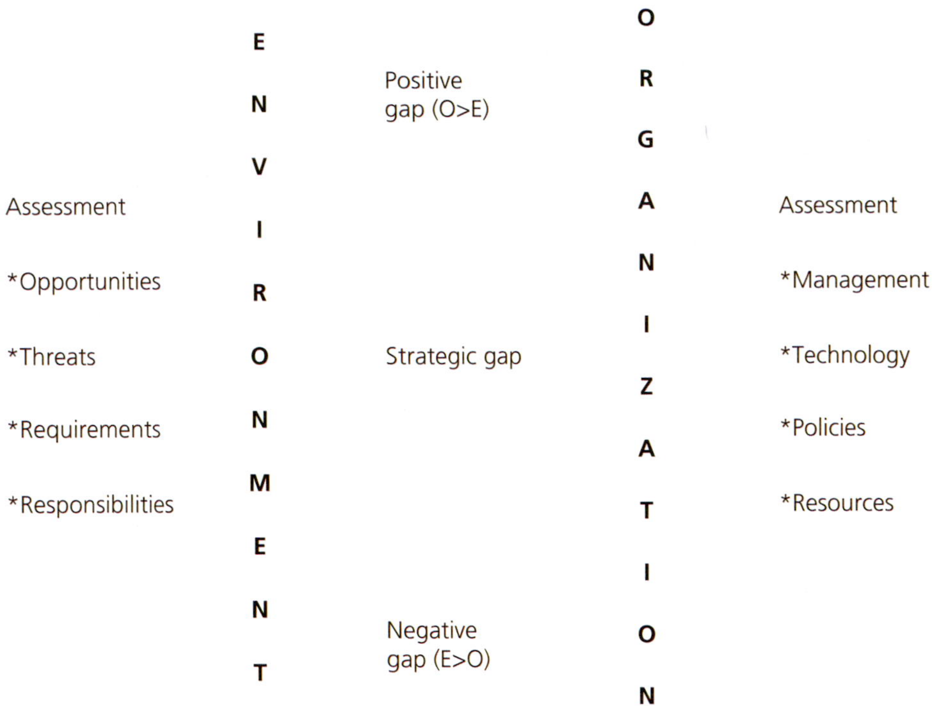

	E			O	
	N	Positive gap (O>E)		R	
	V			G	
Assessment	I			A	Assessment
				N	
*Opportunities	R			I	*Management
	O	Strategic gap		Z	*Technology
*Threats				A	
*Requirements	N			T	*Policies
	M			I	
*Responsibilities	E			O	*Resources
	N	Negative gap (E>O)		N	
	T				

FIGURE 16.2 Strategic gap analysis

The strategic gap – reflects the imbalance between the current strategic position of the organization and the desired strategic position.

KEY TERM

The strategic gap is measured by comparing the organization's capabilities with the opportunities and threats in its external environment (see Figure 16.2). For example, if interest rates are low and a particular industrial sector is growing then it may make sense for a firm to borrow money to upgrade its technologies and resources to take advantage of new opportunities in that sector.

Capability profile – measures the principal capabilities of an organization.

KEY TERM

The four main areas of weakness and strength include:

1. Management: the extent to which existing management has a good decision-making track record.

2. Technology: the extent to which the organization keeps up with state-of-the-art developments in the field.

3. Policies: the extent to which there are clear and well-focused policies covering all aspects of the organization's activities.

4. Resources: the extent to which the organization has the right balance of relevant resources.

> **Environmental assessment** – an organization can carry out a wider environmental assessment to identify the demands of the environment in which it is operating including an important economic assessment.

The environmental assessment examines:

- Opportunities: situations with a potential to enhance the competitive position of the organization. Clearly, opportunities need to be matched with capabilities.

- Threats: there is a range of threats but the most common threats are competition, economic recession and technological obsolescence.

- Requirements: these include statutory requirements, legal codes and other government-related restrictions on strategic choices.

- Responsibilities: these involve expectations on the part of stakeholder groupings including social responsibilities.

A positive strategic gap exists when the organization's capability is greater than its environment (O > E). In this situation the organization is well placed to exploit opportunities, cope with threats, or meet requirements and responsibilities in the external environment.

A negative strategic gap exists when the organization's capability is less than its environment (E > O). This requires management action to reverse the gap because the organization is unable to take up opportunities, respond to threats, or fulfil its responsibilities and requirements in the wider environment.

Perhaps the best state of affairs for an organization is one in which O = E because the organization is in tune with its environment and is taking up appropriate opportunities, responding to threats as and when they arise, and dealing effectively with its requirements and responsibilities because it has the capability to do so. From the point of view of business economics O is most likely to equal E when the business has a full understanding of its economic environment and is responding in an appropriate way to changes in GDP, interest rates, taxes, subsidies, etc.

KEY THEME

Wolseley responds to changing economic environment in France

Wolseley is the world's largest supplier of plumbing materials – ranging from bath taps to kitchen sinks. The company has European operations in the UK, France, Scandinavia and Central Europe. In July 2012 it announced in a press release that it was considering a number of strategic options for its French business. The range of options included selling it off, cutting down the size of the operation, and forming a joint venture with a partner. Wolseley were considering making this move at a time of poor sales due to widespread economic recession in Europe and a cutback in building activity. In addition, there were specific reasons for cutting back in France. Foremost among these is the fact that in other markets where the company operates it is the market leader. However, in France Wolseley does not occupy this position as Saint-Gobain is the dominant company, controlling over a quarter of the French market (Wolseley's share is only 7 per cent).

The building industry (including plumbing) is often used as a general indicator of how economies are doing and there were clear indications at the time that demand was slack across Europe. In July 2012 the French car maker Peugeot Citroën had announced that it was cutting 8,000 jobs. The French government is particularly sensitive to situations where job losses take place in major industries so any move to make major cutbacks at Wolseley would face major political opposition.

- **What major environmental changes were impacting on Wolseley?**

- **To what extent are these changes economic in nature?**

- **Identify the gap that appeared to exist between Wolseley's capability and its environment?**

- **What constraints are placed on Wolseley's choice of actions by the external environment?**

- **What do you think would be an appropriate strategy for the company to pursue, given the conditions in July 2012?**

16.3 Uncertainty in the economic environment

Chapter 9 of this book explored the development of economic ideas and illustrated some of the arguments put forward to justify the effectiveness of market economies.

Over time economists' understanding of how the economy works have improved so that it is possible today for politicians and other economic decision makers to draw on much more detailed knowledge about the economy. Examples of useful additions to our understanding include Keynes' analysis of the way in which investment can be used as a tool to stimulate an economy in a time of recession, and Friedman's contribution to monetary policy theory showing that the money supply should be increased at a steady and transparent rate in line with the growth of the real economy. This level of economic understanding adds to our stock of knowledge. However, it is important to appreciate that our knowledge of economics and the ability of policy-makers to apply knowledge is still limited and subject to error.

Flaws in economic thinking were particularly exposed during the recent financial crisis. Prior to 2007 there had been a period of considerable confidence in economics resulting from what appeared to be a greater ability of market economies to control economic fluctuations. This was referred to as the Great Moderation, as highlighted in the following quote from the then US Federal Reserve Chairman Ben Bernanke (2004). He stated that in the previous two decades there had been:

> not only significant improvements in economic growth and productivity but also a marked reduction in economic volatility, both in the United States and abroad, a phenomenon that has been dubbed 'the Great Moderation'.
>
> Recessions have become less frequent and milder, and quarter-to-quarter volatility in output and employment has declined significantly as well.
>
> The sources of the Great Moderation remain somewhat controversial, but as I have argued elsewhere, there is evidence for the view that improved control of inflation has contributed in important measure to this welcome change in the economy.

However, confidence in economic thinking rapidly evaporated, as outlined in the extract from Steve Keen's book *Debunking Economics* (2011) in the key theme below.

The financial crisis highlighted the potential uncertainty that exists in market economies and alerts business to the importance of monitoring the economy to identify potential changes and the risks that a business is exposed to.

The ideology and economic systems of many countries, including the UK, our European Union partners and the United States, are deeply embedded in a belief that the market economy is the most effective way of organizing the economic system. However, it is important to recognize the potential uncertainty that this system brings with it.

In his book *The Value of Nothing* (2011: 5–6) Raj Patel highlights the potential weaknesses in an over-reliance on the ideas that underpin the market system in citing an exchange between Alan Greenspan, Chairman of the US Federal Reserve (in 2008), and a member of a US Congress Committee:

> *Waxman*: The question I have for you is, you had an ideology, you had a belief that free, competitive – and this is your statement – 'I do have an ideology. My judgement is that free competitive markets are by far the unrivalled way to organise economies. We have tried regulation, none meaningfully worked.' That was your quote. You had the authority to prevent irresponsible lending practices that led to the subprime mortgage crisis. You were advised to do so by many others. And now our whole economy is paying the price. Do you feel that our ideology pushed you to make decisions that you wish you had not made?

KEY THEME

Crisis, an extract from Keen, *Debunking Economics* (2011: 10–11)

Suddenly, everything that neoclassical economics said couldn't happen, happened all at once, asset markets were in free-fall, century-old bastions of finance like Lehman Brothers fell like flies, and the defining characteristics of the Great Moderation evaporated: unemployment skyrocketed, and mild inflation gave way to deflation.

Confronted by a complete disconnect between what they believed and what was happening, economists reacted in a very human way; they panicked. Suddenly, they threw their neoclassical policy rules out of the window, and began to behave like 'Keynesian' economists on steroids. Having eschewed government intervention, budget deficits and boosting government-created money for decades, at their command the government was everywhere. Budget deficits hit high levels that dwarfed anything that old-fashioned Keynesians had ever run in the 1950s and 1960s, and government money flowed like water over the Niagara Falls. Ben Bernanke, as Federal Reserve chairman, literally doubled the level of government-created money in the US economy in five months, when the previous doubling had taken thirteen years.

- **What do you understand by the term the Great Moderation?**

- **How did the financial crisis seem to put an end to the Great Moderation?**

- **Why do you think that the US Federal Reserve resorted to printing money as the impact of the recession hit hard?**

Greenspan: Well, remember though, what an ideology is. It's a conceptual framework with the way people deal with reality. Everyone has one. You have to. To exist, you need an ideology. The question is, whether it is accurate or not. What I am saying to you is, yes, I found the flaw, I don't know how significant or permanent it is, but I have been very distressed by this fact.

Waxman: You found a flaw?

Greenspan: I found a flaw in the model that I perceived is the critical functioning structure that defines how the world works, so to speak.

Waxman: In other words, you found that your view of the world, your ideology, was not right, it was not working.

Greenspan: Precisely. That is precisely the reason I was shocked, because I had been going for 40 years or more with very considerable evidence that it was working exceptionally well.

What this quote indicates is that if someone like Alan Greenspan, a passionate supporter of free market economics, has come to question whether the model works in all situations then it is important for businesses to be aware of potential risks and uncertainties in the economic system.

Corporate governance requirements in the UK outline the need for companies to assess their principal risks and uncertainties. These should be set out in the Company Report and Annual Review. Companies are required to focus on their principal risks, and prioritize and identify the relative weight they give to different risks. This report then provides information for investors (and other stakeholders) to base their decisions on in terms of whether to invest in the business or not.

Internally a company will keep a risk register with the purpose of identifying the company's significant risks, monitoring its risk management performance, allowing the identification of emerging risks and reassuring shareholders and stakeholders regarding the company's risk management and control systems.

In its most detailed form, the risk register could be set out in a table with a number of rows and columns, starting on the left with all the major objectives of the company and its business units, and for each objective – moving to the right and down – all key risks that might affect those objectives. So it could be set out as follows – for each risk:

- Its name (e.g. exchange rate risk).

- Its category (e.g. economic risk).

- A description, including answers to questions such as 'What can happen?', 'How can it happen?' and 'How would it affect the objective?'

- The date the risk was identified, added or modified.

- The owner of the risk.

- The likelihood of the risk happening using a predefined qualitative scale (e.g. almost certain, unlikely).

- The impact on the objective if the risk happens, using a monetary equivalent amount (e.g. £1 million) or a predefined qualitative scale (e.g. severe).

- The trend of the risk (e.g. increasing, decreasing, stable).

- The velocity of the risk (from slow-moving to fast-moving trend).

- The degree of the preparedness of the company regarding that risk.

- If applicable, the existing risk 'treatment', and confidence in the risk treatment.

- The company's appetite for that risk.

All of the above analysis leads to the priority the company should give to that risk. Then the following need to be established:

- The new risk treatment being pursued in light of its priority and the gap between the risk appetite and the existing risk treatment.

- An action plan to achieve it, including a cost–benefit analysis of the measures to be taken.

- The future residual risk left after the treatment has been put in place.

- Deadlines.

- Performance measures and reporting (for assurance).

If companies put in place effective risk management measures they will be best placed to deal with risks and uncertainties such as those stemming from the economic environment.

KEY TERMS

Risk register – document setting out the risks and uncertainties facing an organization that threaten the achievement of its objectives.

Risk owner – the person responsible for managing particular risks.

Risk treatment – approach to treating a particular risk. A '3Ts' approach is helpful here: terminate the risk, treat the risk, tolerate the risk.

Risk appetite – how much risk a company is prepared to accept as a normal part of being enterprising. Some companies have higher risk appetites than others.

Residual risk – original risk minus reduction of the risk through treatment leaves the residual risk.

The risk register needs to be updated regularly so that it matches the velocity of the high-priority risks. The nature of business and risk is that some businesses and some industries will have a higher risk tolerance than others. A good example of this is in the banking industry. Investment banking typically has a higher risk tolerance than traditional high street banking. Unfortunately the distinction between these two sectors had become increasingly blurred in the period leading up to the financial crisis. In the UK the government has recently called for a separation of these two elements of banks to ensure that the funds saved and invested by ordinary households are not being unnecessarily risked in what has been termed 'casino banking'.

The economic arena is an uncertain place with so many variables that are subject to fluctuation – for example, exchange rates, economic growth rates, balance of payments, inflation rates and unemployment rates. It is essential that businesses not only understand changes and inter-relationships between these variables, but that they also put in place risk mitigation strategies and plans to make sure that risks are manageable. In a complex global world it is also essential that those in charge of the international financial system show equal responsibility for the management of risk. This would include those leading the IMF, the Federal Reserve, the European Central Bank (ECB) and the Bank of England.

A key step that has been taken to mitigate risk in the wake of the financial crisis has been that the ECB and the Bank of England have required banks to hold a larger reserve of liquid assets to meet withdrawals from customers. Another form of risk mitigation has been in the separation between different types of banking business in order to protect customers.

16.4 Institutional economics

Perhaps in responding to the recent financial crisis we need to develop a better understanding of how we can shape economic institutions, including local, national and international ones, in order to be more resilient and responsive to economic shocks.

Throughout this book there has been a focus on how markets, government and other economic institutions impact on business. The study of how institutions shape the economy is particularly helpful in understanding how economic relations can be 'improved' to create better outcomes. It is helpful then to examine some of the ideas set out by institutional economists, which provide us with an alternative way of looking at economics and key institutions in the economy, including business.

The study of institutional economics and 'new institutional economics' is an important branch of economics. Some of the key approaches to institutional economics were first set out by the economist Douglass North.

KEY TERMS

Institutions – North (1990: 3–4) defines institutions as 'any socially imposed constraint upon human behaviour. Institutions are the "rules of the game" for human interaction.' North noted that institutions 'are a guide to human interaction, so that when we wish to greet friends on the street, drive an automobile, borrow money, form a business, bury our dead, or whatever, we know (or can easily learn) how to perform these tasks'.

New institutional economics – refers to attempts to understand contemporary economic institutions by systematic analysis of existing institutions as well as being able to make recommendations about how to modify these institutions.

North's view was that the key role of institutions in society 'is to reduce uncertainty by establishing a stable (but not necessarily efficient) structure to human interaction' (1990: 4).

In an economic context institutions can and do vary considerably from society to society – for example, ways of making a transaction (or borrowing money) in Bangladesh might follow substantially different institutional patterns compared to the UK. Institutions therefore limit the set of choices that individuals and businesses can make. Over time institutions are likely to change. The key institutions of market economies such as the UK are the market itself, the firm, and the way in which contracts are made (e.g. in the buying and selling of goods). North's research (into the development of societies over time) led him to the view that institutions determine the performance of economies. Traditions such as hard work, honesty and integrity help to lower the cost of doing business in a society and therefore make it more competitive. Institutions such as the rule of law and private property, as well as opposition to corruption, help to keep costs down in the economy.

For a society to be efficient it is important that contracts are enforced. This works well when individuals in society engage in a process of self-enforcement – they abide by the rules. Where the government has to step in as a third-party enforcer then problems can arise. The third-party requires resources to carry out their work and the claims of the enforcer may become inflated over time. This is one of the central issues related to the role of the state in markets. North set out this dilemma: 'You cannot live without a State and you cannot live with a State!' (1990: 4).

North developed institutional economics partly because he felt (1993) that 'the tools of neoclassical economic theory were not up to the task of explaining the kind of fundamental societal change that has characterised European economies from medieval times onwards'. Perhaps this is particularly true within the context of the financial crisis. Market economists were able to explain ways in which markets could be arranged to minimize risk and to ensure that those seeking to take higher risks could cover themselves by spreading their risks through a range of new financial products that markets had developed. However, what neoclassical economics was not able to take into account was the spread of corruption and greed in the investment banking sector – what Vince Cable (the Secretary of State for Business in the UK) has since referred to as a culture of greed.

Institutional economics has become more popular in recent times partly as a reaction to neoclassical economics. The analysis of institutional economists has been particularly helpful in developing insights related to some major changes that have taken place in economic society. Their view is that in order to successfully facilitate change it is important to understand the existing institutions in society rather than to impose a model (such as a free market model) on a blank sheet of paper. For example, from the time of the October Revolution in 1917 until late 2001 it was impossible for Russian citizens to buy and sell land. Institutional economists argued against the idea of abruptly imposing a free market model on a society which had so little knowledge or experience of how the free market works.

Recently institutional economists have studied institutional factors such as property rights and governance structure, showing how these affect economic transactions and activities. The aim of many modern institutional economists has been to identify ways of reducing petty restrictions that push up costs, to create a more stable legal and commercial framework in markets and to improve social benefits through coordinated institutional activity.

The financial crisis of 2012 came as a shock to many people who had been lulled into a false sense of security about a 'Great Moderation'. In this respect it is interesting to read one of North's statements that: 'all the interesting questions in the world . . . are concerned

KEY THEME

Creating effective institutions for economic development

In a journal article published in *This is Africa* (June/July 2012), Tim Besley, Professor of Economics at the London School of Economics made the following points about the institutions required to create economic development.

In the article he sets out to try and explain why good ideas such as building roads in developing countries are not put into practice even though the argument has been logically set out. For example, cost–benefit analysis might point to the net benefits, and as the case clearly sets out this will lead to a raising of rural population incomes. So why don't these things happen?

His view is that political economy factors 'account for a large fraction of the problems of development'. His work asks:

> what the right political institutions for development might look like. Cohesion is a vital trait. 'The idea is that as far as possible, you want the political process to focus on broad-based policies – those that benefit a large number of citizens rather than narrowly focused policies . . .'

> While identifying institutions that promote cohesiveness is a country specific question, some trends can be asserted. 'One is parliamentary democracy. I genuinely think presidential systems find it much harder to generate cohesiveness, for a variety of reasons; whereas parliamentary systems on the whole invite broad-based coalitions to form, and broad-based coalitions are more likely to operate in a broader public interest. That is just not the nature of the settlement that happens in a presidential system where too much power is placed in the hand of a winner.'

Professor Besley also sees institutions such as an independent judiciary as key – it is certainly a vital feature. Professor Besley's work shows that we need to understand the political decision-making process if we are to better understand why what appear to be rational economic decisions are not made. Besley's work therefore echoes North's attempts to explain why inefficient rules tend to exist and be perpetuated. North, like Besley, was interested in political processes that lead to inefficient institutions.

- **In what way does Tim Besley suggest that institutions can enable economic growth?**

- **How does this fit into a broader perspective of institutional economics?**

with dynamic change and with a world in a continuous flux' (2002: 4). Institutional economics therefore alerts us to the need to be constantly aware of changes in society. We cannot assume that because a system appears to be working that it will continue to do so.

Reflective question

1   To what extent do the institutional economists provide ideas about the organization of market societies which are additional to those presented in neoliberal thinking?

16.5 The importance of competitive advantage

A key institution of the market economy is competition between businesses. This is an important driver towards efficiency and enables a business to achieve abnormal profits. It is therefore important to explore in greater detail the nature of competition because it is such a fundamental concept in market economics.

KEY TERMS

Abnormal profit – any surplus that a business can make over and above the minimum profit required for it to remain in an industry.

Direct competition – where a firm competes head-to-head with another firm providing an identical goods or service (e.g. between two toothpaste manufacturers).

Indirect competition – where firms compete with each other although their goods or services are not directly similar. There are different levels of indirect competition – for example, sellers of pizza/pasta are not identical to sellers of burgers and chips although they are often competing for similar sets of customers. Perhaps competition is even more indirect between coffee shops and pasta and pizza outlets but they are competing for the same money in the customer's pocket.

Many industries in the UK are highly competitive (e.g. mobile phone service providers, budget airlines, online travel agents, competition between universities for students). Actions by one competitor lead to reactions by another, which trigger further actions and reactions. The resulting situation is often described as competitive chaos.

John L. Thompson (2001) suggests that there are three main skills required by organizations in such an environment:

*   The ability to discern patterns in this dynamic environment and competitive chaos, and spot opportunities ahead of their rivals.

For businesses to understand adequately the nature of the competition they face, they must define their market accurately. This involves recognizing a broad base of competitors. In the informal eating out (IEO) sector there are many different types of competitors, as illustrated in Table 16.2.

TABLE 16.2 Informal eating out

Firms operating in quick service sector	Typical range of products
Subway	Sandwiches, rolls, snack, drinks
McDonald's	Burger, buns, salads, chips, drinks
KFC	Fried chicken products, salads, deserts, drinks
Pizza Express	Pizza, drinks
Pizza Hut	Pizza, drinks
Domino's Pizza	Pizza, drinks
Pret-a-manger	Sandwiches, rolls, snack meals, drinks
Costa Coffee	Drinks, cakes, rolls, sandwiches
Starbucks	Drinks, cakes, rolls, sandwiches
Ethnic meals including Chinese and Indian	Take away ethnic meals, drinks
Independents	Fish and chip shops, sandwich bars, coffee shops

Table 16.2 demonstrates the range of outlets each with direct competition in its own segment (e.g. Pizza Express, Pizza Hut and Domino's Pizza all in the Pizza sector). Each of these businesses is seeking to win a share of the market. Businesses need therefore to develop competitive strategies that set them apart from rivals (e.g. Costa Coffee aiming for a high quality and service image with good quality products).

All of these organizations need to be in touch with their business environment in order to make sure that what they do fits with customer expectations. These expectations change over time. Moreover the IEO market in which Pizza Hut and Costa Coffee operate is becoming increasingly competitive. This market is defined as: casual places where consumers buy a quick, inexpensive prepared meal or snack that they eat there, take with them, eat in the car or have delivered.

It doesn't take long for leading firms to copy the ideas of their rivals. At the same time they will seek to promote ideas of their own.

- To what extent should the IEO sector be seen as a single market? Are there distinct sections to this market?

- What can competing firms in this market do to differentiate themselves from rivals and thus to give themselves some element of monopoly power?

- What do rivals do? Use examples from your own experience to limit the extent of this differentiation.

- The ability to anticipate competitor actions and reactions.

- The ability to use this intelligence and insight to lead customer opinion and outperform competitors.

Gaining and maintaining a competitive advantage

Michael Porter (1985) suggested that effective strategic management involves positioning an organization relative to its rivals in such a way that it maintains and sustains competitive advantage. For example, Costa positions itself as a premium provider, and McDonald's positions itself as a quick service family restaurant. Porter focused on two main aspects of an organization's position relative to competitors:

- The number of firms in the relevant market segments, their size, relative power, rate of growth and ways in which they compete. Organizations need to be in the right industries and market segments given their competitive capabilities.

- The size and market share of the firm are important in creating competitive advantage, and whether it has an appeal to particular segments of its markets.

In short, competitive advantage will be gained by being in the right industry and in the right position within that industry. Successful competitors will:

- Create value by giving customers what they want, and by developing clear advantages at every stage of the value chain.

- Develop competitive advantage in creating this value.

- Run their businesses well: meeting their objectives and using resources efficiently.

KEY TERM

Value chain – the series of activities that make finished products more desirable to the end consumer, enabling the producer to sell more goods and generate more profit. Porter identified two sets of activities. Primary activities are those involved directly in the production process (e.g. acquiring raw materials, processing them into finished products and delivering them to the consumer). Secondary activities include a range of support activities (e.g. marketing, providing customer service, etc.).

Clearly, therefore, for a business to gain competitive advantage it will need to plan and organize its business and do things better than rivals. Porter (1980) argued that, given similar abilities to supply goods, the customer will choose to buy from one supplier rather than another because:

- The price of the product or service is lower than that offered by rivals.

- The product or service is seen by the customer to offer better 'valued added' than that offered by a rival.

Value added – the results of applying processes that make a good more desirable to the consumer (e.g. branding it, making it better, advertising it).

Compare firms in the following industries in terms of whether they are seeking competitive advantage through lower price or through more valued added:

- Cosmetics industry
- Newspaper publishing industry
- Book publishing
- Computers
- Tinned food

Porter showed that the best way to gain and maintain competitive advantage is not to be average. The low-cost firm can make higher than average profits by selling a lot more than its rivals and employing economies of scale. The differentiating firm can gain competitive advantage by giving its customers more value added.

Competitive strategies

Porter identified four possible favourable competitive strategies.

1. Broad differentiation strategy. This strategy involves selling a differentiated product to the mass market. Coca-Cola does this – its main drink products (e.g. Coca Cola, Diet Coke) are differentiated through advertising and marketing as well as the product itself.

2. Focused differentiation strategy. This strategy involves selling a differentiated product to a narrow market segment or niche market, rather than to the total market – for example, a specialist high-quality magazine such as Vogue, or an Audi or BMW motor car. Here the manufacturer is saying to the target customer: 'our product is designed for you, we are not going to cut corners to lower quality and will charge you a price that is appropriate to the experience that you are looking for'.

3. Broad low-cost strategy. This strategy involves selling a largely undifferentiated product to a mass market using low cost to drive sales – for example, bags of sugar with simple packaging (e.g. Tate & Lyle or Silver Spoon sugar). It is important to recognize that when Porter examined low-cost strategies he wasn't implying that products would necessarily be cheap. Yes, they will be cheaper than rival products (on account of cost advantages) but they are not necessarily going to be cheap products.

4. Focused low-cost strategy. This strategy involves selling an undifferentiated product or service to a smaller market segment. Again the principal way the producer or seller will gain advantage over rivals will be through being more efficient than rivals.

Many businesses today seek to gain advantage through a differentiation strategy, for example through:

- Offering a more personalized service

- Building relationships with customers

- Built-in extra features

- Speed and reliability of service

- Superior design

- More sophisticated technology

The implication of Porter's competitive models which are of significance for economics and business are that:

- Firms can gain competitive advantage by being highly efficient producers. Business analysts have identified a range of ways of achieving this, including cutting out waste from production processes. The concept of lean production and zero waste targets are very important in suggesting ways of reducing costs. The concept of total quality is also important.

- Firms can gain competitive advantage through differentiating their products. Differentiation should be based on customer expectations (i.e. it should be driven by marketing).

- Firms should focus primarily on either cost leadership or differentiation. Try to blend these and a firm runs the danger of getting 'stuck in the middle'. This creates problems for customers because they are more likely to choose to deal with firms and buy products when they can understand the competitive position of the firm. I buy a Rolex watch because it is top of the range and fly Ryanair because it will get me on time from A to B with no frills but at a value for money price.

KEY TERMS

Lean production – simplification of production processes to cut out activities that do not add value.

Zero waste – the elimination of any processes that lead to waste of resources and time.

Total quality – giving everyone in the workplace the responsibility for improving production, particularly through making suggestions about improvements. Everyone in the organization becomes a quality manager.

In 1990 Porter transferred his attention to identifying factors leading to competitive advantage between nations. He identified four attributes, referred to as Porter's diamond identifying factors, that promote or retard the creation of international competitive advantage (see Figure 16.3).

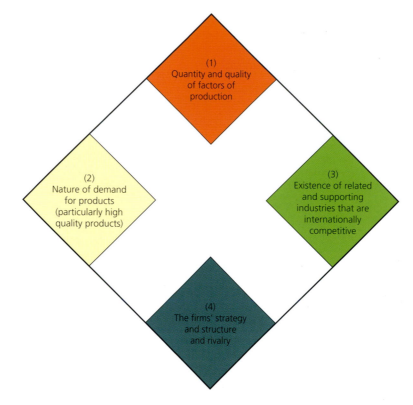

FIGURE 16.3 Porter's diamond

CASE STUDY Ongoing success at Microsoft

In July 2012 Microsoft, the world's largest software producer, reported record fourth-quarter sales.

At a time when the PC industry had reported weak consumer demand, Microsoft figures were driven by a large volume of sales to business. Microsoft reported these findings at a time when it was just about to launch a range of new products including Windows 8, Windows Phone 8, Windows Server 2012 and Office 2013.

In June 2012 Microsoft had succeeded in selling 85 million units of Windows. However, with no major game releases in the offing the company's revenues were expected to decline. Announcing its results Microsoft was upbeat about its social, collaborative, video and voice efforts, relating to its Lync communication tools and Skype and Yammer acquisitions.

- What evidence is provided in this case study that Microsoft has a competitive advantage in terms of the range of products it produces?

- What actions are Microsoft taking to build on this competitive advantage?

In relation to the fourth factor Porter believed that domestic competition (rivalry) is very important in ensuring that firms are competitive in international markets. Rivalry will pressurize organizations to be efficient. Porter showed that Japan, which had done particularly well in the period leading up to the publication of his book, was characterized by intense competition between a number of domestic camera manufacturers, car manufacturers, TV manufacturers, etc.

The key finding from Porter's research is that where firms do particularly well in their home market they can also be successful on a world stage.

16.6 The size of firms in the market

There are many different businesses in Britain ranging from small sole trader business to giant multinationals. In 2009 figures from the Office for National Statistics reveal that there were:

- Over half a million sole traders with a turnover of less than £100,000.

- About 300,000 partnerships.

- About one and a quarter million companies (and public corporations). Of these about 13 per cent have turnovers of more than £1 million.

The picture therefore shows that there are many small firms, and a number of larger firms that are major players in their markets.

Why do small firms exist?

There are several reasons for the existence of small firms, many of which are important for their country's economy:

- Some are new businesses that have just set up, hoping to play an increasingly important role as they grow.

- They may supply a local market (e.g. a local corner shop, restaurant or hairdresser).

- They provide essential components and supplies for larger businesses.

- There may be only a limited demand for their product. An example might be suppliers of specialist medical supplies for patients with rare diseases.

- Their owners may prefer to run a small enterprise.

- Personal services requiring attention to detail, such as hairdressing, are often suitable for small businesses.

Why do large firms exist?

There are various reasons why large businesses exist:

- To meet demand. Large companies (e.g. Procter and Gamble in the US) supply household goods such as washing powder, toothpaste and soap worldwide. Bao Steel (China) produces steel worldwide for construction projects, particularly in the rapidly growing Chinese economy.

- When there are considerable economies of producing on a large scale. Coca-Cola distributes cola-based drinks and bottled water on a huge scale worldwide. It is able to operate from large factories with very low average unit costs.

- When the supply of goods depends on employing large sums of capital. Nuclear energy can only be developed economically on a large scale. This also applies to motor vehicle manufacture, aircraft and ship building, and major construction projects.

16.7 The growth of firms in the market

To integrate means to join together. In business integration may be in the form of a takeover or merger. A merger occurs when two businesses combine to form a single company. It is similar to a takeover except that the existing shareholders of both businesses retain a share in the new business. A takeover occurs when one business gains control of, or acquires part of, another business. A business may be prepared to sell off one of its divisions which it no longer wishes to keep.

Mergers and takeovers take place because:

- There is too much supply in the market, relative to demand. A firm may take over part of a rival in order to control supply to the market.

- To gain access to new markets, perhaps in other countries.

- To acquire new technologies from other businesses.

- To acquire dynamic products.

Table 16.3 sets out different ways in which businesses can merge or integrate.

KEY TERM

Joint venture – a business organization that is set up by two separate business organizations. The joint venture is jointly owned by the two companies.

TABLE 16.3 Ways in which businesses merge or integrate

Horizontal integration	Firms join together at the same stage of production. They can learn from best practice in each company and concentrate on processing activities in the most efficient plants. The increased size of the business provides economies of scale.
Vertical integration	It may be forward – that is, taking over a firm at a later stage of production (e.g. a business with tea estates taking over a company that processes tea) – or backward – that is, taking over a firm at an earlier stage of production (e.g. a firm that advertises and markets tea taking over one that processes it). The advantage of this sort of integration is that the firm gains control over its supply chain.
Lateral integration	Occurs when there is a merger of firms that use the same distribution channels. For example, a company selling tea may join with a firm selling coffee so that the goods can be distributed together to supermarket chains.
Conglomerate integration	For example Tata Industries (an Indian multinational), which is able to spread interests and risks over many industries. Profits from one established business can be used to develop a new business area. So, for example, profits from Tata Steel and Tata Tea could be channelled into the growing Tata IT company. A large conglomerate also builds up a high profile, enabling it to raise finance more easily.
International integration	Global companies like Tata buy from other companies world-wide. In China, for example, Tata Tea has invested in Chinese tea companies producing green tea. A joint venture is a good way of entering a new international market. In this case a new company is set up owned by Tata and a Chinese Company.

16.8 Economies of scale

The economic concept of 'economies of scale' is particularly important in providing an explanation of how large firms have come to dominate international markets – for example, Amazon in bookselling, Google as a web browser, Intel in supplying microchips to computer manufacturers, Microsoft in supplying computer software, Dell in manufacturing computers, Sony in consumer electronics, Ali Baba in supplying an online market for manufacturers, Tata in steel manufacture, the list goes on.

The basic principle on which economies of scale are based is that it is cheaper and more efficient to produce on a large scale than a small one. It is not dissimilar to the process of bulk buying by a household. If you buy a single can of Coca-Cola you will probably pay around 80 pence but if you buy a 12-pack of Coca Cola each can will work out at something like 40 pence. Buying is cheaper for us on a larger scale.

Businesses experience similar advantages from operating on a large scale. The higher the level of production the lower the average cost of production. Fixed costs per unit of production fall as production rises. Larger firms are able to benefit from discounts for bulk purchase when buying raw materials or components. Larger production is more efficient than small-scale production in many instances. For example, the giant US multinational retailer Wal-Mart is able to charge lower prices than rivals because it purchases from suppliers in thousands or millions of units.

There are a number of economies of scale that can be categorized under six main headings:

1. Marketing economies

2. Managerial economies

3. Financial economies

4. Technical economies

5. Indivisibility economies

6. Risk-bearing economies

In **marketing economies** larger firms are able to afford to carry out extensive market research to find out what their customers want. For example, Tesco supermarkets have one of the most sophisticated databases for analysing consumer data. They are able to electronically analyse the buying decisions their customers make. The Tesco Clubcard enables marketers at Tesco to identify which customer is making which transaction. Offers can then be made to individual customers depending on their buying patterns. A small corner shop or supermarket doesn't have this level of knowledge about their consumers.

Other examples of marketing economies include advertising. A company like Coca-Cola is able to spend millions of pounds on an advertising campaign. However, the cost of the advertising campaign is spread across the world (e.g. through national television campaigns). The cost of the advertising campaign is then spread over billions of cans of drinks, so the cost of advertising per unit sold is close to zero.

Larger organizations can also employ specialist marketing staff and management who are skilled in marketing, whereas small firms may have to rely on non-specialists.

In **managerial economies** big companies are able to attract the best managers worldwide by offering them attractive remuneration packages. They can employ specialist managers with just the right skills that the business is looking for. For example, if Tesco wants to enter a new national market it can employ the best possible talent with knowledge of that market.

In **financial economies** if you or I ask a bank for a loan and we are accepted, we are unlikely to have much room for negotiation with regard to the interest rate charged. That is because although the loan may seem large to us, to a bank it is small change. In contrast, if a large firm approaches a bank for a large sum of money, banks will attempt to offer the most attractive deal. Firms can consequently negotiate with a number of banks to get the most attractive loan deals possible, and the larger the firm is the more muscle it has in its negotiations, as it will have substantial assets to offer as security.

Also, since large firms have substantial assets they are in a better position to raise finance by means of share issues. The number and value of shares that a firm may issue depends to a large extent on the value of the firm, and large firms are more valuable than small ones. Consequently a large firm is able to raise money more easily through issues of shares, and this is an ideal way of borrowing for a firm as it does not have to make repayments, only provide dividends to shareholders. Large firms, therefore, can raise finance more cheaply and easily than small firms.

In **technical economies** large firms can benefit from using better techniques of production. Automated plant and equipment (e.g. in a confectionery manufacturing company or bottling plant) may be so expensive to install that only large companies can afford it. Automated production lines enable very high production at low unit costs and can be run 24 hours a day, 7 days a week.

In **indivisibility economies** some production processes are not possible or are not financially viable on a small scale, such as the production of aircraft or trams, and therefore firms have to become large to contemplate moving into such areas.

In **risk-bearing economies** large firms can spread their risks in various ways:

- Product diversification – producing and selling lots of different products.

- Market diversification – producing and selling in many different countries and regions.

- Supplier diversification – using several different suppliers in case one is unable to supply on time.

- Production diversification – having several different production plants.

Economists also use the term economies of scope to describe the advantages that large firms have from offering more products in more markets. Economies of scope therefore relate not just to spreading risk but to being able to sell more products. Table 16.4 illustrates ways in which firms have been able to benefit from economies of scope.

TABLE 16.4 Ways in which firms have been able to benefit from economies of scope

Name of company	Economies of scope
Tesco (originally a UK-based retailer)	Selling a wider and wider range of goods and services (e.g. the development of Tesco bank and insurance). Moving into more and more countries (e.g. Thailand, and China).
Amazon	Originally an online bookseller. Moving into more and more product lines for global distribution (e.g. toys, electronics, jewellery, watches).
Tata (an Indian multi-product, multinational)	Increasingly diversifying into more core products (Tata Tea, Tata Steel, Tata IT, etc.) and into more countries, to become a global company through buying global brands such as Tetley Tea.
Google (starting out as US-based, editing applications)	Branching out into more and more applications that can be used worldwide (e.g. Gmail, movie download, home photography search engine).

Internal diseconomies of scale

If an organization is too large, managers may not be able to manage it effectively. There may be technical problems with complicated equipment. If a firm is producing more than it can sell, the proportion of advertising costs may increase. If the business produces too many products for too many markets and a number of them fail, the losses may have a damaging effect on the development of the company's other products.

KEY TERM

Internal diseconomies of scale – these occur when a firm becomes too large and inefficiencies lead to rising costs per unit of production.

External economies of scale

KEY TERM

External economies – these arise from the growth of an industry rather than a particular firm. As the industry grows the firm is able to produce at a lower unit cost.

All firms benefit from external economies of scale, such as:

- Improved communications and transport links (e.g. a new railway line that cuts distribution costs).

- Improved educational facilities (e.g. a new college or university training people in the skills needed by local businesses).

- The development of suppliers, supplying components to all the firms in an industry.

- Improved housing and social amenities that encourage workers to move to an area.

- The development of banking and insurance services in an area.

External diseconomies of scale

There can be problems arising from the growth of an industry. Labour and other costs can increase as more competitors hire more labour and buy more land and machinery. There may also be congestion and pollution from business activities.

International economies of scale

What is clear in the modern world is that major companies such as Nestlé, Unilever, BP, Shell, Amazon, Google, Haier, Microsoft, Google, Tata, Kraft, Barclays, HBOS and many more have been able to take advantage of international economies of scale and economies of scope. The scope today of these companies is global. The thought processes underpinning strategy at these companies involve identifying new market opportunities and ways of

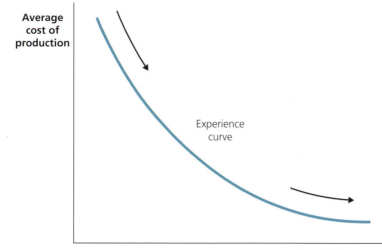

FIGURE 16.4 The experience curve

building competitive advantage in existing markets. Economies of scale and scope play a key part in this process.

The more experience that a business has of operating in a global economy the better the opportunity that it has for driving economies based on this experience.

> **Experience curve** – the benefits of experience that a firm derives from producing and selling a good enabling it to become more effective at doing so.

KEY TERM

Figure 16.4 shows a phenomenon known as the experience curve. It shows that the greater the cumulative output of a particular business the lower the cost of production.

Big multinational companies are therefore able to play a leading role in the global economy:

- Through economies of scale; and
- Through experience curve effects.

The outcomes for large firms of these advantages are that they are able to:

- Grow their market share over time;
- Benefit from continued low unit costs; and
- Develop competitive advantages over rivals.

16.9 Summary

The economic environment in which businesses operate is a complex and dynamic one. Businesses need to be constantly alert to changes in this environment. By scanning the economic environment using tools such as the SWOT analysis they are best placed to build a risk register enabling them to manage risk in line with the risk appetite of the business.

In the period leading up to the financial crisis there was growing confidence among the economics profession that economic fluctuations had been tamed using appropriate economic management tools. However, the scale and severity of the crisis has banished this self-confidence and also our confidence in market economics. Institutional economics provides an alternative way of analysing institutional structures in order to get a better understanding of economic processes.

A key aspect of the market economy is its emphasis on the benefits of competitive advantage. The chapter demonstrates ways in which businesses can gain competitive advantage over rivals. This can be achieved both through differentiation and through cost efficiency. Economies of scale and economies of scope have proved to be of immense significance in enabling major global companies to dominate particular product areas as well as geographical areas. The experience curve coupled with economies of scale are major drivers of international competitive advantage.

KEY IDEAS

Matching business strategy with the organizational environment
- A SWOT analysis enables a business to match its capabilities and resources to the external environment.
- Opportunities and threats arise in a business's external environment.
- Economic opportunities and threats relate to changes in economic growth, and in indicators such as exchange rates and interest rates.

Uncertainty in the economic environment
- Changes in the macro-economy are unpredictable.
- In the period leading up to the financial crisis there was a general feeling among many economists and politicians that the economic cycle had been tamed.
- The financial crisis exposed some fundamental fault lines in the economic system.

Institutional economics
- Institutions affect the performance of economies over time.

- Change is the norm and if we are to manage economic change then it is necessary to understand how institutions impact on economic relationships.

- Free market systems can only work within the context of existing institutions – so, for example, if corruption is institutionalized in some components of the economy then it will be difficult for the free market to work smoothly in that sector.

- A fuller understanding of how institutions work is required alongside the traditional tools of the economist.

The importance of competitive advantage

- Competition is a key institution of the market economy.

- Competing firms seek to achieve competitive advantage over rivals.

- Key ways to achieve competitive advantage are through differentiation and through being a low-cost producer.

- It is important for businesses to establish a competitive position that is understood by customers.

The size of firms in the market

- The UK economy is made up of many small firms and many large firms. The largest firms have very large turnovers.

- There are advantages from being a small firm in some contexts. There are advantages from being a large firm in other contexts.

The growth of firms in the market

- Firms can grow through merger and acquisition.

- Firms can grow horizontally, vertically or laterally.

Economies of scale

- Economies of scope and scale help a firm to gain competitive advantage, particularly in international markets.

- Some economies are internal (i.e. stemming from the growth of a business), while some economies are external (relating to the growth of an industry).

- Internal economies of scale relate to the advantages that large firms have in marketing, financing, risk spreading, management and technology.

- A firm can grow too large and experience diseconomies of scale.

- Economies of scale enable a firm to produce a larger output at a lower unit cost, compared to the smaller firm producing a smaller output at a higher unit cost.

- The experience curve shows that as the cumulative output of a company increases over time so does the unit cost of production.

REVIEW QUESTIONS

1. Identify five key ways in which the external economic environment can impact on business.

2. What are the key economic risks facing companies in the building and construction industry? What actions could these firms take to mitigate these risks?

3. What is a risk register and how does this enable a business to manage economic risk?

4. What is a market economy and why might such an economy be exposed to fluctuation and change?

5. What are institutions? What are the principal institutions in a market economy? To what extent do these institutions encourage stability or change?

6. How is institutional economics different from neoclassical economics? What new dimensions does institutional economics bring to the study of economic change?

7. How can competitive advantage enable a business to succeed in a market economy? What are the principal sources of competitive advantage?

8. Can a firm concentrate on both differentiation and cost leadership?

9. Analyse ways in which economies of scale can enable a global business to dominate a range of international markets.

10. Explain how economies of scale coupled with economies of scope and the experience curve can together enable a firm to achieve competitive advantage.

RECOMMENDED READING

Patel, R. (2011) *The Value of Nothing*, London, Portobello Books.

This work provides an interesting alternative view of economic thinking. For example one of the key questions posed by the book is 'What is the real price of a Big Mac – taking into account the social, health and environmental costs?' The book cites evidence from a report by the Centre for Science and the Environment in India, that 'a burger grown from beef raised on clear-cut forest should really cost about two hundred dollars' (p. 44). Part 1 of the book starts out by exploring the basic 'flaw' in market economies.

REFERENCES

Bernanke, B. (2004) 'The Great Moderation: Remarks by Governor Ben S. Bernanke at the Meetings of the Eastern Economic Association, Washington, DC, February 20, 2004', Eastern Economic Association, Washington, DC, Federal Reserve Board.

Besley, T. (2012) 'Creating Effective Institutions for Economic Development', *Africa Today*, June/July: 24–7.

Green, A. (2012) 'Interview with Tim Besley, Professor of Economics, London School of Economics', *This is Africa a Global Perspective*, June/July.

Keen, S. (2011) *Debunking Economics: The Naked Emperor Dethroned*, London, Zed Books.

North, D. (1981) *Structure and Change in Economic History*, New York, Norton.

North, D. (1990) *Institutions, Institutional Change and Economic Performance*, Cambridge, Cambridge University Press.

North, D. (1993) 'Autobiography', *Nobel Prize website*. Available at: www.nobelprize.org/nobel_prizes/economics/laureates/1993/north-autobio.html (accessed January 2013).

North, D. (1995) 'Douglass C. North (autobiographical sketch)', in Breit W. and Spencer R. (eds) *Lives of the Laureates: Thirteen Nobel Economists*, Cambridge, MA, MIT Press.

North, D. (2002) 'Leon Kozminski Academy of Entrepreneurship and Management and TIGER Distinguished Lecture Series', No.7, Warsaw, 16 May 2002.

Patel, R. (2011) *The Value of Nothing*, London, Portobello Books.

Porter, M. (1980) *Competitive Strategy*, New York, Free Press.

Porter, M. (1985) *Competitive Advantage: Creating and Sustaining Superior Performance*, London, Collier Macmillan.

Porter, M. (1990) *The Competitive Advantage of Nations*, London, Macmillan.

Thompson, J. L. (2001) *Strategic Management*, 4th edition, London, Chapman and Hall.

USEFUL WEBSITES

www.guardian.co.uk/business/economics – *The Guardian* newspaper runs some of the best up-to-date stories about economic issues that impact upon business.

17 Financial planning and investment appraisal

CHAPTER OBJECTIVES

After carefully reading and engaging with the tasks and activities outlined in this chapter you should have a better understanding of:

● What is meant by investment and why and how investment is important to individual businesses and to the economy as a whole

● How to appraise investment using the payback method and the strengths and weaknesses of this approach

● How to appraise investment using the discounted cash flow method and the strengths and weaknesses of this approach

● How to appraise investment using the accounting rate of return method and the strengths and weaknesses of this approach

● The main sources of finance for a business

17.1 Introduction

The final chapter of this book looks at the very important concept of financial planning for business. The financial planning that a business carries out needs to be tailored to the economic climate in which the business is operating. When the economy is growing there will be more scope for business expansion, including accessing more business finance and engaging in investment activities. When the economy is in a recession then a business may want to cut back on investment decisions and to restructure its financing – for example, by reducing its exposure to external finance with fixed interest repayment obligations.

The first part of the chapter looks at a key financial planning decision: whether or not to invest and how to appraise an investment opportunity. Investment involves using scarce resources to create capital to enable future growth. An investment decision is thus important both from the perspective of the economy and for the business carrying out the investment. In evaluating investment opportunities it is important to use investment appraisal methods. The chapter therefore explores different ways of appraising investment: the payback method, discounted cash flows and accounting rate of return.

Finally, the chapter outlines financial planning within the context of the various sources of finance that are available to a business. Some sources of finance expose a business to greater risks than others, and this can be particularly dangerous when an economy is in recession and funds flowing into a business may be reduced.

17.2 What is investment?

Investment is a particularly important aspect of economic growth. Economists identify investment as an expenditure on (or purchase of) items that increase productive capacity (e.g. the purchase of a machine or machine tool). In addition, social investment involves investment in the capacity to increase social welfare (e.g. by building a new school or hospital). Investment is particularly important as it typically creates jobs and new expenditure in an economy which acts to boost growth. Investment is carried out by both the public sector and the private sector of the economy. This chapter focuses on various economic techniques that can be used to appraise the effectiveness of investment projects.

The development and growth of a business usually takes place in a series of separate steps or projects. These can range from the purchase of an additional delivery van to the complete takeover of another business. These projects are investments because they involve adding to or replacing some of the operating assets of the business.

Investment objectives

KEY TERM

Investment objective – an investment objective is the end that a business seeks to achieve as a result of carrying out investment (e.g. to replace an existing asset based on old fashioned technology).

The aim of an investment may be to:

- Increase efficiency.

- Expand capacity.

- Replace existing assets that are no longer economical to use, or are technologically obsolete.

- Comply with health and safety regulations.

Surveys carried out into the motives of UK businesses to invest regularly show that business people state that increasing efficiency is the main motive for investing, followed by the need to replace capital and then to expand capacity. Investment enables business to replace existing technologies with more advanced technologies and to replace less efficient factors of production such as some types of labour with labour-saving equipment and machinery.

Net and gross investment

Economists make an important distinction between gross and net investment.

Gross investment – new investment in fixed assets (e.g. buildings, machinery, equipment, plant and vehicles).

Net investment – gross investment minus any replacement investment (i.e. investment to replace obsolete plant and equipment).

The level of net investment provides an indication of what is happening to the stock of fixed capital in an economy that is available for production. Every year existing capital will depreciate and lose value. Net investment therefore gives a much better indicator of how effective the economy will be in terms of its productive capacity. The same principle applies at the level of a firm. A firm will need to have positive net investment if it is going to be able to improve its production capacity.

Autonomous and induced investment

From an economic perspective it is important to identify the extent to which investment in capital goods arises from changes in GDP or whether this investment is independent of changes in GDP. Induced investment is investment that arises as a result of changes in GDP. As GDP grows, more productive capacity is required to respond to rising consumer demand. However, in addition some investment will take place irrespective of the level of GDP and we call this autonomous investment.

From the standpoint of economic analysis the level of autonomous investment is very important because it is this type of investment that can have a really positive impact in terms of creating a fresh impetus to the economy (e.g. in a period of recession). For example, in 2012 Apple invested in retooling to launch the new iPhone5 and this had a really positive impact on GDP in the United States during a period of recession.

Economic theory suggests that expectations on the part of producers are the major determinant of investment decisions. When business people are confident about the future state of the economy they are most likely to invest. Common sense (as well as economic theory) tells us that this is the case. When business people expect demand to pick up in the future then they are more likely to invest now in order to reap future rewards. Their expectations of future returns will be higher.

Keynes (see Chapter 9) and many other economists have pointed to the importance of investment as a key variable in the economy. The implication of this is that it is important to create a sense of optimism in the economy in order to encourage autonomous investment. Government ministers can help to achieve this by giving out positive messages about the state of the economy and future economic growth. In addition the government can, through its economic policies, establish an environment that encourages business investment (e.g. through incentives and tax reductions for capital spending, or by encouraging a low rate of interest within the monetary system). Profit-seeking businesses in the private sector will be encouraged to invest when they believe that projected future returns on their investment will yield returns higher than the opportunity cost of using their capital in alternative ways (e.g. by saving their money). The analysis that follows therefore explores the decision to invest by a business.

The decision whether or not to invest in a particular project should be based on a financial appraisal to check that benefits outweigh costs, and that the return is sufficient to meet the organization's objectives.

Appraising an investment

A particular feature of most investment situations is that an outflow of cash today is to be measured against benefits to be received in the future, sometimes over many years. This raises a number of issues.

Firstly, because the future is never predictable estimates of future revenues and costs are likely to be less accurate the further into the future we look. Secondly, there are factors that can affect the project's success, including:

- Changes in government and the law.

- Fluctuating economic conditions such as interest rates, exchange rates and unemployment.

- Changing market conditions such as competition and consumer trends

Thirdly, measured in cash terms benefits in the future are not as valuable as benefits received today. This 'time value' of money is illustrated by the fact that the business will incur interest charges on debt used to finance the project.

The planning horizon

There are a number of possible ways to appraise an investment opportunity. A common approach is to set a realistic planning horizon beyond which benefits are not taken into account. This planning horizon will depend on the nature of the project. For example, the appraisal of a new power station is likely to require at least a ten-year planning horizon; an advertising campaign may look just one or two years ahead.

We can now look at different ways of appraising investment.

17.3 The payback method

A commonly used investment appraisal technique is the payback method. The payback period is the time required for a project to repay the initial investment. The calculation is based on cash flows and not profits. The annual cash flows are accumulated and the payback period is reached when the cumulative cash flow reaches zero.

The formula for payback can thus be set out in the following way:

$$\text{Payback period} = \text{Negative years} + \frac{\text{Deficit remaining}}{\text{Cash flow in relevant year}} \times 12 \text{ months}$$

We can illustrate this for an investment project (Project A) that costs £45,000 and where the project is expected to yield £15,000 in the first year, £25,000 in the second year and £20,000 in the third year. The column in Table 17.1 showing cumulative cash flow shows the net cash outflow or inflow in specific years.

We use the term Year 0 to signify the start of the project (when there is the initial cash outlay).

The payback period can then be calculated from these data in the following way. We know that the payback will take place between Year 2 and Year 3.

$$\text{Payback} = 2 \text{ years} + \frac{£5,000}{£20,000} \times 12 \text{ months} = 2 \text{ years and 3 months}$$

TABLE 17.1 Illustrating payback for Project A

	Year	Project cash flow (£)	Cumulative cash flow (£)
Investment in fixed assets	0	−45,000	−45,000
Net inflows of cash	1	15,000	−30,000
	2	25,000	−5,000
	3	20,000	15,000

CASE STUDY An alternative cash flow

Analysts have identified an alternative way of investing the £45,000 outlined above (Project B). This will yield the following cash flows: £5,000 in Year 1, £40,000 in Year 2 and £10,000 in Year 3.

- Which of the projects should the company invest in if it is going to use the payback method? Show your working.

The payback will be particularly helpful in comparing the time taken to pay back alternative projects. The project with the shortest payback period is the best investment proposition, as the shorter timescale reduces the risk of unforeseen circumstances.

KEY TERM

Payback method – a way of appraising investment projects in terms of the amount of time that it takes to pay back an initial cash investment in terms of cash inflows from the project.

17.4 Discounted cash flow to find net present value

A second technique for appraising an investment is to use discounted cash flow. The discounted cash flow approach is a way of valuing the future returns on investment by assessing the value of these returns in terms of their present value. It places emphasis on the cost of funds tied up in a project by considering the timing of cash flows.

For example, we all instinctively know that £1 in the hand today is worth more than a promise of £1 in the future. This is because:

- There is always a risk that unforeseen circumstances will prevent you receiving the amount you have been promised.

- Inflation may lower the real value of money.

- The money cannot be put to constructive use in the meantime. The delay in payment therefore incurs an opportunity cost.

The 'time value' of money is often represented by a composite annual percentage rate. Bank deposit rates, for example, often include amounts to cover the elements described above.

Discounted cash flow works on the same principles as compound interest.

TABLE 17.2 The value of £100 today in terms of future balances (discounted at 10%)

Year	10% interest	Balance (£)
0	–	100.00
1	10.00	110.00
2	11.00	121.00
3	12.10	133.10
4	13.31	146.41

Calculating discounted cash flow can be illustrated by an example. Consider a sum of £100 that is invested in a savings account that yields interest at 10 per cent per annum. Assuming that the interest is left in the account at the end of each year, the savings account balance for the next four years will be that shown in Table 17.2.

What does this mean in terms of net present value? Using an interest rate of 10 per cent:

- £110 in a year's time is worth £100 today.

- £146.41 in 4 years' time is worth £100 today.

By reducing all future cash flows to a common measure in this way enables comparisons to be made between projects.

Compound interest – this arises when interest is added to the principal (initial sum borrowed or lent) so that from that moment on, the interest that has been added also earns interest. Adding interest to the principal is termed 'compounding'.

KEY TERM

Calculating net present value

Net present value (NPV) – the total of all cash flows restated in today's money terms.

KEY TERM

Net present value is based on actual cash flows. These will include **inflows**:

- Sales revenues, phased according to when they are actually received.

- Sales proceeds from the disposal of fixed assets at the conclusion of a project.

- The release of amounts invested in stocks at the end of a project.

- Government grants.

TABLE 17.3 A simple discount table for different rates of interest and time periods

Year	5	6	7	8	9	10	11	12	13	14	15	20
							Interest rate (%)					
1	0.9524	0.9434	0.9346	0.9259	0.9174	0.9091	0.9009	0.8929	0.8850	0.8772	0.8698	0.8333
2	0.9070	0.8900	0.8734	0.8793	0.8417	0.8264	0.8116	0.7972	0.7831	0.7695	0.7561	0.6944
3	0.8638	0.8396	0.8163	0.7938	0.7722	0.7513	0.7312	0.7118	0.6931	0.6750	0.6575	0.5787
4	0.8277	0.7921	0.7629	0.7350	0.7084	0.6830	0.6587	06355	0.6133	0.5921	0.5718	0.4823
5	0.7835	0.7473	0.7130	0.6806	0.6499	0.6209	0.5935	0.5674	0.5428	0.5194	0.4972	0.4019
6	0.7462	0.7050	0.6663	0.6302	0.5963	0.5645	0.5346	0.5066	0.4803	0.4556	0.4323	0.3349
7	0.7107	0.6651	0.6227	0.5835	0.5470	0.5132	0.4817	0.4523	0.4251	0.3996	0.3759	0.2791
8	0.6768	0.6274	0.5820	0.5403	0.5019	0.4665	0.4339	0.4039	0.3762	0.3506	0.3269	0.2326
9	0.6446	0.5919	0.5439	0.5002	0.4604	0.4241	0.3909	0.3606	0.3329	0.3075	0.2843	0.1938

And **outflows**:

- Investment in fixed assets.

- Creation of a working stock balance.

- Operating costs, including material, labour and expenses.

The NPV of a future cash flow is found by multiplying it by a discount factor. The size of the discount factor depends on the discount rate used (cost of capital) and the number of years involved.

The easiest way of finding a discount factor is to look it up in an NPV table (see Table 17.3). This can save a lot of time and effort (discount tables can be accessed on the Internet – simply carry out a search for 'discount tables'). For example, Table 17.3 shows that cash in four years' time discounted at 10 per cent should be multiplied by a factor of 0.6830.

Calculating the discount factor

When calculating NPV it is also possible to calculate the discount factor without having to rely on NPV tables (however, in the days of rapid calculation and access to computerized tables there would be little point in doing so). The calculation is shown below:

$$\text{NPV discount factor} = \frac{1}{(1 + r)^n}$$

Where:

r = Discount rate

n = Number of years

For example, cash received in four years' time to be discounted at 10 per cent is calculated as follows:

$$\text{NPV discount factor} \quad = \quad \frac{1}{(1 + 0.1)^4} \quad = \quad 0.6830 \quad \begin{array}{l}\text{(check this out in} \\ \text{the discount table)}\end{array}$$

We can now illustrate how discount factors are used to calculate NPV in Table 17.4. Note that we are using the same figures that we used for Project 1 when we used the payback method earlier.

CASE STUDY Supercolour Printers

Supercolour Printers Ltd currently has to turn work down because it has insufficient print capacity. A new printing press would cost £400,000, but would enable £500,000 worth of additional work each year to be processed. Annual running costs will be two operatives at £25,000 each and materials amounting to £100,000.

- Calculate the payback period.

- Calculate the NPV, assuming the company's policy is to discount four years' worth of cash flows at 20 per cent per annum.

Supercolour Printers has another investment opportunity. Currently, the work of cutting out card from printed sheets has to be done out-of-house. To do the work in-house requires a die-cutting machine that would cost £300,000. Although the machine would cost £100,000 a year to run, it would erase the annual cutting charges of £325,000.

- Calculate the payback period.

- Calculate the net present value based on a 20 per cent discount rate.

Unfortunately the company does not have sufficient financing facilities to fund both the printing press and the die-cutting machine.

- Which investment opportunity should the company pursue, based on the numbers presented here?

TABLE 17.4 Calculating net present value for Project 1

	Year	Cash flow (£)	10% factor	NPV (£)
Investment in fixed assets	0	−45,000	1.000	−45,000
Net inflows of cash	1	15,000	0.909	13,635
	2	25,000	0.826	20,650
	3	20,000	0.751	15,020
Total		15,000		4,305

The NPV here is positive: £4,305. This indicates that the project earns a rate in excess of the firm's 10 per cent cost of capital. As an individual project, this investment would be given the go-ahead. Where a number of projects are competing for the financial resources of a company, the project chosen would be the one with the highest NPV. The relative merits of the payback and net present value methods are set out in Table 17.5.

TABLE 17.5 Comparing investment appraisal methods

	Advantages	Disadvantages
Payback	Simple to calculate	Takes no account of timing of cash flows other than within or outside payback period
	Simple to understand	Does not consider cash flows after the payback period
	Bias towards early payback – minimizes risks	Does not consider the cost of capital
Discounted cash flow (NPV)	Theoretically 'correct' as it considers • Timing of cash flows • Inflation • Cost of capital	Complex calculations Results are highly sensitive to assumptions such as discount rate and planning horizon

17.5 Accounting rate of return

A third investment appraisal technique is the accounting rate of return (ARR) method. Accounting profit is routinely used to measure business performance, so it makes sense to use it as a basis for appraising investment projects too. The ARR compares profits of a business with the capital invested in the project. Just as a personal investor might compare interest rates between building societies, a business will choose the project with the highest ARR.

The formula for ARR is:

$$ARR = \frac{\text{Average annual profits}}{\text{Average capital employed}} \times 100\%$$

TABLE 17.6 How ARR can be calculated

	Year	Project cash flow (£)	Capitalise asset and depreciate (£)	Project profit (£)
Investment in fixed assets	0	−45,000	45,000	
Net inflows of cash	1	15,000	−15,000	0
	2	25,000	−15,000	10,000
	3	20,000	−15,000	5,000

Table 17.6 shows how ARR can be calculated using the figures used in earlier examples for Project 1. (However, note that the figures have been converted from cash flows to accounting profit by depreciating the original investment over the next four years.)

$$\text{Average profit per annum} = \frac{£0 + £10,000 + £5,000}{3} = £5,000$$

Average capital employed – calculated by taking a simple average between the capital invested at the start of a project and the balance at the end of it.

KEY TERM

For average capital employed, in the example shown the capital invested at the start of the project is £45,000 – and at the end of the project there is a nil residual figure.

$$\text{Average capital employed} = \frac{£45,000}{2} = £22,500$$

Now it is possible to work out the ARR.

$$\text{Accounting rate of return} = \frac{£5,000}{£22,500} \times 100\% = 22.2\%$$

Project rates of return are compared with the business's cost of capital (e.g. the cost of borrowing) before commencing. Where choices have to be made between competing projects, the project with the highest ARR is preferred.

The main advantage of the ARR approach compared to other methods is that it is relatively easy to understand. The profit can simply be extracted from the income statement (statement of profit) for a company. However, a weakness is that the method is not based on cash flows. As a result the figures presented will vary according to the methods that are used by the company accountants for presenting their profits. Methods adopted by company accountants to calculate profit are notoriously subject to variation and eccentricities despite the existence of accounting standards.

> ### Reflective question
>
> **1**   Which of the methods for appraising investment that have been outlined above do you think will be most useful in taking into account the real return on investment? In what situations do you think analysts will prefer to use other methods of investment appraisal?

17.6 Sources of finance for a business

In order for a business to invest it will first of all need to raise capital. Capital comes from two main sources:

1.   Internal finance. Finance from the owners of the business.

2.   External finance. Finance raised from outside the business.

Decisions about the relative proportions of these two sources of finance is particularly important. The term gearing is used to describe the relationship between externally sourced finance and internally sourced finance. A company which raises a high proportion of its capital externally is described as being highly geared. A company which raises only a small proportion of its capital externally is described as having a low gearing ratio. Getting the right gearing balance is an important business decision.

The advantage of internal finance is that the business does not have a legal requirement to pay a reward to its main group of shareholders – those possessing ordinary shares. The reward to ordinary shareholders is called a dividend. The company can pay high dividends when its profits are high and lower dividends (or no dividends at all) when its profits are low.

In contrast a company has a fixed legal obligation to pay interest (and to repay loans and other liabilities when they fall due) to those providing external finance. The higher the gearing ratio therefore the bigger the commitment to external lenders. Because the economy is subject to cycles of boom and recession, there will be years in which profits will be low for most companies. Having too high a gearing ratio therefore exposes a company to the vagaries of the business cycle.

Interest cover

Another valuable measure of financial risk is the relationship of interest payments to the profits generated by the business.

$$\text{Interest cover} \quad = \quad \frac{\text{Profit before interest}}{\text{Interest payments}}$$

KEY THEME

Financial planning

How a business is financed is often subject to constraints determined by the financial market and the state of the economy. However, where possible the financial strategy should be decided after due regard to:

- Duration – how long the finance is required.
- Cost – relative to alternative sources of finance.
- Gearing – the proportion of fixed return finance to equity capital.

Duration. In the same way that individuals do not purchase houses with bank overdrafts or finance home computers with a 25-year mortgage, business should match the source of finance with the need for finance. This makes sense for:

- The business – as it ensures finance is guaranteed for as long as the need exists;
- The investor – as it ensures adequate security can be obtained for the duration of the loan, for example a 20-year loan may be secured against property that will continue to have value in 20 years' time.

Typically long-term finance comes from share capital, earnings retained in the business, and from commercial mortgages (to acquire property). Medium-term finance typically involves some form of bank loan. There is a range of sources of short-term finance (see below).

Cost of finance. Raising finance invariably results in a cost and so it follows that the financial benefits arising from a particular project should outweigh the cost of using the funds.

Gearing. Gearing is the term used to describe the relationship between finance that enjoys a fixed rate of return and equity (capital that enjoys profit-related returns). It is important to get the gearing right because companies that are overgeared (having too much finance with a fixed interest obligation) can find themselves in a difficult position in a period of recession when profits are low.

- **Why might a business require finance for a long period of time? How might it raise this finance?**

- **Why might a business require finance for a short period of time? How might it raise this finance?**

- **How is the cost of raising finance likely to impact on investment appraisal?**

A low interest cover ratio indicates that interest payments are a burden. The larger the profits earned in relation to interest commitments, the less risk there is of interest payments pushing the business into a loss situation.

Businesses that are heavily influenced by economic cycles, such as capital goods suppliers, would not normally wish to be highly geared. On the other hand stable industries, such as food producers, may be able to provide adequate interest cover at all stages of the economic cycle. They are unlikely to make losses for ordinary shareholders even if highly geared.

Figure 17.1 provides a useful picture of financial risk.

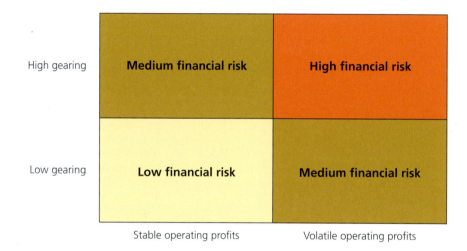

FIGURE 17.1 Illustrating financial risk

Different sources of business finance

Owner's capital

There are two main types of shares: ordinary and preference shares. Each offers a different right to dividends (returns) and capital repayment.

Holders of **ordinary shares** are entitled to a share in the profits of the business after all other investors have been paid their dues. They are able to vote at general meetings of the company and to exert influence in direct proportion to the number of shares they hold.

Items requiring shareholder authorization include:

- The appointment of the board of directors.

- The amount of profit distributed by way of dividends to shareholders.

- The issue or repurchase of share capital.

Ordinary share capital is often called **equity capital** and can be likened to an owner's equity in a private house. Equity for the householder is the difference between the value of the house and the mortgage secured against it. In the case of a company, equity (the value of ordinary shares) represents the difference between the value of assets owned by the business and the value of any outstanding loans and liabilities to other parties.

Assets – what a business owns or is owed by others.

Liabilities – what a business owes to others.

Table 17.7 shows how the equity value of a company is calculated.

TABLE 17.7 How the equity of a business is calculated

Holders of **preference shares** are entitled to receive a fixed dividend out of profits before payment is made to ordinary shareholders. But they usually have no voting rights, and so have less influence on company policy.

	£000s
Assets: fixed and current	2,000
Liabilities	500
Equity	1,500

Third-party finance

Large amounts of business finance are provided by investors who do not want to take the risk of becoming a shareholder in a company. These third-party investors include banks, insurance companies and pension funds, who for some of their investments at least require stable income and greater security for their capital investment.

The basic principle of **loan stock** is that a loan is made to a company in accordance with terms set out in a certifying document. Typically, loan stock involves a fixed rate of interest and is repaid (redeemed) by the company on a predetermined date. Sometime loan stock is 'secured' on specified assets of the business in case the company runs into financial difficulties.

Loan stock is a loan to a company typically for a medium or long-term period. Loan stocks are financial securities that can be traded in the same way as a company's shares. Loan stocks are also referred to as 'debentures' and 'company bonds'.

Long-term finance – over five years.

Medium-term finance – 1–5 years.

Short-term finance – up to 12 months.

Bank finance. Banks are risk averse and, as well as requiring detailed business plans, will generally not lend more than the owners are putting into the business themselves. Security is also usually required. In the case of small businesses, this is often in the form of a personal guarantee secured by the personal assets of the major shareholders.

Loans can be for the short, medium or long term. There is a range of financial products provided by clearing banks including overdrafts, loans, credit cards, mortgages and sale and leaseback.

- Bank loans are taken out for a fixed period with repayment being either in instalments or in full at the end of the term.

- Overdrafts are a more flexible form of finance. However, while interest is only charged on debit balances, amounts are legally repayable on demand.

- Most small businesses use credit cards as a form of finance at some stage. The user of the card receives credit up to an agreed limit and must pay instalments on the outstanding balance each month. If they pay off all of the credit received during a month before a fixed date then no interest is charged. However, if they retain a credit balance outstanding then they will be charged interest on the outstanding balance (at a relatively high rate of interest which is calculated using compound interest).

- Mortgages are loans secured by land and buildings and are an exception to the general rule that banks do not provide long-term finance. The funds provided may be used to purchase the property or, in the case of property already owned, to provide security for a loan which is being used for some other purpose.

- Sale and leaseback is another form of finance for land and buildings. This involves the business selling its freehold property to an investment company and then leasing it back over a predetermined period of time.

Hire purchase (HP) allows the business to use an asset without having to find the money immediately. A finance house buys the asset from the supplier and retains ownership of it until the business has made the payments required under the HP agreement. At the end of the HP agreement, ownership of the asset passes to the business.

Leasing works in the same way as HP in that a finance house (the lessor) allows the business (the lessee) to use an asset without having to buy it outright. The real distinction between the two forms of finance is that leasing does not confer an automatic right to eventual ownership. It is a very popular form of finance for company vehicles, office equipment and factory machinery.

There are two types of lease:

- An operating lease is a rent agreement for a short period of time relative to the asset's useful life. For example, in the case of a car a two-year agreement is fairly typical.

- A finance lease tends to run for longer. The agreement will cover most of the asset's economic life and so payments under the agreement will, like HP, exceed the cash price of the asset.

Factoring. A major problem for many businesses is the length of time taken by customers to pay – the credit period. Typically this is 30–60 days, and in some cases considerably longer. Factors provide finance against a business's trade debt by advancing up to 80 per cent of the value of the invoices outstanding, with the remainder payable as and when

CASE STUDY Financing issues

Palmer Software Ltd required £100,000 for computer hardware to re-equip its programming facilities with the latest computer technology.

- **Identify appropriate sources to finance the purchase.**

Brightwell and Rugman Ltd ran into temporary cash flow problems when disruption to work flow was caused by a delay in the introduction of a new production line. The situation was aggravated by unpaid creditors who stopped supplying materials.

- **What measures could have resolved the short-term situation?**

Eurotunnel's ordinary shares were worth £1 billion when they were issued in 1996 but because of cost over-runs in building the Channel Tunnel it owed its bankers £9 billion. Such high gearing left the company with interest payments it could not afford to pay.

- **Explain what the term gearing means.**
- **What type of new finance was needed to reduce the company's gearing ratio?**

customers pay at the end of the their credit periods. Factors receive interest on the amounts they advance. They also charge an administration fee for taking over the credit control function of a business.

Trade credit. Suppliers are a valuable source of finance for many businesses. Just as the business may give credit to its own customers, the firm may be able to negotiate credit terms with its suppliers. Credit terms are typically 30 days from date of supply or 30 days from the end of the month following the month of delivery (i.e. 30–60 days).

17.7 Summary

This chapter has examined the important topic of business investment both from an economy-wide and a business perspective. Autonomous investment decisions made by the business community can have a substantial impact on the economy. Business people are most likely to invest when the economy is growing and hence when there is more optimism about profitability. In order to invest, business will need to acquire capital either from internal sources (e.g. ploughed back profits or shares) or by raising money externally. How a business finances itself (sources of finance) impacts on the exposure of a business to risk, including the risk of a downturn in the economy. This chapter has outlined the main types of investment appraisal to show how business analysts will identify the potential returns on investment projects.

KEY IDEAS

What is investment?

- Investment is an expenditure that increases the productive capacity of an organization (e.g. the purchase of a machine).
- Investment usually takes place in a series of steps or projects over time.
- It is important to appraise the return on different types of investment.

The payback method

- The payback period is the time required for a project to repay the initial investment.
- The calculation is based on cash flows, which are accumulated over the payback period until cumulative cash flow equals zero.

The discounted cash flow method (DCF)

- The DCF method values future returns on investment by assessing the value of these returns in terms of their present value.
- All future cash flows are recorded in terms of their present value.
- The NPR of a future cash flow is found by multiplying it by a discount factor that can be accessed from a table.
- When comparing projects using the NPV method you would select the project with the highest NPV.

Accounting rate of return (ARR)

- The ARR method compares profits of a business with the capital invested in the project.
- Average annual profits are calculated as a percentage of the capital employed in the project.
- In comparing alternative projects (that involve similar amounts of capital) using the ARR method the preferred project will be the one that is calculated to yield the highest return (i.e. the anticipated profit as a percentage of the capital investment will be the highest).

Sources of finance for a business

- It is important to distinguish between long-term (e.g. share capital), medium-term (e.g. bank loan) and short-term (e.g. overdraft) finance.
- An important distinction can also be made between finance which commands fixed interest repayment and other sources of finance.
- The gearing ratio measures the exposure of a business to fixed rate repayments.
- There is a danger of businesses exposing themselves through a high gearing ratio in a period of economic downturn.

- Interest cover measures the profit made before interest by a business with interest repayments that the business needs to make.
- Interest cover is a useful indicator of a business's ability to deal with a period of economic difficulty.

REVIEW QUESTIONS

1. Outline the key advantages of using the payback method for investment appraisal.

2. What is the purpose of carrying out investment appraisal?

3. Describe two main methods of carrying out investment appraisal.

4. Why do different investment projects have different planning horizons?

5. How does the timing of returns on investment impact on the certainty with which these benefits can be calculated?

6. Outline three main factors that are likely to impact on an investment project's success.

7. Show how: (a) the payback method; and (b) the NPV method of investment appraisal is calculated.

8. Explain how the timing of cash flows impacts on the values of these cash flows.

9. What is the purpose of a discounted cash flow table? How does it assist in taking investment decisions?

10. What is the significance of opportunity cost when making investment decisions?

RECOMMENDED READING

Gazely, A. and Lambert, M. (2006) *Management Accounting*, London, Sage.

You will find that Chapter 4 of this book, which looks at different ways of appraising investment, is very helpful and that it is full of practical examples. You should also find Chapter 1 to be helpful in setting out a management accountant's view of costing techniques.

Walker, J. (2009) *Accounting in a Nutshell: Accounting for the Non-specialist*, Oxford, Elsevier/CIMA Publishing.

Chapter 12 of this book 'Making Long-term Investment Decisions' provides a very clear account of different ways of appraising investment projects.

USEFUL WEBSITES

www.businesscasestudies.co.uk/finance/investment-appraisal – *The Times* 100 provides a number of useful case studies in investment appraisal that can be accessed online.

INDEX

Page numbers in **bold** indicate **tables;** page numbers in *italics* indicate *figures.*